THE
PALESTINIANS

THE PALESTINIANS
People, History, Politics

Edited by

Michael Curtis

Joseph Neyer

Chaim I. Waxman

Allen Pollack

Prepared under the auspices of the American Academic Association for Peace in the Middle East.

Transaction Books
New Brunswick, New Jersey

Table of Contents

ACKNOWLEDGMENTS vii
ABOUT THE EDITORS ix
ABOUT THE CONTRIBUTORS ix
INTRODUCTION 1
   Michael Curtis

I

JEWS AND ARABS IN PALESTINE

PALESTINE IN THE ISLAMIC AND OTTOMAN PERIOD 9
   Moshe Sharon
LAND OWNERSHIP IN PALESTINE, 1880-1948 21
   Moshe Aumann
ARAB IMMIGRATION INTO PRE-STATE ISRAEL: 1922-1931 30
   Fred M. Gottheil
ARAB-JEWISH CONTACTS IN PALESTINE: 1923-1931 41
   Frederick H. Kisch
THE JEWISH PEOPLE AND PALESTINE 46
   Chaim Weizmann
MIDDLE EAST REFUGEES 51
   Terence Prittie

II

THE PALESTINIAN ARABS

THE PALESTINIANS: WHO THEY ARE 77
   Ya'acob Caroz
SOCIAL AND POLITICAL CHANGES IN ARAB SOCIETY IN ISRAEL ... 81
   Aharon Layish
WEST BANK SENTIMENTS: 1967-1973 88
   Amnon Cohen

III

PALESTINIAN ARAB NATIONALISM

POLITICAL AND SOCIAL ASPECTS OF ISRAELI
AND ARAB NATIONALISM 97
   Shlomo Avineri
VARIETIES OF PALESTINIAN NATIONALISM 112
   Chaim I. Waxman
THE PALESTINIAN-ARAB NATIONALIST MOVEMENT 121
   Yehoshua Porat
THE EMERGENCE OF YASSER ARAFAT 128
   Joseph Neyer
INSUFFERABLE SILENCE 133
   Muhammad Watad

IV

THE PALESTINIAN ORGANIZATIONS
AND TERRORISM

THE PALESTINIAN ORGANIZATIONS, THEIR LEADERS
AND IDEOLOGIES..139

THE PALESTINIAN NATIONAL COVENANT 143
    Yehoshefat Harkabi
A PALESTINIAN DEMOCRATIC STATE AS THE POLITICAL GOAL OF
THE PALESTINIANS . . . . .154 ✓
    Yehoshefat Harkabi
THE DEBATE AT THE 12th PALESTINIAN NATIONAL COUNCIL . . . . . . .159 ↙
    Yehoshefat Harkabi
THE POSITION OF THE PALESTINIAN ORGANIZATIONS ON THE
ESTABLISHMENT OF A PALESTINIAN STATE AND ON PEACE . . . . . . .166 ✓
    Zahir Mukhsan (PLO and Saiqa)   Salah Khalaf (Abu Iyad) (Fatah)
    George Habash (PFLP)   Nayef Hawatmeh (PDFLP)

V
ISRAELI VIEWS ON THE PALESTINIAN PROBLEM

ON THE PALESTINIAN PROBLEM 175
    Yitzhak Rabin
ON A PALESTINIAN IDENTITY 180
    Yigal Allon
PALESTINIAN NATIONALISM: AN ESTABLISHED FACT 183
    Amnon Rubinstein
THE PALESTINIAN OPTION 187
    Uri Avneri
A PALESTINIAN STATE — WHERE? 194
    Moshe Maoz

VI
GENERAL

PALESTINIAN NATIONALISM: ITS DEVELOPMENT AND GOAL 199
    Marie Syrkin
ON ISRAEL'S EAST 209
    David Pryce-Jones
ISRAEL AND THE PALESTINIAN QUESTION 213
    Terence Prittie
MOSCOW AND THE PALESTINIANS: A NEW TOOL OF SOVIET
POLICY IN THE MIDDLE EAST 228
    Augustus R. Norton

VII
APPENDICES

MAPS 251
PALESTINIAN ARAB TERRORIST ACTS AGAINST INTERNATIONAL
CIVIL AVIATION: 1968-1973 254
PALESTINIAN ARAB TERRORIST ACTS: 1968-1974 260
THE POLITICAL PROGRAM OF THE PALESTINE
NATIONAL COUNCIL 267
SELECTED BIBLIOGRAPHY 269
INDEX 273

ACKNOWLEDGEMENTS

"Palestine in the Islamic and Ottoman Period" by Moshe Sharon. Reprinted from *The Arabs and Palestine,* Institute Symposia No. 1, Institute of Jewish Affairs, (London). The Symposium was held at University College, London, March 19, 1972. Reprinted by permission.

"Land Ownership in Palestine 1880-1948" by Moshe Aumann. Reprinted by permission of the *Israel Academic Committee on the Middle East,* Jerusalem. Also appeared in *Middle East Information Series XXIV,* Fall 1973, A.A.A.P.M.E., N.Y.

"Arab Immigration into Pre-State Israel: 1922-1931" by Fred M. Gottheil. Reprinted by permission of *Middle Eastern Studies* (London) Vol. 9, No. 3, Oct. 1973. Also appeared in *Middle East Information Series XXIV,* Fall 1973.

"Arab-Jewish Contacts in Palestine, 1923-1931" by Frederick H. Kisch. Reprinted by permission from *Palestine Diary,* Victor Gollancz (London), 1938.

"Middle East Refugees" by Terence Prittie. Reprinted by permission of *Britain & Israel,* (London) Commentary No. 26, 27, 28. Sept. 1973.

"The Palestinians: Who They Are" by Ya'acob Caroz. Reprinted from *Yediot Aharonot* (Israel) July 19, 1974. Reprinted by permission.

"Social and Political Changes in Arab Society in Israel" by Aharon Layish. *The Arabs and Palestine,* Institute Symposia No. 1. A paper read at a Symposium arranged by the Institute of Jewish Affairs (London) at University College, London, on March 19, 1972. Reprinted by permission.

"West Bank Sentiments 1967-1973" by Amnon Cohen. *The Arabs and Palestine,*

Institute Symposia No. 1. A paper read at a Symposium arranged by the Institute of Jewish Affairs (London) at University College, London, on March 19, 1972. Reprinted by permission.

"Political and Social Aspects of Israeli and Arab Nationalism" by Shlomo Avineri. Reprinted by permission of *Midstream,* N.Y., January 1973.

"Varieties of Palestinian Nationalism" by Chaim I. Waxman. Reprinted from *Middle East Information Series* XXV, Winter 1973-74, A.A.A.P.M.E., N.Y.

"The Palestinian-Arab Nationalist Movement" by Yehoshua Porat. Reprinted from *Middle East Information Series* XXV, Winter 1973-74, A.A.A.P.M.E., N.Y.

"Insufferable Silence" by Muhammad Watad. Reprinted by permission of *New Outlook,* (Israel) Vol. 17, No. 6 (152), July 1974.

"The Palestinian Organizations, Their Leaders and Ideologies" Reprinted from *Middle East Review* I Fall 1974, A.A.A.P.M.E., N.Y.

"The Palestinian National Covenant" by Yehoshefat Harkabi. Reprinted from *Maariv,* Israel, December 12, 1969. Reprinted by permission.

"The Debate at the 12th Palestinian National Council" by Yehoshefat Harkabi. Reprinted from *Palestinians and Israel* by Y. Harkabi, by permission of Keter Publishing House, Jerusalem, Israel, 1974. Also appeared in *Middle East Review* I, Fall 1974, A.A.A.P.M.E., N.Y.

"Palestinian Nationalism: An Established Fact" by Amnon Rubinstein. Reprinted from *Ha'aretz* (Israel) July 19, 1974. Reprinted by permission.

"The Palestinian Option" by Uri Avneri. Reprinted from *Ha'aretz* (Israel) July 21, 1974. Reprinted by permission.

"A Palestinian State—Where?" by Moshe Maoz. Reprinted from *Ha'aretz* (Israel) July 21, 1974. Reprinted by permission.

"On Israel's East" by David Pryce-Jones. Reprinted by permission of *The New Republic,* Washington, Aug. 31, 1974.

"Israel and the Palestinian Question" by Terence Prittie. Reprinted by permission of *Britain & Israel.* (London) Commentary No. 35 and 36, Sept. 1974.

"Moscow and the Palestinians" by Augustus R. Norton. From *Occasional Papers in International Affairs.* Reprinted by permission of the Center for Advanced International Studies, University of Miami, 1974.

Acknowledgement is due to Dr. Martin Gilbert and Weidenfeld and Nicolson Limited (London) for permission to reproduce the map on page 49 taken from *The Arab-Israel Conflict. Its History in Maps,* 1974 History Atlas, for the map reproduced in this book on page 63.

About The Contributors

ABOUT THE EDITORS

Michael Curtis is Professor of Political Science at Rutgers University, New Brunswick.

Joseph Neyer is Professor of Philosophy at Rutgers University, New Brunswick.

Allen Pollack is a member of the Department of History at Yeshiva University.

Chaim I. Waxman is a member of the Department of Sociology at Brooklyn College.

ABOUT THE AUTHORS

Moshe Aumann is an Israeli specialist in the history of Palestine.
Shlomo Avineri is Dean of Social Sciences at the Hebrew University, Jerusalem.
Uri Avneri is an Israeli journalist and editor of *HaOlam Hazeh,* a Tel Aviv Weekly, and a former member of the Israel Knesset (Parliament).
Ya'acob Caroz is an Israeli journalist and Middle East specialist.
Amnon Cohen is Lecturer in the History of the Muslim Countries in the Institute of Asian and African Studies at the Hebrew University, Jerusalem.
Fred M. Gottheil is a member of the Dept. of Economics at the University of Illinois, Urbana.

Yehoshefat Harkabi is Associate Professor of the History of Islamic Countries and International Relations at the Hebrew University, Jerusalem.

Col. Frederick H. Kisch was a British Jewish leader who became a member of the Executive Committee of the Jewish Agency in Palestine in the 1920s.

Aharon Layish teaches Modern Middle East History in the Institute of Asian and African Studies at the Hebrew University, Jerusalem.

Moshe Maoz is Associate Professor of History of the Muslim Countries in the Institute of Asian and African Studies at the Hebrew University, Jerusalem.

Augustus R. Norton is Assistant Professor of International Relations at the University of Illinois at Chicago Circle.

Yehoshua Porat is Chairman of the Dept. of the History of the Muslim Countries at the Institute of Asian and African Studies of the Hebrew University, Jerusalem. Translated from the Hebrew by Aryeh Greenfield.

Terence Prittie is a noted British journalist and author. He is the editor of *Britain & Israel,* a Newsletter (London).

David Pryce-Jones is a noted British journalist and author.

Amnon Rubinstein is Professor in the Faculty of Law at Tel Aviv University.

Moshe Sharon is Lecturer in the History of the Muslim Countries in the Institute of Asian and African Studies at the Hebrew University, Jerusalem.

Marie Syrkin is Professor Emerita, Brandeis University, author, journalist and the editor of the Herzl Press.

Muhammad Watad is an Arab journalist on the editorial board of *Al-Mirsad* and *New Outlook* (Mapam monthly), and producer of Arab-language programs on Israeli Television.

Introduction

By Michael Curtis

This book consists, to a large degree, of papers contained in two 1973 issues of the *Middle East Information Series* and the first issue of the *Middle East Review* (Fall 1974), published by the American Academic Association for Peace in the Middle East. The various papers and statements not only examine the historical and political dimensions of the Palestinian problem but also provide a picture of the realities of demography, land ownership and Arab-Jewish relations in Palestine and analyze the nature, personalities and intentions of the Palestinian Arab movement.

The essence of the conflict between Israel and the Arab states has been the refusal of those states to acknowledge the existence and legitimacy of the State of Israel and to accept it as a member of the family of nations in the Middle East. The major outstanding political problems of occupied territory and of displaced Arabs have resulted from that refusal which has produced four wars, a war of attrition by Egypt, unending terrorist attacks on both Israel and on civilians in the outside world, an Arab economic, diplomatic and cultural boycott of Israel, and Arab breaches of international agreements on armistice and freedom of navigation issues.

A just and lasting peace between Israel and the Arab states is possible only if the three issues—the existence of an Israel with secure borders, the territorial integrity of the Arab states, and the displacement of Arab refugees—are resolved. The complex history of the area, the tangled web of inter-Arab rivalries and hatreds, the intricate maneuvering and ambition of outside powers, and bitter intransigence have all contributed to the difficulty of finding a resolution. An end to the tragic conflict between Arabs and Jews arising from competing claims to right and

1

justice in the same land and a just solution can be obtained only by compromise and concessions.   It is essential that secure and permanent borders be determined in the Middle East. In the four hundred years of control by the Ottoman Empire between 1517 and 1917, boundaries in Palestine, which was governed as Southern Syria, had little significance for the nomadic groups of the region. The mandate entrusted in 1921 by the League of Nations to Britain, which had conquered the area in 1917, to govern Palestine comprised the areas of what is now Israel, Jordan and the West Bank and Gaza. Legally, the term "Palestinian" refers to all the residents, Jewish and Arab, of the former mandate area. As a consequence of the political machinations in the area between Britain, France and local Arab sheiks, the mandate area was partitioned in 1922. On the East Bank of the River Jordan, "the Transjordan province of Palestine," Britain established the Arab Emirate of Transjordan under Emir Abdullah, though Britain still remained as the mandatory power in the whole of Palestine. The new Emirate comprised 32,640 sq. miles out of the original mandate area of 43,075 sq. miles.

On November 29, 1947, the General Assembly of the United Nations recommended the partition of the rest of Palestine and the creation of two sovereign states. The Jewish Agency, the political representative of the Jewish community in Palestine, accepted the recommendation and announced the establishment of the state of Israel in the territory allocated to it. But the Arab governments unanimously rejected the recommendation. Arab terrorists attacked the Jewish community after the U.N. Resolution and the armies of the Arab states attacked the new state immediately after Israel was proclaimed on May 14, 1948.

It was this attack that led to the creation of the Palestinian Arab refugee problem as well as to the redefinition of boundaries as a consequence of the war. The Gaza Strip was occupied until 1967 by Egypt, which refused to accord the right of citizenship to the inhabitants. Transjordan occupied the West Bank and the Old City of Jerusalem which thus became a divided city. Israel acquired the Negev, extending to the Gulf of Aquaba and the port of Eilat: its total area was 18% of the mandate area of 1922. In 1950 Transjordan annexed the territory it occupied and transformed itself into the Hashemite Kingdom of Jordan which now constituted 77% of the mandate area.

Since 1948 the Arab states have refused both to acknowledge the existence of Israel and to provide a home for all the Arab refugees, as Israel has done for the Jews who fled Arab countries. Border warfare against Israel, in the form of incessant raids from the Gaza Strip, the West Bank and the Golan Heights, helped produce the 1956 war. The blockade by Egypt of international waterways through which free passage for Israel had been guaranteed by the maritime nations of the world led to the 1967 war which, like the outcome of the 1973 war, produced new borders in the Sinai and the Golan Heights. For twenty six years the Palestinian refugees have been used as a political instrument by the Arab states in the continuing war against Israel rather than treated compassionately or assisted in any significant fashion by fellow Arabs.

All proposals for a peaceful compromise—in 1949 when Israel at the Lausanne Conference offered to readmit 100,000 refugees and pay compensation to others, in 1951 when the Conciliation Commission proposed a peace declaration and when the United Nations suggested a plan for the resettlement of refugees, in 1955 when the Johnston Plan proposed use of the waters of the Jordan, Yarmuk and Litani rivers, in 1959 when Secretary-General Hammarskjold proposed resettlement—have been rejected by the Arabs. The Arab position has been one of total intransigence, regarding the negotiation of peace through direct discussions as the ultimate humiliation.

The territory of Palestine has been conquered by many different armies—the Seljuks, the Crusaders, the Mongols, the Mamelukes, the Turks, the British—and settled by many different peoples throughout history. But history does not validate the proposition that the Arab population is necessarily indigenous or that the whole of Palestine belonged to the Arabs. In 1917, the date of the Balfour Declaration, there were 640,000 Arabs in the whole mandate area. The economic opportunities provided by Jewish immigration stimulated an even larger Arab immigration into Palestine, especially into the urban areas from drought-stricken Southern Syria in the early 1920s, from Sinai, and from Transjordan and other Arab countries. Between 1922 and 1939, the non-Jewish population in Palestine increased by 75%, apart from natural increase and a decrease in infant mortality. Between 1922 and 1947 the Arab population increased by 90% in Jerusalem, 134% in Jaffa and 216% in Haifa. In the time between the Balfour Declaration of 1917 and the establishment of Israel in 1948, the Arab population of Palestine doubled, a rate of increase very much greater than that in neighboring Arab countries. The roots of the majority of the Arab population in Palestine are no deeper than those of the Jewish population.

The Ottoman Empire did little to secure land tenure for the inhabitants of Palestine. Land ownership fell increasingly to the wealthy, the moneylenders and the Muslim Religious Endowment Fund (Waqf). The combination of taxation, Bedouin raids which wiped out whole villages and clan blood feuds led to the *fellahin* (peasants) becoming increasingly landless. The development of Jewish enterprises in the towns attracted some of those landless peasants. The new farming techniques, increasing the economic absorptive capacity of the country, were introduced by Jewish settlers on land previously considered unsuitable and largely bought from absentee owners whose homes were in Arab capital cities. Large Arab landowners bought land and resold it at speculative prices. Of all Jewish land purchases, only 27% was bought directly from the *fellahin*.

The State of Israel was established on territory over 70% of which had been vested in the mandatory power and therefore reverted to the new state as the legal heir. This land had not been owned by Arabs under either Turkish Ottoman rule or the British Mandatory government. In 1948, 16.5% of Israeli territory was abandoned by its Arab owners who fled the country during the war, another 3.3% was owned by Israeli Arabs and 8.6% was owned by Jews.

If the view that Arabs owned the whole of Palestine is fallacious, equally mistaken is the belief that most Palestinians are refugees from their homeland. In fact, according to most reliable estimates and up to date statistics, the majority of the Palestinian Arabs live in the area of mandatory Palestine, if not in all cases in their original villages. About 420,000 live in Israel as citizens of Israel and another 80,000 inhabit East Jerusalem. In Jordan there are 643,000 Palestinians who are citizens of that country and constitute 50% of the population of the East Bank. At the Geneva peace talks in December 1973, seven of the eleven Jordanian delegates were Palestinians. The family of the Prime Minister and Foreign Minister of Jordan came from the West Bank as do the majority of the Cabinet and half of both the elected House of Representatives and the appointed Senate. On the West Bank the 670,000 Palestinians are treated as citizens of Jordan, the laws of which apply in civil matters, though the area is administered by the Israeli authorities. On the two Banks of the Jordan, Palestinians form over 70% of the population.

The 400,000 inhabitants of the Gaza Strip, also administered by Israel, have the status of refugees. Outside Palestine live some 90,000 refugees in camps in Lebanon and another 60,000 in the rest of Lebanon, another 138,000 live in Syria and about 277,000 Palestinians live and work in other countries.

Much of the current discussion in the Middle East controversy centers on the possibility, meaning and nature of a Palestinian Arab entity. Arab nationalism in general is of recent vintage. No independent state with Arabic as its official language existed before 1914. An inhabitant of the area might define himself as a Muslim or a Christian, a member of a tribe or clan or as an inhabitant of a particular village before thinking of himself as an Arab. Palestinian Arab nationalism, stimulated by and reacting to the Jewish national liberation movement of Zionism, is even more recent. It has lacked the comprehensive coherence, the positive approach, the cooperative spirit, the belief in self-reliance, the popular electoral support that characterized Zionism. Its chief impetus has come from opposition to Jewish settlement and to the State of Israel.

In recent years a group of self-appointed individuals, heading groups financed and militarily trained by Arab states and encouraged by the Soviet Union, have emerged as spokesmen for Palestinian nationalism. The Palestine Liberation Organization, formed by the combination of these groups which have the destruction of Israel as their only common bond and the use of terror as their only common tactic, has been accepted by the Arab states as "the sole representative of the Palestinians," a status upheld on October 14, 1974 by the United Nations General Assembly which invited it to participate in the deliberations of the General Assembly on the question of Palestine in plenary meetings.

As a tactical move, though not as an indicator of their true, more ambitious intentions, the PLO sees the West Bank as the main base of a Palestinian entity. The West Bank has never formed a geo-political entity of its own in modern times and the Palestinian Arabs refused to establish a state of their own in that area when given the opportunity by the U.N. in 1947. But suggestions for some form of Palestinian entity have been made. In 1967 Yigal Allon, at that time Israeli Deputy Prime Minister, proposed the return to Jordan of most of the West Bank, except for East Jerusalem, some largely uninhabited strips of the Jordan Valley and the Judaean Desert-Dead Sea coast and other areas, on the condition that it be completely demilitarized. In 1972 Hussein suggested a federated state of Jordan consisting of two semi-autonomous regions—the present East Bank, whose regional capital would be Amman, and the West Bank whose capital would be Jerusalem. The new regional executive and legislative bodies would be subordinate to the federal governmental bodies in Amman.

Theoretically there are five possible solutions to the Palestinian problem: an independent state, a federation of the West Bank with Jordan, a federation with Israel, incorporation in a Jordanian state, or a binational state in which Jews and Arabs would be equal citizens. The last two seem impossible and the third has been by-passed by history. It is arguable whether an independent Palestinian state, almost certainly irredentist in nature, small in size and landlocked, could be economically and politically viable. The rational choice would seem to be an entity which linked itself in some way to Jordan.

Yet the PLO has refused to accept any such solution, arguing for a separate state as a minimum and for a secular, democratic Arab state for Muslims, Christians and Jews in the whole area to be liberated as the final solution. Since this constitutes a denial of the Jewish population as a national, political entity and presumes the liquidation of Israel it is an unacceptable position. Indeed the PLO objective of seeking the liquidation of Israel, and possibly the dispersion of its population, is contrary to the principles of the U.N. Charter and of international law. The call in Article 15 of the Palestine National Covenant for the liberation of Palestine as "a national duty to repulse the Zionist, imperialist invasion from the great Arab homeland and to purge the Zionist presence from Palestine" is hardly an indication of future pacific intentions. It is ironic that the U.N. should issue an invitation to an organization which, in the words of its chairman Yasser Arafat on December 3, 1973, has refused to recognize the 1947 U.N. Resolution partitioning Palestine into a Jewish and an Arab state.

It is doubtful at the present time that the inhabitants of the West Bank or Palestinians in general can choose a body truly representative of their interests but clearly the PLO, by its unrepresentative and undemocratic nature and by its intransigent, destructive attitude toward Israel, cannot be seen as the body likely to help bring peace to the Middle East.

It should be the objective of United States foreign policy to encourage the emergence of a moderate Palestinian point of view by individuals and groups democratically chosen and prepared to enter into negotiations, either with Jordan or on its own, with Israel. The United States cannot condone an organization and group which not only have engaged in terror as a way of life, but also seek the elimination of a neighbor state.

In addition the United States must make clear its determination to prevent the liquidation of Israel. The United States, by its diplomatic readiness to act as peacemaker, by its forceful pressure to overcome the use of the Arab oil weapon, by its clear message to the Soviet Union that the preservation of detente is dependent on Russian restraint in the Middle East, by its effort to dissuade Western Europe and Japan from acts of appeasement, and by its military and economic assistance to Israel, must now play a leading part. To leave events to the outcome of a United Nations debate, dominated by those who, for differing reasons, have either refused to exchange or have broken diplomatic relations with Israel, or only to a Geneva Conference in which the Soviet Union would be a major participant, is to invite the Arabs to militant extremism.

I

Jews and Arabs in Palestine

Palestine in the Islamic and Ottoman Period

By Moshe Sharon

It is extremely difficult, if not completely impossible, to talk about a political history of Palestine after the destruction of the Jewish state in A.D. 70 and the suppression of the Bar Kokhba revolt in A.D. 135[1]. The country became a province and not a very important one, within the Roman Empire. From that date onward its fate was decided by the fortunes that befell the Empire or kingdom in whose boundaries it happened to be incorporated. First it was the Roman Empire and then successively: the Byzantine Empire until the seventh century, a short Persian rule (614-629), the Ummayyad Caliphate until the middle of the 8th century, the Abbasid Caliphate until the middle of the ninth, and from then onwards it came under masters that ruled it from Egypt. Two local Egyptian dynasties, the Tulumids and the Ikhshids held it until the second half of the 10th century; the Fatimid Caliphate, also from Egypt governed it until the end of the 11th century. For a short period in the seventies of the 11th century great parts of Palestine were subdued by the Seljuq Turks.

The Crusaders remained in the Holy Land for about two hundred years, and under them Palestine became once again an independent political unit (the Latin Kingdom of Jerusalem), the political activity of which had such far-reaching international implications that it is not surprising that the literature about it in verse and in prose, in fiction and in scholarly studies, in novels and in drama exceeded anything that has ever been written about this country.

After the defeat of the Crusaders by Saladin in 1187, great parts of Palestine

9

again came under Islamic rule, and once more the country's fate was decided either by Damascus or by Cairo. The Ayyubids were its masters until the middle of the 13th century, then came two hundred and sixty six years of Mameluke rule from Egypt. At the beginning of the 16th century the Ottoman Empire took over and ruled the country until the beginning of the present century. Palestine became once again part of a great Empire but this did not necessarily mean the improvement of its fortunes. It was now ruled from the distant imperial capital Istanbul via the provincial capital Damascus, which served for centuries as the traditional seat of the governor of Syria in which Palestine was included in a form of several sub-districts.

In the course of the almost 1,300 years between the Arab conquest and the British one, Palestine was governed, wholly or partly by more than *ten* different Empires, Governments and dynasties. I mention this chronological list not so much in order to show the obvious instability of government which had in its turn a devastating effect on the country, but more in order to emphasize the fact that the history of Palestine under the Muslims cannot be separated from the general history of the different powers that acquired it throughout the ages.

The province of Palestine was so insignificant during most of the Islamic rule that one hardly finds it mentioned in the Arabic sources. The earliest work dedicated to Palestine which is available to us dates as late as the 14th century[2], although earlier accounts of the country are scattered in works of the Muslim geographers. These accounts, with all their importance, contain, on the whole, very scanty historical information. The first major historical work (with noticeable elements of the former guide books) was not written until the end of the 15th century.

Thus, the task of the historian of Palestine under Islam is especially difficult, for he is obliged to patch up an artificial history of a country that for almost 1,300 years was in the dark corner of the historical arena.

However, although very little can be said about the political history of Palestine, the study of the impact of Islam and Arab rule on its social, economic and cultural development is of extreme importance. It has many significant implications, both cultural and political, for modern times.

In order to comprehend the historical consequences of the long Islamic presence in the country one must review its situation under its previous rulers—the Byzantines.

A major and most decisive historical event took place under the Byzantines in the 4th century; its results for world destiny can never be overestimated. It was probably one of the very few most important turning points in human history, if not the most important one. This was the acceptance of Christianity by Emperor Constantine (306-337 A.D.) first as a tolerated creed and later as the religion of the state. This event, which determined the whole future of Western civilization in general, also decided dramatically the destiny of Palestine for the centuries to come. The decision of Constantine transformed the country from a half neglected sub-district of Syria into the most important place in the Christian world, which became very soon identified with the Roman Empire and its inheritors. The Byzantine government increased tremendously its interest in the welfare and security of Palestine. A strong and efficient military administration was established in it. The fortifications of its main cities were strengthened and the two Roman lines of defense, the *Limes Arabia* and the *Limes Palestinae* were reactivated and fortified to enable the efficient protection of the sedentary areas from the incursions of the nomads from deserts which encircled the country from the East and the South. Churches, basilicas, convents and other Christian religious buildings appeared all over the country. Pilgrims from every corner of the Christian world poured into it, commerce was enhanced and encouraged by the excellent security provided by the government and so, too, was agriculture. The sedentary population grew in number and most of the country's soil, even in semi-deserts and desert areas, was brought under cultivation. The study of the contemporary sources leaves no doubt that Palestine under the Byzantines achieved prosperity and growth of population unequalled in history. Its population is estimated to have numbered between 3.5 and 4 million people. The country was packed almost to its utmost capacity with villages and towns. Agriculture, based in many places on complicated systems of irrigation, commerce, and the services and facilities given to pilgrims and tourists, were the main branches of its economy.

As far as the composition of the population is concerned, it is in my view of lesser importance to discuss the different groups that built it up. The line should rather be drawn between the sedentary population and the nomad one. The tension and the clashes between these two ways of life, or better, cultures, always had a fatal effect on the history of Palestine, and especially so under Islam.

Although we can detect in the population of Byzantine Palestine—Jews, Samaritans, some Greeks and some Hellenized groups in the coastal towns, these had, however, a high degree of cultural unity within the sedentary populations, which was demonstrated by the fact that the spoken language was Aramaic whilst the official language of the administration and clergy was Greek. The Arab tribes that had erupted time and again out of the vast "oceans" of the Arabian deserts, were kept in check by the effective Byzantine military force. Those of them that managed somehow to enter into the sedentary areas were rapidly assimilated into their population.

To sum up, when the Islamic conquest of Palestine began in 633 A.D., the country was fully occupied by a well-protected, prosperous, sedentary and urban—mainly Christian—population. Around that year this population numbered approximately 4 million. However, by the middle of the 16th century, when the first Ottoman census was made, it numbered no more than 300,000.

These two numbers cannot possibly suggest anything but that throughout the Islamic rule, Palestine underwent a steady process of decay.

This phenomenon is due mostly to one major fact and this is that under Islam, Palestine lost, almost completely, the special status which it had enjoyed under both Jewish and Christian rule, and more specifically the sacred position it had occupied in Christianity. The shrines of Islam were far away from it, situated in Arabia, whereas Jerusalem, which had been regarded as the heart of both Judaism and Christianity was given by Islam, even in later ages, a status secondary to that of Mecca and Medina. Naturally, the interest of the various Islamic governments and rulers in the country was not motivated by the ideological and spiritual considerations that had characterized the interest of the previous Christian state. The Islamic attitude toward Palestine was, therefore, formulated mainly in accordance with the political circumstances and vicissitudes of power. Thus the Islamic traditions concerning the sacredness of Jerusalem, Palestine and even the whole of Syria, which developed in the course of time, were the product of political conditions and political necessities. The fact that the first great dynasty of Caliphs, the Umayyad, established itself in Syria and ruled the Islamic Empire from Damascus and the fact that the oppositional forces to this dynasty were active in the Holy cities of Arabia and in Iraq created the need to supply Syria with a proper *Islamic* holy status. The key word in the last sentence is *Islamic,* for although Jerusalem, Palestine and some places in Syria had been sanctified either by Judaism or by Christianity or by both, nevertheless Islam, that regarded itself as the ultimate manifestation of the truth of the two previous revelations, had to find for them its own meaning. Since nobody could or would challenge the supreme holiness of Mecca and Medina, where the Prophet was born, acted and taught, the Islamic tradition managed to create its own version of the sanctity of Jerusalem and Palestine. It was done mainly in three ways: (a) by inventing, reconstructing and Islamizing traditions about places connected with Qur'amic personalities, who are mainly biblical figures, the most prominent of whom is Abraham. (b) by the exegesis of certain verses in the Qur'an in such a way that they could be identified with places in Palestine and especially in Jerusalem. The most important of all those exegetical identifications is the one of the famous sura 17, verse 1. The night journey of the prophet from the nearer to the "further mosque" was said to have been made from Mecca to Jerusalem—to the Rock of the Temple Mount of Moriah. (c) by Islamizing Jewish (and to far lesser extent Christian) traditions on Jerusalem and Palestine, and especially such traditions related to the Day of Judgment, and to the advantages of residing or even sojourning in Jerusalem and Palestine.

The development and elaboration of hundreds of traditions along these lines was a process that continued for hundreds of years. The wars with the Crusaders in the twelfth and thirteenth centuries supplied an excellent atmosphere for more traditions of the kind. From that time onward a special form of literature developed known as the *Books of the Praises,* which were collections of traditions praising Jerusalem, Palestine, Damascus, the whole of Syria and many other places.

The techniques involved in the creation of Islamic traditions were quite simple, so that practically any *Alim,* that prepared his homework in the *Madrasah* well, and learned by heart several scores of chains of transmittors, could provide, to order, traditions on practically anything.

To return to the Umayyads, there is little doubt that they were the first to encourage officially the creation of traditions institutionalizing Islamic holy status to Jerusalem and later to the whole of Syria.[3]

Political situations and circumstances were, therefore, the cause and not the outcome of Palestinian sanctity under Islam. If we compare it, once again, with the previous periods, this "conditional holiness" of Palestine and Jerusalem could be influential as long as it served the purposes that brought it forth. Even at the height of the clash between Islam and Christianity, in the time of the crusade of Emperor Frederick II, the Ayyubid Sultan of Egypt ceded Jerusalem in treaty to the Emperor in 1228, guided by military and political considerations.[4] Ten years previous to that, the Ayyubid al Mu'azzam 'Isa destroyed the city of Jerusalem and caused the expulsion of most of its inhabitants because he felt that he could not protect it against the Franks.

Scores of additional examples can be brought in order to demonstrate this status of the conditioned holiness of Palestine and Jerusalem in Islam, but the most striking perhaps is the one which is a slip of the tongue of the great Muslim geographer Yaqut (died 1229). Talking about the city of Multan in India Yaqut remarked that Multan was holy for the people of the East in the same manner that Jerusalem was holy for the Jews and Christians. Let us not forget that this was written whilst the Franks were still ruling great parts of Syria and Palestine.

To sum up, Palestine under Islam lost most of the spiritual advantages that it had enjoyed under the previous Christian rule; therefore the attitude of the Islamic rulers toward it was dictated mainly by practical considerations. Internal political developments within the Islamic state decided the destinies not only of Palestine but of the whole of Syria as we shall see later. The speedy deterioration of the central power of the Caliphate from the 9th century onward and the shift of the centers of power far away from the borders of Palestine first to Baghdad and later to Cairo, were additional causes for the neglect and swift deterioration of the country.

The process that followed is a well known one in the history of Palestine. It is already to be found in ancient times. The neglect of the country's internal security and defense followed the growing lack of real interest on the part of the government in it. Heavy taxation with no reward in the form of maintenance of public enterprises resulted in the quick desertion of cultivated lands. Once the borders of the deserts were thrown open, those lands fell as easy spoil into the hands of the Arab tribes. This was by no means a process peculiar to the Islamic period, it had happened time and time again in the history of Palestine. One can recall the same situation in the ancient time of the Judges, when the deterioration of the power of the various central authorities in the sedentary areas of Palestine enabled the Midianites to fall on the fertile fields of the country like locusts. In the 15th century, the great Muslim historian Ibn Khaldun regarded this endless strife between the *imran,* the civilization developed in the sedentarized regions, and nomads as the main pattern in the movement of human history—in the growth and decline of civilizations. This process had its supreme manifestation in the case of Palestine.

When outlining the pattern of development, the question to be asked is—from what period can we talk about the real Arab occupation of Palestine, and in what circumstances?

One fact is beyond all doubt, and that is, that the Arab conquest of the 7th century did not change in any drastic form the composition of the population that had existed under the Byzantines. It was quite a while before the Arabs colonized parts of the country and it took much longer before it was Arabized. The *Islamization* of Palestine was never really achieved. In fact Syria as a whole, including Palestine and Lebanon, contains to our day the highest percentage of non-Muslims in the whole of the Middle East. Even before the establishment of the State of Israel, only Egypt had larger Christian and Jewish populations than Syria—and that was only in absolute number, but not in percentage of the population. We cannot say the same, for instance, about Persia, which was completely Islamized in a matter of a few generations, but never Arabized.

We can think of many reasons for the fact that the Arab tribes did not settle in the country immediately after its conquest, but two reasons seem to me the most important:

I. Very soon after the beginning of the Islamic invasion in 633-634, and due to extraordinary successful campaigns, the fronts and battlefields of the Muslim forces were quickly pushed far beyond the borders of Palestine. In the north, the front against the Byzantine Empire was formed for many centuries to come on the northern borders of Syria. In the East, the Muslims overran Iraq and were pushing eastwards toward the borders of India and Transoxania where their front was ultimately formed in the second half of the 7th century.

In the West their forces moved into Egypt and securing its swift occupation continued westward toward the Atlantic and Spain. Most of the Arab warriors who took part in the occupation of Palestine moved in the direction of the new fronts where fresh spoils and hopes for the pleasure of Paradise were waiting. Most of these warriors, who were organized in their original tribal groups and had their families with them, moved either to the north or to the south west, to Egypt. Very soon after its conquest, therefore, Palestine was left to its original inhabitants, Christians, Jews and Samaritans, whilst its conquerors moved to new battlefields. As long as the momentum of the conquests continued, most of the fresh tribal manpower went in the same directions. This process was demonstrated by the new military towns that were established by the Arabs. These towns—the *Amsar*—were erected along the route of the conquests or as an immediate support to them. In Iraq, Basrah and Kufa, these were towns that served both as bases from which warriors went forth to Persia and as link posts with the great reservoir of manpower of Arabia. In the West, a line of such towns sprang up along the route of the advancing army—Fustat in Egypt, Qayrawan in what is today Tunisia and Ribat (Rabat) on the Atlantic coast in Morocco. On the Northern front, which was the first to be stabilized, a line of fortresses was built, known in later ages as the *Thughur* and the *Awasim.* For many generations to come, these fortresses would be a major attraction for Muslim fighters, long after the conquests had come to a standstill. In Palestine, not a single military town was erected. The only battle front of the country during the whole of the Islamic period was the coast. The sea was the Muslim's main enemy in the two senses of the word—firstly, it was from the Mediterranean that the Christian fleets could effectively threaten Syria, as they in fact did; and secondly, because of the fear that the Arabs had of the sea and which they never managed to overcome. Throughout the ages the Islamic Army remained basically a land army of cavalry and infantry. The resentment and the feelings of fear of the sea are reflected in many Islamic traditions which compare the sea to Hell or to fire. A martyr who has fallen on the sea, one tradition says, will receive the reward of two martyrs fallen on land and will have all his sins forgiven.[5]   The problem of fortifying the Syro-Palestinian coast has always been the *Achilles-heel* of the Muslim states, and for a long time after the conquests, the main defenders of Syrian coastal towns and the bulk of their population were either non-Arabs or even non-Muslims, such as elements of the local population and Persians who were transferred to them.

One town was built in Palestine by the Arabs. This was the city of Ramlah, established in 717 A.D. It was not a military town, but a purely commercial, industrial center and the administrative capital of Palestine, prospering from its location on the main route between Syria and Egypt. Its population was an ethnic conglomerate of Jews (and later Karaites), Samaritans, Christians and some Muslims. At the time of its establishment, its founder, Prince Sulayman, the Governor of Palestine, had no intentions of populating it with Arab tribes but forced the local population of Lodd to move into it, by actually destroying their town. The town grew as a cosmopolitan trade center where a large and prosperous Jewish community grew and flourished until the Crusades. With the establishment of Ramlah, Jerusalem was almost completely neglected. The Jewish community in Jerusalem that was reestablished after the Islamic conquest deteriorated with the deterioration of the town and its remnant in the tenth century was completely dependent on the rich, prosperous community of Ramlah.

The fact that immediately after the conquest Palestine was left to its former inhabitants is reflected in the Arabs' attitude to the native population. They did not embark on a policy of exile, a policy which was widely followed by previous conquerors from the Assyrians down to the Persians. The Arabs most probably were aware of the advantages of such policy but they used it even elsewhere very seldom, and on a very small scale. They simply did not need such a policy, since most of Syria fell into their hands without local resistance of any significance. Once the main body of the Byzantine army was crushed, in two decisive battles in 634 and 636, the local population did not oppose them, to say the least. In one case, we are told, the inhabitants of one of the Syrian cities went out to welcome the advancing Muslims with music and song.

The peace treaties that were drawn up between the conquerors and the inhabitants of various towns in Syria and Palestine reflect this lack of a deliberate policy of colonization on the part of the Muslims. The peace treaty that was made with the inhabitants of Tiberius is typical of all the other treaties and it is worth citing. The treaty guaranteed the following: "Security (Aman) for the people of Tiberia, for their lives, their property, their children, their churches and their houses, excluding these (houses) which were left and abandoned by their owners".[6]

II. The establishment of the Umayyad dynasty soon after the conquest was achieved, brought to Palestine direct and in many ways enlightened rule. Mu'awiyyah, the first Umayyad caliph (661-680) who had served as the Governor of Syria since 640, long before he ascended the throne, governed his Empire from Damascus. He and two of his great successors Abd al-Malik (685-705) and Hisham (724-743) shared between themselves sixty of the ninety years of the dynasty.

Naturally, the Umayyads were concerned about the welfare of Syria, which provided them with their loyal army and which was their main stronghold against the rebellious Iraq. Mu'awiyyah followed almost to the very detail the Byzantine policy of protecting the sedentary population and keeping the nomads in check. Irrigation projects and other public works, such as the maintenance of roads and the development of the Imperial Post were carried out under him at least as efficiently as they had been under his predecessors. It was also due largely to the fact that the administrative machine was not only manned and managed by the same Byzanto-Christian personnel, but also in the Greek language. Jews and Christians enjoyed under him and under most of his successors religious freedom, which amongst the Jews kindled as it seems new Messianic hopes. When Caliph Abd al-Malik built in 691 the Dome of the Rock, the act was hailed by many Jews. An old midrash hails Abd al-Malik almost in the same words that were used to praise Koresh (Cyrus) more than a thousand years earlier: "and he also . . . will build the House of the Lord the God of Israel"[7].

Jews were appointed by Abd al-Malik to supply certain services to the new edifice: to manufacture glass lamps, to provide the oil for them and light them, and to keep the place clean. "It is very difficult to understand", says Prof. Saitein—"how Jews undertook at that period such duties, and even regarded it as a merit, had they not observed the revival of Temple peace (under the Muslims) as the beginning of the Redemption."

The building of roads in Palestine, or at least the maintenance of the Roman —Byzantine roads by the same Caliph also had its echoes in the Midrash which praised the Caliph saying: "And he will pave the way of Jerusalem."

As far as keeping the Arab tribesmen in check was concerned, that was not a difficult task for the Umayyads. In the first half of this period the continued momentum of the conquests drew many of the Arabs to areas which promised fresh spoils. But probably more important was the fact that many Arab tribesmen did not wish to settle in the cities and villages of Syria and Palestine in great numbers.

The nomad detested as much as he feared sedentary life. The *Tatun*, the plague, so frequent in the towns was the thing he dreaded most. In order that the Arab tribes actually occupy the country, one condition was essential and this was the retreat of the rural civilization. As long as the country was fully occupied and cultivated by a sedentary population well protected by the central government the Arab nomad would keep out, both voluntarily and by force. Favorable conditions for the Bedouin developed, however, very rapidly once the Umayyads fell and were replaced by the Abbasids in 750.

However, although the Umayyad strove to preserve and protect the local sedentary population that provided their treasury with handsome revenue, they realized very soon that the situation was somewhat unnatural. They were Arab rulers of the Islamic Empire, yet the provinces that formed the backbone of their empire, their own capital, their administration, were all Christian. The official language of the State was Greek, the coinage Byzantine. Abd al-Malik was the first to take practical steps against this situation and to embark on a preconceived policy of *Arabization* and *Islamization*. This policy was part of the strife between Christianity and Islam; it had cultural and administrative motives and aims but had very little, if anything, to do with the ethnic composition or social order of the local population. Abd al-Malik started with the reform of the administration. Arabic was established as the official language in all the state documents, the administrative posts were gradually closed for non-Muslims, the new coins were struck and put into circulation instead of the Byzantine ones.

The inscriptions on the coins were clearly directed against Christianity while stressing the supremacy of Islam.

"There is no God but Allah alone, He has no co-partners. Muhammad is the Messenger of Allah. Allah has sent Him with guidance and the religion of truth in order that He may set it above all the other religions." For many centuries to come, this was the standard inscription on all gold and silver Islamic coins.

The Arabic inscriptions dating from Abd al-Malik on all the state enterprises were all written in the same spirit. The eight hundred feet long inscription inside the Dome of the Rock is entirely composed of anti-Christian and Islamic missionary verses (mostly from the Qur'an).

The main attack was on the Christian dogma of the Trinity and of the divine nature of Jesus. The pure Islamic monotheism was stressed over and over again accompanied by the emphasis on the true prophetic message of Muhammad. No direct reference was made to the Jews, for the simple reason that the Jews though mentioned in the Qur'an as being worse enemies of Islam than the Christians, did not actually constitute a direct threat to the Islamic state, as the Byzantine Christian Empire did. Besides, it seems that at the early stages of Islamic rule the Jews regarded the Muslims as their deliverers from the Christian-Byzantine yoke, and as the forerunners of the ultimate *géullah* (Redemption).

In the different stages of the Islamic campaign, the Jews extended help to the invaders, and many of them that converted to Islam were to be found among the inner circles of the new rulers. The Jewish community did not cut its relations with these converts, and in all probability acquired through them many concessions for the renewal of Jewish life, especially in Jerusalem.

The policy of cultural and administrative Islamization began with Abd al-Malik, was carried further by Caliph Umar II (717-720) who imposed further discriminatory legislation against non-Muslims, which undoubtedly brought in turn new converts. The exemption of the newly converted from poll-tax and at the beginning of his reign also from land tax, also encouraged conversion.

But despite all, Islamization under the Umayyads fell far behind Arabization. The policy of Islamization in such a Christian country as Syria could not be very successful for the inhabitants there had developed religious communal institutions with well invested clergy, and their links with the other parts of the Christian world, though badly affected, were not interrupted. The policy of Islamization under most of the Umayyad caliphs was not applied to the individual and not even to the community; it was directed more against *Christianity* and *Christiandom* than against *Christians*, and much less against Judaism. Taking this fact into consideration and the strength of Christianity in Syria and Palestine, one can well understand why Islamization had only a partial and limited success.

Different, however, was the case with Arabization. The acceptance of the Arabic language as the colloquial and the language of cultural activity, was not a traumatic experience for a population which spoke, wrote and read various semitic dialects and especially Aramaic. The introduction of Arabic as the language of administration speeded a process which had already begun a few centuries before with the contacts between the Syrian and Palestinian population and the Arabic speaking tribes that had occupied the deserts on the borders of these countries.

In the case of Persia — to continue with a comparison we have started — the conditions and circumstances were completely different. There, the local administration was left in the hands of the indigenous Sahamiah notables (*dihqans*) who carried out their diverse administrative tasks in Persian. The country was vast and far away from the main centers of the Arab-speaking territories. In many places the contact with Arabic speaking peoples was minimal, in others completely non-existent. The Persians were able, therefore, to absorb Arabic into their language in the same way that they assimilated within them the Arabs who had come with the various waves of the conquests.

In Syria and Palestine, with their immediate contact with Arabia, and with Arabic effectively replacing the Greek, which was a completely alien language to the Syrians, the cultural Arabization was profound, rapid and durable. Arabic became the language of the intellectuals — no matter what their creed was. Jews and Christians developed their own form of Arabic, known today by the technical terms of Judaeo-Arabic and Christian Arabic respectively. In the case of the Jews and Karaites, most of the works in any branch of intellectual endeavor were produced in Arabic, and this includes the interpretation of the Law. It can be compared only to the phenomenon that had taken place in the previous centuries, when Aramaic was used, somehow in the same manner, to produce the Talmud and different *Targumim*. I have no doubt that at the beginning Arabic characters were used side by side with Hebrew letters in the text, but later, the Rabbinical Jews wrote in Hebrew characters, whereas the Karaites used, to a large extent, Arabic characters, even in pure theological works. It is possible, as some scholars hold, that this is a sign of the cultural assimilation of the Karaite society.

To sum up: toward the end of the Umayyad period we can speak about Syria and Palestine being populated mainly by their earlier inhabitants, and undergoing a quick process of cultural Arabization without the infiltration of much Arab blood.

The whole situation was catastrophically altered with the fall of the Umayyads in A.D. 750 and the establishment of the Abbasid Caliphate.

The site of the new government was transferred to the east, to Iraq where the city of Baghdad was established in 762. The new dynasty, depending completely on the eastern provinces of the Empire, deliberately neglected Syria, which had been the home and mainstead of their predecessors and enemies. The deterioration of Syria and Palestine, as a result, was very quick. In a matter of a few years cultivated areas were being deserted, and by the end of the eighth century the central government in Baghdad of Harun ar-Rashid was alarmed by the drop of revenues in land tax. The deterioration of agriculture was not a phenomenon typical of Palestine alone; it was part of the death of agriculture under Islam everywhere throughout the Empire. But in the case of Palestine the process was enhanced by the official neglect of the country. That meant first of all that the Government was no longer interested in protecting the rural population against the incursions of the nomads. With more cultivated areas deserted, the nomads began to have the upper hand. Side by side with the process of the deterioration of the sedentary civilization from within, great changes were taking place in the deserts that border Palestine. In the ninth century, when the country was brought under the Egyptian rule of the Tulumids, a huge eruption of Arab tribes from the Arabian Peninsula had started. Two big tribes, Banu Hilal and Banu Sulaym moved from the heart of Arabia northwards and then across Sinai westward toward Egypt. They moved first along the Nile to southern (upper) Egypt and later they pushed westward to North Africa where they landed in the 11th century. The destruction which they caused wherever they passed was tremendous, and its signs were seen very clearly even in the 15th Century. They influenced Ibn Khaldun's entire attitude to human history. The migration of Banu Hilal and Banu Sulaym was such a tremendous event and such a traumatic experience for the people of the area, and especially for the inhabitants of Egypt, that the legends and popular stories about them form, to our own day, the main repertoire of any professional Arab storyteller. Palestine was affected first by this migration, albeit indirectly. The movement of such big tribes was bound to cause an upheaval in the desert. Many smaller tribes were pushed in front of them, and these tribes could now break into the unprotected sedentary areas of Syria and Palestine. Very swiftly, the coastal plains and the fertile valleys fell into their hands. The more the pressure of the desert continued the quicker was the retreat of sedentary life. The population was drained out first from the countryside to the urban centers where plagues took their toll in thousands every year, and then from the local urban centers out of the country to the main centers of political and economic activity. It was around this time that the Jewish population in Palestine had its final exile either to Egypt (where a great Jewish community had existed for centuries) or to Babylonia.

With the death caused by Islam to agriculture everywhere, the Jews in Palestine died also as an agricultural people but were reborn into the new commercial, bourgeois society in the main political centers of the Empire. In Jerusalem, the remnants of the Jewish community lived under most difficult economic conditions and were completely dependent on the donations that were collected for them in the rich community of Egypt.

But still, until the arrival of the Crusaders, a considerable number of Jews chose to live in Jerusalem even in the worst conditions. In a letter from 1054 we read about Jerusalem:

"Its food is scarce and its livelihood limited, and many (people) came to it rich and became impoverished."[8]

The successive masters that ruled Palestine from Egypt paid more attention to their capital Fustat than to the whole province of Syria—Damascus and Jerusalem included. Under the Fatimids, who captured Palestine in 969 and ruled it until the coming of the Crusaders 130 years later, the country acquired the appearance which characterized it until the beginning of the present century: the remnants of the rural population retreated to the hilly areas of Judaea and Samaria or to the fortified towns, the rest of the countryside was abandoned to the Bedouin.

The increasing destruction of Palestine in the 9th and 10th centuries was due also to the fact that the country assumed once again its tragic historical role as a border land between conflicting powers, and became the battlefield of wars that intensified the process of its desolation. By the beginning of the 11th century the Arab tribes in it, led by the powerful tribe of Tayy, grew so bold that they denounced the authority of the central Fatimid government and set up a counter-caliph of their own, and though they were defeated by a strong army sent against them, they were able to rebel once again in 1024 and actually rule the country for another five years. The continuous disturbances and wars that marked the end of the Fatimid rule, the Seljuq invasion of 1070, the Crusaders, the unstable Ayyubid rule of Saladin's successors in Syria, all had, in their turn, additional ruinous consequences for Palestine.

When it was taken over by the Mamelukes in the middle of the 13th century, nomadism, destruction and lawlessness increased to yet a higher degree. Special attention and intensive measures were required in order to restore security and order but the Mamelukes, more than any other government which had ruled Palestine from Egypt, dedicated their main interest to Egypt and, in particular, Cairo. The policy of neglecting Syria and Palestine was continued almost as a policy of state. The province of Syria was regarded as a second rate province once the Crusaders were expelled (1291). Unable to defend the coastal towns, for lack of a naval force, and because they depended solely on cavalry, the Mameluks followed the example set by Saladin himself and began destroying systematically all the coastal towns and fortifications. The mass annihilation of the Palestinian shore was the last and worst blow dealt to the country, for by destroying the coast, the Mamelukes added to the annihilation of the agriculture — the extinction of trade.

Although many sacred buildings and pious institutions were established in Jerusalem by the Mamelukes, Syria and Palestine were regarded as places of exile where out of favor Mameluke officers were sent.

The real rulers of the country were the Arab tribes that brought travel many times almost to a complete standstill.

Even the Hajj caravan was frequently attacked and robbed by the Bedouin, and travel between Egypt and Gaza, between Gaza and Jerusalem and even between Jaffa and Jerusalem on the main route was rejected as highly perilous.

The state of destruction of the country was summed up by the Ramban in the second half of the 13th century, when he came to Jerusalem and revived Jewish life in it.

"Whatever is holier is more destroyed" he wrote — "Palestine is destroyed more than the other countries, Judaea is the most devastated in the whole of Palestine and Jerusalem is the most destroyed of them all."

At the end of the 15th Century, Rabbi Meshullam of Voltera wrote, on his v
age from Cairo to Gaza:

"From Cairo to Gaza there are 'miles of murder'—and how much we arⳑ
indebted to God who rescued us from the dangers that lurk between Cairo and
Gaza."

The same picture continued throughout most of the Ottoman period
(1516-1918). The revival of modern Palestine was due to both the great zeal of the
Jewish pioneers and to the introduction of modern government and security
measures mainly by the British after the First Word War, though the last two or
three decades of Ottoman rule saw some improvement in the administration and
internal security. To be sure, the greater proportion of the modern Arab population of Palestine entered the country in the present century.

But when the first Jewish pioneers came into the country at the end of the last
century they were met by destruction which was caused mainly by the indifference of the Muslim rulers to the Holy Land. Wars, plagues, earthquakes and,
probably above all, the quick and general deterioration of the Islamic civiliza-tion,
added their share.

FOOTNOTES

1. It is, however, possible to study the history of the *Jews* in Palestine until the eve of the
Arab conquest, as has been brilliantly done by Prof. M. Avi-Jonah in his *B'yme Romi
u-Byzantion*. Although the Romans sent into exile many of the most influential families and
people regarded by them as rebellious, the majority of the Jewish population remained in
the country and cherished hopes and aspirations for the renewal of its political freedom.
These hopes sometimes took the form of Messianic movements and sometimes burst out in
the form of rebellions whose center was mainly in the Galilee — the home of the main Jewish
activity after the destruction of the Temple. The Persian conquest of the early seventh century in which the Jews placed all their hopes turned out to be a disastrous disappointment
which resulted in the loss of any hope and in the mass migration of the Jews into the diaspora
(then mainly in Iraq and Egypt).

2. This was a guide book composed for the benefit of the pilgrims to the Holy Places,
mainly in Jerusalem. The author, Jamal ad-Din Ahmad, wrote his book *Muthir al-Gharam
. . .* ("*The Exciter of Desire for Visitation of the Holy City and Syria*") *in 1351. A similar work, based
on the former, was written in 1430. See, Le Strange, Palestine under the Moslems, 1890, p. 11.*

3. Historical tradition was also colored accordingly. It is highly possible that the message
of Abu Bakr, the first Caliph to his General in Mesopotamia which read, according to a
famous account "Haste to Syria for one village in it is more important for me than the whole
of Iraq," date from the same period.

4. cf. K. Setton (ed.) *History of the Crusades*, Philadelphia, 1962, II, pp. 454-55.

5. see, Y. Friedmann, "Minor problems in al-Baladhuri's account of the conquests of
Sinai". *RSO*, 1970, p. 255.

6. Baladhuri, *Futuh al-Buldan*, (ed. de Geoje), p. 116.

7. *Sefer Hayyishuv, II*, 69.

8. *Ibid.* p. 18.

Land Ownership in Palestine 1880 – 1948

By Moshe Aumann

A great deal has been spoken and written over the years on the subject of land ownership in Israel—or, before 1948, Palestine. Arab propaganda, in particular, has been at pains to convince the world, with the aid of copious statistics, that the Arabs "own" Palestine, morally and legally, and that whatever Jewish land ownership there may be is negligible. From this conclusions have been drawn (or implied) with regard to the sovereign rights of the State of Israel and the problem of the Arab refugees.

The Arab case against Israel, in the matter of Jewish land purchases, rests mainly on two claims: (1) that the Palestinian Arab farmer was peacefully and contentedly working his land in the latter part of the 19th century and the early part of the 20th century when along came the European Jewish immigrant, drove him off his land, disrupted the normal development of the country and created a vast class of landless, dispossessed Arabs; (2) that a small Jewish minority, owning an even smaller proportion of Palestinian lands (5 percent as against the Arabs' 95 percent) illegally made itself master of Palestine in 1948.

Pre-1948 Conditions in Palestine

A study of Palestine under Turkish rule reveals that already at the beginning of the 18th century, long before Jewish land purchases and large-scale Jewish immigration started, the position of the Palestinian fellah (peasant) had begun to deteriorate. The heavy burden of taxation, coming on top of chronic indebtedness to money-lenders, drove a growing number of farmers to place themselves under

21

the protection of men of wealth or of the Muslim religious endowment fund (*Waqf*), with the result that they were eventually compelled to give up their title to the land, if not their actual residence upon and cultivation of it.

Until the passage of the Turkish Land Registry Law in 1858, there were no official deeds to attest to a man's legal title to a parcel of land; tradition alone had to suffice to establish such title—and usually it did. And yet, the position of Palestine's farmers was a precarious one, for there were constant blood-feuds between families, clans and entire villages, as well as periodic incursions by rapacious Bedouin tribes, such as the notorious Beni Sakk'r, of whom H. B. Tristram (*The Land of Israel: A Journal of Travels in Palestine*, Society for Promoting Christian Knowledge, London, 1865) wrote that they "can muster 1,000 cavalry and always join their brethren when a raid or war is on the move. They have obtained their present possessions gradually and, in great measure, by driving out the fellahin (peasants), destroying their villages and reducing their rich corn-fields to pasturage." (p. 488)

Tristram goes on to present a remarkable and highly revealing description of conditions in Palestine on both sides of the Jordan River in the middle of the 19th century—a description that belies the Arab claim of a tranquil, normally developing Palestinian rural economy allegedly disrupted by Jewish immigration and settlement.

> A few years ago, the whole Ghor was in the hands of the fellahin, and much of it cultivated for corn. Now the whole of it is in the hands of the Bedouin, who eschew all agriculture, except in a few spots cultivated here and there by their slaves; and with the Bedouin come lawlessness and the uprooting of all Turkish authority. No government is now acknowledged on the east side; and unless the Porte acts with greater firmness and caution than is his wont . . . Palestine will be desolated and given up to the nomads.
>
> The same thing is now going on over the plain of Sharon, where, both in the north and south, land is going out of cultivation, and whole villages rapidly disappearing from the face of the earth. Since the year 1838, no less than 20 villages have been thus erased from the map and the stationary population extirpated. Very rapidly the Bedouin are encroaching wherever horse can be ridden; and the Government is utterly powerless to resist them or to defend its subjects. (p. 490)

For descriptions of other parts of the country, we are indebted to the 1937 Report of the Palestine Royal Commission—though, for lack of space, we can quote but the briefest passages. In Chapter 9, para. 43 the Report quotes an eye-witness account of the condition of the Maritime Plain in 1913:

> The road leading from Gaza to the north was only a summer track suitable for transport by camels and carts . . . no orange groves, orchards or vineyards were to be seen until one reached Yabna village . . . Not in a single village in all this area was water used for irrigation. . . . Houses were all of mud. No windows were anywhere to be seen. . . . The ploughs used were of wood. . . . The yields were very poor. . . . The sanitary conditions in the village were horrible. Schools did not exist. . . . The rate of infant mortality was very high. . . .
>
> The area north of Jaffa . . . consisted of two distinctive parts. . . . The

eastern part, in the direction of the hills, resembled in culture that of the Gaza-Jaffa area. . . . The western part, towards the sea, was almost a desert. . . . The villages in this area were few and thinly populated. Many ruins of villages were scattered over the area, as owing to the prevalence of malaria, many villages were deserted by their inhabitants.

The Huleh basin, below the Syrian border, is described as "including a number of Arab villages and a large papyrus swamp draining south into Lake Huleh . . . a triangular strip of land some 44 sq. miles in area . . . This tract is irrigated in a very haphazard manner by a network of small, primitive canals. It is, owing to over-irrigation, now the most malarious tract in all Palestine. It might become one of the most fertile."

With regard to yet another region in Palestine—the Beisan (Beit Shean) area—we quote from the report of Mr. Lewis French, Director of Development appointed by the British Government in 1931:

> We found it inhabited by fellahin who lived in mud hovels and suffered severely from the prevalent malaria. . . . Large areas of their lands were uncultivated and covered with weeds. There were no trees, no vegetables. The fellahin, if not themselves cattle thieves, were always ready to harbour these and other criminals. The individual plots of cultivation changed hands annually. There was little public security, and the fellahin's lot was an alternation of pillage and blackmail by their neighbours the Bedouin.

This, then, was the picture of Palestine in the closing decades of the 19th century and up to the First World War: a land that was overwhelmingly desert, with nomads continually encroaching on the settled area and its farmers; a lack of elementary facilities and equipment; peasants wallowing in poverty, ignorance and disease, saddled with debts (interest rates at times were as high as 60 per cent) and threatened by warlike nomads or neighboring clans. The result was a growing neglect of the soil and a flight from the villages, with a mounting concentration of lands in the hands of a small number of large landowners, frequently residing in such distant Arab capitals as Beirut and Damascus, Cairo and Kuwait. Here, in other words, was a social and economic order that had all the earmarks of a medieval feudal society.

Who Dispossessed the Palestinian Peasant?

The Palestinian peasant was indeed being dispossessed, but by his fellow-Arabs: the local sheik and village elders, the Government tax-collector, the merchants and money-lenders; and, when he was a tenant-farmer (as was usually the case), by the absentee-owner. By the time the season's crop had been distributed among all these, little if anything remained for him and his family, and new debts generally had to be incurred to pay off the old. Then the Bedouin came along and took their "cut," or drove the hapless fellah off the land altogether.

This was the "normal" course of events in 19th century Palestine. It was disrupted by the advent of the Jewish pioneering enterprise, which sounded the death-knell of this medieval feudal system. In this way the Jews played an objective revolutionary role. Small wonder that it aroused the ire and active opposition of the Arab sheiks, absentee landowners, money-lenders and Bedouin bandits.

Jewish Land Purchases

It is important to note that the first enduring Jewish agricultural settlement in modern Palestine was founded not by European refugees, but by a group of old-time families leaving the overcrowded Jewish Quarter of the Old City of Jerusalem. (According to the Turkish census of 1875, by that time Jews already constituted a majority of the population of Jerusalem and by 1905 comprised two-thirds of its citizens. The *Encyclopedia Britannica* of 1910 gives the population figure as 60,000, of whom 40,000 were Jews.)

In 1878 they founded the village of Petah Tikva in the Sharon Plain—a village that was to become known as the "Mother of Jewish Settlements" in Palestine. Four years later a group of pioneering immigrants from Russia settled in Rishon le-Zion. Other farming villages followed in rapid succession.

When considering Jewish land purchases and settlement, four factors should be borne in mind:

1. Most of the land purchases involved large tracts belonging to absentee owners. (Virtually all of the Jezreel Valley, for example, belonged in 1897 to only two persons: the eastern portion to the Turkish Sultan, and the western part to the richest banker in Syria, Sursuk "the Greek.")

2. Most of the land purchased had not been cultivated previously because it was swampy, rocky, sandy or, for some other reason, regarded as uncultivable. This is supported by the findings of the Peel Commission Report (p. 242): "The Arab charge that the Jews have obtained too large a proportion of good land cannot be maintained. Much of the land now carrying orange groves was sand dunes or swamp and uncultivated when it was purchased . . . there was at the time at least of the earlier sales little evidence that the owners possessed either the resources or training needed to develop the land."

3. While, for this reason, the early transactions did not involve unduly large sums of money, the price of land began to rise as Arab landowners took advantage of the growing demand for rural tracts. The resulting infusion of capital into the Palestinian economy had noticeable beneficial effects on the standard of living of all the inhabitants.

4. The Jewish pioneers introduced new farming methods which improved the soil and crop cultivation and were soon emulated by Arab farmers.

The following figures show land purchases by the three leading Jewish land-buying organizations and by individual Jews between 1880 and 1935.

From the Table below it will be seen that the proportion of land purchased from large (usually absentee) owners ranged from about 50 to 90 percent.

"The total area of land in Jewish possession at the end of June 1947," writes A. Granott in *The Land System in Palestine* (Eyre and Spottiswoode, London, 1952, p. 278), "amounted to 1,850,000 dunams; of this 181,00 dunams had been obtained through concessions from the Palestine Government, and about 120,000 dunams had been acquired from Churches, from foreign companies, from the Government otherwise than by concessions, and so forth. It was estimated that 1,000,000 dunams and more, or 57 percent, had been acquired from large Arab landowners, and if to this we add the lands acquired from the Government, Churches, and foreign companies, the percentage will amount to seventy-three. From the fellahin there had been purchased about 500,000 dunams, or 27 percent, of the total area acquired. The result of Jewish land acquisitions, at least to a considerable part, was that properties which had been in the hands of large and medium owners were converted into holdings of small peasants."

JEWISH LAND PURCHASES, 1880-1935

(in dunams*)

Organization	Total land acquired	Government conces- sions	From private owners	Large tracts**	
				Dunams	Percent (approx.)
PICA (Palestine Jewish Colonization Assoc.)	469,408	39,520	429,887	293,545	70
Palestine Land Development Co.	579,492	66,513***	512,979	455,169	90
Jewish National Fund****					
Until 1930			270,084	239,170	90
1931-1947			566,312		50
Individual Jews			432,100		50

* 4 dunams = 1 acre.

** The large tracts often belonged to absentee landlords.

*** Land situated in the sandy Beersheba and marshy Huleh districts.

**** ". . . created on December 25, 1901, to ensure that land would be purchased for the Jewish workers who were to be personally responsible for its cultivation.

"Since the J.N.F. was as concerned with conforming to socialist ideals as with intensive economic exploitation of land, its Charter was opposed to the use of lands purchased by it as private property. The J.N.F. retained the freehold of the lands, while the people working it are only life tenants. . . .

"The capital of the Jewish National Fund was essentially raised from small regular donations from millions of Jewish craftsmen, labourers, shop-owners and intellectuals in Central and Eastern Europe where the shadow of genocide was already apparent, who felt concerned about the return of Jews to Zion. . . .

"Contrary to colonialist enterprises, which were seeking an exorbitant profit from land extorted from the colonized peoples, Zionist settlement discouraged private capital as its enterprise was of a socialist nature based on the refusal to exploit the worker." (Kurt Niedermaier, *Colonisation Without Colonialism*, Youth and Hechalutz Dept., Jewish Agency, Jerusalem, 1969).

The League of Nations Mandate

When the League of Nations conferred the Mandate for Palestine upon Great Britain in 1922, it expressly stipulated that "The Administration of Palestine . . . shall encourage, in cooperation with the Jewish Agency . . . close settlement by Jews on the land, including State lands and waste lands not acquired for public purposes" (Article 6), and that it "shall introduce a land system appropriate to the needs of the country, having regard, among other things, to the desirability of promoting the close settlement and intensive cultivation of the land." (Article 11)

British policy, however, followed a different course, deferring to the extremist Arab opposition to the above-mentioned provision of the Mandate. Of some 750,000 dunams of cultivable State lands, 350,000, or nearly half, had been allotted by 1949 to Arabs and only 17,000 dunams to Jews. This was in clear violation of the terms of the Mandate. Nor, ironically enough, did it help the Arab peasants for whose benefit these transactions were ostensibly carried out. The glaring examples of this policy are the case of the Beisan lands and that of the Huleh Concession.

Beisan Lands

Under the Ghor-Mudawwarra Agreement of 1921, some 225,000 dunams of potentially fertile wasteland in the Beisan (Beit Shean) area were handed over to Arab farmers on terms severely condemned not only by Jews but also by such British experts as Lewis French and Sir John Hope-Simpson. More than half of the land was irrigable, and, according to the British experts, eight dunams of irrigated land per capita (or 50-60 dunams per family) were sufficient to enable a family to maintain itself on the land. Yet many families received far more than that: six families, of whom two lived in Syria, received a combined area of about 7,000 dunams; four families (some living in Egypt) received a combined area of 3,496 dunams; another received 3,450 and yet another, 1,350.

Thus the Ghor-Mudawwarra Agreement was instrumental in creating a new group of large landowners. Possessing huge tracts, most of which they were unable to till, these owners began to sell the surplus lands at speculative prices. In his 1930 Report, Sir Hope-Simpson wrote of the Agreement that it had deprived the Government of "the control of a large area of fertile land eminently suited for development and for which there is ample water available for irrigation," and that "the grant of the land has led to speculation on a considerable scale."

Huleh Area

For twenty years (from 1914 to 1934) the Huleh Concession — some 57,000 dunams of partly swamp-infested but potentially highly fertile land in northeastern Palestine — was in Arab hands. The Arab concessionaires were to drain and develop the land so as to make additional tracts available for cultivation, under very attractive terms offered by the Government (first Turkish, then British). However, this was never done, and in 1934 the concession was sold to a Jewish concern, the Palestine Land Development Company, at a huge profit. The Government added several onerous conditions concerning the amount of land (from the drained and newly developed tracts) that had to be handed over — without reimbursement for drainage and irrigation costs — to Arab tenant-farmers in the area.

All told, hundreds of millions of dollars were paid by Jewish buyers to Arab landowners. Official records show that in 1933 £854,796 was paid by Jewish individuals and organizations for Arab land, mostly large estates; in 1934 the figure was £1,647,836 and in 1935, £1,699,488. Thus, in the course of only three years £4,202,180 (more than 20 million dollars at the prevailing rate of exchange) was paid out to Arab landowners (Palestine Royal Commission Report, 1937).

To understand the magnitude of the prices paid for these lands, we need only look at some comparative figures. In 1944, Jews paid between $1,000 and $1,100 per acre in Palestine, mostly for arid or semi-arid land; in the same year rich black soil in the state of Iowa was selling for about $110 per acre (U.S. Department of Agriculture).

Effects on Arab Population

In those instances where as a result of such transactions Arab tenant-farmers were displaced (on one year's notice), compensation in cash or other land was paid, as required by the 1922 Protection of Cultivators Ordinance; the Jewish land-buying associations often paid more than the law required (Pollack and Boehm, *The Keren Kayemeth Le-Israel*). Of 688 such tenants between 1920 and 1930, 526 remained in agricultural occupations, some 400 of them finding other land (Palestine Royal Commission Report, 1937, Chapter 9, para. 61).

Investigations initiated in 1931 by Mr. Lewis French disposed of the charge that a large class of landless or dispossessed Arab farmers was created as a result of Jewish land purchases. According to the British Government report (Memoranda prepared by the Government of Palestine, London 1937, Colonia No. 133, p. 37), the total number of applications for registration as landless Arabs was 3,271. Of these, 2,607 were rejected on the ground that they did not come within the category of landless Arabs. Valid claims were recognized in the case of 664 heads of families, of whom 347 accepted the offer of resettlement by the Government. The remainder refused either because they had found satisfactory employment elsewhere or because they were not accustomed to irrigated cultivation or the climate of the new areas (Peel Report, Chapter 9, para. 60).

Purchases of land by Jews in the hill country had always been very small and, according to the investigations by Mr. French, of 71 applications by Arabs claiming to be landless, 68 were turned down.

Arab Population Changes Due to Jewish Settlement

Another Arab claim disproved by the facts is that Zionist "colonialism" led to the disruption and ruin of the Arab Palestinian society and economy.

Statistics published in the Palestine Royal Commission Report (p. 279) indicate a remarkable phenomenon: Palestine, traditionally a country of Arab emigration, became after World War I a country of Arab immigration. In addition to recorded figures for 1920-36, the Report devotes a special section to illegal Arab immigration. While there are no precise totals on the extent of Arab immigration between the two World Wars, estimates vary between 60,000 and 100,000. The principal cause of the change of direction was Jewish development, which created new and attractive work opportunities and, in general, a standard of living previously unknown in the Middle East.

Another major factor in the rapid growth of the Arab population was, of course, the rate of natural increase, among the highest in the world. This was accentuated by the steady reduction of the previously high infant mortality rate as a result of the improved health and sanitary conditions introduced by the Jews.

Altogether, the non-Jewish element in Palestine's population (not including Bedouin) expanded between 1922 and 1929 alone by more than 75 percent. The Royal Commission Report makes these interesting observations:

> The shortage of land is, we consider, due less to the amount of land acquired by Jews than to the increase in the Arab population. (p. 242)
>
> We are also of the opinion that up till now the Arab cultivator has benefited, on the whole, both from the work of the British administration and from the presence of Jews in the country. Wages have gone up; the standard of living has improved; work on roads and buildings has been plentiful. In the Maritime Plains some Arabs have adopted improved methods of cultivation. (p. 241)

Jewish development served as an incentive not only to Arab entry into Palestine from Lebanon, Egypt, Syria and other neighboring countries, but also to Arab population movements within the country—to cities and areas where there was a large Jewish concentration. Some idea of this phenomenon may be gained from the following official figures:

Changes in towns: The Arab population in predominantly Arab towns rose only slightly (if at all) between the two World Wars: in Hebron—from 16,650 in 1922 to 22,800 in 1943; Nablus—from 15,931 to 23,300; Jenin—from 2,737 to 3,900; Bethlehem—from 6,658 to 8,800. Gaza's population actually decreased from 17,426 in 1922 to 17,045 in 1931.

On the other hand, in the three major Jewish cities the Arab populations shot up during this period, far beyond the rate of natural increase: Jerusalem—from 28,571 in 1922 to 56,400 (97 percent); Jaffa—from 27,437 to 62,600 (134 percent); Haifa —from 18,404 to 58,200 (216 percent).

Changes in rural areas: The population of the predominantly Arab Beersheba district dropped between 1922 and 1939 from 71,000 to 49,000 (the rate of natural increase should have resulted in a rise to 89,000). In the Bethlehem district the figure increased from 24,613 to about 26,000 (after falling to 23,725 in 1929). In the Hebron area it went up from 51,345 to 59,000 (the natural increase rate dictated a rise to 72,000).

In contrast to these declines or comparatively slight increases in exclusively Arab-inhabited areas, in the Nazareth, Beit Shean, Tiberias and Acre districts —where large-scale Jewish settlement and rural development was underway —the figure rose from 89,600 in 1922 to some 151,000 in 1938 (by about 4.5 percent per annum, compared with a natural increase rate of 2.5-3 percent).

In the largely Jewish Haifa area the number of Arab peasants increased by 8 percent a year during the same period. In the Jaffa and Ramlah districts (heavily Jewish populated), the Arab rural population grew from 42,300 to some 126,000—an annual increase of 12 percent, or more than four times as much as can be attributed to natural increase (L. Shimony, *The Arabs of Palestine,* Tel-Aviv, 1947, pp. 422-23).

One reason for the Arab gravitation toward Jewish-inhabited areas, and from neighboring countries to Palestine, was the incomparably higher wage scales paid there, as may be seen from the Table below.

The capital received by Arab landowners for their surplus holdings was used for improved and intensive cultivation or invested in other enterprises. Turning again to the Report of the Palestine Royal Commission (p. 93), we find the following conclusions: "The large import of Jewish capital into Palestine has had a general fructifying effect on the economic life of the whole country. . . . The expansion of Arab industry and citriculture has been largely financed by the capital thus obtained . . . Jewish example has done much to improve Arab cultivation . . . The increase in Arab population is most marked in areas affected by Jewish development."

During World War II, the Arab population influx mounted apace, as is attested by the *UNRWA Review,* Information Paper No. 6 (September 1962):

DAILY WAGE SCALES, 1943

(in mils)

	Unskilled labor	Skilled labor
Palestine	220—250	350—600
Egypt	30— 50	70—200
Syria	80—100	150—300
Iraq	50	70—200

Source: A. Khoushy, *Brit, Poalei Eretz-Israel,* 1943, p. 25.

A considerable movement of people is known to have occurred, particularly during the Second World War, years when new opportunities of employment opened up in the towns and on military works in Palestine. These wartime prospects and, generally, the higher rate of industrialization in Palestine attracted many new immigrants from the neighboring countries, and many of them entered Palestine without their presence being officially recorded.

Land Ownership in 1948

The claim is often made that in 1948 a Jewish minority owning only 5 percent of the land of Palestine made itself master of the Arab majority, which owned 95 percent of the land.

In May 1948 the The State of Israel was established in only part of the area allotted by the original League of Nations Mandate. 8.6 percent of the land was owned by Jews and 3.3 percent by Israeli Arabs, while 16.9 percent had been abandoned by Arab owners who imprudently heeded the call from neighboring countries to "get out of the way" while the invading Arab armies make short shrift of Israel. The rest of the land—over 70 percent—had been vested in the Mandatory Power, and accordingly reverted to the State of Israel as its legal heir. (Government of Palestine, *Survey of Palestine, 1946*, British Government Printer, p. 257.)

The greater part of this 70 percent consisted of the Negev, some 3,144,250 acres all told, or close to 50 percent of the 6,580,000 acres in all of Mandatory Palestine. Known as Crown or State Lands, this was mostly uninhabited arid or semi-arid territory, inherited originally by the Mandatory Government from Turkey. In 1948 it passed to the Government of Israel.

These lands had not been owned by Arab farmers—neither under the British Mandate nor under the preceding regime. Thus it is obvious that the contention that 95 percent of the land—whether of Mandatory Palestine or of the State of Israel—had belonged to Arabs has absolutely no foundation in fact.

There is perhaps no better way of concluding and summing up this study than to quote from an article entitled *Is Israel a Thorn or a Flower in the Near East?* by Abdul Razak Kader, the Algerian political writer, now living in exile in Paris (*Jerusalem Post*, Aug. 1, 1969):

"The nationalists of the states neighboring on Israel, whether they are in the government or in business, whether Palestinian, Syrian or Lebanese, or town dwellers of tribal origin, all know that at the beginning of the century and during the British Mandate the marshy plains and stony hills were sold to the Zionists by their fathers or uncles for gold, the very gold which is often the origin of their own political or commercial careers. The nomadic or semi-nomadic peasants who inhabited the frontier regions know full well what the green plains, the afforested hills and the flowering fields of today's Israel were like before.

"The Palestinians who are today refugees in the neighboring countries and who were adults at the time of their flight know all this, and no anti-Zionist propaganda—pan-Arab or pan-Muslim—can make them forget that their present nationalist exploiters are the worthy sons of their feudal exploiters of yesterday and that the thorns of their life are of Arab, not Jewish, origin."

Arab Immigration into Pre-State Israel: 1922 – 1931

By Fred M. Gottheil

As an historical event of major consequence, it is not surprising that there are at least two conflicting accounts concerning immigration into Palestine prior to the formation of the State of Israel. One account, for example, depicts Jewish immigration into Palestine primarily in terms of filling up vast empty spaces of sparsely populated land.[1] Much of this description centers upon the drainage of the northern marshes and the reclamation of the desert. Essentially, it is an account of man versus nature. Only parenthetically does it consider Arab immigration or the impact of Jewish immigration on the resident Arab population.

By contrast, a second version shifts the focus of discussion to population displacement. It describes the same Jewish immigration as creating in Palestine a demographic overcapacity situation with the indigenous Arab population being forced off the settled land.[2] In this case it is an account of man versus man for control and ownership of extremely limited natural resources.[3] Both descriptions survive today as historical summaries of pre-Israel Palestine.

Although there is substantial disagreement in the two accounts concerning the *impact* of immigration, there is no disagreement as to its *source*. Both emphasize its Jewish origins. Almost completely lost in these accounts is an analysis of concurrent Arab immigration. References to such immigration are made only *in passim* and the conclusion reached is that for purposes of permanent settlement, Arab immigration was insignificant.[4]

This conclusion, however, has not gone completely unchallenged. The Royal Institute for International Affairs, for example, commenting on the growth of the

Palestinian population prior to World War II, states: "The number of Arabs who entered Palestine illegally from Syria and Transjordan is unknown. But probably considerable."[5] Professor Harold Laski makes a similar observation: "There has been large-scale and both assisted and unassisted Jewish emigration to Palestine; but it is important also to note that there has been large-scale Arab emigration from the surrounding countries."[6] Underscoring the point, C. S. Jarvis, Governor of the Sinai from 1923-1936, noted: "This illegal immigration was not only going on from the Sinai, but also from Transjordan and Syria and it is very difficult to make a case out for the misery of the Arabs if at the same time their compatriots from adjoining States could not be kept from going in to share that misery."[7] Even the Simpson Report acknowledged Arab immigration in this form:

> Another serious feature of immigration is the number of persons who evade the frontier control and enter Palestine without formality of any kind. It is exceedingly difficult to maintain any effective control of the various frontiers of Palestine. At the present time such controls as exists is carried out at police posts on the roads. The immigrant who wishes to evade the control naturally leaves the road before reaching the frontier and takes to the footpaths over the Hills . . . The Chief Immigration Officer has brought to the notice that illicit immigration through Syria and across the northern frontier of Palestine is material.[8]

Other writers make this same point.[9] Although Arab immigration has been described as "considerable," "large scale," and "material," such descriptions are nonetheless lacking in precision.[10]

This paper presents some statistical evidence concerning Arab immigration into Palestine. The following issues will be considered: What was the Arab population size in Israel in 1922 and how rapidly did this population grow? What percent of this growth can be attributed to natural increase and what percent to immigration? How do the demographic patterns in pre-State Israel compare with those in non-Israel Palestine during the 1922-1931 period, and what explanations can be offered to explain divergent patterns? Although data will be presented for all of Palestine, a distinction will be drawn between Arab immigration into the part of Palestine that later becomes Israel and the non-Israel sector of Palestine. The analysis will emphasize the former.

The Application of Palestine Census Data to Pre-State Israel: 1922-1931

Census data for Palestine is available only for the years 1922 and 1931. Prior to 1922, there existed at best, educated guesses.[11] Since 1931, population estimates were derived by applying natural rates of growth and *registered* immigration to the 1931 numbers.[12] Because these population estimates make no attempt to measure unrecorded immigration, the reliability of these numbers is considerably less than those of the census years.[13] For this reason, the analysis here is restricted to the census period 1922-1931.

The transfer of this census data to pre-State Israel is complicated by the character of the Israel borders which were not entirely aligned with the administrative subdistricts of Palestine upon which the statistical reporting of population was made. In 1922, population data for Palestine was arranged by the British Mandatory Government in 18 subdistricts according to urban or rural location and according to religion. The relationship between these subdistricts and the State of Israel is illustrated in Table 1.

Table 1

PALESTINE AND ISRAEL

(by subdistrict)

Subdistricts entirely within Israel	Subdistricts partially within Israel	Subdistricts entirely outside Israel
Safad	Jenin	Nablus
Acre	Tulkarm	Ramallah
Nazareth	Jerusalem	Jericho
Haifa	Hebron	
Beisan	Gaza	
Jaffa	Bethlehem	
Ramle		
Beersheba		
Tiberias		

SOURCE: *Survey of Palestine*, Vol. I, 1946, p. 145.

The problem of identifying the 1922 Arab population as pre-State Israel or non-Israel Palestine is thus reduced to an intra-subdistrict analysis of population allocation in the 6 subdistricts that are only partially included in the State of Israel. A disaggregation of the census data from the subdistrict level to the village level for those subdistricts whose domain includes the Israel border permits a reclassification of the Palestine census data into Israeli Arab and non-Israeli Arab population. The results are seen in Table 2.[14]

Arab Population in Pre-State Israel: 1922-1931

Total Arab settled population in the pre-State Israel sector of Palestine increased during the 1922-1931 period from 321,866 to 463,288, or by 141,422. This population increase reflects both natural increases and increases through immigration. Since natural rates of growth for the Arab population of Palestine are available for the 1922-1931 period (Table 3), the relative contributions of natural increase and immigration can be measured.

Applying these rates to the 1922 population, we derive, for 1931, a population size of 398,498. Other estimates of rates of natural increase for the Muslim population have been made:

The 1931 Arab population that would obtain using the substantially higher estimates of the *Reports* modifies our results only slightly. The 11.8 percent of Arab immigration to 1931 actual Arab population is reduced to 9.2 percent; the 38.7 percent of total population growth 1922-1931 that is immigration is reduced to 30.2 percent; and the 36.8 percent of total immigration for 1922-1931 that is Arab is reduced to 31.1 percent. This compares with Horowitz and Hinden's estimate of 23 percent for 1922-1936 non-Jewish immigration as a percent of total non-Jewish population growth 1922-1936. *Economic Survey of Palestine*, Hapoel Hazair Cooperative Press. Tel-Aviv, 1938, p. 22.

Table 3 would obtain if natural increase were the only source of population growth. The actual 1931 population, derived from the 1931 census data however, is 463,288 or 64,790 more than can be explained by the natural increase. Since 10,000 represents simply a transfer of territory from Syria to the subdistrict of Safad, the 54,790 residual is imputed to the Arab immigration from the non-Israel sector of Palestine and from the surrounding Arab countries.[15]

Arab immigration thus appears to be substantial, as Laski, Jarvis, Simpson and others suggested. The 1922-1931 Arab immigration alone represents 11.8 percent of the total Arab settled population of 1931 and as much as 38.7 percent of the total 1922-1931 Arab population growth. This immigration size is no less impressive when compared to the 94,162 Jewish immigration during the same period.[16] The Arab immigration accounts for 36.8 percent of total immigration into pre-State Israel.

Table 2

Arab Settled Population 1922 and 1931
in Pre-State Israel and Non-Israel
Palestine (by subdistricts)

Subdistrict	Pre-State Israel		Non-Israel Palestine	
	1922	1931	1922	1931
Safad	18,720	35,751		
Acre	34,276	43,465		
Nazareth	20,713	24,090		
Haifa	45,712	69,136		
Beisan	9,925	13,087		
Jaffa	39,866	73,927		
Ramle	44,465	61,329		
Beersheba	2,258	2,948		
Tiberias	14,245	18,877		
Jenin	5,430	7,014	27,978	34,239
Tulkarm	13,424	17,016	21,477	28,581
Jerusalem	18,799	29,201	35,272	45,266
Hebron	11,246	14,359	41,881	53,114
Gaza	42,563	52,763	29,055	42,288
Bethlehem	224	325	22,554	21,444
Nablus			56,482	68,477
Ramallah			28,948	37,771
Jericho			1,888	3,192
Totals	321,866	463,288	265,535	334,372

SOURCE: Barron, J. B., *Report and General Abstracts of the Census of 1922*, Jerusalem, Government Printer, m.d. Mills, E., *Census of Palestine 1931, Population of Villages, Towns, and Administrative Areas*, Jerusalem, 1932.

Table 3

Annual Rates of Natural Increase of Moslem, Christian, and
Other Non-Jewish Settled Population
(1922-1931)

	Moslem	Christian	Others		Moslem	Christian	Others
1922	2.49	1.91	2.48	1927	2.10	1.84	2.20
1923	2.15	1.98	2.15	1928	2.34	2.10	2.38
1924	2.47	2.34	2.03	1929	2.34	1.96	1.63
1925	2.18	1.81	2.63	1930	2.81	2.21	2.47
1926	2.90	2.16	1.84	1931	2.74	2.28	3.35

SOURCE: *Survey of Palestine,* Government of Palestine, Government Printer, Palestine, 1946, Vol. III, p. 1176. These rates, averaged, for 1922-1925 and 1926-1930, appear in *Palestine Blue Book,* 1938, Government Printer, Jerusalem, p. 144 and Palestine, Office of Statistics, *General Monthly Bulletin of Current Statistics of Palestine,* Jerusalem, January, 1937, p. 4.

	Palestine and Trans-Jordan Reports	Survey of Palestine "true-rate"		Palestine and Trans-Jordan Reports	Survey of Palestine "true-rate"
1922		na	1927	2.85	1.44
1923	2.18	na	1928	2.50	1.32
1924	3.37	na	1929		1.77
1925	2.97	na	1930	2.90	2.12
1926	3.48	1.67	1931		2.02

SOURCE: *Report: Palestine and Trans-Jordan,* His Majesty's Stationery Office, London: *Reports* 1922 through 1931. *Survey of Palestine,* Vol. III, Government of Palestine, Government Printer, Palestine, 1946, p. 1177.

Pre-State Israel and Non-Israel Palestine Immigration: A Comparison

The demographic character of the pre-State Israel 1922-1931 period contrasts sharply with that of non-Israel Palestine. This is shown in Table 4.

The population increase for non-Israel Palestine was 4,677 greater than what would have been obtained through natural increase alone. This number compares with the 54,790 immigration for pre-State Israel. The 1922-1931 immigration to non-Israel Palestine constitutes only 1.4 percent of its 1931 population size and 6.8 percent of the total increase for the period. The conclusion derived from the comparative analysis is that while immigration was an important contributor to

Table 4

ARAB SETTLED POPULATION IN PRE-STATE AND NON-ISRAEL PALESTINE (1922-1931)

	Population Measure	Pre-State Israel	Non-Israel Palestine
1922	actual	321,866	265,535
1931	actual	463,288	334,372
1931	natural	397,728	329,695
1931	immigration 1922-1931	54,790	4,677

population growth in pre-State Israel, it was of minor consequence in the non-Israel sector of Palestine.

Although the contrast between the two sectors of Palestine is clear, still, both sectors record for the period a net inflow of population. This outcome contrasts with the experience of the surrounding Arab countries, where, for the 1922-1931 period, emigration in some cases of substantial numbers, are reported.

—

ESTIMATES OF SYRIAN AND LEBANESE EMIGRATION (1921-1939)

	Origin	Gross emigration
1921-28a	Syria	89,407
1922-27b	Syria	46,500
1925-38c	Syria	38,302
1925-38c	Lebanon	49,586
1920-39d	Syria	54,000
1923-31e	Syria and Lebanon	97,892

SOURCE: (a) Hurwitz, D., "The Agrarian Problem of the Fellahin," *Jews and Arabs in Palestine*, Ed., Sereni and Ashery, Hechalutz Press, New York, 1936, p. 54; (b) *The Jewish Plan for Palestine: Memoranda and Statements Presented to the United Nations Special Committee on Palestine*, Jerusalem, 1947, p. 115; (c) Granott, A., *The Land System in Palestine*, Byre and Spottiswoode, London, 1952, p. 47; (d) Helbaoui, Y., *L'Economie Syrienne et les Problems de son Developpement*, BOSC Freres, Lyon, 1955. (e) Widmer, R., "Population," *Economic Organization of Syria*, Ed., Himadeh, S., American Press, Beirut, 1936, p. 16.

Immigration and Economic Development

The explanation for these diverging patterns of population growth and immigration can be found in the growing disparities of economic performance in pre-State Israel, non-Israel Palestine, and the Arab States.

That migration is highly synchronized with international investment and with disparities in the rates of economic growth in different regions has been well established.[17] Although the statistical record of economic activity in the Middle East is severely limited for the period 1922-1931, a consensus of economic reporting does appear to suggest that an Arab migration of 54,790 to pre-State Israel and 4,677 to non-Israel Palestine should be considered as something less than a total surprise.[18]

In contrast to the "economic paralysis" that seems to have characterized the Arab economies,[19]Palestine had been undergoing substantial economic growth. Capital stock, largely imported, increased by 327 percent while net domestic product rose, at constant prices, by 410 percent.[20] The importance of Jewish-owned enterprises, located primarily in pre-State Israel, can hardly be overstated. Their number increased during 1922-1937 from 1,850 to 6,007.[21] Moreover, 75 percent of the entire industrial work-force in 1927 was employed by such firms and 60 percent of the force was Arab.[22]

The rapid economic development in Palestine was not the exclusive property of the Jewish sector. The extent of Arab participation in the industrialization process is reflected in the growth, from 1918-1928, of 1,373 new Arab-owned enterprises.[23] Although clearly of a smaller scale than the Jewish enterprise, these nonetheless represented over 60 percent of the total enterprises established during the 1918-1928 period.[24]

Table 5

Per Capita Income, Relative Wages, Consumption of Foodstuffs, Net Productivity Per Male Earner in Agriculture, and the Value of Agricultural and Industrial Machinery Imports in Selected Middle East Economics (1932-1936)

	Per capita income (£) 1936 [a]	Industrial daily wages 1933-1935 (mils) [b]	Per capita Consumption of foodstuff (I.U.) 1934-1936 [a]	Net productivity per male earner in agriculture (I.U.) 1934-1936 [a]	Machinery imports (Palestine = 100) 1932-1934 [c] agricultural	industrial
Egypt	12	na	16.0	90.1	10	16
Syria	13	50-310	19.0	97.6	23	17
Iraq	10	40-60	13.8	93.2	10	16
TransJordan	na	na	na	90.1	na	na
Palestine: Arabs	19	70-500	22.9	186.3	100	100

SOURCE: (a) Alfred Bonne, *Economic Development of the Middle East*, Kegan Paul, Trench, Truber & Co., London, 1943, pp. 21, 47, 62. The International Unit (I.U.) is defined as the amount of goods and services that could be purchased for one dollar in the USA over the average of the decade 1925-1934. (b) David Horowitz and Rita Hinden, *Economic Survey of Palestine*, *Hapoel-Hazair Co-operative Press*, Tel-Aviv, 1938, p. 207. 1933 for Syria and Iraq; 1934 for Palestine and 1935 for Lebanon. (c) David Horowitz, "Palestine and the Middle East: An Essay in Regional Economy," *Palestine and the Middle East Magazine*, Tel-Aviv, October/November, 1943, p. 8. 1935-1938 for Iraq.

Economic conditions in Syria, Iraq, Lebanon, and Trans-Jordan appear to have been substantially different. In Syria, for example, the growth of new industry and the conversion of handicraft production to mechanization had been insufficient to absorb the surplus labor generated by the decline in overall industrial and handicraft production.[25] In the agricultural sector, progress appeared to have been equally unattractive. The persistence of agricultural backwardness is attributed to the continuation of primitive technology, excessive peasant indebtedness, climatic conditions, and the skewed distribution of land holdings.[26]

Similar descriptions are offered for Iraq[27] and Trans-Jordan; the latter described as "a parasite existing on the permanent subsidy of Britain and the civil administration of Palestine" with no attempts being made toward industrialization or the modernization of agriculture.[28] Industrial activity in Egypt appeared to have been hardly more successful. Capital in corporate enterprise increased by two percent annually between 1920-1930 and although investment in agriculture did increase, per capita agricultural output actually declined.[29]

Although comparative statistics for the Middle East for 1922-1931 is virtually impossible to construct because of limited comparable data, some regional estimates for 1932-1936 can serve at least as an indicator of comparative economic performance for the few preceding years. Such a comparison is offered in Tables 5 and 6.

The economic portrait shown in Tables 5 and 6 seem clear enough. Consumption of foodstuffs in Palestine among Arabs was 143 percent of the Egyptian, 121 percent of the Syrian, and 166 percent of the Iraqi consumption. Net agricultural productivity was 207 percent of both the Egyptian and Trans-Jordanian, 191 percent of the Syrian and 200 percent of the Iraqi.

Since a capital goods industry was virtually non-existent in the Middle East, the value of machine imports indicates, to some degree, the rate of increase in industrialization and mechanization of agriculture. Syrian, Egyptian and Iraqi agricultural machinery imports were 23, 10 and 10 percent of the Palestine imports; industrial machinery imports were 17, 16 and 16 percent.

Disparities between Palestine and the Arab States appear also in the investment outlays in the public sector.

Table 6

AVERAGE PER CAPITA GOVERNMENT EXPENDITURE (1929)
(in Palestine Mils)

Item	Palestine	Iraq	Syria	Transjordan
General Adm.	608	377	537	400
Army and Police	610	525	460	410
Total Unproductive	1290	902	997	810
Education	150	80	80	70
Health	110	70	40	40
Economy	80	115	30	57
Survey	80	14	63	30
Public Works	330	142	283	110
Total Productive	750	421	496	307

SOURCE: Grunwald, K., *The Government Finances of the Mandated Territories in the Near East*, Palestine Economic Society, May 1932, p. 100.

On almost every budget item, and particularly on items of industrial and social overhead capital, per capita expenditures in Palestine were higher than in any of the Arab States. Productive expenditures were, in 1929, for Palestine, 151 percent of the Syrian, 178 percent of the Iraqi and 244 percent of the Trans-Jordanian expenditures. In terms of government revenues, Palestine's per capita tax was 156 percent of Syria's, 167 percent of Iraq's and 295 percent of Trans-Jordan's.[30]

While the comparative evidence offered above is admittedly incomplete, the simple observation that significant disparities in economic activity between Palestine and the Arab States existed is clearly not without substance.

Conclusions

Arab immigration into Palestine, and specifically into pre-State Israel during the census period 1922-1931 reflects, to some degree, the different levels of economic activity within Palestine and between it and the contiguous Arab States. Arab immigration accounted for 38.7 percent of the total increase in Arab settled population in pre-State Israel, and constituted 11.8 percent of its 1931 population. Although less numerically than the Jewish immigration during the period, the significance of Arab immigration is nonetheless emphasized by its comparison with the Jewish population inflow. Arab immigration composed 36.8 percent of the total immigration into pre-State Israel. The situation in non-Israel Palestine was somewhat different. There, Arab migration was positive, but inconsequential.

FOOTNOTES

1. "Regions that but a few years ago were barren sand dunes, bare hills or pestilential swamps, have been converted into fertile agricultural land dotted with pleasing villages, and where people can live in the faith of their fathers and the children grew up happily. The labour was arduous, but it was cheerfully, even joyfully undertaken and it was lightened by the generous help given by Jews all over the world." Sir John Russell in forward to Lowdermilk, W. C., *Palestine: Land of Promise,* London, Gollancz, 1945.

2. "The increase in Jewish immigration was accompanied by large scale acquisition of land and large-scale dispossession of Arabs. Thousands of Arab farm families, driven from the land on which they and their ancestors had lived, were forced to go to the towns. The Jews aimed at controlling the economic life of the country. A landless and distorted class was created." Rousan, Mahmoud, *Palestine and the Internationalization of Jerusalem,* The Ministry of Culture and Guidance, Government of Iraq, Baghdad, 1965, p. 31.

3. It is this second version that is reflected in the Shaw (*Palestine Commission on the Disturbances of August, 1929,* Cmd. 3530, London, 1930) and Simpson (*Palestine Report on Immigration, Land Settlement, and Development,* Cmd. 3686. London 1930) Commission Reports which subsequently formed the basis of British policy restricting Jewish immigration into Palestine during the 1930s and 1940s.

4. It is noteworthy that this conclusion is represented in Arab, Jewish, and British writing alike. See, for example, Hopkins, L., "Population," *Economic Organization of Palestine,* edited by Himadeh, Sa'id, American Press, Beirut, 1938, p. 19; Ruppin, A., "Population of Palestine," *Palestine and Near East Economic Magazine,* Nos. 5 and 6, 1927, p. 130; and *Survey of Palestine,* Vol. I, Government of Palestine, Government Printer, 1946, p. 212.

5. *Great Britain and Palestine,* 1915-1945, Royal Institute for International Affairs, Information Papers no. 20, London, p. 64.

6. "Palestine: The Economic Aspect," *Palestine's Economic Future,* Ed., J. B. Brown, P. L. Humphries and Company Limited, London, 1946, p. 34.

7. United Empire, Vol. 28, p. 633.

8. *Palestine Report on Immigration, Land Settlement and Development,* London, 1930, pp. 126 and 138.

9. See Horowitz, D., "Arab Economy in Palestine," *Palestine's Economic Future,* P. L. Humphries Co., London, 1946, p. 65; Gervasi, F., *To Whom Palestine?* D. Appleton-Century, New York 1946, p. 79; Nemirovsky, M., "Jewish Immigration and Arab Population," *Jews and Arabs in Palestine,* Ed., Sereni, E., and Ashery, R., Hehalutz Press, New York, 1936, p. 81; Jewish Agency for Palestine, *Memorandum submitted to the Palestine Royal Commission,* London, 1936, p. 109.

10. The few estimates offered simply mention numbers. No documentation is presented. Nonetheless, the numbers are of interest: Gervasi mentions 60,000-80,000 for 1926-1946, *op. cit.*, p. 79, 20,000-30,000 is recorded for 1922-1927 by the *Jewish Plan for Palestine: Memoranda and Statements presented by The Jewish Agency for Palestine to the United Nations Special Committee on Palestine,* Jerusalem, 1947, p. 115. 40,000 for 1919-1944 is mentioned in Nathan, R., Gass, O., and Creamer, D., *Palestine: Problems and Promise,* Public Affairs Press, Washington, 1946, p. 136. David Horowitz and Rita Hinden write: "The official net immigration figures are obviously an underestimate, as they include neither illegal Jewish immigrants nor the steady influx of Arabs from the surrounding countries. The official net immigration for 1922-1936 is about 250,000, whereas the figure we arrive at . . . was 322,000—a difference of nearly 30 percent." *Economic Survey of Palestine,* Hapoel-Hazair Co-operative Press, Tel-Aviv, 1938, p. 28.

11. A. M. Carr-Saunders, for example, estimates Arab population in Palestine in 1919 at 642,000 *World Population,* Carendon Press, 1936, p. 307.

12. See *Survey of Palestine,* Government of Palestine, Government Printer, Palestine, 1946, Vol. I, p. 140; Hovne, A., *Labor Force in Israel,* The Maurice Falk Institute for Economic Research in Israel, Jerusalem, 1961, p. 29.

13. "There has been unrecorded illegal immigration both of Jews and of Arabs in the period since the census of 1931, but no estimate of its volume will be possible until the next census is taken." *Report by His Majesty's Government on Palestine and Transjordan.* London, 1937, p. 221. No census was taken.

14. The transformation of population data in the form of Muslims, Christians and other non-Jews to Arab population was made according to the equation: Arab Population = 0.82 Christian + 1.00 Muslim + 0.90 other non-Jews. *Palestine Blue Book 1938.* Government Printer, Jerusalem, n.d., p. 328. The distinction between settled and total population is made by excluding the nomadic tribes of the Beersheba subdistrict, Mills, E., *op. cit.,* Preface to the Census of Palestine, 1931.

15. Although no analysis was made of such a residual, it was nonetheless recognized in the Royal Commission Report of 1937. The Report states: "A discrepancy arose at the census of 1931 between the expected and enumerated population due to incomplete recording of births and deaths and of migration, and possibly to faulty enumeration of suspicious and primitive people." *Memoranda prepared by the Government of Palestine for the use of the Palestine Royal Commission,* His Majesty's Stationery Office, London, 1937, Colonial no. 133, p. 2.

16. *Ibid.,* p. 8.

17. See, for example, Thomas, B. "Migration and International Investment," *Economics of International Migration,* Ed., Thomas, B., McMillan, London, 1958; and Kuznets, S., and Dorothy S. Thomas, "Internal Migration and Economic Growth," *Selected Studies of Migration Since World War II,* Milbank Memorial Fund, New York, 1958, p. 199.

18. There is no way of separating out the migration from non-Israel Palestine to pre-state Israel although it is clear that such migration did take place. The *Survey of Palestine,* for example, comments: "Internal migrations have probably operated in the same way, the coastal plain and other regions *of more rapid economic development* attracting immigration from the hill regions," Vol. III., *op. cit.,* p. 1150. *My italics.*

19. The term "economic paralysis" belongs to Z. Y. Herschlag, *Introduction to the Modern Economic History of the Middle East,* E. J. Brill, Leiden, 1964, p. 231. Herschlag's is perhaps the best analysis of Middle East economic development for the pre-World War II period, but here too, the scarcity of statistical evidence is apparent. See his section "The Economy of the Mandated Territories—Syria, Lebanon, Iraq and Trans-Jordan—Between the Two World Wars," pp. 225-275.

20. Szereszewski, Robert, *Essays on the Structure of the Jewish Economy in Palestine and Israel,* The Maurice Falk Institute for Economic Research in Israel, Jerusalem, 1968, p. 82.

21. Gervasi, F., *op cit.,* p. 104.

22. Grunwald, K., "The Industrialization of the Near East," *Bulletin of the Palestine Economic Society,* February, 1934, Volume 6, Number 3, pp. 78-79.

23. Horowitz, D., and Hinden, R., *op. cit.,* p. 208.

24. Himadeh, S., "Industry," *Economic Organization of Palestine,* Ed., Himadeh, S., American Press, Beirut, 1938, p. 230.

25. Himadeh, S., "Industry," *Economic Organization of Syria,* Ed., Himadeh, S., American Press, Beirut, 1936, p. 172.

26. *Ibid.,* p. 115.

27. *Progress of Iraq 1920-1931: Special Report,* Colonial no. 58, His Majesty's Stationery Office, London, 1931, pp. 205-217, 235-240. See also, Young, E. H., *Reports on Economic Conditions and Policy and Loan Policy,* Government Press, June 1930, Baghdad, p. 4. Young, lamenting the lack of statistical data, "surmises" a process of slow accumulation of wealth.

28. Herschlag, Z. Y., *op. cit.,* p. 237.

29. O'Brien, P., *The Revolution in Egypt's Economic System,* Oxford University Press, 1966, p. 210.

30. Grunwald, K., *The Government Finances of the Mandated Territories in the Near East,* Palestine Economic Society, May 1932, Volume 6, Number 1, p. 97.

Arab-Jewish Contacts
In Palestine: 1923 – 1931

Efforts to build relations between the Arabs and the Jews in Palestine were initiated by the *Yishuv* (the Jewish community in Palestine) from the earliest period of modern Jewish settlement. The Yishuv's most concerted efforts began in the early 1920s and continued until its War of Independence in 1948. Some of the first contacts of this period, from 1923-1931, are recounted in the *Palestine Diary,* of Colonel Frederick H. Kisch, a British Jewish military engineer and Zionist leader who became a member of the Jewish Agency's Executive and was delegated the task of cementing Jewish-Arab relations. Below are excerpts from the *Diary*.

April 15, 1923. A two hours' interview at my flat with Sheik Assad Shoukair with whom I discussed the possibility of forming a more or less popular party to support the Mandate . . . A remarkable old man of strong personality . . . . He works in close concert with Ragheb Nashashibi. . . . The official leaders of such a party might be Ragheb Nashashibi and Arif Pasha Dajany, both of whom are *bien vus* by the Government. They might really effect a change in Arab opinion, if only the Government would give them some encouragement.[1]

May 20, 1923. All sections of the population have today been staggered by the publication in the press of the following cable received on May 18th by Musa Kazem Pasha from King Hussein:

"I desire to inform you of the truth concerning the Anglo-Arab Treaty on the occasion of this Holy Feast, the contents of which are based on fundamental decisions, and which are recognized by His Majesty the King of Great Britain.

His Majesty recognized the freedom of the Arabs in Arabia and in other lands, and pledges himself to support us effectively in the foundation of an All-Arab Union in these lands, viz. Mesopotamia, Palestine, Transjordania and all other Arab States, which are in the Arabian Peninsula (except Aden).

This is one of the great blessings of God, which shows that I have realized my assurances to the Arabs in the protection of their rights. There is no doubt that this Holy Feast will remain a National Feast; the Feast of Liberation of the Arab Nation.

I think it necessary to warn you against any activities which might disturb the peace and security of the country in any form whatsoever, as this might cause loss to our rights.

I will keep you informed with regard to future developments. Signed, Hussein."

I asked urgently for an appointment with the High Commissioner and informed him that the Jewish Community viewed the substance of King Hussein's telegram with grave concern. Whatever might be the real facts of the case it was clear that the British Government had been negotiating with King Hussein on a matter vitally affecting the future of the National Home without keeping the Jewish Agency informed of their intentions. Such action seemed inconsistent with Article IV of the Mandate.

H.E. stated that in his opinion there was no reason for perturbation. King Hussein's telegram was wholly unauthorized, and contained inaccurate statements. . . .

May 20, 1923. There is no doubt that the pan-Arab movement is at present a danger and will remain so until we succeed in coming to terms with the Arabs and bringing our respective national aspirations into harmony with each other. . . .

January 27, 1924. Left Jerusalem . . . for Amman[2] . . . I . . . greeted the King in the name of the Jews throughout the world . . . I declared that Jews were determined to realize their national revival in friendship and cooperation with their Arab kinsmen. I begged the King to accept an address setting forth the declaration of our highest National Institution to this effect . . . The text ran as follows:

(Translation form Hebrew)

"We beg to offer to Your Majesty our respectful greetings. We wish to express the belief that the two great Semitic peoples, united of yore by the bonds of common creative civilization, will not fail in the hour of their national regeneration to comprehend the need to combine their vital interests in a common endeavour. The Jewish people are determined to live with the Arab people on terms of concord and mutual respect, and together with them to make the common home into a prosperous land, the building-up of which may assure to each of its peoples undisturbed national development. The desire of the Jewish people to cooperate with the Arab people in the regeneration of the Orient was authoritatively expressed in the following Resolution of the XIIIth Zionist Congress of 1923:

'The Congress sees in the awakening of the Orient one of the most important factors in the reconstruction of the eastern world. The Jewish people who are beginning to rebuild their National Home are resolved with all their spiritual, moral and material powers to associate themselves with this new world now only coming into being, but so rich in energies and possibilities, and to collaborate on a footing of equality with the peoples whose destinies they share, in close communion and fruitful harmony of interests.'

Further, the Congress explicitly declared that the rights of all communities in Palestine will in all circumstances be regarded as equally sacred. It is in this spirit of cooperation and goodwill towards our Arab kinsmen that the resolve of the Jewish people for the establishment of their National Home is being executed.

Together with the above-quoted authoritative statement we wish to bring to Your Majesty's notice the indisputable fact that Palestine occupies a unique position in the hearts of the Jewish people by virtue of historical association, of the love of the Jewish people for the land and their will to rebuild it, of their work in the country, and now also by virtue of international recognition. We believe, moreover, that national harmony and concord between Jews and Arabs in Palestine will prove a positive and valuable factor in the general restoration of the ancient prosperity of neighbouring lands."

. . . the King stated that the Arabs would always stand for justice. . . . and the Jews should now help to defend the rights of the Arabs. The Arabs were ready to accept the help of the Jews towards that end . . . the Jews had nothing to fear from the Arabs. . . .

Amir Abdullah asked: "What is the Balfour Declaration?"

I replied as follows: "The Balfour Declaration is a recognition of certain historical facts. . . ."

The Amir said . . . did not the Jews threaten the political rights of the inhabitants? I replied that the proceedings of the Zionist Congresses proved that it was the intention of the Jews, while re-establishing their own national rights, not only to safeguard the rights of the Arabs but also to help them . . .

January 28, 1924. . . . the King asked me to explain the Zionist problem. I began with an explanation of the nature and intensity of the sentiment which was the foundation of the Zionist ideal . . . I said that in the eyes of the Jews the essential feature of the position was the *right* of any Jew to come to Palestine as his fatherland . . . The corollary to this was the right of the Jews in Palestine collectively to develop a national life of their own . . . I expressed the hope that before long the Arabs would recognize them also. As regards the Holy Places, I said that the Jewish leaders, both religious and secular, had made the most formal declarations that they regarded the Holy Places of the Muslim and Christian faiths as entirely outside the Jewish sphere of interest. . . . The Jews felt themselves very close in sentiment to the Arabs. . . . If a real understanding were reached, the King would see that the Jews were both ready and able to help the Arab cause.

King Hussein expressed his appreciation of the depth of the Jewish sentiment with regard to Palestine which he regarded as most honorable to the Jews. But, before he could help in a practical manner, it was necessary that we should gain the confidence of the Arabs. He suggested . . . that an endeavor be made to formulate definite proposals . . . the fact that we have now established direct and sympathetic relations with King Hussein may open possibilities which did not exist before.

March 2, 1924. A visit from a member of the Dajany family of whom a small contingent . . . have been visiting King Hussein. The latter had said that there could be no question of his attempting to expel the English from Palestine . . . while as regards the Jews, it must be remembered that they had received pledges no less than the Arabs. He therefore wanted the Arabs of Palestine to come to an understanding with the Jews.

March 22, 1924. Entertained Hassan Sabri to lunch . . . we were joined first by Aziz Bey Ali and . . . Said Kiamil Pasha, . . . the son of Abdul Hamid's Grand Vizier . . . these three men . . . all Muslims and true Orientals, were equally emphatic in their pro-Zionist declarations . . . each . . . for a somewhat different reason, recognized that the progress of Zionism might help to secure the development of a new Eastern civilization.

June 2, 1924. A visit from Musa H'deb,[3] leader of the Peasants' Party at Hebron, who are combining with the peasants of the Nablus region for a joint conference. The program should be published in the Arabic press this week, and I am told it will not be unfavorable. Progress in our relations with the Arabs is not unsatisfactory and should develop naturally from the bankruptcy of the policy of the extremists.[4]

January 13, 1931. Conference with representatives of the *Histadrut,* Golomb and Burla, with regard to Arab-Jewish relations . . . In outlining their standpoint, Golomb contended that of the various sections of the *Yishuv* Labor is the most realistic and sincere in its approach to the Arab question. He believes that ultimately the Labor people will be successful by their example and influence in securing that no section of the *Yishuv* will be content with mere declarations of good intentions. In the Labour sphere there is a natural community of professional interests between Jews and Arabs. . . . Burla then outlined a program of practical activities: the issue of informative pamphlets in Arabic; the establishment in Jerusalem and Jaffa of joint Arab-Jewish workers' clubs as existing at Haifa; credit facilities for Arab workers and fellahin under joint Arab-Jewish auspices; cultural work including Hebrew and Arabic classes for Arabs and Jews respectively . . ., etc. In his concluding remarks Burla touched upon the fundamental aspects of the matter, namely the recognition of the existence of Arab national aspirations. This, he submitted, cannot be ignored, and we have to seek to reconcile Arab aspirations with our own through some project for the association of Palestine with an Arab Confederation . . . I welcomed this wise approach on the part of the *Histadruth,* having always myself urged that we will never solve our political problem so long as we treat Palestine as if it were an island.

May 12, 1931. A long visit . . . from one of the leaders of the Arab *Istiklal* or Independence Party. I assured my visitor that the leaders of the Arab revival would find a considerable measure of support among Zionists and Jews generally, if on their part they would recognize the idea underlying the conception of the Jewish National Home in Palestine and its logical consequences . . . Unfortunately all our efforts had hitherto met with a negative response. Here I suggested that if at this stage conversations were difficult in Palestine, it might perhaps be practicable and useful for Arab and Jewish leaders to meet informally somewhere in Europe. I received no response . . . but understood that it would be considered among the persons concerned. My visitor mentioned several leaders of the Syro-Palestinian Committee as being anxious to seek an understanding with the Jews. I repeated that progress in the matter presupposed mutual confidence, which unfortunately was still lacking . . . On the other hand, the general tendency of the Zionist Movement was definitely in the direction of seeking understanding with the Arabs on the basis of reciprocal guarantees against domination, and mutual recognition of the legitimate aspirations of the two peoples.

FOOTNOTES

1. See Colonel Richard Meinertzhagen, *Middle East Diary*, 1917-1956 (New York, Thomas Yoseloff, 1959), esp. pp. 55-56, for the role played by British officers in encouraging Arab violence. The *Diary* is a rich source of material bearing upon the role of the British Administration in sabotaging the purposes of the Mandate. Meinertzhagen, a Britain of Danish origin, served as chief political officer in Palestine and Syria from 1919 to 1920 and as Military Adviser to the Middle East Department of the Colonial Office from 1921 to 1924.

2. To visit King Hussein (Sheriff of Mecca and father of King Abdullah of Transjordan). *Eds.*

3. Murdered in 1929 as a result of his friendship with the Jews.

4. This forecast proved incorrect as will be seen hereafter owing to the unaccountable support accorded by the Government to the Arab extremists, of whom the Mufti of Jerusalem, Hajj Amin al-Husseini, became the leader after the death of Musa Kazem Pasha.

The Jewish People and Palestine

By Chaim Weizmann

Excerpted from the statement made before the Palestine Royal Commission in Jerusalem on November 25, 1936 by Dr. Weizmann as President of the Zionist Organization and of the Jewish Agency for Palestine.

What did the Balfour Declaration mean? It meant something quite simple at that time, and I am saying so advisedly. It meant that Judaea was restored to the Jews or the Jews were restored to Judaea. I could submit to the Commission a series of utterances of responsible statesmen and men in every walk of life in England to show that this Declaration was at the time regarded as the *Magna Charta* of the Jewish people; it was in a sense comparable with another Declaration made thousands of years before, when Cyrus allowed a remnant of the Jews to return from Babylon and to rebuild the Temple. To the ordinary man at that time reading the Declaration, what it meant is broadly indicated by the various speeches at a solemn meeting at the Opera House in London, where (among others) Lord Cecil spoke and said:—"Arabia for the Arabs, Judaea for the Jews, Armenia for the Armenians." Much water and much blood have flowed under the various bridges of the world since that time, and not all of his predictions have been realized; but we read into the Declaration what the statesmen of Great Britain told us it meant. It meant a National Home, "National" meaning that we should be able to live like a nation in Palestine, and "Home" a place where we might live as free men in contradistinction to living on sufferance everywhere else. To English people I need not explain what the word "home" means, or what it does *not* mean, to us everywhere else.

The meaning was clear, and the Jewry of the world, in the trenches of Europe, in the pogrom-swept area of Russia, saw it like that. Tens of thousands of Jews marched before the house of the British Consul in Odessa at the time. Behind them were half-organized bands of marauders and murderers sweeping the countryside and destroying everything in their wake. But those Jews poured out their hearts in gratitude to the one accessible representative of the British Government, whom they had never seen, of whom they had never heard, whose language they could not speak, whose mentality they could not understand. They felt that here something had been done for us which, after two thousand years of hope and yearning, would at last give us a resting-place in this terrible world. I can only refer the Commission to the numerous newspaper articles in the British and American press. On the other hand the German Government, when they got to know of it afterwards, were sick at heart that the British had stolen a march on them. They called together our representatives in Germany and tried to explain to them that of course they would have done it, but they could not do it, because they were linked up with Turkey and had to go slowly. Perhaps the German Government considered it a piece of propaganda, but neither the British Government nor the Jews ever conceived of it as such. There was nobody to win over. As I have said, the rich Jews, who could have helped with their influence or money,—to them it meant nothing. The poor Jews had nothing to give.

It meant, as I say, at that time, and speaking in political parlance, a Jewish State; and when I was asked at the Peace Conference, quite impromptu, by Mr. Lansing, "What do you mean by a Jewish National Home?" I gave this answer: "To build up something in Palestine which will be as Jewish as England is English." Of course, we have always borne in mind, and our teachers and mentors at that time, British statesmen, repeatedly told us: "There is a second half to the Balfour Declaration. That second part provides that nothing should be done which might injure the interests of the non-Jewish communities in Palestine." Well, I must leave it to the Commission to test this and to ascertain whether, throughout the work of these last sixteen years, we have done anything which has in any way injured the position of the non-Jewish population. I go further than that. The Balfour Declaration says that the civil and religious rights of the non-Jewish communities should not be interfered with. I would humbly ask the Commission to give the broadest possible interpretation to that, not merely a narrow interpretation of civil and religious rights; put it as broadly as the Commission may wish, and test it, and I think I can say before the Commission, before God, and before the world, that in intention, consciously, nothing has been done to injure their position. On the contrary, indirectly we have conferred benefits on the population of this country. I should like to be perfectly frank: We have not come for that purpose. We have come for the purpose of building up a National Home for the Jewish people; but we are happy and proud that this upbuilding has been accompanied by considerable benefits to the country at large.

A certain time elapsed, My Lord, between the issue of the Declaration and the reign of peace in the world—a precarious peace—before we were allowed, under the terms of the Declaration, to begin our work; and I should like briefly to describe to the Commission what were the conditions under which we had to begin this kind of work. I think it will be admitted, after the Royal Commission has had an opportunity of surveying what we have done, that for the first time in the history of colonization work of this kind has been carried out by a private body, a body which had no treasury at its back, no State organization to aid it, so that we began our work, so to speak, with our right hand tied. Russian Jewry, that Jewry which was the natural carrier of the Zionist ideal and Zionist tradition, was broken, non-existent to all intents and purposes. As I have already mentioned, the rich Jews in the Western communities were, with a few exceptions, either skeptical or opposed. One of the exceptions, whose work you will no doubt have plenty of opportunity of seeing, was Baron Edmond de Rothschild, who began his work in Palestine when it was still under the rule of the Turk. He began his work here roughly sixty years ago. With perhaps the exception of him and a few others—very few—the powerful Jews were either indifferent or against us. In order to get funds for immigration, settlement, acquisition of land, we had to go hat in hand to the Jews of the world, to the poor, and get their contributions.

It is, if I may say so with respect, a fallacy to think that what has been built up in Palestine (with the exception which I have mentioned) has been built up by the rich Jews. When people speak of Jews, My Lord, they often have in mind the sort of conventional, not to say vulgar, picture of the Jew—powerful, greedy, rapacious, grasping. Here he is, he will throw himself upon a country like a vulture, and will tear it to bits. I have no such opinion even of the rich Jews (I think they are much better than they are made out to be), and certainly not of the poor.

I was instrumental in raising a great part of the public funds which have been sunk in this country. Between 1920 and the present day I have been in America eleven times, once in South Africa, innumerable times in various parts of Europe, and I know my clientèle, so to speak. They are the poor and the lower middle-class; and when I speak of the poor Jew, he is very poor. Only since 1929, since the formation of the extended Jewish Agency, has Palestine become a sort of practical proposition—when people think of practical things nowadays, they do not reckon with imponderables, and do not understand that money is much less than the ideal, the impulse, the self-sacrifice of thousands and thousands who are ready to go to Palestine at the first opportunity—it became a sort of practical proposition, and we began to get the support of the so-called practical men; but at the beginning we had to work in a small country, impoverished, ruined after the War, ruined after four hundred years of misrule by the Turk. Very often British officials used to look at me, and you could feel they were thinking: Dr. Weizmann is not a bad fellow, but he is running his head against a brick wall; what can he make out of this impoverished, difficult country? In 1930, Lord Passfield, a very practical man, a great economist, said to me, "But Dr. Weizmann, do you not realize there is not room enough to swing a cat in Palestine?" I do not want to be facetious, but many a cat has been swung in Palestine since then, and the population of the country has increased, since that talk of mine with Lord Passfield, by something like 200,000.

Those were the conditions under which we had to start: no treasury, no funds, no experience, no training, a broken-up people; a people which for centuries had been divorced from agricultural pursuits, from what is called, in the English language, pioneering. They were petty traders, middlemen, intellectuals—but we began. After fifteen years we stand before an achievement on which I think one can look with a certain amount of respect, and on which, I will not hide from you, we look with a certain amount of pride.

In the material which has been submitted to you and to which no doubt the Commission will give careful attention, you will see our achievements from the concrete facts and figures. I have before me a Table, but I do not wish to weary you with its details. The Jewish population of Palestine has increased from something like 55,000 at the end of the War to something (to take the official figures) in the neighborhood of 400,000—perhaps 375,000, perhaps a little more. I was in

Palestine in 1918, while the War was still going on. I had the honor of being attached to Lord Allenby's headquarters, and I saw the sort of Jewish people who were here then—the old people who came to Palestine to pray and to die and to have the privilege of being buried in the Holy Land. These 375,000 are mostly of a different calibre.

We have acquired a certain amount of land. Now a word about that. Our Arab friends always tell us: "Yes, you may not have acquired much but what about the future?" The basis of the National Home today is 350,000 acres. In England, in America, in Canada, there are many private estates almost as big as that. The total acquisition of land by the Jews since our early beginnings, during the past sixty years, amounts to something like 1,400,000 dunams. Divide that by four and it will give you the acreage. It is said that all the land which has come into the hands of the Jews is good land, but it is not added that it is good land now, because the sweat and blood of our pioneers has been sunk into it, and a good deal of money. It was not good land at first. It was the land about which the British officials in 1919 had said to me that we would not be able to make anything out of it, and I daresay that if some of them had had a look at the land upon which Tel Aviv and Rishon-le-Zion are built they would have said: "No, it is no good, nobody can settle on that."

We have met with all these difficulties, and I may say that everything which tended toward embarrassing the position of Great Britain in this part of the world has used Zionism and the Jews as a convenient stick with which to beat a dog, and the Jews have lent themselves magnificently to being the stick. Another difficulty with which we had to contend, was that the very causes which might have hastened the issue of the Balfour Declaration also produced resisting forces. One of these forces is the growth of Arab Nationalism. The Arab race emerged out of the War more conscious of itself, and rightly so; and they look upon Palestine as an Arab country and upon us as intruders. This is not the time to discuss it, but by implication, I think, I have answered this particular charge. It may perhaps be interesting to read to you a quotation from a speech by the late Lord Milner in a debate in the House of Lords in 1923:

"If the Arabs go to the length of claiming Palestine as one of their countries in the same sense as Mesopotamia (the name of Mesopotamia was then current) or Arabia proper is an Arab country, then I think they are flying in the face of facts, of all history, of all tradition and all associations of the most important character, I had almost said, the most sacred character. The future of Palestine cannot possibly be left to be determined by the temporary impressions and feelings of the Arab majority in the country at the present day."

I should like to add that as soon as the Balfour Declaration was issued, and even before that, British statesmen and those who had negotiated with British statesmen, were well aware both of Arab susceptibilities and of the necessity for making our position clear to the Arabs. The difficulty with which we were faced, and are unfortunately still faced to-day, is that there were and are very few Arabs who can really speak authoritatively on behalf of the Arab people. In 1918 there was one distinguished Arab who was the Commander-in-Chief of the Arab armies which were supporting the right flank of Allenby's army, the then Emir Feisal—subsequently King Feisal. At the suggestion of General Allenby, I went to the camp of the Emir. I frankly put to him our aspirations, our hopes, our desires, our intentions, and I can only say—if any oath of mine could convince my Arab opponents—I can only say that we found ourselves in full agreement; and that first meeting was the beginning of a lifelong friendship. Our relationship was expressed subsequently in a treaty—perhaps treaty is too ambitious a word—I was not a contracting party—but in a document whose moral value cannot be contested. It lays down the lines of relationship between the Jews in Palestine and the Arabs in Palestine and their general relationship with the Arabs at large. I may submit to the Commission that, as far as we are concerned, that has not changed.

One feature of this treaty to which I refer is that the intermediary who negotiated it and actually contributed to its drafting was the late Colonel Lawrence. He also acted as interpreter. Of this treaty I gave cognizance to the Foreign Office and to the various authorities who dealt with us at that time.

It may be that we have come to this country as a people which was looked upon primarily as a western people with western training. We have been engaged too much and too deeply with our own work, which has taxed all our energies, and it may be that we have not done all that we could have done in normal circumstances, to find our way to our Arab friends. History will have to judge of that; but many attempts were made by us, here, in Cairo, in Damascus, in Beirut, to make the Arabs understand our point of view, to ask them to co-operate with us, to help to find a *modus vivendi*. The hand which we repeatedly stretched out was always repelled, and today we stand in this position which the Royal Commission faces. Anything which my Organization or myself or our friends can contribute towards helping the Royal Commission, if they need our help, in finding a solution of this thorny problem, you will find us only too ready to offer.

*   *   *

Before I conclude, I should like for one moment to revert again to the Arab problem. Here we are. It is quite true that the Arabs have perhaps not got one hundred per cent satisfaction out of the War. But, if I understand rightly, what the War settlement considered was the Arab problem as a whole, and not any particular group—this, that, or the other group of Arabs; and the Arab nation emerged out of the War with something like three kingdoms: Hedjaz, Iraq, and Trans-Jordan. Well, it may not be all that human beings could wish for, but who in this world has got the satisfaction of all his wishes? We have this small land to work in—not all of it—and I thought that the old tradition of co-operation between Jews and Arabs which gave a great deal to Europe and enabled these peoples to transmit to Europe in the Dark Ages treasures of science, of art, and philosophy—I had hoped that this old tradition of co-operation might still prevail, and help us in finding a way out. So far we have not succeeded, but I confess I have not given up hope.

I have mentioned Trans-Jordan and I should like to make only one brief reference to it and to preface my remarks by saying that it will not enter my mind to discuss the present political status of Trans-Jordan. No Jew in his senses would now demand any alteration in it; but it should be made clear to the Commission that when this project was adumbrated, when the Balfour Declaration was made, and almost five years subsequently when it began to work, Trans-Jordan was part and parcel of Palestine. For reasons into which I need not enter and which are not my business, it was thought wise to separate them, to truncate Palestine and to separate a country which is larger than Palestine, just as good (or just as bad) climatically, ethnically and physically as Palestine, and it is somewhat hard on us that you should turn round and say—"Palestine is a small country and you are creating a very considerable congestion in the country." . . .

Middle East Refugees

By Terence Prittie

The Palestinian Arabs: A Historical Note

The starting point of the Palestinian Arab refugee problem was the adoption of the U.N. Partition Resolution—proposing the setting up of an Arab and a Jewish State in Palestine—on November 29, 1947. On the next day Arab riots and attacks on the Jewish community began. The Resolution was fiercely rejected by the Arabs of Palestine, and accepted, with some hesitation and misgiving, by the Jewish community. Arab attacks on the Jewish community were stimulated by the infiltration of guerrillas from neighboring Arab countries, and on January 25, 1948, formal command of them was assumed by Fawzi el Kawakji, who arrived from Syria to lead the main, mixed, Palestinian-Syrian "Army of Liberation". A number of other guerrilla armies, chief among them the force operating round Jerusalem under Abd el Kader Husseini, cooperated with Kawakji. Jewish settlements all over Palestine were attacked and the Jewish community in Jerusalem—which had constituted a majority of the city's inhabitants since 1872—was completely cut off from the outside world and placed under bitter siege. A U.N. Commission reported on April 10, 1948, that "armed Arab bands from neighboring Arab States have infiltrated into the territory of Palestine and together with local Arab forces are defeating the purpose of the Partition by acts of violence". Five months earlier the Arab League had openly stated its plan "for the occupation of Palestine and the forcible prevention of the establishment of the Jewish State".

The fighting which began in November 1947 was plainly forced upon the Jewish community. It was the prelude to the second phase of Israel's War of Independence, which followed the end of the British occupation of Palestine and the

51

proclamation of the State of Israel on May 14, 1948, in accordance with the U.N. Partition Resolution. In this second phase, Israel was attacked by the armies of Egypt, Jordan, Syria and Iraq. In place of the confused fighting which had gone on all over Palestine, actual military campaigns had to be fought along the borders of areas of Israeli occupation. These military campaigns only ended finally early in 1949.

The two-phase War of Independence resulted in the flight or ejection from their homes of several thousand Jews. The whole population of the Jewish Quarter of the Old City of Jerusalem was forced to leave its homes when the Old City fell into the hands of Jordan's Arab Legion (commanded, incidentally, by an Englishman, General Sir John Glubb). All four Jewish settlements at Etzion, and other settlements in the lower Jordan valley were overrun by Arab troops and had to be evacuated. But the Jewish exodus was very small compared with that of the Palestinian Arabs. This exodus took the following form:

- In the weeks immediately after the announcement of the U.N. Partition Plan about 30,000 Arabs left their homes. They were mainly members of wealthy or well-to-do families. They believed that a civil war was inevitable and that an early Arab victory would enable them to return home.
- After the early Jewish victories against Kawakji's irregulars at least 200,000 more Arabs left their homes, or were driven from them during the fighting. Most of them came from urban areas which fell under complete Israeli control—thus perhaps 70,000 from Jaffa and 60,000 from Haifa.
- Another 300,000 Arabs were displaced after May 15, 1948, when the armies of other Arab states invaded Palestine, and fighting took place in whole new areas which had been relatively quiet until then. This third exodus ended almost completely in November 1948. There was no large-scale fighting after that.

How Many Refugees?

The three figures given above add up to a total of about 530,000 Palestinian Arab refugees in all. In some quarters this figure is regarded as too high. One has noted, for instance, that Emil Ghory, the Secretary of the Palestine Arab Higher Committee, assessed the total number of refugees as only 300,000 at the time of the second truce, in July 1948. It is doubtful whether as many as 150,000 left after that date. But it would be wise to give as liberal an estimate as possible, in the light of the much larger and often utterly unrealistic claims which have subsequently been made. These, then, are the relevant figures for a fair and careful calculation:

1. There were rather less than 1,200,000 Arabs in the whole of Palestine before the War of Independence began.

2. Of these, at least 450,000 lived in areas which were not occupied by Israel when fighting ended in 1949. This is a highly conservative figure; other estimates are of 550,000, or more.

3. The maximum number of Arabs who could have been living, before the war, in areas which were subsequently incorporated into the State of Israel, was 750,000.

4. About 160,000 Arabs either remained in their homes in Israel or were enabled to return to their homes there.

5. This leaves 590,000 as the absolute maximum number of Palestinian Arab refugees who were displaced between 1947 and 1949. A figure of 550,000, or something under this, would be rather more probable.

These figures are given, not in order to minimize the extent of the Palestinian Arab refugee problem, but to put it in the right statistical perspective. One should note that the Economic Survey Mission, set up in 1949 by the Conciliation Commission for Palestine, early on gave a total figure of 726,000 refugees. Three years later, the U.N. relief agency UNRWA was estimating the number of Arabs whom it supplied with free food rations at around one million. It is, of course, impossible that a refugee community of about 550,000 could increase by nearly one third in a few months, or nearly double in three years.

One Jewish estimate may be mentioned in passing which was published in the "Jewish Observer and Middle East Review" in December, 1969. This gave the total number of Palestinian Arabs who lost their homes in 1947-49 as 539,000. Of these, about 40,000 emigrated to countries far off and never claimed refugee status and assistance; while 70,000 settled in the four Arab countries contiguous to Israel and similarly did not claim assistance. This left a balance of 430,000 genuine refugees (Lebanon 90,000, Syria 78,000, Jordan 156,000 and the Gaza Strip, which was under Egyptian military rule, 106,000).

Why did the Arab Refugees leave?

The most wildly contradictory statements have been made about the causes of the flight of more than half a million Palestinian Arabs from their homes in 1948-49. Israeli spokesmen have pointed out a number of contributory causes, but have on the whole laid most of the blame at the doors of Arab governments and Arab propagandists, who proclaimed a war of annihilation but washed their hands of the consequences. The Arab case is, by contrast, ingenuously simplistic—the Jews set out to drive hundreds of thousands of Arabs from their homes, and carried out their intention with the utmost ruthlessness and brutality. Even the most ostensibly "moderate" Arabs accept this explanation, whereas there are all sorts of nuances of view among Israelis.

One reasonably well-documented case-history is that of Haifa, from whose port and environs about 60,000 Arabs fled during the War of Independence. Haifa was the biggest evenly-mixed Arab-Jewish community in Palestine, outside Jerusalem. Its Jewish Mayor, Shabetai Levi, implored the Arabs of Haifa to stay in their homes and guaranteed to look after them. The answer of the Arab National Committee in Haifa was a memorandum sent to Arab League governments on April 27, 1948, asking for the transfer of the Arabs of Haifa to neighboring Arab countries. The memorandum said:

"The signing of a truce would be a disgrace to the Arab population of Haifa . . . our delegation proudly refused to sign the truce and asked that the evacuation of the population and their transfer to the neighboring Arab countries be facilitated . . . The military and civil authorities and the Jewish representatives expressed their profound regret at this grave decision. The Mayor adjourned the meeting with a passionate appeal to the (Arab) population to reconsider its decision."

This statement speaks for itself. The Arabs of Haifa followed the instructions of their own National Committee, and left. Even the woman hijacker, Leila Khaled, who claimed that she had been "driven" from her home, admitted that she was in fact driven thence in a taxi—ordered by her mother in direct disregard of her absent husband's instructions to the family to stay where they were. The British Port Officer in Haifa, Harry Stebbens, had this to say in a letter to the *Evening Standard* of January 10, 1969:

"Long before the end of the British Mandate, between January and April 1948, practically all my Arab Palestinian staff of some 200 men and women and all of the 1,800 labor force had left Haifa, in spite of every effort to assure them of their safety if they stayed. They all left for one or more of the following three reasons:

1. The Arab terrorism engendered by the November 1947 U.N. Partition Resolution frightened them to the death of their imaginative souls, and they feared Jewish retaliation.

2. Propagandists promised a blood bath as soon as the Mandate ended, in which the streets of all the cities would run with blood.

3. The promised invasion by the foreign Arab armies (which started with the Arab Legion massacre of some 200 Jewish settlers at Kfar Etzion) was preceded by extensive broadcasts from Cairo, Damascus, Amman and Beirut to the effect that any Arabs who stayed would be hanged as collaborators with the Jews.

The Palestinians were the victims then, as in 1967, of their own propaganda, and having on the average no stomach for violence they ran. I have met many of my Palestinian Arab friends since in Beirut, Damascus, Amman and the Persian Gulf States, and they have all without exception told me that they wished they had listened to me and stayed."

The British Port Officer's version merely confirms the statement of the Arab National Committee, but the case of Haifa is not necessarily typical of what happened elsewhere. Thus a regular "front line" grew up in the fighting in Jerusalem, with Arabs on one side of it and Jews on the other. The road from the coast to Jerusalem was cleared by the Israeli armed forces and many Arabs in the Ramlah-Lydda area were driven from their homes by the advancing troops. Acts of terrorism on both sides led to panic flights, but always of Arabs. As Harry Stebbens put it:

"It is true that the massacre of Deir Yassin (always quoted by the Arabs) caused some of the refugees. But the massacre of Kfar Etzion, the massacre of the hospital convoy which killed 48 Jewish doctors and nurses, the continued shelling and blasting of Jewish settlements for more than 20 years, has not caused one single Israeli to move away. They sit tight . . . How long will the Palestinian Arabs continue the myth that they were kicked out, every time they ran away from trouble and got themselves into more trouble?"

A fair summing-up of the causes of the flight of the Palestinian Arabs might be as follows:

- Some left because they were forced, physically, from their homes during the fighting. This was a small proportion of all refugees.
- Some left because they heard of Jewish acts of violence, chief among them the massacre of Deir Yassin. This, again, was a small proportion.
- Many more left because they believed their own Arab propaganda, promising a blood-bath, and visualized that victorious Jews would be sure to treat them in the same way.
- Many, again, left because as the Commander of British troops, General Sir Hugh Stockwell, put it: "The Arab leaders left first, and no one did anything to stop the mass exodus, which became first a rush and then a panic".
- Many left, especially in the early stages, in the belief that they should keep out of the fighting and would be able to return in a very short time, after total Arab victory.

The more basic causes of the exodus are more obvious; they were the Arab guerrilla warfare which began in November 1947, and the invasion of Palestine by the armies of outside Arab states in May, 1948. These set the scene for bitter and desperate warfare in which the weakest were bound to go to the wall. The weakest were the Palestinian Arabs, lacking a strong sense of identity and purpose, ready to bolt in the belief that they would be enabled to return by other Arabs fighting their battles for them. The Jews, on the contrary, stood and fought, trusting in themselves and aware that the only alternatives to victory were annihilation or, at the very least, ejection from what they regarded as the only possible homeland for them.

The Fate of the Palestinian Arab Refugees

Refugees in other parts of the world have generally been successfully integrated in the national communities to which they belong. They have established new homes there, intermarried with the people living around them, and brought up their children to "belong" with their neighbors. Generally speaking, too, they have shown only a temporary desire, or no desire at all, to maintain a separate identity or to cherish hopes of an eventual "return" to homes irretrievably lost—homes which have often ceased to exist in a physical sense.

The Palestinian Arabs are a striking exception to this rule, for three main reasons:

1. With the exception of Jordan, no Arab "host" country automatically offered them citizenship and a full place in the community.

2. Far too little material help was given to them; in particular, oil-rich Arab states have done shockingly little for these, the least fortunate of their Arab brethren.

3. Resettlement was not carried out, partly in order to ensure that they retained "refugee status". Armed with this, they constituted an enduring accusation against the State of Israel and could be expected to maintain their demand to return to their old homes.

There is no material reason, and there never has been, for hundreds of thousands of Palestinian Arabs to eke out wretched existences in the fifty or so refugee camps which were set up in the countries adjacent to Israel and as near Israel's frontiers as possible.

In 1950 U.N.-sponsored plans for moving up to 150,000 refugees from the Gaza Strip to Libya were blocked by Egypt. In 1951 Egypt first agreed to allow 70,000 refugees from Gaza to be resettled in Sinai, but then withdrew permission. In 1952-54 Syria turned down U.N. proposals for the resettlement of 85,000 refugees, to be paid for with international funds. In 1955, UNRWA reported that its rehabilitation fund of $200 million, set up in 1952 to provide homes and jobs, remained completely unused.

It is fair to say that, given a reasonable degree of Arab cooperation, at least 400,000 of the original refugees could have been resettled by the mid-1950s—and in Arab lands where they would have been living among fellow-Arabs.

Since resettlement was actively discouraged by the Arab States—Jordan, again, was to some extent an honorable exception—the numbers of Palestinian Arabs claiming "refugee status", and drawing rations and other benefits from UNRWA, was bound to increase. By the beginning of the present decade Arab spokesmen were claiming that there were more than one and a half million refugees, and even higher figures were sometimes quoted. This inflation of numbers was due to the following factors:

- The UNRWA authorities who tacitly accorded refugee status to applicants by giving them food rations and other services were unable to check effectively on their identity. Large numbers of Arabs gained refugee status who were not entitled to it.
- There was a total lack of cooperation in checking numbers of Arab governments which, indeed, openly refused on occasion to help UNRWA in this respect.
- Deaths of refugees were very often not recorded, and other people drew the rations of the dead. One investigator was told: "We hold our funerals quietly; it would be foolish for a family to give up a ration-card, simply because one of its members dies."
- Births in the refugee camps were often multi-recorded, a baby being passed from one family to another and "registered" as belonging to several.

A spot-check carried out in one refugee camp by U.S. Senators in November 1959 revealed that out of 145 names of receivers of rations which were checked, 61 were of people who were ineligible or did not exist. When Israeli forces took over the Gaza Strip in 1967 UNRWA figures showed that there were 312,000 refugees and 118,000 "indigenous" Arabs there. The Israelis conducted a census, the first since the 1948-49 war, which showed that there actually were 222,000 refugees and 134,000 indigenous population. In fact, 90,000 refugees, or nearly one-third of those on UNRWA's rolls, were non-existent. An independent investigator, the New York businessman, Ira Hirschmann, estimated the nonexistent "ghost" refugees among UNRWA's 1,300,000 registered names in 1967 at anything from a low of 200,000 to a maximum of 500,000. Like other investigators, his view was that over half of those who claimed refugee-status had been re-settled, were in full employment and did not come within the U.N. definition of being "still in need".

This is not to under-estimate the very real need of genuine refugees, and this side of the refugee question will be dealt with more fully later. Jordan was the only Arab state which readily granted full citizenship to Palestinian refugees, but Jordan was the poorest of Israel's neighbors. The refugees of the Gaza Strip were not only denied Egyptian citizenship and placed under Egyptian military jurisdiction up to 1967; they were not allowed freedom of movement and were penned into what became virtually a refugee ghetto. In Jordan, Gaza, Lebanon and Syria a large proportion of refugees, something over 500,000 in all, continued to live in camps, although an increasing number of them began to find worthwhile employment—especially in Israeli-occupied territories after the 1967 war. But the conditions under which these people lived were mainly wretched in the extreme, causing frustration, bitterness and near-despair. It has often been pointed out that UNRWA has provided housing (of a very meagre kind), food, education and medical facilities for the camps; refugees there were in some respects better off than the population outside the camps. But such material benefits do not compensate for the lack of a real home.

Up to the beginning of 1972 six Western Powers had contributed $735 million to UNRWA. Nineteen Arab states contributed $23 million, or less than five per cent of the U.S. contribution alone! The contribution of the five richest Arab oil-states was a mere $8½ million. This was the measure of Arab readiness to help fellow-Arabs in need. It goes without saying that the two Western Powers who have contributed 85% of UNRWA funds (U.S.A. and U.K.) have never received one word of thanks or even recognition. It goes without saying, too, that the Soviet

Bloc—which has posed as the friend of the Arabs—contributed precisely nothing. Israel, the "enemy", gave $4 million.

To Sum-Up

The Palestinian Arab refugee problem was caused primarily by the war of 1948-49 forced upon Israel by neighboring Arab states, and by the state of civil war which preceded it, and was largely the result of the invasion of Palestine by guerrilla forces from other countries. Efforts to ameliorate the situation were rejected by the Arab side and the problem was exacerbated by the inflation of the numbers of refugees, their retention in camps which were the breeding grounds of resentment and hatred, and the sitting of most of these camps close to Israel's pre-1967 borders. Unlike Indian, Pakistani, German and other post-1945 refugees, the Palestinians were not systematically resettled in their "host" countries. Their "refugee status" was deliberately maintained in order to encourage them to believe that they would one day return to their old homes.

So much, for the moment, for the political side of the problem. The human side cannot be divorced from it and is equally revealing. Its salient features have been widespread suffering and insufficient efforts to alleviate it. But whereas the Western Powers have spent freely in order to keep UNRWA in existence, the Arab world—and in particular the oil-rich section of it—has done terribly little. Human sufferings have been unnecessarily prolonged and increased—one has to say, for political ends, however justifiable these may have seemed to be to much of the Arab world. And the weight of Arab complaint has been such that the problem of the Jewish refugees from Arab countries has been almost entirely forgotten.

Refugees who were resettled

Refugee problems, arising out of war, are as old as history itself. They are the by-products of human misunderstanding and folly. When such problems have arisen, they have invariably been "solved" by the resettlement refugees in those countries where they have sought refuge. There has been no instance in history of a substantial number of refugees-from-war being quickly returned to their country of origin. The Palestinian refugee problem is unique, in that Arab "host countries" to the initial 550,000-580,000 Palestinian refugees have, in the main, failed or even refused to give them permanent new homes. Instead, the Palestinian refugees have been systematically encouraged to demand the right to return to old homes which, in a physical sense, disappeared decades ago.

The Table below gives approximate figures of refugees from different countries who, since 1945, have been resettled elsewhere. World opinion has accepted the terms of their resettlement, and in no instance has there been any outside backing of a "return" to the former homeland. Any such return has, in fact, been castigated as the worst kind of irredentism.

From India and Pakistan—15 million refugees.
From Finland (1945)—400,000 refugees.
From Czechoslovakia (1945)—1.5 million refugees.
From Poland (1944-45)—2.8 million refugees.
From East Germany (1945)—7.5 million refugees.
From the DDR (1945-73)—3.8 million refugees.
From Roumania (1945)—1.2 million refugees.

This, of course, is an incomplete list. There have been a great many other movements of refugees, of a minor nature. But this short list indicates that up to 35 million refugees have been successfully absorbed in the countries in which they have found refuge. In no single case has a claim to repatriation been supported, let alone upheld. The figures which have been given are in all cases those of "original" refugees, not of refugees and all subsequent progeny. Here, again, the Palestinian claim is unique, in that it covers all future generations as "refugees" with a "right" to return to "homes" which they have never seen.

* * *

The Forgotten Million

They were called the Forgotten Million: the Jews of the Arab world who lived in ancient settlements from the Atlantic seaboard to the mountains of Kurdistan. Twenty-five years ago they numbered nearly one million; today there are fewer than 60,000.

As they poured into Israel they changed the face of the new State. In 1948 only one Israeli in ten was Oriental; today one in two. A nation created by Russian, Polish and other European Jews was suddenly flooded by Jews from Arab lands.

The Western Jews in Israel look askance at many of the newcomers with their dark complexions and Arab culture. The West had been virtually ignorant of the existence of these Oriental communities. It is small wonder that they were called the Forgotten Million.

Western Jews were often unaware, too, of the deep religious faith which inspired the Oriental Jew; of the glories of Babylonian Jewry in Iraq; of the famous academies, scholars and sages; of the Hebrew poets in the farthest villages of the Sahara and the Atlas Mountains. Though Oriental Jews had been isolated for centuries from their co-religionists, they had retained their piety and their love of Zion.

We should first define our terms:

Oriental is the term now accepted as describing Jews from Arabic-speaking countries. Geographically it means little (Morocco, for instance, is a long way from the Orient) but it serves its purpose. "Eastern" and "Sephardi" are other terms used to define these communities.

Sephardi strictly means those Jews who were expelled from Spain ("Sepharad" in Hebrew) and their descendants. Some quarter of a million moved in the 15th century to North Africa, Italy, Turkey and other countries. But Sephardi has also come to apply to those Middle East communities which had no connection with Spain—the Iraqis and the Yemenites, for example. The practice began when two Chief Rabbinates were established in Palestine during the British Mandate and the Oriental communities identified with the Sephardi religious authorities.

Ashkenazi (from the Hebrew word for Germany) refers to Jews of European stock, most of them from Russia and Poland. They are also called "Western" or "European" Jews.

Oriental Jews had come to the Land of Israel long before 1948. Throughout history there were waves of immigration. But the great surge of Oriental immigration came after the State of Israel was established. For the first three years the balance of immigrants was even - 300,000 Europeans and 300,000 Orientals - but in the next years the balance shifted to the Orientals.

The Myth of Arab Tolerance

Arab and pro-Arab propagandists have tried to cast a warm glow over the history of Jews in Arab countries by proclaiming the myth of Arab tolerance. But the Arab record looks good only in comparison with the much worse Christian record.

The situation varies by country and century, but one thing is certain: there was no real equality between Jew and Muslim, in theory or in practice. If the Arab ruler was tolerant, the laws governing minorities were interpreted lightly; if the ruler was tyrannical, the Jew was reduced to the role of slave.

The Jew was expected to recognize his inferiority. When outbursts occurred it was usually because the Arab thought that the Jew had failed to keep his place. At times throughout history tyrannical Arab rulers invented ways to stigmatize the Jew.

One Sultan ordered them to wear black cloaks and pointed hats; an Egyptian ruler forced Jews to wear wooden blocks around their necks; in some countries they had to walk with head downcast, or squat when they talked to a Muslim. The oath of a Muslim automatically nullified the oath of a Jew, so he was always at the mercy of hostile Muslim neighbors.

The Jewish quarter in Oriental towns was often surrounded by a wall and the gates were closed at night. The inhabitants of the medina, the Muslim town, did not allow Jews to live with them. In Morocco the Jewish district was the mellah; in Tunisia, the hara; and in other North African countries the zanqua. In Yemen it was the qu'a and in Kurdistan the mahalla.

Particularly in North Africa, the ghettos were miserable and squalid. A distinguished North African historian wrote; "Humiliation was accepted by the Jew as part of life. He learnt to endure the slap in the face with which he was rewarded when he paid his tax, the blow administered as he walked down the street, the deliberate jostling, the insult. He was an outcast of inferior status."

Why They Left

Whatever the so-called "boundless tolerance" of Muslims towards their Jewish minorities in the past, Arab conduct since the Palestine conflict began shows how thin was the veneer of that tolerance.

Why did the Oriental Jews leave? The reasons were as complex as the countries from which they came. In the Yemen there was a surge of messianic fervor among people who had previously had little contact with their fellow-Jews. In Iraq there was a mixture of traditional messianic feelings and Zionism. In North Africa, the departure of the French, the political chaos and the uncertainty about their future under the new nationalist regimes made many Jews look toward Israel (and France).

Arab propagandists blame Zionist agitators for stirring up trouble among the peaceful and happy Jews in Arab countries. In fact most Jews in such countries paid little attention to Zionism and no Zionist propaganda reached the Jews in the interior of Morocco, Yemen and Kurdistan who formed the bulk of those who emigrated to Israel.

The Jews who were killed by Muslim mobs in the Baghdad riots of 1941; the Egyptian, Syrian and Libyan outbreaks of 1945; and the Aden and Aleppo massacres of 1947, were not Zionists; they were inoffensive victims of mass violence.

So Orientals Jews came to realize that there was no future for them in Arab countries, either as individuals or as Jewish communities. Under the new nationalist regimes they felt themselves robbed of legal status, stripped of whatever rights they had possessed, and potential future victims of Arab political extremists.

Nazi Germany's anti-Jewish campaign in Arab countries after 1933 met with success. The Nazis made extensive use in their propaganda of the notorious forgery "The Protocols of the Elders of Zion," which was supposed to be proof of a Jewish conspiracy to rule the world. The Egyptian Government published an official edition of the Protocols and it was included in the curriculum of many Arab schools. President Nasser commended it to a visiting Indian editor.

Bookshops in Arab countries were stacked with copies of "Mein Kampf," the Protocols, and anti-Jewish magazines. The Arab Press was steeped in crude anti-Semitism; some of the cartoons would have done credit to the Nazi newspaper *Der Sturmer*.

If before the State of Israel was established, Jews in Arab countries were victims of occasional anger, after 1948 they became hostages. Whenever Arab fortunes suffered a reverse, Jews under Islam paid the price.

The Dwindling Communities

• MOROCCO. There were 300,000 Jews in Morocco in 1948. After Israel was established, Jews were attacked in Djerada and Oujda; 43 were killed and 155 injured, despite Government attempts to protect them. More were killed in 1953 and 1954. Some 30,000 Jews remain but there is nervousness among them, in spite of reassurances from King Hassan's government.

• ALGERIA. Most of Algeria's 150,000 Jews left with the French exodus; they had suffered in the FLN and OAS reign of terror. The new regime imposed heavy taxes on Jews and many synagogues were destroyed or converted into mosques.

• TUNISIA. Anti-Jewish riots have occurred; in 1967 mobs set fire to the Great Synagogue in Tunis and tore up Torah scrolls. President Bourguiba did his best to stop them but the riots, and the government's Arabization policy, caused nervousness in the Jewish community, which has steadily dwindled.

• LIBYA. In 1945 Arab mobs massacred 130 Jews in Tripoli; Jewish property was destroyed and shops pillaged. In 1948, 14 Jews were killed and synagogues were desecrated. In 1967 there were riots in Tripoli and Benghazi, 18 Jews were murdered. From 40,000 the community has been reduced virtually to nil.

• EGYPT. Of the 75,000 Jews, 35,000 fled in 1948, abandoning all their property. A further exodus took place in 1956. When the Six-Day War began, all Jewish males over 17 were arrested and many were kept in terrible conditions, suffering torture and cruelty. Now only a handful of Jews remain in Cairo and Alexandria, living in abject poverty.

• LEBANON. Jews have generally been well treated but of the 1948 total of 20,000, 90 per cent have left.

• SYRIA. Vicious oppression of the Jews caused most of them to flee. In 1967 a ban on emigration made the remaining Jews virtual prisoners. They need special permits to travel inside Syria; they may not be employed in government jobs; their property is confiscated on death; and there is clear evidence of torture and rape.

• IRAQ. During the Second World War a large-scale program was launched under the pro-Nazi Rashid Ali regime: 150 Jews were murdered and 400 injured. Pressure on the community led to an exodus in 1951. The Six-Day War brought further persecution to the small community which remained: nine Jews were publicly hanged in Baghdad on false spy charges in 1969.

• YEMEN. One of the oldest communities, living under rigid Muslim rule which forbade Jews to ride on horseback, wear brightly-colored clothes, or sit in the presence of a Muslim. The Jews left in a mass exodus in 1948.

Absorbing the Immigrants

The absorption of the Oriental immigrants is one of Israel's greatest achievements. The Jewish Agency was given the responsibility for immigration and absorption of all immigrants as early as August 1948, three months after Israel was founded.

At first the immigrants were housed in settlements abandoned by the Arabs, and later in immigrant camps. In 1950 it was decided to set up *ma'abarot* (sing. *ma'abara*) so called after the Hebrew word meaning "transition." They were intended to provide temporary housing for the immigrant, who had to support himself and his family with aid from the Jewish Agency and the Government.

The inhabitants of the ma'abarot were housed at first in tents and afterwards in canvas huts—*badonim*(from the Hebrew word for cloth). Wooden huts were built for clinics, schools, and the labor exchange. In northern Israel, which is exposed to strong storms, tin shacks were built.

During the first months of mass immigration the immigrants flocked into former Arab towns; North Africans concentrated in Jaffa, the Wadi Salib district of Haifa, Lod, Ramlah and other places. Those who arrived early were lucky enough to move into the habitable buildings but from the winter of 1949 they had to take over ramshackle houses which were on the verge of collapse. The absorption authorities were not yet geared for immigration on a vast scale and were unable to supervise the movement of many of the immigrants. There were great mistakes as well as great achievements.

The North African masses who arrived in Israel were desperately poor. Their elite—the intellectuals, the businessmen and the wealthy—had gone elsewhere, mostly to France. The poverty from which they came was of a level difficult for the Western mind to grasp. In Casablanca the Jews were crowded together on a basis of 870 to an acre; in parts of Tunis, 1,000 per acre. There were hovels where there was not room to stretch the legs.

The health of these Jews reflected their living conditions; in southern Algeria, eight out of ten had eye disease; tuberculosis and alcoholism were rampant. In southern Tunisia and Morocco, malnutrition made them an easy prey to epidemics and infant mortality. The raising of the health standards of these immigrants was a brilliant medical feat by the Israeli authorities. Of course, to speak of the whole Oriental community as backward is incorrect. It included immigrants who were well-educated businessmen, doctors and lawyers from countries like Egypt and Iraq; most of them continued their successful careers after arrival in Israel.

During the 1950s the ship-to-village scheme was introduced so that many immigrants could by-pass the transit camps. They were taken direct from the ship to the moshav (agricultural village) or the development town.

The development towns had been planned as part of the government policy of population dispersal, to prevent the immigrants from flocking to the big cities. The ma'abarot in the Negev and Galilee served as nuclei for the new development towns, like Yeruham and Dimona. The Halsa ma-abara became Kiryat Shmonah and the Gabim Dorot ma'abara became Sderot.

But the rate of construction could not keep pace with the influx of immigrants and the ma'abarot became fixtures—the Hatzerim Ma'abara at Beersheba, for instance, one of the worst slums in the country, was still there when the Six-Day War broke out in 1967.

Small wonder that the ma'abarot created social problems. Worst of all for the Oriental immigrant was the disintegration of the family. In the old country the father was king; his wife was his servant and his children looked on him with awe. Now the father lost status; he could not speak Hebrew; his children learned it quickly. He probably could not get a job; his wife was more likely to get a job first and she became the bread-winner. From being a patriarch he was suddenly a nobody.

Closing the Gap

At the beginning of 1971 there were 54,000 Israeli families living in sub-standard housing—three or more people per room. About 30,000 more families were living in houses substandard in respects other than overcrowding. Some 8,000 families were living in huts and other temporary houses; 5,000 young couples had no housing of their own. A high proportion of all these categories were Orientals.

But these figures must be set against the achievements in providing accommodation. Most of the Oriental immigrants arrived in the early years of the State, when money was short and resources were few. They were given the only accommodation which Israel could afford at the time—usually cramped apartments with a couple of rooms.

At the time they accepted it gratefully; now, when they see more spacious and well-equipped housing being provided for new immigrants, they naturally feel discontented. There have been cases of Oriental Jews who arrived in the early 1950s and still live in sub-standard housing, seeing relatives arriving 20 years later being given modern apartments.

Though the accommodation that the Orientals received when they arrived 20 years ago was the same as that given to European families, the larger size of the Oriental families led to severe over-crowding in accommodation which was adequate for the smaller European families.

Catching up with arrears of slum clearance has been hampered by the need to provide housing for new immigrants but the pace has been stepped up: 9,500 apartments were built during 1972, exceeding the total built during the whole of the previous 12 years for slum clearance.

During the next five years 9,500 apartments will be built each year for slum clearance; 60 per cent will be for rent. More money will be spent on improving existing housing estates.

The scale of achievement is this:

• Of the Oriental families who arrived in Israel before 1948, 37 per cent were living in overcrowded conditions in 1960; by 1970 the figure was reduced to 12 per cent. Of the Oriental families who came after 1948, 49 per cent were overcrowded in 1960; by 1970 the figure was 17 per cent.

• The Ministry of Housing built 390,000 apartments between 1949 and 1970, of which more than half were intended for young marrieds, slum clearance and other needy cases.

• In the moshavim there were 19,000 families in 1965 living in unfit houses; by 1972 more than 9,000 had been brought up to standard or rehoused, and 3,000 more had rehabilitated their homes by their own efforts.

• The number of children sleeping three or more per room had declined from

231,000 (26 per cent) to 190,000 (20 per cent) during the years 1969 and 1972.

There are other ways in which the gap is closing:

• The increase in Oriental ownership of household appliances: in 1960 only 17 per cent of Oriental families had refrigerators; within ten years the figure had risen to 92 per cent. In 1960, 8 per cent had washing machines; in 1970, 46 per cent.

• The gap between the income of Oriental and European families is narrowing. Between 1963 and 1970 the income of European families rose by 34 per cent; that of Oriental families by 46 per cent.

• Despite differences in background, Israelis regard themselves as belonging to a single nation; for young people in the Army and the universities, origins are of little importance. One Israeli marriage in five is between Europeans and Orientals; and the rate of mixed marriages is growing at 1 per cent every year.

The Jewish exodus from Arab Countries

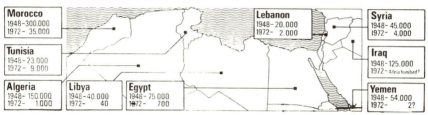

| Morocco 1948-300.000 1972- 35.000 | | | | Lebanon 1948-20.000 1972- 2.000 | | Syria 1948- 45.000 1972- 4.000 |

| Tunisia 1948-23.000 1972- 9.000 | | | | | | Iraq 1948-125.000 1972-A few hundred? |

| Algeria 1948-150.000 1972- 1.000 | Libya 1948-40.000 1972- 40 | Egypt 1948-75.000 1972- 700 | | | | Yemen 1948-54.000 1972- 2? |

Getting an Education

As in most countries, Israel's under-privileged have had the greatest difficulty in getting a good education. Children who live in overcrowded homes often with illiterate parents are most likely to be school drop-outs. There are no facilities for studying, no books to read, no help with homework.

Schools in remote development towns or slum areas have greater difficulty in attracting teachers than those in old-established neighborhoods. A survey of 280 new towns and immigrant settlements in 1965 showed that more than half of the teachers had not received full teaching diplomas. Many were on their first teaching assignments and their encounter with the profession was a shock, causing many to leave. These constant staff changes naturally had a bad effect on school performance.

The consequences were inevitable. Eighty per cent of children under 14 who do not attend any school are Oriental, as are 82 per cent of youths who neither attend school or work. These reflect the fact that 90 per cent of all children who live in substandard housing are Oriental.

By the ninth year of schooling, only 24 per cent of the Oriental children have stayed the course, compared with 55 per cent of the Europeans; at matriculation stage, only 6 per cent of Orientals compared with 35 per cent.

The gap between Oriental and European children occurs from the first year in primary school and the problem becomes more pronounced each year unless it is tackled. Even in pre-school years the Oriental child in a poor home is at a disadvantage, either because of parental ignorance or parental difficulties in coping with a large number of children.

That is the problem which Israel has had to face. These are some of the steps she has taken to solve the problem:

Long school-day. The child stays at school for two or three hours after the formal classes have finished. He does his homework under supervision and engages in art, handiwork and games. During 1971/1972, 71,600 children benefited from this scheme.

Extended school year. The living conditions of many Oriental families mean that the child's educational progress is harmed during the long summer vacation. To keep such children off the streets their school year is lengthened: the lessons are held in an informal atmosphere, with no examinations or homework. During 1971/72 there were 843 classes, with 45,000 pupils taking part.

Widening the horizons. Underprivileged children are introduced to outstanding works in music and drama to widen their cultural horizons.

Graded tuition fees. Secondary education is fee-paying in Israel but in practice many Oriental children are exempted: 65,000 secondary school pupils enjoyed full exemption during the 1970/71 school year and of these 65 per cent were Oriental.

Higher education. Special pre-academic courses lasting nine months are given to Oriental soldiers in the Hebrew University and the Haifa Technion to bring them up to university entrance level. Of those who graduated during the first six years of the scheme, 40 per cent went on to do a second degree.

The role of the Army. The Army's role in education is vital and has been recognized by the award of the Israel Education Prize, the highest distinction in this field that the State can bestow. The young "Oriental" soldier acquires assurance, a feeling of absolute equality and a thirst for more education. Half of the soldiers on squad commander courses are of Oriental origin.

Teaching the parents. Efforts are being made to educate illiterate mothers so that they can help with the education of their children.

The results have been impressive. In the 14-17 age group only 130 of every 1,000 Oriental children were enrolled in school in 1956. By 1970 the number had risen to 442 per thousand.

The Black Panthers

Israelis were shocked early in 1971 by the sudden emergence of the Black Panthers. They were a group of Oriental Jewish youths from Musrara, a slum district of Jerusalem, with a few hangers-on from extreme Left-Wing organizations. They borrowed the name Black Panthers (Panterim Shchorim) from the anti-Semitic Afro-American group of that name but had no connection with it. Most were school drop-outs; many had been refused admission into the Army because of records of petty crime.

The Panthers applied for a permit to demonstrate on March 2nd, 1971, about their alleged grievances. They demanded more action to clear the slums, provide better education and more jobs, stop so-called discrimination against Oriental Jews, and admit to the armed forces those who had been rejected for non-medical reasons. They were refused the permit and on the night before the demonstration was due to take place, several of them were arrested. The demonstration took place reasonably peacefully, with about 300 youths taking part.

On May 18th, 1971 another Panther demonstration took place in Jerusalem. It turned into a seven-hour riot in Zion Square and petrol bombs were thrown. The resultant publicity lent the Panthers an importance which was not borne out by their lack of organization and political ideas.

At their high point they had 2,000-3,000 supporters and could attract hundreds of people to meetings. Within a year they had dwindled to a couple of dozen youths and had been reduced to such publicity stunts as hijacking a milk cart to distribute its contents to the poor.

Many of the former Black Panthers were given jobs; some are to be found working in the police garage. One of the leaders of a demonstration outside the office of the Mayor of Jerusalem in 1971 returned there this year—to receive an award for his work as a youth club leader. The army relaxed some of its more rigid rules in accepting recruits.

In late 1971 Mrs. Golda Meir established a special commission to study the conditions under Dr. Israel Katz, director of the National Insurance Institute and an expert on the problems of poverty.

A Place in Politics

The number of Oriental members in the Israeli Parliament is low but rising slowly. In local politics, the Orientals have made a great breakthrough in the political parties, trade union branches and local councils.

In 1950 there was only 13 per cent Oriental membership of local government bodies; by 1969 the figure had grown to 44 per cent. Inside the Labor Party 51 per cent of the local councilors were Orientals.

Orientals have replaced mayors of European background in towns throughout Israel: today 30 per cent of all municipalities have Oriental mayors. Of the 48 regional councils, which group together smaller villages, 10 are headed by Orientals.

Beersheba, Israel's fourth most important city, is a typical case. The town was controlled by the "old guard" of European stock but the influx of newcomers from Arab countries soon changed that. They gained a majority in the executive body of The Labor Party, which controlled the city, ousted the party secretary, the Histadrut (trade union) secretary, and eventually the Mayor. The present Iraqi-born mayor is one of the most able in Israel.

Conclusions

1. The arrival of three-quarters of a million refugees from Arab countries saddled Israel with a massive burden. Most arrived when the new state was least able to cope with them; since much of the immigration was of the "rescue" type, it could not, by its very nature, be planned ahead. Israel is still paying the price of the years which these immigrant masses spent in tent towns and ma'abarot.

2. The standard of life for Oriental families has improved dramatically: higher incomes, better housing, greater ownership of consumer goods, and better education. Despite the progress towards economic and political equality, however, a gap between Europeans and Orientals still remains; it has produced social problems which will not be totally solved for many years to come.

3. The suggestion that Israel is irrevocably split into "two Israels" and that the state will "break up from within" is the product of ignorance or wishful thinking. The clear evidence is that the Oriental Jews are integrating and that the whole structure of Israeli society is changing as a result of that integration. The shared Jewishness of Israelis is much stronger than any divisive influence. The loyalty of Orientals to Israel and pride in the state's achievements are beyond doubt.

4. Although many of the Oriental refugees came to Israel voluntarily, many others came because of persecution, uncertainty about their future under Arab nationalist regimes, and centuries of treatment as second-class citizens.

5. The Jews left behind property worth thousands of millions of pounds. In Baghdad alone the Iraq Government in 1951 confiscated £35 million in cash from Jewish accounts in banks, plus vast quantities of other assets and property. In Egypt £350 million of property was left behind. Jewish property left in Algeria alone was many times greater than that abandoned by Arab refugees in Palestine.

6. Resettlement in Arab countries is obviously unthinkable. The Oriental Jews are now fully-fledged Israelis and would not think of returning; and there is no indication that the Arab regimes would restore the money and property which they took from the Jews. Persecution, discrimination and brutality in such countries as Syria and Iraq have poisoned any relationships which might have existed.

7. The solution of the Middle East refugee question must be based on a recognition that an exchange of population has taken place. Though the circumstances varied, the exchange is irrevocable. Arab refugees should be resettled and rehabilitated in Arab countries in the same way that Israel has resettled her Orientals refugees. In any event, present conditions in Arab countries clearly make it impossible for Jews to return there.

In Search of a Balance-Sheet

The Palestinian Arabs "right" of return to homes lost twenty-five years ago has been for years past the main talking-point in the Middle East refugee problem. Other, often much larger groups of refugees have either never asserted a "right of return," or have long ago dropped their claim. Given the circumstances of a continuing state of war in the Middle East—due to the fact that Arab states have so far found themselves unable to sit down at the conference table with Israel—the Palestinian Arab claim of a right of return is understandable. Human suffering has been prolonged, even perpetuated, so that their claim should lose nothing of its force. Israel has been accused of turning a deaf ear to the legitimate grievances of the Palestinian Arab refugees. No state's record is impeccable, and Israel has been much preoccupied since 1949 with commensurately overwhelming problems of her own, including the resettlement of hundreds of thousands of Jews who have come from Arab countries because, baldly stated, they had no future there.

Efforts to Help Solve the Arab Refugee Problem

These can be put under the following headings:

1. Israel accepted back, after the 1948-49 war, Arabs who wished to rejoin their families and applied to do so. An estimated 70,000 Arabs returned forthwith, bringing the number of Arabs living in the State of Israel to about 160,000. This was a comparatively painless operation, in the sense that Israel did not attach difficult, let alone impossible conditions to the return of individual Arab refugees.

2. Israel offered to make the refugee problem the first item on the agenda of peace talks. This offer was refused by the Arab states, which insisted on a "return" of a different kind, to the political situation which obtained before the State of Israel was set up and before Israel had to fight a bitter and bloody battle to ensure its own right of existence.

3. In August 1949 Israel offered to take back 100,000 refugees, and the offer was immediately rejected by the Arab states. Acceptance just might have opened the way to further negotiation between the Middle East disputants. Although Israel reiterated her readiness to negotiate, diplomatic channels were closed by the Arabs, who imposed a political and economic blockade on her. Once again, the

Arabs had an arguable case—that any acceptance of an Israeli offer could prejudice the "all or nothing" demands which were genuinely regarded as legitimate.

4. In 1950 UNRWA (United Nations Relief and Works Authority) proposed moving refugees from the Gaza Strip (administered by Egypt and maintained as a refugee ghetto) to Libya. The aim was to resettle 150,000 out of the estimated quarter of a million refugees there; the proposal was blocked by Egypt.

5. In 1951 UNRWA managed, temporarily, to secure the agreement of Egypt to move 70,000 refugees from the Gaza Strip to the El Arish area of the Sinai Peninsula. Sinai is a natural appendage to Palestine, but has been quite fortuitously Egyptian as a result of Egypt's "suzerain," Britain, penetrating into the area 70 years ago. Egypt withdrew from the agreement with UNRWA, possibly because of not wanting "to be seen" to be cooperating in a resettlement of Arab refugees in another part of the Arab world than Palestine.

6. From 1952 onward Israel released bank balances held by Arab refugees, and hitherto blocked, to an amount of more than $10 million. This was done "without strings," and it should be noted that Arab governments did not respond by releasing bank balances held in their countries by Jews who had emigrated to Israel. There was no *quid pro quo*; the Israelis had not sought one, but had made a purely practical gesture.

7. In 1952-54 UNRWA tried to negotiate an agreement with Syria, for the resettlement of 85,000 Palestinian refugees who were already either in Syria or Lebanon. Resettlement was to be financed by international funds, and one can well imagine that Jewish money would have been contributed. But Syria refused to cooperate.

8. On a number of occasions Israel has offered to pay compensation to Arabs who lost their homes in the 1947-49 hostilities. These offers have invariably been rejected, and it is worth noting that they went outside the normal terms of reference of a State which was under siege by its neighbors, who declared themselves to be still in a state of war.

9. In 1955 the special envoy of President Eisenhower of the USA, Mr. Eric Johnston, obtained the agreement of technical experts of Israel, Jordan, Syria and Lebanon on a scheme for the irrigation of the Jordan valley, which was designed to facilitate the resettlement of 240,000 refugees. In October 1955 the Arab League, politically motivated, rejected a scheme which could have been of great value to the region, as well as easing the material lot of the refugees.

10. In 1959 UNRWA was obliged to report that its rehabilitation fund of $200 million, set aside in 1952 to provide homes and jobs for Palestinian refugees, had been boycotted. This, of course, was the decision of Arab governments and not of the refugees themselves.

11. In 1959 the UN Secretary-General, Dag Hammarskjold, carried out a personal investigation into the possibilities of an overall resettlement scheme in the Middle East, designed in the area's economic and social interest. As a result of Arab opposition he dropped his proposals.

12. At the 18th session of the UN Special Political Committee in November 1963 Mrs. Golda Meir, Israel's Foreign Minister, offered direct negotiations with Arab governments on the refugee problem, as an urgent priority. The Israeli Prime Minister, Mr. Levi Eshkol, did the same two years later. As Prime Minister, Mrs. Meir repeated her offer; so did her Foreign Minister, Mr. Abba Eban. All offers from the Israeli side have been ignored or denounced.

The United Nations View on the Palestinian Refugees

The United Nations have frequently expressed their views about the Middle East refugee question. In all cases these views have dealt only with the Palestinian Arab refugees. Since Jewish refugees from Arab countries have not the slightest desire to return to them, it has been blandly assumed that their problems are the sole responsibility of Israel and that the outside world can wash its hands of them. Today this viewpoint might seem quite natural; in the late 1940s and early 1950s it was otherwise, for almost all immigrants into Israel went through a long period of hardship and want.

Between November 1948 and the War of 1967 the UN General Assembly adopted 23 resolutions on the subject of the Palestinian Arab refugees, urging either resettlement or compensation for them. The UN Security Council did not adopt a resolution concerning the refugees until November 1967, and then only within the context of an overall settlement of the Middle East dispute. Virtually all of the resolutions adopted by the General Assembly quoted UN Resolution 194 of December 11, 1948, and called for the implementation of the Resolution and in particular of its paragraph 11. This paragraph reads:

"Resolves that the refugees wishing to return to their homes and live in peace with their neighbors should be permitted to do so at the earliest practicable date, and that compensation should be paid for the property of those choosing not to return, and for loss of or damage to property which, under principles of international law or in equity, should be made good by the Government or authorities responsible."

"Instructs the Conciliation Commission to solicitate the repatriation, resettlement, and economic and social rehabilitation of the refugees, and the payment of compensation."

The following points about this key Resolution are operative:

• The question of compensation of refugees not wishing to return to their old homes was left open for negotiation. Israel repeatedly made plain that she was prepared to negotiate over compensation. The Arab states have rejected her offers to do so.

• The Conciliation Commission has rejected any attempts to isolate the refugee problem, or any parts of the refugee problem, from an overall peace settlement. This was explicitly stated in its report of 1951, which stated: "The Conciliation Commission, while fully recognizing the extreme urgency of the refugee question, both from the humanitarian and political points of view, did not consider it possible to separate any one problem from the rest of the peace negotiations or from the final peace settlement."

• Resolution 194 stated specifically that refugees who wished to return to their homes should be prepared to "live in peace" with their neighbors there, in fact with the Israelis. This condition of peaceful coexistence has been reinforced in subsequent resolutions, and the UN Conciliation Commission pointed out in Paris in 1951 that Israel could not be expected to make any commitments on the refugees "unless, at the same time, she received reasonable assurance from her neighbors as to her national and economic security."

Peaceful Coexistence and National Security

Israel, as already stated, offered to do more than prescribed by the UN. She offered to pay compensation to refugees not wishing to return home, irrespective of whether a final and overall peace settlement were reached, and she offered to take back an initial number of refugees in August 1949. Plainly, she could have attached conditions to these offers. But she chose not to do so, regarding them rather as goodwill gestures which could do something toward improving the political climate and making serious peace negotiations more acceptable to her Arab neighbors.

The following views, from the Arab side, show what her neighbors thought of the two questions of peaceful coexistence with the State of Israel and the underwriting of Israel's national security:

- Dr. Mohammed Salah ed-Din, Egyptian Foreign Minister: "In demanding the restoration of the refugees to Palestine, the Arabs intend that they return as the masters of their homeland, not as slaves. More explicitly, they intend to annihilate the State of Israel." October 11, 1949.
- "Al-Said," Lebanese newspaper: "The return of the refugees should create a large Arab majority that would serve as the most effective means of reviving the Arab character of Palestine, while forming a powerful fifth column for the day of revenge and reckoning." April 6, 1950.
- "Falastin," Jordanian newspaper: "The Arab refugees will not be returned to Palestine except by war, which will preface their return. Palestine Arabs demand only arms, mobilization and training. The rest they will do themselves." January 28, 1956.
- Resolution adopted by Conference of Arab Refugees, at Homs, Syria: "Any discussion aimed at a solution of the Palestine problem which will not be based on ensuring the refugees' right to annihilate Israel will be regarded as a desecration of the Arab people and an act of treason." July 11-12, 1957.
- Iraq Government Radio, Baghdad: "The refugees are Arabs who seek to expel Zionism from their land." November 14, 1958.
- Jordan Government Radio, Amman: "Jordan will accept no solution to the Palestine Problem that does not involve the liquidation of Israel." December 26, 1960.
- President Nasser of Egypt, in interview with "Neue Zuercher Zeitung": "If the refugees return to Israel, Israel will cease to exist." September 1, 1960.
- Egyptian Government Radio, "Voice of the Arabs": "It is obvious that the return of one million Arabs to Palestine will make them the majority of Israel's inhabitants. Then they will be able to impose their will on the Jews and expel them from Palestine." September 13, 1961.
- Abdullah al-Yafi, Lebanese Prime Minister, to newspaper "Al-Hayat": "The day of the realization of the Arab hope for the return of the refugees to Palestine means the liquidation of Israel." April 29, 1966.

These statements, and dozens like them have been the Arab answer to the U.N. demands for peaceful coexistence and the guaranteeing of Israel's national security. It is not necessary to reproduce here the statements of George Habash, Yasser Arafat and other Palestinian terrorist leaders. Nor, with a few exceptions, were Arab spokesmen of a more official kind any more accommodating. In 1967 the states of the Arab League decided at the Khartoum Conference that there should be no negotiation with Israel, no recognition of Israel and no peace treaty with Israel. Mahommed Heykal, accepted then as the "mouthpiece" of Nasser, openly preached his theory of the "two-stage" destruction of the State of Israel

—first the consequences of the 1967 war should be "eliminated," and then the consequences of the war of 1948-49. The Palestinian National Covenant laid down conditions which made it plain that the State of Israel should cease to exist, and only those Jews should be allowed to remain in Palestine whose families had been settled there before 1917. The popular Arab view remained that Israel should at least be "eliminated," but preferably "liquidated" or "annihilated."

The Hard Core of the Palestinian Refugee Problem

Today, twenty-five years after the Palestinian refugee problem was created, it is still not easy to assess what "hard core" of this problem remains. Spokesmen for the refugees claim that more than 1½ million still possess "refugee status." Since Arab states have consistently refused to conduct a census, a detailed breakdown into categories must be based on approximate figures only:

1. Roughly two-fifths of the refugees have settled in the Kingdom of Jordan, only a minority of them in camps. The Kingdom of Jordan, it should be remembered, was an integral part of the area of Palestine taken over by Britain after the First World War. It was detached from the remainder of Palestine in order to give a domain to the Emir Abdullah, the brother of King Faisal of Iraq and, like him, a member of the Hashemite family which sought freedom from Turkish rule and as a result threw in its lot with Britain. Although displaced from their own homes, refugees in Jordan are still living in Palestine.

2. Rather more than one-fifth of the refugees settled in Syria and Lebanon, in fact in Arab states and among fellow-Arabs in areas immediately contiguous to Palestine. Roughly half of these refugees are still living in camps.

3. Under one-fifth of the refugees are under temporary Israeli administration, as a result of Israel's military victory in the 1967 war. They are, in fact, living in "Palestine proper," although not in their old homes. The number living in camps is being steadily reduced, as a result of the Israeli policy of resettling a proportion in new homes. The likelihood is that these Palestinians will merge gradually with their fellow-Palestinians among whom they live; this trend is being encouraged by the virtual disappearance of unemployment and the raising of living standards.

4. Well under one-fifth of the refugees are scattered far and wide, mainly in more distant parts of the Arab world, but some in Europe and the New World. Most of these refugees have settled for good outside their former country.

From these approximate figures it is possible to draw two main conclusions. At least three-fifths of those enjoying refugee status are living on the soil of Palestine today, and are in gradual process of resettlement there. Of the remainder, a majority are living close to the old borders of Palestine. Those in camps, who approximate to the popular concept of homeless exiles, may comprise 15,000 to 20,000 families. Some estimates are of 10,000 to 12,000 families only. These are the Palestinian Arabs who today have the worst of all worlds, inhabiting camps which UNRWA is finding increasingly difficult to maintain, discouraged from leaving them, generally unable to look forward even to the prospect of being resettled locally, but still in exile. Here is the "hard core" from which the bulk of the Palestine Liberation Army and the different terrorist groups have been recruited—certainly since King Hussein drove the "fatah" out of Jordan three years ago.

It is understandable that this hard core contains the most bitter, frustrated and forlorn of the Palestinian Arab refugees. Something has been done for them by the outside world, but not enough. Far too little has been done by their Arab "hosts." Lebanon is a relatively rich country and could have settled all resident refugees on its soil long ago. With adequate financial aid, Syria could have done likewise. It would have been perfectly possible to find employment for them. The Annual Report of the Director of UNRWA of 1959-60 pointed out that "over two-thirds of the *urban* refugee population (20% of the total populace) almost immediately became self-supporting in other Arab countries because they possessed skills which were useful in those countries." And the Lebanese daily "Al Hayat," wrote in June 1959 that of 120,000 refugees who had entered Lebanon only 15,000 remained in camps. The paper went on: "Taking into account a natural growth of 15,000, we may conclude that 120,000 refugees have been absorbed in Lebanon and have become an integral part of her inhabitants, her society and her economy."

One obvious conclusion is that the problem of the hard core could be solved much more easily than is generally supposed. A six to eight year program, entailing rehousing, the finding of jobs, and the creation of educational and social services in areas of resettlement, would eliminate the problem of the hard core in human terms.

Some Further Thoughts on the Palestinian Arab Refugee Problem

"Since 1948 Arab leaders have approached the Palestine problem in an irresponsible manner. They have not looked into the future. They have no plan or approach. They have used the Palestine people for selfish political purposes. This is ridiculous and I could say, even criminal." One might imagine that this is an Israeli judgment; in fact, it was contained in a statement made by King Hussein of Jordan to the Associated Press in January 1960. An even more outspoken statement, by a neutral, was that of Ralph Galloway, former head of UNRWA in Jordan, in August 1958—"The Arab States do not want to solve the refugee problem. They want to keep it as an open sore, as an affront to the United Nations and as a weapon against Israel. Arab leaders don't give a damn whether the refugees live or die."

These statements may sound extreme; the sources of them, however, are unimpeachable. The Arab refusal to work for a settlement of the refugee question is, of course, based essentially on the contention that the refugees should be allowed to return to their old homes. This contention gives rise to the following considerations:

• The "old homes" of Palestinian refugees no longer, in most cases, exist. Their simple dwellings have vanished, the very contours of the land they once farmed have changed. Palestinian smallholders and tenant farmers generally operated on a "subsistence" basis; the intensive farming methods of Israeli collectives and cooperatives are more akin to those used in Holland or Denmark. Were Palestinian refugees to return, in real numbers, to Israel, they would almost certainly drift to the towns and into jobs least wanted by the Israelis themselves.

• Refugees who returned would find themselves living in a still predominantly Israeli community. The unique situation would be created, of Arabs removing from fellow-Arabs in order to enter an alien community.

• Refugees who returned should be committed to living in peace with their neighbors. But it is precisely the Palestinian refugees in the camps who have been taught to believe that the State of Israel must be wiped off the map, and a new

Arab State of Palestine set up in its place. The Israelis would be taking in primarily people pledged to destroy their community. They have been taught this by activist groups, by a large section of the Arab Press, and in the UNRWA schools in the camps.

● It follows that Israel's leaders are averse to admitting the "right" of Palestinian refugees in return. Nor can they take a more charitable view of Arab intentions than that indicated by the Arabs' public pronouncements. These have usually denied Israel's right of actual existence. When more favorable, they have generally not gone beyond the granting of a "peace arrangement" conditional on a regulation of the refugee question which would enable all refugees to return who wished to do so.

Conclusions

In 1957 the Adviser on Refugees to the World Council of Churches, Dr. Elfan Reese reported that: "I hold the view that, political issues aside, the Arab refugee problem is by far the easiest post-war refugee problem to solve by integration. By faith, language, race and by social organization they are indistinguishable from their fellows of their host countries. There is room for them in Syria and Iraq. There is a developing demand for the kind of manpower they represent. More unusually, there is the money to make this integration possible . . . That money remains unspent, not because these tragic people are strangers in a strange land—because they are not—not because there is no room for them to be established—because there is —but simply for political reasons."

It is difficult to fault this view. But the phrase "political issues aside" touches the heart of the problem. A large section of the Palestinian Arab refugees have been encouraged not to seek resettlement in host countries, and to maintain the fixed belief that they will be helped to return to their former homes in sufficient numbers to ensure the disappearance of the State of Israel and its replacement by a state of their own. They are, in fact, being cruelly misled a second time—just as they were misled in 1947-49 to believe that Israel would be annihilated and they would at once return to their homes in triumph.

No account whatever is taken in the outside world of the lot of Jews who have left Arab countries, largely as a result of discrimination and persecution. Yet these Jews now constitute a majority of the population of Israel, of the so-called "Oriental" Jews who regard themselves as the under-privileged half of the community. This, as has already been pointed out, is by far Israel's biggest social problem, which she must tackle without any help from the outside world. Indeed, the very existence of the problem is often held against Israel, as a slur on her record and an imagined indication of her failure to ensure total social equality. Waiting to come to Israel—when allowed to do so—are small, badly scared and periodically brutally bullied Jewish communities in Egypt, Syria and Iraq. These people are never going to be allowed a decent existence in those Arab countries.

While the overall refugee question cannot be solved by any single act of statesmanship or grace, the following are some of the steps which could be taken to ameliorate the problem:

1. There should be a massive aid program, to which the outside world should contribute, to help resettle Middle East refugees—wherever they are—and give them a better and more civilized existence. The oil-rich Arab states can make a major contribution to such a program, but there is good case for the Jewish world making a contribution too.

2. A regional plan for such resettlement could be drawn up, indicating suitable areas of settlement and economic programs which could be coordinated. Thus, the "Johnston Plan" for the waters of the Jordan and Yarmuk could be revived, enabling perhaps 200,000 Palestinians to be settled in the Jordan Valley. A similar plan could be evolved for the use of the much greater flow of the Litan River in Lebanon. Something of the same kind could be done in Syria.

3. UNRWA budgets, at present showing deficits of several million dollars a year, should be supplemented by the outside world. Here, too, the oil-rich Arab states can help; so can the Communist bloc, which has hitherto done nothing more than shed crocodile tears over the refugees and use their sufferings as a means of stirring up trouble.

4. A Refugee Claims Conference could examine the whole question of losses of property, of Jews as well as Arabs. A balance-sheet could be drawn up, on the basis of the value of property at the time that it was lost, or at present-day prices. Israel and Arab states should undertake to reach an "equalization agreement" for mutual compensation; if a residual sum is left over, owing either to the Palestinian Arabs who left their homes or to Jews who left Arab countries, this should be covered by an international loan.

5. Jews still living in Arab countries and wishing to leave them, should be granted this elementary human right. These people are living in perpetual apprehension, or even terror.

6. Pending a peace settlement, the Israelis should be encouraged to go on doing everything possible to improve the lot of refugees in Arab territories which they are temporarily occupying. They have already done much, by eliminating unemployment, raising living standards, and building some new homes. A supplementary program could be launched under U.N. or other international aegis.

There are other steps which could be taken, when there is a final peace settlement—and one should recall that U.N. resolutions have always envisaged a regulation of the refugee problem as a part of such a peace settlement. But a great deal can be done in the meantime. Countries like Britain have a duty to point this out, unless their purpose is only to treat the refugees as political pawns. The basic consideration governing the whole Middle East refugee problem is that an irrevocable exchange of populations has taken place and that a maximum effort must be made to improve the lot of all displaced persons, Arab and Jew alike.

II

The Palestinian Arabs

The Palestinians: Who They Are

By Ya'acob Caroz

The Palestinian problem apparently will not lose its position as a prominent issue in the next few months. It is, therefore, advisable that we clarify to ourselves who the Palestinians are, especially in light of the impression among many circles in the world that the Palestinians are only the inhabitants of refugee camps in Lebanon, represented politically by the Palestine Liberation Organization (PLO) and actively—violently—by the terrorist organizations which comprise the PLO.

Until May 15, 1948, all the Palestinians were residents of the territory of the Mandate of Palestine. This mandate was granted to Britain by the League of Nations after World War I. In 1922, the British Government divided the territory into two parts. It gave Trans-Jordan to the then Emir, and later on King, Abdullah. Since then the name Palestine has applied only to the western part of the country, from the Jordan river to the sea. The word Palestine was printed in the three official languages in British passports held by residents of the country—"Palestinian" Jews and Arabs. The initials for Land of Israel appeared in Hebrew. Throughout the world, holders of these passports were identified as coming from a region in which Jews lived. In one of the European ports where holders of these passports used to call on their visit to the continent, they were nicknamed "Sabbath Englishmen."

On both banks of the Jordan river

The majority of Jews there were ready for a territorial compromise on the West Bank of the Jordan River. The Arabs always demanded all for themselves. After the termination of the Mandate, the larger part of the area west of the Jordan became part of Israel and the smaller part was annexed to Jordan. All the Jews, including those who had formerly resided in the areas annexed to Jordan were concentrated in the Jewish state. Most Palestinian Arabs who, on the eve of the War of Independence numbered 1,278,000, remained on both banks of the Jordan River, namely in the original territory of the Mandate. A considerable number of those who had resided in areas on which the State of Israel was established fled and settled down in Jordan, on both banks of the river. All of them received Jordanian nationality. Some of them moved to the Gaza Strip, or became refugees in other Arab countries.

The Six Day War did not radically change the map of Arab Palestinian settlement. As was the case elsewhere, their number increased as compared to 1947 and amounted to 2,360,000 according to the following breakdown:

Judaea and Samaria	650,000
The Gaza Strip	400,000
Jordan	600,000
Lebanon	150,000
Kuwait	150,000
Syria	130,000
Saudi Arabia	100,000
Egypt	20,000
Libya	10,000
Other countries in the region and in the world	150,000
	2,360,000

This number does not include the 450,000 Arabs living in Israel, including East Jerusalem.

It follows that 1,050,000 former Palestinian Arabs and their descendants—excluding citizens of Israel—are currently living in Judaea, Samaria and the Gaza Strip. If we add to them those who reside in Jordan—some of whom also lived there before the termination of the Mandate—the total number will come to 1,650,000. This means that a great part of Palestinian Arabs did not leave the boundaries of the original territory of the Mandate. Most of the remainder live in Arab countries, in an environment not alien to them; 1,250,000, over half of those who lived outside Israel before June 1967, are Jordanian citizens.

False registration

As for the refugees among the Palestinians, the High Commissioner of UNRWA made an enlightening distinction in his 1972-73 report. He differentiated between registered refugees—holder of refugees cards—numbering 1,540,694 and persons listed in refugees camps, totaling only 457,300. The report itself treats the former with skepticism. According to the report, for instance, deaths are not registered and many registrations were false. The number of refugee cards does not tally with the number of persons residing in the camps. As for the listed residents of refugee camps, many were absorbed, economically and socially, in their countries of residence. Even if camp inmates were refugees to all intents and purposes, they would constitute only sixteen percent of the total Palestinians. This, despite the efforts exerted by Arab governments not to solve the problem of the refugees, to let it "simmer" for more than twenty-six years.

These figures clearly narrow the issue—the solution of which does not seem to incur unsurmountable difficulties—to its right dimensions.

In view of this demographic deployment it would seem natural that efforts for the solution of the Palestinian problem would be exerted in the country in whose boundaries their largest number is found. It is in the areas under Israel rule. Today the contention is heard in Israel that during the seven years which elapsed since the Six Day War, no attempt was made to create a stratum of leaders to represent the residents of the administered areas and serve as an authoritative party in negotiations toward a settlement.

This contention ignores the real facts of the situation. Until September 1970 most residents of Judaea and Samaria supported their return to the Hashemite Kingdom. Hussein's liquidation of the terrorist organizations undermined—were it only temporarily—their loyalty to Jordan. What solution could they come up with? It is difficult to imagine that any leadership would have proposed, say, annexation of the area to Israel or the establishment of an independent state. Without attachment to Jordan, such a state—not durable in itself—would have been considered an Israeli satellite. Even if leaders were prepared to agree to that, it is doubtful whether they would have dared voice their plans aloud, both for concern over their isolation in the Arab world and their fear of Jordan and the terrorists.

Negation of Zionism

Who is speaking on behalf of the Palestinians? Jordan, which until 1967 ruled Judaea and Samaria, considers itself the legal representative of their population. The West Bank inhabitants are Jordanian nationals, just like the Palestinians who live on the East Bank. Jordan's "qualification" is further strengthened by the fact that twelve of the twenty ministers in the present cabinet of Amman and seven of the twelve members of its delegation to the Geneva Conference are Palestinians. The Jordanian authorities also feel that they are empowered by Security Council resolutions 242 and 338 to negotiate the future of the administered areas and also to determine the form of their future relationship with Jordan.

The second pretender to the right to represent the Palestinians is the PLO. It was never chosen by those on whose behalf it presumes to speak. Its "voters" were members of the Arab League who decided on its establishment, at Egypt's recommendation, in 1964. The summit conference held in Algeria in October 1973 recognized—with the exception of Jordan—its existence as the sole representative of the Palestinians.

The PLO is currently the roof institution of all terrorist organizations. Its objectives—the "legitimate rights of the Palestinian people," the implementation of which is demanded by the Arab states—are defined in the Palestinian National Covenant, as amended in 1968. The Covenant negates Israel's right to exist. It states that only the Palestinian people have the right of self-determination and only they "have a legal right to their homeland." It rejects the historic links of the Jews to the country, arguing that contentions of such a link contradict historic truth, Judaism is a religion, not a nationality. Jews are citizens of the countries in which they live and have no right of self-determination. The Zionist movement is illegal and all governments in the world should forbid its existence and activities. Only Jews who lived in the country before the "Zionist invasion" which began in 1917 are entitled to remain. The Balfour Declaration and the mandate given by the League of Nations are to be considered null and void, because they opened the gates of the country to "invaders." The Arabs are duty bound to "clear Palestine of the Zionist existence."

"Final Solution"

After outlining its ideological foundations and determining the aims of the PLO, the treaty reveals the way to implement them. It specifies that "armed struggle is the only way to liberate Palestine." This struggle will be conducted through "fedayeen activity," which constitutes the nucleus of "the Palestinian popular war of independence." "Fedayeen activity" is simply an act of terror.

One who reads the full text of the Palestinian National Covenant cannot evade the awkward feeling that there is something irrational in all these pretentious determinations, formulated as though coming straight from a divine source —what is historic truth and what is not; which national movement is legal and which is not; which is nationality and which is not; who has the right of self-determination and who has not; which historic documents are valid and which ones are null and void. One may argue that Hitler's Mein Kampf was an insane document, but there was a holocaust nevertheless. Actually, just as Hitler wanted a "final solution" for the Jewish people, the PLO is striving for a "final solution" for the State of Israel.

Ways and Means of Implementation

The Palestinian National Council—the PLO's supreme institution—which convened at the beginning of June 1974, did not at all moderate the extremist demands expressed in the National Covenant. On the contrary, the Council's resolutions are based on the Covenant. It did not discuss a change in the organization's objectives but only ways and stages for their implementation. It expresses readiness to set up national rule in any area evacuated by Israel so that it would serve as a base for the continuation of the armed struggle for the attainment of the final objectives.

The Council also lent expression to the additional PLO objective—the annihilation of Jordan. The state of the terrorist organizations is, thus, to range on the two banks of the Jordan River.

In the past, too, Palestinian leaders wished to attain the impossible and, rejecting the possible, lost everything. They have apparently learned nothing.

Social and Political Changes in Arab Society in Israel

By Aharon Layish

Most of the social and political changes which the Arabs of Israel are undergoing are intensified by the direct encounter with a western type Jewish society and the tensions caused by the state of Israel's relations with the Arab countries. These changes are shaped in an Israeli version unknown in the Arab countries.

The Arab population of Israel increased from 108,000 in May 1948 to 477,000 in 1970. Components of the increase were: (1) 31,000 inhabitants of the "Little Triangle", a narrow strip along the Jordanian border, incorporated into Israel under the 1949 Rhodes Armistice Agreement; (2) 40,000 refugees who entered Israel under the Families' Reunion Scheme or as infiltrators whose presence was legalized *ex post facto*; (3) the 69,000 inhabitants of East Jerusalem added when the city was reunited after the Six-Day War; (4) the remainder, 229,000, is natural increase (at one of the highest rates in the world). The Arabs form today about 16 per cent of the population of Israel. [1973 figures]

The demographic balance, characteristic of a traditional society, between a high birth rate and a high death rate, has been drastically upset since Israel came into existence. The death rate has dropped to 6 per thousand (1972)—one third of what it was at the end of the British Mandate period — as a result of improved, and preventive, medical services. The birth rate has remained high (about 45 per thousand) and even increased. Consequently, the rate of natural increase, 39 per thousand, is among the highest in the world (it was even higher — 45 per thousand — in the mid sixties; in the last few years, there has been a decline in the birth rate).

The Arab woman in Israel has made great strides toward emancipation. Measures were enacted to end discrimination based on religious law (e.g., polygamy, and divorce against the wife's will, were banned; natural guardianship of both parents over their children and equal rights of succession for both sexes were established). Women enjoy full equality in respect of any legal act, in voting, social legislation etc.; considerable progress has been made in the education and vocational training of girls. Yet, the Arab woman is still far from enjoying real partnership in all spheres of life, owing to social and religious obstacles; her social emancipation still lags behind the changes in her legal status.

The patriarchal extended family has disintegrated almost completely, and its place is being taken by the biological family unit. The causes of this phenomenon are the high proportion of "commuters" among Arab labor; fragmentation of property by inheritance (especially in Muslim society) and the curtailment of landed property through take-over by the Custodian of Absentees' Property and expropriation by the Development Authority; the diminished importance of extensive agriculture as a source of income and consequent non-cultivation of large areas; the broadening of education and the adoption of modern ways of life.

The position of the clan *(hamula)* is weakening, though at a slower pace. The rate of endogamous marriages within the *hamula* is steadily increasing but this does not reflect, necessarily, the position of the *hamula*. The development of local government in Arab villages has created a new medium for the display of the *hamula's* political power, but the mode of operation and democratic election of the local council will ultimately weaken the *hamula* organization.

The Arab population of Israel is remarkable for its multi-communal character: there are Muslims (75%), Christians of various denominations (17%) and Druze (8%). Most of the Muslims and Druze live in villages, most of the Christians in towns. The communal framework is also weakening. Modernization and secularization weaken the religious community in general. The Muslim community is affected, additionally, by the decline of the status of the *Shari'a* (Islamic Law system) and its functionaries in a non-Muslim state; the lack of a tradition of Muslim communal organization in the Ottoman period and the collapse of the communal organization of Mandatory days; the nationalization of the management of most of the Muslim *Waqf* (endowment) property, which became absentees' property in 1948; the lack of a religious and political leadership on a national scale; the severance of the links with the center of religious law and leadership abroad. However, the *Shari'a* Courts still have the widest powers of any religious court in Israel.

The Druzes were not recognized as a separate community until 1957, and the establishment of their religious-legal system and communal leadership was completed only a few years ago. Druze communal cohesion is weakened by the lack of a tradition of communal organization, the lack of religious experience of most of the members of the community owing to the secret nature of their religion, and the service of Druze youth in the Israel Defense Forces.

The most important Christian communities in Israel are the Greek Catholic, the Greek Orthodox, the Latin (Roman Catholic), the Maronite and the Evangelical-Episcopal (the local branch of the Anglican Church). Until recently, the Protestant churches had no communal judicial autonomy; after the reunification of Jerusalem, the government granted the Episcopalians and the Bahais the status of a recognized religious community.

The Greek-Orthodox are the weakest organizationally. The reasons for this lie in the Orthodox doctrine, which is less dogmatic, authoritarian and activist than the Catholic (there is no missionary activity, for instance); the absence of a firmly-knit clerical hierarchy; the national antagonism between the higher clergy, which is Greek, and the members of the community and the lower clergy, which are Arab; and the existence, alongside the ecclesiastical organization, of a secular communal organization (Majlis Milli), which is more accessible to external influences tending to erode the traditional frameworks. The Greek-Catholic community, on the other hand, is the most closely-knit.

Israel has about 44,000 Bedouin, two-thirds of them in the Negev and one third in Galilee. These Bedouin, especially the Galilean ones, are on the threshold of complete sedentarization. This is due to the restriction of their movement by political boundaries (though one should admit that these boundaries are not hermetically closed so far as the Bedouin are concerned); the establishment of control by various government agencies especially the military government in the Negev; changes in the employment structure, especially gravitation toward centers of employment in Jewish localities; the diminished income from agriculture and flocks owing to frequent droughts in the Negev; and State development plans in Bedouin areas designed to encourage their settlement.

Following sedentarization, the tribal framework tends to break up into *hamulas* (clan) units, and the social, economic and political status of the sheiks declines. At Bosmat Tiv'on, a new Bedouin settlement near Haifa, the settlers, skipping the village stage, have become towns' people in all respects. The importance of orthodox Islam is increasing among the settled Bedouin (observance of religious commandments and recourse to *Shari'a* Courts in matters of personal status).

About three-quarters of the Arab population of Israel lives in villages. The Israeli Arab village has undergone radical changes. The irrigated area has increased, diversified marketable crops have been introduced, and the means of agricultural production have been improved (*i.e.,* by mechanization); the agrarian system has changed fundamentally; large-scale basic investments have been made. The standard of living has risen. Several large villages, such as Tayyiba and Umm al-Fahm, have become thriving townlets. A surplus labor force has come into being in the villages, these commuters — about one-half of the Arab labor force and in some villages two-thirds and more — travel to work outside their villages, most of them being in agriculture, the building trade, and services in the towns.

Until the Six-Day War, about 25% of the Arab population was urban — distributed over two Arab towns, Nazareth and Shafa 'Amar, and five mixed towns: Haifa, Acre, Tel Aviv-Jaffa, Lod (Lydda) and Ramlah. The urban Arab population has not significantly increased in Israel, as the process of urbanization has been hindered, even halted, by social, economic, cultural and political obstacles: there were no well-established Arab urban centers to attract rural migrants (East Jerusalem may well become the metropolis of Israel's Arabs); most of the commuters are unskilled, and about one third of them work in the towns only temporarily, in the dead seasons of agriculture; closer contact (in housing, education etc.) with Jewish society in the mixed towns, is feared as a disintegrating factor; easier communications and the construction of approach roads to most of the villages make daily commuting more desirable than migration to the towns; and the cost of housing and subsistence in town is appreciably higher.

Side by side with the collapse of clan and community organizations and the blurring of traditional ecological divisions, new occupational and social strata —laborers, intellectuals, liberal professions—are emerging. A growing awareness of the Arab cultural and historical heritage, owing to the increasing spread of education, and a sharpened national consciousness may lead, because of the Arab-Israel conflict, to a conflict of loyalties, aggravated by the fact that the Israeli Arabs' nationalism is or at least was until recently pan-Arab, Nasserist rather than local. There are, moreover, internal factors of tension: the recent transformation of the Arab population from a majority in the territory of the British Mandate into a minority in Israel; mutual prejudices; the social, economic and cultural differences between the two sectors which are easily translated into political terms.

This process is reflected in the political organization; in parliamentary elections, Arabs vote either for the general, not specifically Arab parties of which only the Communists, Mapam and splinter groups have Arab candidates on their lists— or for specifically Arab lists, of which there have usually been two to four, mostly linked to the Labor Party (Mapai), and based on regional, local, communal and clan alignments. Most Arab members of the Knesset have been elected on these lists and on the Communist ticket. The first Knesset had three Arab members (among 120); there have been seven or eight Arab members in every Knesset since.

All the political parties active in Israeli Arab society, except the Communists and to some extent Mapam, adapt their methods to the traditional patterns, e.g. in the selection of candidates to elective office so as to represent clans and communities. Yet the proportion of Arab votes cast for the Zionist parties, though still high, declines from election to election, parallel with the disintegration of the traditional social patterns. At the 1973 Knesset elections, the Zionist parties still obtained about two-thirds of the total Arab vote. About 24% of Israel's Arabs voted Communist in 1949, 11-15% did so in 1951-59, about 22-23% in 1961 and 1965, 28-30% in 1969. The Communists gained about one-third of the total Arab vote in 1973.

The Communists are producing a new type of Arab political leader, ideologically and organizationally trained; a radical both politically and socially. They have had some success among the traditional strata as there is no other political framework for airing grievances against the establishment and as the traditional election lists cannot satisfy all claims for clan and community representation. But the Communists are still weak when pitted in local elections—except in Nazareth and a few villages—against lists based on clans, blood relationship and religion. They operate mainly among workers and intellectuals.

The Communist Party is the only political party in which Arabs appear among the active leadership (Mapam has admitted Arabs since 1954, but they are hardly represented in its leadership). The Communists present an Arab nationalist line, sharply anti-Government and critical of the status of the Arab in Israel. In the first years of the State, they also supported the Israeli Arabs' right of self-determination (i.e. secession).Since the split in the party—virtually into a Jewish and an Arab branch—Arab Communists have become even more rigid and extremist.

In the early 1950s, circles close to the government attempted to set up a country-wide Arab political party under the leadership of Muhammed Nimr al-Hawari, but had no success. Equally unsuccessful were attempts by Communists to set up mass front organizations outside the framework of their party, such as the Popular Front (originally called the Arab Front) (1958) and the Muslim General Congress (1961). Another attempt to set up a purely Arab party was made in 1959. Following the rift between Egypt's Nasser and Iraq's Qassem (who was supported by the Communists), young Nasserist radicals ceased co-operating

with the Communists and founded *Al-Ard* (The Land—an association that re-
fused to accept the existence of the State of Israel). After prolonged litigation,
Al-Ard was outlawed. An attempt by the same elements to put up a list for the 1965
Knesset elections also failed.

In the first decade of independence, the government aimed at preserving
separate Jewish and Arab sectors. Military government was severe in the early
years, and movement from the "closed areas" under military control to the
centers of economic life was restricted. Wide autonomy was granted in religious
and cultural matters, e.g. religious jurisdiction in matters of personal status,
recognition of Arabic as an official language and its designation as the language of
instruction in State schools for Arab children and social organizations (such as
the General Federation of Labor (the Histadrut), and political parties (except
Mapam) established separate branches for Arabs rather than admit Arabs to
direct membership.

In the late fifties, there was an increasing tendency to integrate the Arabs into
the economic, political and social organization of the country. Restrictions on
movement were gradually lifted and finally abolished; military government was
also abolished. Arabs were admitted to full membership of the Histadrut (1960)
and the Labor Party has recently opened its ranks to Druzes and to anyone serving
in the Security Forces. The Government accorded the Druzes special attention for
throwing in their lot with the State. They were given the status of a recognized
community with its own judicial-communal institutions etc. (1957). Recently,
Druze affairs were removed from the special departments for Arab affairs in the
various Government Ministries. Five-year plans for the development of Arab and
Druze villages (1962-67; 1967-72) yielded impressive results in the supply of
drinking-water, the construction of approach roads, electrification, the improvement of education, health, housing, etc. Local government in the villages was
encouraged. The Histadrut voluntary bodies made efforts for the social integration of Israeli Arabs by establishing groups for understanding and friendship,
social circles, etc.

The integration of Israel Arabs is still far from complete. Some Arabs and Druze
have been appointed to responsible positions in government service, the
Judiciary and the Legislature (a Muslim is Deputy Speaker of the Knesset). Two
Arab Deputy Ministers have been appointed. But in the economic field, Arabs
have mainly been absorbed into occupations of little social prestige. Their political
integration is technical-organizational (the formation for election purposes of
separate Arab lists attached to general Israeli Zionist parties or the canvassing of
direct votes for those parties) and does not commit them to the doctrinal ideological program. The State does not wish to subject the Arabs to severe loyalty tests:
they are not required to identify with the State and its aims; Muslims and
Christians are not liable to conscription into military service.
All that is required of the Arab citizen is to accept the existence of the State
passively and obey its laws. The government views with suspicion any attempt
to organize separate national groups with programs not consistent with the
existence of the State. The traditional leadership, identified with the *status quo*,
enjoys the support of the establishment.

What is the attitude of Israeli Arabs toward the State? Up to the 1967 war, this
question did not arise with full poignancy for several reasons; the political elite
had left the country during the War of Independence; the Arab towns, which
had been the centers of activity, had dwindled; the proportion of the rural popu-

lation had increased. In the traditional society the attitude toward the State is not expressed in political terms.

The war preceding the establishment of the State created for many Israeli Arabs distressing problems, such as the division of families by the new borders; the expropriation of lands belonging to absentees, including technical absentees, i.e., refugees who in some manner had returned to the State; the expropriation of lands for purposes of security settlement and development, especially in border areas, involving for instance, the evacuation of the villages of Irqit and Bir'am on the Lebanese border; land ownership problems; the restriction of movement and the permits system operated by the military government; the problem of unemployment among the intelligentsia, etc.

Most personal problems have been somehow solved. A reunion of families has taken place—with or without permits; most of the persons affected by land expropriations, including the people of Irqit (but not those of Bir'am) have been compensated in money and/or land; military government has been abolished. Yet, no solution has been found to problems closely bound up with political questions, such as that of unemployment among the white-collar workers; the inaccessibility of top-level positions of power and responsibility to the Arab intelligentsia (this is not a question of providing the Arabs with an adequate representation in the establishment according to their proportion size); or problems of the contents and aim of the curriculum of state Arabic schools.

The physical severance of Israeli Arabs from the Arab countries up to the Six Day War (though not including communication media such as radio and television) facilitated integration. The Arab-Israel struggle was conducted by the sovereign Arab states while Israel Arabs were not required actively to participate. Their well-being was linked to the interest of the State: its economic prosperity, the distribution of refugee lands as compensation for expropriated property, the advantages of the welfare state and the rule of law. There were those who tried to rationalize the existing situation as a bi-cultural nation-state and believed in the possibility of integrating Israeli Arabs while preserving their national identity. Some cherished an Israeli-Arab consciousness (and even tried to organize a group by that name), based on negative ideological reasoning (such as the harm likely to befall Israeli Arabs if the Israel-Arab conflict escalated). On the eve of and during the Six Day War, most Arab Israelis threw in their lot with Israel and showed their identification with the State. The radical leftist leadership, despite its growing influence, was not able to change this.

The Six Day War greatly upset this balance. The crushing defeat of the Arab countries exacerbated the Israel-Arab conflict. Physical contact with the centers of activity of the Arab world, and first and foremost the Palestinians on the West Bank, was resumed; the complete isolation of Israel's Arabs was broken and they were exposed to increasing pressure to define their attitude to Arab nationalism and the State of Israel. Meeting the Arabs of the Israel-occupied territories, the Israeli Arab could point to the social and economic achievements of his rural society, but his social-political position could not compare with that attained by the Palestinians in Jordan. As a result, there are signs that a Palestinian consciousness, dormant for the past twenty years, is reawakening. Jerusalem and several West Bank towns, with their large and able middle-class, may supply the cadres for a political leadership. (The inhabitants of East Jerusalem took part in the 1969 and 1973 municipal elections, but are not entitled to vote in elections to the Knesset until they acquire Israeli citizenship). The liberal policy of the military government in the occupied territories, facilitates the emergence of a leadership whose influence may exceed the local level. On the other hand, the Israeli authorities and public have become less tolerant toward Israeli Arabs as a result of acts of sabotage. Arab society reacts by shutting itself off, and the achievements of the highly successful integration policy are seriously threatened.

Arab society in Israel is in a transition stage. Its traditional structure, though cracks are appearing in it, has not yet collapsed. The intensity of change is not equal in all parts of the social fabric. In view of the uncertainty of political developments in the region, especially since the war of October 1973, it is too early to assess the future.

West Bank Sentiments
1967 – 1973

By Amnon Cohen

Only some 30,000 of the Arab inhabitants of the West Bank, a very small minority indeed, are Christian, all the rest are Muslim. While two-thirds of the population is rural, there are seven or eight big cities, towns, main urban centers in which there are about 35 per cent to 40 per cent of the total population of the West Bank. Another statistical item to be added, which is of importance in my view, is that the West Bank population also includes about 50,000 to 60,000 refugees, namely people who actually live in refugee camps. A distinction should be made between this and another category, that of legally identified refugees: this latter group is much larger, but a high percentage of those who carry the refugee cards can hardly be distinguished from any other elements within the local population; they live in towns, they are integrated in the urban society, they are married into deep-rooted families; they engage in practically the whole spectrum of economic and social activity, and do not tend to indicate any specially-tailored, distinct political concepts different from either the ordinary town dwellers or rural society. Those who live in camps in the whole of the West Bank are not more than 10 per cent of the entire population.

If we try and look at the 4½ or 5 years of Israeli rule and administration of the West Bank we might discern three to four stages. The first one was that of the initial shock which they suffered immediately after the Six Day War. The general feeling shared by the whole of the population of the West Bank was that of a shock, which emanated from different sources, the most important of which was that nobody, at least on the West Bank, and perhaps in other parts of the Middle East as well, had thought that things would turn out the way they did. Only very few people, if any, among those who did not exclude the possibility of Egyptian defeat would have envisaged that King Hussein would have erred so fatally as to drag Israel into an unpredicted war culminating in the occupation of the West Bank. The local population was completely taken by surprise by these results. The shock was further aggravated by the fact that Israel did not behave exactly as it was supposed to, that is to say, as the ruthless, frightening, occupying soldiers. The Arabs discovered Israelis had neither tails, nor horns on their foreheads, but were ordinary human beings, treating them too as such. Given the intensive propaganda they were subjected to during the last 20 years or so, they were not only ignorant of, but also suspicious toward Israel; in their heavy hearts they were afraid that Israel might behave in the same malicious manner they had been taught it would, and treat the local population with utmost cruelty. When the war was over, they looked around, listened to what their relatives in distant places told them and found out that nothing of this sort happened. I shall not elaborate here upon the reasons, interesting as they may be. Suffice it to say that this whole complex of unsubstantiated fears was yet another cause for shock. The third reason was that whereas all the aforesaid was relevant with regard to the personal behavior of the Israeli soldiers, it turned out that it was a part of a wider scheme which was later worked out, a part of a general policy, which on the face of it was illogical. We shall be more explicit at a later stage about the logic which underlies this illogical policy; we use this term in this context as a purely subjective one, as regarded or initially reacted upon, by the local population. It seemed illogical because it contradicted all their previous concepts. Having been brought up on feelings of contempt, hatred and hopes of vengeance, once faced with the reality which did not give them the slightest outlet — I am referring, for the moment, to any national aspirations — or justification for that hatred, the only result was a certain feeling of uneasiness and apprehension, culminating in an increasing awareness of the fact that once again they were let down, not only militarily and politically, but emotionally as well. And they were shocked for another reason as well. They suddenly found out that not only were all the things they were told about Israel and its intentions wrong, or at least most of them, but one more thing proved to be untrue. Statistics they used to read wherever they read them were wrong, namely they knew, or they thought they knew that there were something around 2 million Israelis and they found out, to their bewilderment, that there were many more than 5 million! One very prominent Arab political leader once told a high-ranking Israeli friend of his: "Well, after all, between you and me, no journalists present, why do you insist that you are somewhat more than 2 million Jews in Israel, while I am sure that you are more than 5 million"? When asked what made him doubt official well established statistics, he said that to judge by the multitudes who flooded the West Bank every Saturday with their wives and children, he wouldn't say there were anything less than 5 million Israelis! As things stood in the first weeks after the war, the ordinary Israeli discovered the West Bank, and there were so many cars, so many visitors, so many Israeli tourists throughout the West Bank that no Arab would believe there were only 2 million Israelis.

The first stage of the shock, deep and paralyzing as it may have been, did not last very long. Within a few months they managed to overcome it and woke up to the second stage, which lasted for two years, from the end of 1967 to the end of 1969, sometimes overlapping the beginning of 1970 and could best be termed as the stage of active resistance, both political and military, to the Israeli rule. In retrospect it seems quite natural, almost self-evident. It is natural to assume that once a state of shock ends it should be followed, almost by definition, by a gradual return to normal behavior. As weeks went by the local population got used to the fact that Israelis were human. Quite logically and expectedly they said to themselves: why not try and do something about the unhealthy state of affairs and start acting in a way which might facilitate the accomplishment of national, personal and communal hopes and beliefs. In other words, let the Arabs take the opportunity and get rid of the newly inaugurated occupation in one way or another. Nationally minded, as they surely have been for the last decades, they were not only hoping to get rid of Israel but they had all the justification and reasons to try and think and believe that they might achieve their aim which, during the years 1968, 1969, consisted of shaking off Israeli rule, as benevolent as it might appear to be. The terrorist organizations were then at full flood, not much militarily but rather in the public's mind, if one is to judge by the front pages in all sorts of newspapers all over the world. In fact, this was not sheer propaganda, for it was during that period that the terrorist organizations accomplished some real achievements from their point of view, one of which I witnessed personally; this was the bomb which blew up in the Jerusalem University cafeteria within the campus. The cafeteria bomb, the Mahane Yehuda market bomb and many others were real successes to them as well as a painful reminder to Israel. Moreover, even though I would not suggest that the future historian doing any serious work on the terrorist organizations' activities across the Jordan River use their newspapers and announcements on the radio as source material, because many of them were false, and others exaggerated to a large extent, but many of them tried and in some cases they even succeeded in crossing the Jordan River, attacking Israeli villages, thereby scoring some points to their advantage. This stage did not last long. Within a year or two Israel succeeded in stamping out the acts of violence by a combination of different methods. On the one hand it managed to block the way across the Jordan River by installing a sophisticated military net which practically put an end to the infiltration across that border. This was coupled with the discovery of most of the saboteurs engaged in espionage, and whatever else they were doing on the West Bank. On the other hand Israel proved to them that strikes and demonstrations of high-school students would not serve their cause in any way. The result in a nutshell was that these measures, combined with the impasse on the international political level, hastened the end of terrorist activity. Toward the end of 1969 there was not any practical, real action by terrorist organizations, either across the border running along the Jordan River, or within the territories.

This started the third stage, which was the stage of disappointment and reappraisal of their future. On the one hand, the Jordan River was blocked; inside the West Bank they could not establish any real underground network of value. Then King Hussein, in September 1970, dealt them a very severe blow in Amman and the whole of the Hashemite Kingdom of Jordan, which damaged not only their real cause but also their image. Then came another very sad event in the modern history of Arab nationalism, which was the death of Nasser at the end of September 1970. Then there was the cumulative effect of the gradual disappointment with all the international attempts to solve the problem through political measures; consultations, mediation, the talks of the Four, and the Security Council of the United Nations. All of these and many others added up to a deeper sense of failure and a growing consciousness of the fact that this was not going to be the way to get rid of Israeli rule. To sum up, they were both deceived and disappointed on the military as well as on the political level with the various courses they had been trying for almost three years without any substantial success. Thinking of it over and over again, faced with the eternal problem, "quo vadis", they could not perceive, generally speaking, any particularly new hopeful vista. It was then, gradually, that the fourth stage started. I call it the stage of normalization. Let me try and describe the main features of this phenomenon, the stage of normalization. Let me cite only two or three examples. The first one concerns work and workers, at present [1972] about 35,000 to 40,000 workers — statistics are never really accurate — cross "the Green Line" (the old border between Israel and the West Bank). About 40,000 workers daily cross the Green Line to go and work in Israel and cross the same line again when they go back home in the evening. Mainly male workers with an incessant, slow growing of the number of females, work throughout Israel in most of the economic enterprises. They do it in spite of recurrent threats from all sorts of media of the terrorist organizations and some Arab states. Arab propaganda tends to depict this work in Israel in very sombre colors, regarding it as a "betrayal" of the national cause. These were elements which tried in the past to implement the threats against these workers, but this proved to be useless as well. The fact that they can earn in Israel twice as much as they could earn within their own society proved stronger than any other factor in influencing the decision of more than a quarter of the actual man-power of the West Bank. At present it is mainly an economic process, but it engenders far-reaching social developments, and possibly some ideological and political ones as well.

The second sphere to be mentioned here is education. Not-withstanding former difficulties, the whole network of primary and secondary education is thriving. About one fourth of the entire population goes regularly to schools, which are run by their own teachers and headmasters, according to the actual Jordanian curriculum and textbooks. Israeli intervention is limited mainly to the financing of the system as a whole, as well as to paying attention to any help asked for. It seems it is within the scope of this field that the greatest achievement has been made. The overwhelming atmosphere of learning, devoid of any active involvement in politics, should not be related to any fundamental deterioration of the nationalistic zeal among the pupils or, for that matter, their teachers. Having tried the militant arena and realized that Israeli authorities had not the slightest intention of forcing them to attend school, it was from within, from among the parents and leaders of the society that the most efficient and effective course was chosen. A positive decision on its own merits, it was another contribution toward a normalization of life.

The third and the last example to be cited here is the municipal system. Having taken it for granted and probably underestimated its importance for a long time, I found out that the normal way in which municipal councils have been functioning on the West Bank was not self-evident at all. In 1972 I accompanied a very prominent British politician, who was on a visit to Israel, through the West Bank, trying my best to draw his attention to the most instructive facets of Israel's rule there, and I did not find it of any interest or importance to mention to him that all the towns on the West Bank were run completely by Arabs. When I mentioned it *en passant*, he was really astonished, and assured me that he regarded it as an outstanding phenomenon. I should say here that the municipal administration of all the cities and towns on the West Bank is entirely and exclusively Arab without any Israeli interference. They are run [1972] by the same Mayors as under Jordanian rule and have the same municipal councils regulating the same Jordanian law. This applies to taxation as well, in that taxes are levied according to Jordanian law, be it municipal taxes or taxes accruing to the Government. It is on this issue as well as on any other that regulations are carried out to the letter in accordance with the Jordanian law, which is still valid and fully implemented on the West Bank.

There are many other examples of normalization, but I hope that the two or three I have cited are sufficient, to prove how normalization has worked and is still the main phenomenon which characterizes the general atmosphere on the West Bank. It is also the main concrete contribution to the present stage of Arab-Israeli relations within the wider framework of time and place. This is a stage which started somewhere around 1969-70 and which could be witnessed whenever one met any part of the society, be it town or village, whether one spoke to a student, a worker, or an ex-minister; the latter and his peers, for instance, might not be very happy to acknowledge the fact but if they spoke their minds they would admit that these were the facts.

I would like to dwell for some time on another aspect of the situation on the West Bank, namely the main political trends prevailing within its territory. Minor, marginal or dormant tendencies excluded, and with all inevitable reservations as to the validity of every generalization born in mind, the main political inclinations of the population could be divided and scrutinized according to three criteria: (a) Hashemite identification; (b) guerrilla organization identification; (c) Palestinian entity identification; (d) Israeli identification.

As to Hashemite identification: this brings us back in a sense and to a certain extent, to the question of the relationship between political and national identity. I think that I may state with a large amount of certainty that pro-Hashemite feelings among the politically conscious are still very strong on the West Bank. Maybe I should not have used the word 'feelings', I should have said political identification because there might be rather important elements in the population which may feel themselves Palestinians but which identify themselves with the Hashemite Kingdom of Jordan either for reasons of tradition, or expediency, or, because of a faith in an identity, as artificial as it may sound. The faith in Jordan, with which they were incorporated for only seventeen years, (Jordan formally annexed the West Bank in April, 1950) created some sort of an identification, a sense of belonging to the State or rather of the State belonging to them, which is the same thing, at least theoretically. They regard themselves as identified to a large extent with that State. This may lead them to the conclusion that they should try their best to change its future, to modify it or to agree to the present situation, but a deep sense of a common interest, past and future, is there. They have, of course, family ties with that State, they still are Jordanian citizens, judged by my criteria of International Law, and whenever they go abroad they travel on their Jordanian passports. They have Jordanian identity cards as well, even though they also have Israeli identity cards, which they are supposed to carry with them while they are on the West Bank. Many of them still get their salaries either directly or through bank-accounts from the Jordanian Ministry of Finance. Their bonds are not only financial or historical; they are closely related to the future as well. When encountering people from the West Bank one may quite often hear the following: "We may not like very much the idea of belonging to this political entity called the Hashemite Kingdom of Jordan, or as it is termed at present the United Arab Kingdom, but this is the only practical way in which we could get rid of you Israelis and for reasons of expediency we had better stick to that reality." The result is that even though there is a certain sentiment of resentment which has increased during the last five years, especially after what happened in September 1970, still most, or a large and overwhelming percentage of the present population of the West Bank, regard themselves as politically identified with Jordan, either in its present form or in a whole variety of different political shades.

A second focus of identification which might be present on the West Bank is to the terrorist organizations. This political identification had to undergo many changes in the last five years. If we are asked to sum it up in one or two sentences, we would regard the present situation [1972] as follows: many members of the Arab population of the West Bank hoped until 1969 that they might be saved from Israeli rule by what they regarded as "their" guerrilla organizations. They found out, to their regret, and in some cases to their shame, that this solution was not a very practical one.

If again I try to look back for four or five years I should say that there has been a certain growth of feeling of Palestinian distinctiveness, entity, self-assertion as such, but it should still be regarded and seen within the context of feeling rather than within the context of political factors or effective forces. The politically minded people who are ready to back this idea politically are still a minority.

To sum up, and here I come back to the fourth possibility: are there, perhaps, some Arabs, who are neither pro-Hashemite, nor pro-fatah, nor pro-Palestinian-entity, and who might think that the fourth possibility, that of backing Israeli rule will be the lesser of the other evils? Nobody on the West Bank has become pro-Zionist, let alone Zionist.

The inhabitants of the West Bank are part and parcel of a national movement, proud of their dreams and aspirations, not ready to trade any of them for the most liberal, enlightened Israeli rule. There is no pro-Zionist identification within the Arab population on the West Bank but on the other hand there is a great and increasing feeling and, what is more important, a more mature evaluation of day-to-day facts. After all, they think, the Israelis are here on the West Bank, perhaps for rather a long period, we can't get rid of them even though some of us might feel very inclined to do it. The Arab States cannot help us, the great powers will not help us, the Israelis will not withdraw of their own free will without first reaching a general settlement, so the only practical way is to try and live as normally as possible. People prefer to get more education for their children and to be able to send them abroad to study in an Arab University. This does not mean any discredit to the alleged memories of all that the Jews have done — including the 1967 war, and the possession of the West Bank and does not impinge on their hope for the future. But, until that "day of salvation" comes, they strive to do their best not only to survive but also to lead a normal life, as normal as possible, under the circumstances, of which one of the main implications is complete co-operation with the Israelis on the economic, social and even cultural level while waiting for a brighter future.

III

Palestinian Arab Nationalism

Political and Social Aspects of Israeli and Arab Nationalism

By Shlomo Avineri

In 1905 a volume appeared in Paris that was to become one of the classic expressions of Arab nationalism. Its author, Neguib Azoury, was, like many other early Arab nationalists, a Christian. He founded in Paris the *Ligue de la Patrie Arabe,* whose avowed aim was the liberation, with French assistance, of Syria and Iraq from Turkish rule. In his book, the following remarkable passage occurs:

> Two important phenomena, of the same nature and yet antagonistic, manifest themselves nowadays in Turkish Asia but have drawn very little attention to themselves. They are the awakening of the Arab nation and the latent effort of the Jews to reconstitute on a large scale the ancient kingdom of Israel. These two movements are destined to fight each other continually. . . . On the final outcome of this struggle may well hinge the destiny of the whole world.

How much more farseeing and realistic this is than the naïvely harmonious visions one usually encounters in most of the early Zionist writings. For example, in his *Judenstaat,* published in 1896, Herzl devoted entire chapters to a detailed description of the social organization of the future Jewish state, but had only one short paragraph about its army. The Jewish state, he argued, would be neutral and have no enemies; hence it would need only a small professional army to maintain internal and external security. Unlike Azoury, with his vision of ever-lasting strife, Herzl saw no conflict or confrontation in store for the Jewish state.

It is not my intention to discuss here the conflict between the two national movements, the Arab and the Jewish, nor to present a detailed history of their respective developments. I shall limit myself to an analysis of two aspects of their intellectual and social structures. But this account may have a bearing on

97

the possibility of an adequate understanding of the conflict, and what I have to say may also serve as an attempt to provide an explanation for the relative success of one of the two movements and the relative failure of the other to achieve similar ends.

Both Arab and Jewish nationalism originated under the impact of Western enlightenment and secularization upon two ancient and traditional societies. Though there have been Arabs and Jews for centuries and millenia, and though in the past both communities had expressed their consciousness through the establishment and maintenance of political commonwealths, the emergence of a secular, politically-oriented nationalism among both is basically a 19th century phenomenon. It was prompted in both cases by the impact of the West on their traditional religious structures: for the Arabs it was the emergence of the West as an intellectual, political and technological challenge to their traditional way of life. It started most dramatically with Napoleon's Egyptian expedition—certainly one of the bizarre by-products of the French Revolution—and the consequent penetration into the Middle Eastern countries of Western merchants and missionaries, bearing Western ideas, at precisely the time when the traditional religious legitimacy and political paramountcy of the Ottoman Empire was being undermined.

For the Jewish communities of Eastern and Central Europe, the disintegration of the traditional communal way of life and the emergence of modern, secular nationalisms among the general population posed a number of similar problems concerning identity, self-consciousness and sheer survival. Thus both Jewish and Arab nationalism, though drawing on long national and religious histories, are the children of Western enlightenment and have to be viewed in this context.

Oddly enough, the major push toward a cultural and national Arab renaissance was given by a group of American Presbyterian missionaries. In 1823 the American Board of Commissioners for Foreign Missions, a Boston organization established a mission and a school in Beirut. The original idea was to have the station in Jerusalem, but for political reasons that became impossible, and the group had to content itself with this less exalted venue.

The Mission encountered a number of severe handicaps in its work. It was from the start unable to extend its ministry to the vast Muslim majority of the population: the Turkish authorities, barely tolerant of Western missionaries at all, made it perfectly clear that no proselytizing among this group would be allowed. Furthermore, the Jewish communities were not very receptive, to say the least, to the ministrations of the Boston Brahmins. This left them with basically one target—the Christian Arab communities, mainly the Maronites, the Greek Orthodox and some of the lesser Eastern Rite Christian communities. The function of their missionary activity thus became that of converting to Protestantism Christians of long standing, whose churches could be traced back to the origins of Christianity.

The theological problems such activity raised need not detain us here. What is of interest to us is that it involved the missionaries in an unusual development: for the American Protestants made an appeal to secular Arab consciousness that became for these Christian Arab groups a real alternative to their ambivalent position as second-class subjects in the Muslim Ottoman Empire. The invoking of a secular Arab nationalism turned out to be the only legitimate way the missionaries could challenge the religious nature of a Muslim-dominated society, which they felt had to be saved from whatever sins the infidels were inflicting on it. If political allegiance could be grafted onto the cultural base shared by Muslims and Christian Arabs, the latter could become the political and social equals of Muslims.

As the doyen of historians of Arab nationalism, George Antonius—himself a Christian Arab—put it: "The educational activities of the missionaries . . . gave pride of place to Arabic. . . . They were the pioneers, and because of that, the intellectual effervescence which marked the first stirrings of the Arab revival owes most to their labor." The first Arabic book to be printed in Syria was a new translation of the Bible prepared by the head of the Beirut mission, the Rev. Eli Smith; the press it was printed on had been brought over by the missionaries from a previous base in Malta. This introduction of the printing press into Syria was an event of tremendous importance. It was accompanied by the development of a new Arabic font, which Eli Smith ordered in Leipzig, and which became known as *American Arabic.*

The most interesting and influential figure of this period was Butrus Bustani, in whose career the shift from a national self-consciousness that was cultural to one that was political is most clearly discernible. Born in 1818 into a Maronite Christian family, Bustani became one of the first Christian Arabs to be converted to Protestantism by the Beirut mission. He not only assisted Eli Smith in his translation of the Bible, but also wrote the first history of Lebanon, composed several Arabic grammars, and compiled the first modern Arabic dictionary and the first Arabic modern encyclopedia. For a while, in 1857, he served as acting U.S. consul in Beirut. He taught for years in the mission school, and later established the first Arabic secular schools, called 'national schools' (*madrassah wattaniyah*). He also translated numerous European books into Arabic (notably *Robinson Crusoe*), set up his own printing press and publishing house and founded a number of periodicals devoted to Arab cultural themes. In 1866 under his initiative, the mission established the Syrian Protestant College, later to become the American University of Beirut, one of the main intellectual centers of Arab nationalism to this day.

Around 1845, Bustani founded the first literary society, *Majma' at-tahdhib*. It had 14 charter members, headed by Bustani. Eleven of them were Christian Arabs converted to Protestantism, two were missionaries (Dr. Cornelius Van Dyke and Dr. Henry de Forest), and one, Nasif al-Yaziji—famous in his own right as one of the most important modern writers in Arabic—was a Maronite who did not embrace Protestantism but who was a teacher in one of the mission schools. In less than two years the society had about fifty members, none of them Muslim.

It was not until 1857 that there was established, also on Bustani's initiative, an Arab Learned Society that included Muslim and Druze members and thus became the first non-sectarian Arab intellectual society.

The efforts of the group around Bustani and the Beirut mission were given a tremendous political impetus by the 1860 Lebanese communal riots, in which mainly Maronites and Druzes were involved in a series of mutual massacres. Bustani published many impassioned appeals, calling upon the various communities to unite in a non-sectarian patriotism as the only alternative to bloodletting. Only through a non-sectarian patriotism—*wattaniya*—based on their common Arabism, could members of the various communities learn to discover their common cause under the aegis of a non-religious allegiance to the Turkish Empire. Arab national self-consciousness, albeit within the Turkish Empire, was thus raised from a mere particular remedy for the ambivalent position of Christian Arabs within a Muslim realm to a focus for general political allegiance, embracing Muslims, Christians and Druzes alike. Despite this, its main appeal, through the rest of the 19th century, remained much stronger to Christian than to Muslim Arabs.

A different source for Arab nationalism is to be found in Egypt, whose semi-autonomous position on the periphery of the Ottoman Empire brought forth what Bernard Lewis has called the only territorial, non-confessional patriotism of the 19th century in the Middle East. This patriotism was centered much more on Egypt than on the common Arab heritage, and the emergence of Muhammad Ali and his son Ibrahim Pasha as reformers and modernizers greatly enhanced the position of Egypt as an independent entity. Nor was the Egyptian regime averse, throughout the 19th century to extending asylum if not outright assistance to various Syrian and Lebanese intellectuals, again mostly Christians, who were calling for an Arab cultural and political renaissance in the lands still under direct Ottoman rule. This became entangled with the movement for Islamic reform: while such reformers as Jumal ad-Din al-Afghani called for a purification of Islam in a way that became very easily utilized by the Pan-Islamic notions of the Ottoman Caliphate, a different development took place in Egypt. While reformers like Muhammad Abdu' were of extreme importance, for our purposes the most significant development was the one heralded by Abdul Rahman al-Kawakibi, a Syrian Muslim who found refuge in Egypt and who evolved a concept of Islamic reform and purification based on the restoration of its pristine Arabic character. In his *Excellences of the Arabs* (1901), Kawakibi argued that the Arabs, rather than the Turks, were the legitimate rulers of Islam. Al-Afghani's Pan-Islamism was implicitly pro-Ottoman, but Al-Kawakibi argued that only the Arabs could truly represent Islam in its purity. He enumerated twenty-six reasons for Arab superiority over any other Islamic nation and especially over the Turks. Despite this strong blend of Islam and Arabism, Al-Kawakibi also called for the separation of religion and state; he thus qualified, in Sylvia Haim's opinion, as the first intellectual precursor of modern, secular Pan-Arabism. He also prefigures some of the inherent ambiguities of the relationship between Arab nationalism and Islam.

The major transition, however, from the cultural to the political realm occurred in the aftermath of the 1908 revolution of the Young Turks. For the Arabic-speaking population of the Ottoman Empire, this revolution signified not so much the attempt to modernize the Empire as a conscious effort at political centralization—a shifting of political allegiance in the Empire from its Islamic base to a predominantly Turkish one. What to the outsider appeared as sensible centralization and modernization manifested itself to the Arab population as the imposition of a conscious, ethnic Ottomanization. So long as the Empire was conceived as one of the successive Muslim Caliphates, it did not basically present a problem to the allegiance of its Muslim population. But once the ethnic Turkish element came to the fore, the Muslim Arabs, already aroused to a consciousness of their linguistic, ethnic and historical tradition through half a century of cultural revival from Bustani to Al-Kawakibi, found themselves for the first time at loggerheads with the Turkish rulers who appeared now as foreign masters and enslavers rather than as co-religionists.

Turkish nationalism was, of course, as recent a phenomenon as Arab nationalism. Originally, it was fostered by groups basically marginal to the ruling elite of the Ottoman Empire. Among its sources were Crimean Tartar refugees who fled in the early 19th century to Constantinople in the wake of the Russian annexation of the Crimea and what was later to become South Russia. It is among them that one finds for the first time the emergence of an ethnic self-consciousness calling for the unification of all Turkic-speaking peoples. Another source, no less interesting, was a number of Polish and Hungarian 1848 refugees who found asylum and employment in the Ottoman Empire, which was only too glad to use them as military advisers. Some of them converted to Islam and reached very high positions in the army and administration. The most interesting among them was Count Konstantyn Borzecki, a Pole who embraced Islam and became prominent in the Ottoman administration as Mustafa Jelaleddin Pasha (his son, Enver, became a member of the Imperial Ottoman General Staff under the Young Turks). In 1869 Jelaleddin published in Constantinople a volume entitled *Les Turcs anciens et modernes,* in which he argued that the Turks are fundamentally a white, European people and the Empire should become a focal point for all Turkic-speaking peoples in South Russia and Central Asia. There were others like him. The most famous European Turcologist of the century, Arminius Vambry, a Hungarian of Jewish origin, lived for several years in Constantinople and also contributed to the growing awareness of Turkish ethnicity among the young intellectuals of the period who began to style themselves 'Young Ottomans.'

The Young Turks' attempt at Ottomanization exacerbated reactions among the Arab elite on account of the suspicion that the Committee of Union and Progress (as the Young Turks' high command was known) was also favoring Jewish immigration into Palestine. The fact that Cavid Bey, the Minister of Finance in the CUP cabinet, was a member of the Sabbataean crypto-Jewish sect of the Dönme, gave rise to all kinds of rumors about the contacts between the Zionists and the Young Turks, culminating in some absurd speculations about the Jewish origins of the whole Young Turk elite.

But this was mainly a side issue. What we find above all is a growing resentment against Ottomanization, and in the years between 1908 and 1914 a number of Arab political organizations sprang up expressing the radicalization of political sentiment among the Arabic-speaking population of the Empire. The Ottoman Decentralization Party *(Hozb al-Lamarkaziya al-Idariya al-Uthmani)* was formed around groups in Damascus, Tripoli, Beirut, Jaffa and Jerusalem, calling for a greater measure of autonomy in the various provinces of the Ottoman Empire. A more radical group, the Young Arab Society *(Jami'at al-Arabiya al-Fatat)* was formed in 1911 in Paris with an outspoken political nationalist program. During World War I, many of the founding members of these organizations were hanged by the Turks as traitors; and the British-inspired Arab revolt in the desert, so romanticized by T. E. Lawrence did in fact cash in on the anti-Turkish feelings of the nationally self-conscious young Arab intelligentsia in Syria, Palestine and Iraq.

For though in its later stages Arab nationalism became basically anti-Western, and as such found temporary allies first in Nazi Germany and later in Soviet Russia,* in its initial political manifestations it usually favored the British and the

---

* President Sadat of Egypt is a case in point. In his autobiography he tells how in 1942, when Rommel was at the gates of Alexandria, he and other members of the 'Free Officers' group sought and established contact with Nazi and Fascist agents against the common British enemy. See Anwar es-Sadat, *Revolt on the Nile,* London, 1957, pp. 34ff.

French as allies in the ousting of the Turks. What was sown by the American Presbyterian missionaries of Beirut was later reaped, in a way, by the British imperial interests who viewed Arab nationalism as a convenient instrument in their anti-Turkish policies during World War I and later.

One of the intriguing aspects of this development is that while modern Arab nationalism, with all its ambivalence about the West, initially welcomed, for political reasons, the Western intrusion into the Turkish Empire, the most fero- cious anti-Western opposition came not from nationalist but from fundamental- ist religious ideologies. Abdul Kadr in North Africa, the Mahdi in Sudan, the Senoussis in Libya—these were the forces that were trying to stem the French, British and Italian incursion into the Arab world. The fact that the only truly national leader Palestinian Arabs ever had, Hajj Amin al-Hussaini, was Mufti of Jerusalem and upheld the holy sites of Islam in Jerusalem as national symbols, is also very much within this tradition; and the emergence of such fiercely nationalist and anti-Western leaders as Qadhafi and Boumedienne, who find in Islam their basic ideological framework, is of immense significance in assessing the nature of Arab nationalism and its development.

Let us now turn to the origins of modern Jewish nationalism. Enlightenment and secularization changed radically the conditions of life of the Jewish com- munities in Eastern and Central Europe. So long as the Jews had lived as a religious community within the *natio Christiana,* there was ultimately very little ambivalence in their basic condition of existence, whatever difficulties and perse- cutions they had to endure. They were living in a society but were not members of it—a situation basically acceptable both to them and to Gentile society. Thus they were able to maintain their identity through generations of sometimes violent persecutions; in a social order based on hierarchy and distinctions, their apartness was in tune with the general *mores* of society.

But the ideas of equal rights brought in by the emancipation and the emergence of modern nationalism in Europe opened a whole Pandora's box of problems: if Jews were equal to other members of society, should they retain their own exclusive customs? Was a Yiddish-speaking Jew from the Pale of Settlement really an equal member of the Polish nation? Could an orthodox Jew really be in communion with republican Frenchmen? Similar questions began to be asked a century later in Arab countries, with the emergence of modern Arab nationalism in Iraq, Egypt, Syria and Morocco; the plight of European Jews in the nineteenth century repeated itself in the Arab world in the twentieth—the anti-Jewish riots in Baghdad under Rashid Ali al-Kailany's nationalist regime in the early 1940s followed similar developments of half a century earlier in Eastern Europe.

The emerging first generation of secularly educated and emancipated Jews was thus faced with a set of agonizing problems wholly unprecedented in Jewish history. If one does not believe any more in the orthodox Jewish way of life, what, then, is one? Is one really a German? But then the 'real' German, even if emancipated, was a Christian—as shown by Bruno Bauer's argument that Jews could be granted equal rights only if they converted first and *then* rejected Christianity like the emancipated Christian Germans themselves. Or could one really identify with the Polish nation without relating to Catholicism or with Mother Russia without being a member of the Orthodox Church? In some coun- tries with emerging nationalist movements, such as Poland and Hungary, the Jews were caught in a crossfire, for their emancipation usually took the form of assimilating to Russian and German, rather than to Polish and Magyar, cultures.

The leaders of the Jewish Sanhedrin convened by Napoleon must have been less than candid when they declared, under Imperial pressure, that they felt more in communion with their Gentile French compatriots than with their co-religionists in other countries. The problem of identity, which in a way never presented itself to Jews leading a traditional life within a Christian—or for that matter a Muslim —society, became an excruciating challenge to the modern, secularized Jew. Add to this the breakdown of the old economic order in which East European Jews had found a traditional niche for themselves, and one gets some idea of the enormous upheavals Jewish communities were undergoing in the 19th century.

Many turned to baptism, not always out of religious conviction but, as Heine put it, to gain 'a passport to European culture' or, like Marx's father, to be able to pursue one's career in a secularized society. Others found a way out of their predicament in Reform Judaism which postulated that the ethnic elements in Judaism were outdated and tried to forge a Jewish 'confession' in the image of enlightened Protestantism. Still others identified with the national and social struggles of their countries, sometimes oblivious to the fact that their participation might hamper the causes they believed in—as in the accusations brought forth first by the Czarist regime and later by the Nazis that socialism and communism were *verjudet*. Millions more emigrated to America and other Western countries. A small minority turned to the secular and cultural aspects of Jewish history in order to find in them a modern, non-religious focus for their identity as Jews.

It is out of these efforts, produced by the ambiguities of the position of the modern, secularized Jew, that there emerged the 19th century revival of Hebrew literature. It was from a combination of Herderianism and classicism that people turned to Hebrew as a medium of intellectual communication among those Jews who left the ghetto and its religion behind them and yet felt themselves to be Jewish. If there can be a Polish or a Czech literature, why not a renaissance of Hebrew? It was German- and Russian-educated intellectuals, not the rabbis in the Pale, who started the revival of Hebrew language and Jewish histori- cal consciousness. In Vilna, the crossroads of Polish, Russian and Lithuanian culture (where German was always in the background as a *Kultursprache*), Avraham Mapu wrote the first two modern Hebrew prose novels, *Ahavat Zion* and *Ashmat Shomron*. A modern Jewish historiosophy, trying to adapt Hegelian schemes to Jewish history, was first suggested by the Galicia-born Nachman Krochmal in his *Guide to the Perplexed of Our Time (Moreh Nevuchei HaZman)*, and a student of German historicism, Heinrich Graetz, wrote the first modern history of the Jewish people.

It is among these secularized, Westernized Jewish intellectuals that one finds the emergence of modern Jewish nationalism: the rabbis and the traditionalists were skeptical if not downright hostile to what appeared to them as a secular political creed contravening the traditional religious quietism associated with orthodox Jewish beliefs in messianism. Who could better epitomize the flower of Central European *Kultur* than journalists like Herzl and Nordau, more imbued with European socialist ideas than the early socialist Zionists were? It was a protest against the failure of the naïve belief in emancipation that modern Jewish nationalism appeared in the 19th century. Nazism was merely the final and most brutal blow dealt to the dream of emancipation as far as Central and Eastern Europe were concerned.

This leads us to the second question we propose to examine in our discussion: the problem of social structures.

Both Jewish and Arab nationalism not only had to contend with problems of national identity and survival, but also were confronted immediately with enormous issues of social structures. It will be my contention in the remainder of this account that while Jewish nationalism was relatively successful in imbuing its ideology and praxis with a vision of social transformation, Arab nationalism remained mainly political and, by ignoring the social dimension, was unable to achieve a degree of social cohesion comparable to the one achieved in the social structures of Israel.

Let us start with the problems of Jewish social structure first. What one discerns quite early in Jewish national writings of the 19th century is an awareness of the lopsided nature of the Jewish social structure. Jews, it was argued, are to be found almost exclusively in positions of social mediation, be it economic or intellectual: from *this* point of view the social structure of the Pale of Settlement did not differ much from that of the emancipated, Westernized Jewish communities, though the exact roles of Jews differed considerably. There were almost no Jews to be found in primary production—there was no Jewish peasantry, hardly any Jewish proletariat (insofar as one found a Jewish proletariat in some urban Polish areas toward the end of the 19th century it was because of the unique conditions of Jewish urban economic development, which was quicker than that of the general society—a development which itself contributed to anti-Semitism among the Gentile middle class and proletariat). A Jewish renaissance, it was argued, would have to be accompanied by a conscious realignment of the social structures of Jewish society. The Return to Zion would not have to be a mere territorial shift in population: in order to be successful, it would have to be accompanied by the development of a Jewish peasantry and a Jewish working class.

The development of these ideas can be traced most dramatically in the career of Moses Hess, Karl Marx's mentor and his so-called 'communist rabbi,' who is also considered one of the founding fathers of Socialist Zionism. He now lies buried in the first kibbutz on the shores of the Sea of Galilee, though he was initially interred in a Cologne cemetery under a tombstone carrying the inscription *Vater der deutschen Sozialdemonkratie*. His private papers are to be found divided between the Central Zionist Archives in Jerusalem and the Institute for Marxism-Leninism in Moscow, and editions of his works are being published by the Zionist Library in Jerusalem and the Academy of Sciences of the German Democratic Republic. He deserves a much closer study than the few footnotes usually referring to him as an 'influence' or 'forerunner.'

Though only six years older than Marx, Hess was born into a strictly Orthodox Jewish family in the Rhineland, while Marx grew up in a family that had been baptized. Unlike Marx who had no Jewish education and knew practically nothing about Judaism, Hess' early education had been a Jewish religious one. It was said of him that he belonged to that generation of Jews who learned their German from Hegel and their Latin from Spinoza.

Like many members of his generation, Hess reacted strongly against his Orthodox upbringing. His repudiation of Judaism became total and fierce. In his first book, *The Holy History of Mankind*, Hess refers to two nations of 'world historical importance' which are nowadays lifeless cadavers: the Jews and the Chinese. Following a somewhat simplified version of Hegel's philosophy of history, Hess characterizes the Jewish people as 'spirit without body' and the Chinese as 'body without spirit.' Judaism's role in history has been completed and though the Jews may experience a revival it will be as individuals totally immersed in universal

Western culture. Spinoza is to Hess an example of this new type of Jew who transcends the narrow limits of his origins and merges into the universal spirit —his anonymous book actually gives 'a Young Spinozist' as author.

The last chapter of the volume is indeed called 'The New Jerusalem': in it Hess paints a picture of a future society organized in communes, in which distinctions between town and country, as well as between man and woman, would disappear. But 'it is in the heart of Europe that this New Jerusalem will be founded.'

In an unpublished draft written around 1840 and called *The Poles and the Jews,* Hess says that one may expect a renaissance among both the peoples, but while the Polish renaissance will be political, the Jewish one will be purely spiritual. The Jews lack the two basic conditions for national life, territory and language; they have repeatedly shown a total lack of national consciousness *(Mangel an National-sinn).* Even traumatic experiences like the Damascus Affair have failed to arouse in them a sense of cohesion, and they are destined to disappear as a separate group through assimilation and integration into the new Europe of the spirit. Similarly in his *European Triarchy* Hess suggests that through their rejection of Jesus, the Jews have become a 'mummy.' And in his essay *On the Essence of Money,* Hess identifies Judaism and the cult of money—an identification which was later taken over and elaborated by Marx in his *On the Jewish Question.*

We thus see that though the Jewish Question comes up quite frequently in Hess' writings, and his well-informed historical account of early Judaism unmistakably shows the signs of his religious schooling, his attitude to Judaism is basically hostile and if he has a message to deliver it is that of total assimilation and ultimate disappearance.

Almost twenty years later, however, Hess experienced a complete transformation in his views on the subject. In 1862 he published his *Rome and Jerusalem,* which he originally intended entitling 'The Rebirth of Israel.' In the Preface he takes up the posture of the prodigal son:

> Here do I stand, after an estrangement of twenty years, in the midst of my people. Only one thought, which I felt I had stifled forever in my breast, presents itself vividly before my eyes: the thought of my nationality, which cannot be separated from the heritage of my forefathers, the Holy Land and the Eternal City, the birthplace of the belief in unity of the divine and the future brotherhood of all men.

The book is written as a series of letters to a fictitious lady correspondent, and Hess finishes one of the letters with a highly emotional outburst that he is happy to revert to his original name Moses and discard his adopted name of Maurice, further commenting: "I only regret that I cannot be called Itzig."

How may one account for such a complete change of attitude? On the evidence of Hess' own account of his conversion, there had been a number of reasons. The success of Italian nationalism, which became a great triumph for the European Left, was certainly one of the main driving forces; the Rome in the title of the book is Mazzini's *Roma Terza,* though the overtones of the Rome of the Pagan Emperors and of the Catholic Popes are, of course, also evident. Whereas for Marx national unity was viewed as purely instrumental (it helps the working class to focus on its true class interest), Hess followed Mazzini in arguing that the nation is a community in which individuals transcend their pure egotism, and on its foundations a socialist international 'community of communities' could be established.

Hess also cites as a reason for his advocacy of Jewish nationalism the increasingly racist overtones of European, and particularly German, nationalism: in this
he is one of the first to discern the catastrophic consequences of the failure of
liberal nationalism in Germany in 1848. German nationalism, Hess argues, is
becoming xenophobic, militaristic and racist, and there is no hope for the Jews of
incorporation into the New Germany.

Another formative influence Hess mentions is a volume by a French radical,
Ernest Laharanne: *La Nouvelle Question d'Orient*. Laharanne became greatly disturbed by the communal riots in Lebanon in 1860 (the same riots which we saw so
instrumental in politicizing Butrus Bustani's thought). He saw in them an ultimate proof of the bankruptcy of the Ottoman Empire. France, he argues, true to
its revolutionary tradition of supporting enslaved people against their oppressors, should now espouse the cause of the new nationalisms in the Levant.
Laharanne envisions, in place of the old Ottoman Empire, the emergence of two
Arab states, one in Syria-Mesopotomia and the other in Egypt. In the area
between the two he envisages the formation of a new Jewish state, and he calls
upon France to help establish *'les empires d'Egypte et d'Arabie et la reconstitution de la
nation Juive.'*

But beyond all these motives, the prime force in Hess' argument is that emancipation has not worked. Bourgeois society has not been able to solve the Jewish
problem, and because of this the Jews in bourgeois society have been put into
invidious positions which made their integration into a future socialist society in
Europe quite impossible. Reform Judaism failed similarly: not only did it, according to Hess, emasculate historical Judaism, but also, by stressing the purely
confessional rather than the national aspect of Judaism, it substituted the eternal
Jewish dream of communal redemption for the Christian message of merely
individual salvation.

In his historical account of Judaism in *Rome and Jerusalem*, Hess similarly takes a
completely different attitude from the one that had informed his early writings, in
which Judaism had been associated with the cult of money. This may or may not
be the case with various Jews in the Diaspora; but Judaism as a system of social
ethics, both in biblical and talmudic times, is in Hess' view a proto-socialist
system.

The romantic idealization here is obvious, but the examples are nonetheless
illuminating, Jewish sabbatarian legislation is portrayed as socially motivated,
as the first historical instance of social legislation in which even slaves were
included. Judaism, Hess argues in a letter dating from the same period, knows
no classes, had no feudalism, is basically 'social democratic.'

The Jewish family figures prominently in this historical account—the family
and not the individual has always been, according to Hess, the focus of Jewish
life. "Judaism never severed the individual from the family, nor the family from
the nation, nor the nation from humanity." The family appears here—in Hegelian
fashion—as a community, in contradistinction to what Hess sees as the fundamental individualism of Christian society. Moreover, whereas Gentile society, be
it pagan or Christian, worshipped masculinity and its attributes, in Judaism it was
the feminine virtues of compassion, suffering, love and understanding, associated with the Jewish mother, that were always dominant: "every Jewish
mother is a *mater dolorosa*." On the evidence of a paragraph in the talmudic tractate
Pirkei Avoth ('Ha-omer sheli sheli v-shelcha, shelcha, zo mida beinonit, ve-yesh omrim zo
midat Sdom')* Hess concluded that "the ordinary bourgeois morality of *chacun pour*

soi is alien to Jerusalem."

But Jerusalem, Hess contends, cannot be rejuvenated in the Diaspora, and certainly not in bourgeois society: the Jewish masses will be able to participate "in the great movement of modern mankind" only when they will have a Jewish homeland, when they will be engaged, like any other nation, in primary production.

It is indeed to the Jewish "masses," i.e. the populace of Eastern European Jewry, and not to the assimilated Western Jew that Hess turns his attention; there, Jewish consciousness is still alive, there, suffering is quite brutal, and it will be from there that the immigration to Palestine will come. It will be the impoverished *Ost-Juden* and the Middle Eastern Sephardim that will make up the bulk of the population of the new society. It is among these communities that the traditional communal spirit of Judaism is still alive, whereas Western Jews have been corrupted by individualism. Hess has, for example, a great, and somewhat naive, admiration for Hasidism: while criticizing what he calls its "religious superstitions," he sees in its way of life a communal togetherness, transcending individual atomism.

With such a background, Jewish immigration to the Land of Israel will not, in Hess' opinion, create another free-enterprise society. The new society will be organized "according to Mosaic, i.e., socialist, principles," there will be no private property in land, agricultural settlements will be formed on a communal basis, industry and commerce will be likewise organized according to co-operative principles. The New Jerusalem will be a socialist Jewish society.

Just as the national liberation of Italy and Poland became a central cause for the 19th century European Left, so the solution of "the last nationality problem" should be espoused by European socialists. Hess' latter-day Jewish nationalism was not a reversal from early socialist principles, though it obviously involved a change of heart about the Jewish question. The recent East German editors of Hess usually ignore his Zionism, briefly referring to it in one instance as an aberration, an inexplicable throw-back to "the religion of his youth." This is obvious nonsense, since Hess is not reverting to Jewish religious orthodoxy but is trying to evolve a concept of Jewish nationalism, and the future Jewish commonwealth envisaged by Hess is postulated in socialist terms.

Despite all the romanticization involved in the Zionist socialist attempt to create a Jewish peasantry and a Jewish working class in Palestine, this ultimately proved to be the main reason for the ability of the new society to maintain itself. Zionism thus became the only migration movement with *a conscious ideology of downward social mobility.* While all the great mass migration movements of the 19th century were motivated by the promise of upward social mobility—and this includes, of course, the three million Jewish immigrants from Czarist Russia to the West during the 1882-1914 period—the handful of Zionist immigrants to the Land of Israel were mainly middle and lower-middle class people who went to their New Zion in order to become laborers and peasants and thus lay the foundations for a new type of Jewish social structure.

Though much of this initial ideology is not as evident today in Israel as it was years ago, it was responsible for the creation of the basic socio-economic structures which characterize Israeli society to this day. The emergence of the kibbutz and the moshav as forms of collective and cooperative organization, the fact that most of the land is publicly owned, the hegemony of the labor movement in Israel's life and the fact that all Israeli governments have been headed by the Labor Party, the evolution of the Histadrut not only as a powerful trade union organization but also as a Labor-owned section of industry, the fact that the command-ing heights of the Israeli economy are publicly owned—all these, together with the basic egalitarianism of Israeli society, are elements that can be traced back to the combination of national ideology and social critique leading to the vision implied in Zionism.

Though Hess was the first to evolve this combination of Zionism and socialism, he was less influential, in the long run, than some later, perhaps less original minds. Mention should be made of only two of them, signifying the different streams of thought that went into Labor Zionism. One was Aharon David Gor-don, who under the influence of Tolstoyan ideals became an agricultural laborer at a very advanced age and in his writings extolled the idea of "the religion of labor," suggesting that physical labor should become part of the life experience of every individual and especially of intellectuals. The other was Dov Ber Borochov, whose amalgam of Plekhanovite Marxism and Zionism was perhaps the most influential in the emergence of Labor Zionism in Israel.

What is interesting is that this awareness of the social dimension in Zionism appears even in the writing of those Zionist thinkers who cannot be called Socialists. Herzl represents the liberal, bourgeois element in Zionist thought, yet even he refers on the first page of the Preface to *Der Judenstaat* to Thomas More's *Utopia* and to the popular utopian novel *Freiland* by his Viennese contemporary, the economist Theodor Hertzka. The social structure of Herzl's *The Jewish State* includes, among other features, public ownership of land and a seven-hour working day. When Herzl came up with a flag for the new state, he suggested an arrangement of seven golden stars on a white field, for "it will be under the banner of labor" that the Jews will return to their land. A few years later Herzl wrote a utopian novel, *Altneuland,* clearly modeled on Hertzka's *Freiland,* in which the new Jewish society in Palestine is based on Proudhonist mutualist principles. Like many other utopian novels. Herzl's abounds with long didactic speeches about the new life, in this case hailing Mutualism as the realization of social justice and the abolition of the power of privately owned capital.

Arab society, on approaching and achieving political independence, was faced with a similar problem of social structure. While it can be said of Jewish society that in the 19th century it was almost exclusively middle class, Arab Muslim society hardly had a middle class for a number of historical reasons. It is my argument that Arab nationalism remained almost exclusively political, had very little to say about the problem of social structures, and hence was almost com-pletely unsuccessful in effecting the transformation of Arab society that would have been necessary for political independence to have been more than a hollow crown.

As the previous remarks on Arab nationalism pointed out, the Arabs lived for centuries under foreign rule before the British and the French moved into the area. Before the establishment of Western paramountcy in the Middle East, Arab society was not a self-governing entity. Ever since the 12th century, the Arabic-speaking population of the Middle East had been ruled by a succession of foreign invaders: first the Crusaders, later Muslim Seljuks, Tartars, Osmanli Turks, Mameluke slaves (in Egypt). It was the Islam of all these conquerors, except the Crusaders, which gave them, as we have seen, legitimacy in Arab consciousness. But sociologically speaking the consequence was that the political elites in Arab societies were not Arabs but members of a foreign ethnic and linguistic group. Arab society, on achieving independence, had hardly a traditional political elite of its own.

Furthermore, because of Islamic precepts and the nature of the Arab Muslim *Conquista* of the Middle East in the 7th century, Muslim Arab society looked with disdain on commercial activity. Because the Arabs appeared in the countries of the Middle East outside the Arabian Peninsula as conquerors, the social structure of Muslim Arab society tended to emphasize a system of values connected with military valor and hence mercantile activity was never considered to be the right thing for a true Muslim to be engaged in. As a consequence, most of the urban mercantile middle classes in Arab society in the 19th and 20th centuries turned out to be composed of non-Muslim minority groups: Christian Arabs, Armenians, Greeks, Jews. The Christian Arabs, as we have seen, had been crucial in the initial steps of Arab nationalism (they still figure very strongly among the most radical nationalist groups: most of the membership of the Popular Front for the Liberation of Palestine comes from among Christian Arabs), but they could not give the movement its social backbone.

Thus Arab society lacked a Muslim Arab middle class, so central to formative stages of nationalism, and it was this gap in the social structure which was responsible for the breakdown of the democratically-oriented constitutions adopted by most Arab countries on achieving independence.

There has been very little in Arab nationalist literature about the need to overhaul the existing social structure. Arab nationalism has generally been focusing its attention on political aims, and there has been no preoccupation parallel to the one which characterized Zionism on the need to transform society as well. In this purely political conception of nationalism an external political enemy was usually viewed as being responsible for the woes of Arab society. First it was the Turkish Empire that was the problem, then British and French and western imperialism in general; now it is the existence of Israel. The degree of self-criticism that went along with Jewish nationalism, the consciousness that political goals by themselves are not enough, never had its counterpart in Arab nationalism.

Hence the role of the army in present day Arab societies. The army did not enter into politics because it was the most modernizing element in society. True, it is in a way that sector which has been exposed more than others to Western influence on a technological level. But this neither changed its basically conservative social structure, nor deprived it of something else which is crucial to its role in society: within Islam, and in Arab society in particular, there is a basic legitimacy to military rule. This goes back both to the ethos of Islam as a religion of conquest, and also to the fact that the historical structures of Arab societies after Islam have all been based on the rule of a military elite. There never was in Arab society the ambiguity characterizing Western societies, as well as Indian society, about military rule. Interestingly enough, there never has arisen in any of the Arab countries now under military rule an opposition even to the idea of the army being the dominant element in politics. There may be criticism of this or that policy of any given military regime; there certainly is opposition to the rule of one or another military group or military leader; but that is as far as opposition to military rule goes. Not one Arab intellectual voice has been raised in protest against it as a principle. In this, Arab society is reminiscent of the Latin American tradition of the army in politics.

As Bernard Lewis has pointed out, modernization in the Arab world was usually tried through the introduction of new techniques into the army. But it is here that the crisis of modernization becomes most felt in Arab society: one cannot modernize a society by modernizing its army. Rather, one cannot achieve a modern army unless one modernizes society from the bottom up. This is the vicious circle in which so many Arab societies find themselves at the moment: whatever one may say about the Egyptian army, for example, it is not that it does not have modern techniques of organization and warfare at its disposal. As a matter of fact, the Egyptian army has been undergoing modernization since the days of Muhammad Ali, though the nationality and politics of the foreign instructors has changed over the generations. If its performance is still problematic, it is not the fault of the army, nor is it to be ascribed to the instructors. The fault goes back to the social structures on which the army is based.

Engels, who was keen on military matters, observed an analogous phenomenon when discussing the 19th century Persian army:

> The fact is that the introduction of European military organization with barbaric nations is far from being completed when the new army has been subdivided, equipped and drilled after European fashion. . . . The main point, and at the same time the main difficulty, is the creation of a body of officers and sergeants, educated on the modern European system, totally freed from the old national prejudices and reminiscences in military matters, and fit to inspire life into the new formation. This requires a long time, and is sure to meet with the most obstinate opposition from Oriental ignorance, impatience, prejudice, and the vicissitudes of fortune and favor inherent to Eastern courts.

It is true that the last decade has seen a remarkable rise in the intensity of radical social ideologies in the Middle East. Very little of this has spilled over into praxis, and the entrenched social class interests of the military elite have been one of the main obstacles in this direction. But even on the ideological level one would be hard pressed to find any comprehensive view of social transformation which manages to overcome the purely political aims common to the various trends of Arab nationalism. Not that on the purely political level one can really find an overall consensus; the very tension between the political patriotism of attachment to any particular Arab country (*wattaniyah*) and the overall attachment to a general Arab nationalism (*qawmiyah*) is too strong to overlook. Hence the largely tentative nature of the various attempts for political unification in the Arab world.

The inadequacy of the social vision, however, is much more pronounced. The Syrian Socialist Ba'ath Party is surely one of the most interesting radical political movements in the Arab world. In its two founders it had a unique combination of the political astuteness of Akhram Hourani and the acute analysis of one of the most sensitive Arab modern thinkers, Michel Aflaq (again, significantly enough, a Christian). But even Aflaq's writings are rather short on questions of social structure: the point is that the Party's rule in Syria has done very little to change the basic traditionalism and quietism of traditional Syrian society.

From archives captured by the Israelis on the Golan Heights during the Six Day War we have now a picture of the social structure of the Ba'ath Party in two districts, Kuneitra and Fiq. The number of members in a district of about 100,000 inhabitants was about 300—surely not that of a mass mobilization party. Moreover, the social composition of the membership is heavily weighted in the direction of the traditional elites. For a party that calls itself socialist, it is quite amazing to find that 77 per cent of the members were civil servants, teachers and students, five per cent employers, landowners and shopowners, and only 13 per cent are classed as workers and peasants. The implications speak for themselves. Similarly, when the Rector of Al-Azhar University proclaims that "the most perfect, complete, useful and profound socialism is that prescribed by Islam" (22 December, 1961), one sees how deep the social conservatism involved is.

There are numerous levels on which Arab and Jewish nationalism can be compared with each other: both are quite problematical movements, with a history in each case quite different from that of not only traditional European nationalisms, but also, to a degree, the new nationalisms of the Third World. Among the burdens they have in common are heritages of distorted social structures: that Zionism was able to combine nationalist goals with a vision of social reconstruction and implement it gave Israeli society, with all its yet unsolved problems, the cohesion and integration it possesses. One may hope that Arab nationalism will be similarly successful in achieving a comparable amalgam, but this is still hidden in the mists of future development. A student of comparative nationalism would not be able to overlook the fact that the differences between the two movements have to be attributed to the different ways in which problems of social structure have been approached in both societies. Where a vision and praxis of social transformation is lacking, the question raised by nationalism itself remains unsolved.

Varieties of
Palestinian Nationalism

By Chaim I. Waxman

Many of the problems which plague Arab nationalism today have been present since its beginnings. Specifically in the century or so since its birth, differing ideologies of nationalism and contradictory goals of leaders have been more decisive than any common objectives.

Arab nationalism emerged during the second half of the nineteenth century, with the growing reactions against the Turkish sultan's harsh treatment of Arabs and the spreading perception of a distinction between Arabs and Turks. Whereas the initial seeds of Arab nationalism were sown by those who called for a return to Islam, in the last decades of the nineteenth century secular bases of nationalist ideas likewise found expression. Significantly, it was the Christian Arabs who were the promulgators of secular nationalism. The common element underlying both religious and secular Arab nationalisms was the insistence that the misfortunes of the Arabs were the result of Turkish negligence and decadence and that the former must break away from the latter's will and achieve autonomy. But differences among the Arabs outweighed their common elements. Not only were they divided as between religious and secular nationalists. In Lebanon, they were also divided as between those who emphasized Arab culture and who aspired to Syrian autonomy, and those who aspired to an independent Lebanon which would have strong ties with the Western Christian world. And throughout the Middle East there was disagreement between those who aspired to a united Arab empire—pan Arabists—and those who looked forward to the rise of independent Arab states loosely linked together, but with autonomy for each state, Syria in particular. Syrian nationalists went so far as to decalre that there is no such thing as an Arab nationalist.

Among these various nationalists were a number of leaders and writers from the area which later came to be known as Palestine. One of these, Neguib Azoury published a book in 1905 in which he stated the inevitability of conflict between Jews and Arabs in determining the destiny of the Middle East. But the notion of Palestine as a separate entity in the Arab world was yet non-existent. Palestine was unanimously conceived of by Arabs to be an inexorable part of Syria. It was referred to as "Souriya Janoubiya"—Southern Syria.[1]

Palestine came into being in 1919, mandated by the League of Nations to Britain. The leading families in the country were the Nashashibis and the Hussainis, and the traditional rivalries between these two families were further intensified by their opposing nationalist ideologies. The dominant Hussainis formed the Palestine Arab Party, which was strongly pan-Arabist, whereas the Nashashibis, who derived their influence from the middle class, formed the National Defense Party, which was localistic in orientation. Throughout the Mandate period (1922-1948) the extremist pan-Arab Hussainis, under the leadership of Hajj Amin al-Hussaini, the British appointed Grand Mufti of Jerusalem and President of the Supreme Muslim Council, had much wider appeal than the more localistic Nashashibis who were not as vehemently opposed to compromise with the British authorities. Thus during this period the leading Palestinian nationalists were not espousing a distinctly Palestinian (as separate from Arab) nationalism. On the contrary, the most vocal and influential of these nationalists were thoroughly pan-Arabist who never imagined a Palestinian entity as distinct from the Arab entity. Even to the localistic Nashashibis, the emphasis on the immediate needs of Palestine was never derived of in terms of an ideology of distinctly Palestinian nationalism; it was rather a submission of ideology to pragmatic interests.[2]

It was the Arab-Israel war of 1948 and especially its aftermath that gave birth to the ideologies of Palestinian nationalism. We may speak of the years 1948-1967 as the pre-natal period, and the post-June 1967 period as the first stages of activity. In the two years following the 1948 war, a number of works were published by Arab intellectuals attempting to fathom the Arab defeat, with the authors' ideologies spanning the right-left religious and political continua. Most noteworthy among these were: Constantine R. Zurayk, *The Meaning of Disaster;* Musa Alami, *The Lesson of Palestine;* and George Hanna, *The Road to Salvation.* (Again, immediately after their 1967 defeat, there appeared such ideologically assorted works as : Constantine R. Zurayk. *The Meaning of Disaster Renewed;* Adib Nassur, *The Setback and Error;* Nadim al-Bitar, *From Setback to Revolution;* and Sabiq Jolal al-'Azm, *Self Criticism After the Defeat.*)

While they differ in their perspectives, a dominant theme in most of these works is criticism of Arab society. Zurayk, for example, writes:

> The explanation of the victory which the Zionists have achieved—and only a person who deceives and blinds himself can deny the victory—lies not in the superiority of one people over another, but rather in the superiority of one system over another. The reason for this victory is that the roots of Zionism are grounded in modern Western life while we for the most part are still distant from this life and hostile to it. They live in the present while we continue to dream the dreams of the past and to stupefy ourselves with its fading glory.

This dramatic statement should not however, be taken as indicating an even remotely benevolent attitude toward Zionism.

The exodus of Palestinian Arabs from the victorious state of Israel and King Abdullah of Jordan's refusal to comply with the United Nations Partition recommendations which called for the establishment of a Palestinian state in the Arab part of the former mandate, established the ensuing conflict as an Arab-Israeli conflict, with the Palestinian Arabs relegated to the status of non-entities. Hiding behind the facade of protectors of the Palestinians, Arab leaders sent their armies to attack the new state of Israel in an effort to enlarge their own domains, with no intention of "upholding the rights of the Palestinians." When Abdullah finally considered a peace settlement with Israel, he was assassinated by Palestinians who recognized his intention to hold on to the West Bank of the Jordan and East Jerusalem.

The war left the Palestinians decimated. The Palestinian elite found refuge in the Arab states and elsewhere, while the masses were left leaderless. Again, despite their claims of being the protectors of their Palestinian brethren, the Arab states made life miserable for the Palestinian masses. They were considered lowly aliens in the states of their "brethren," with only Jordan extending to them the rights of citizenship. Their miserable plight in Lebanon and Syria has been forcefully rendered in a recent personal account by a "Palestinian exile." Fawaz Turki[3] dramatically depicts the niggardly treatment to which he, as a Palestinian, was subjected by his benefactors. "Ben Sharmoota," "khara," and other profanities to which he was subject are strikingly reminiscent of the labels "swine," "dog," "ape," "nigger," etc. to which detested minority out-groups have long been subject.

Their sense of complete frustration, their dream of imminent return shattered, their need for an out of the refugee camps, for excitement—and cash—led many young Palestinians into the hands of the emerging guerrilla organizations. Guerrilla groups (or *fedayeen** as they have come to be known) are not new to the Arab world. They are not a product of the 1967 war, or even of the 1948 war. Probably the earliest twentieth century Palestinian fedayeen group was the Kassamai'in of the early 1930s, named after its leader, Az-el-Din el-Kassam, a Muslim zealot who organized guerrilla bands to kill the British and Jews, and who was himself killed during an assault in November 1935. Of that group, Moshe Dayan recalls, "The case of el-Kassam was the first time I began to regard the gangs as part of a national structure with nationalistic motivation. Individually, the Kassami'in were virtuous men, exceptional idealists."[4] After the 1967 war, the spotlight focused upon a new and fast growing guerrilla organization, *fatah*, and its leader, Yasser Arafat.

Arafat,[5] who was born in 1928, owes his political philosophy largely to his relatives Hajj Amin el-Hussaini, the Grand Mufti, and Abd el-Kader, who achieved fame during "The Great Arab Revolt," (the anti-Jewish riots of 1936-1939), and who was one of the most daring and able Arab leaders during the 1948 war.

Arafat began his political activity in 1951, while he was a student at Fuad I (now Cairo) University. Living almost as an ascetic, he concentrated his efforts on organizing the Palestinian students at the university, and it was there that he developed friendships with a number of those who were later to be his colleagues

---

*Suicide squads—a term based on medieval Islamic concepts, particularly on the Shi'ite Isma'ilis and the hashashiyan (assassins). In the modern terminology it designates commando and sabotage groups, also engaging in political murder.

in the leadership of *fatah*. He founded the Union of Palestinian Students in Egypt, which was the forerunner of the General Union of Palestinian Students (G.U.P.S.) and which had close ties with the Muslim Brothers, the fanatically religious organization which called for a return to Islam, armed revolution and the annihilation of all aliens. The two-year rift between the Muslim Brothers and the military exploded late in 1954, with an unsuccessful assassination attempt on President Nasser, which resulted in swift action by the government and the suppression of the Brothers. This episode accounts for the alleged suspicion and contempt which Arafat never ceased to hold for Nasser.

Arafat received his education in guerrilla tactics through his experiences as one of the fedayeen who carried out operations against the British in the Suez Canal Zone in 1953. In 1954, he conceived, with his colleagues, the idea of sending their own fedayeen forces against Israel, and the idea became crystallized after the 1955 Israeli raid in Gaza (undertaken by Israel to suppress the fedayeen bases there).

Following his departure (or expulsion) from Egypt in 1957, Arafat spent the next year in Kuwait, where he was joined by Khalil el-Wazir, who was later to become his right-hand man in *fatah*. It was during this period that Arafat and his colleagues developed and began implementing their methods of "raising Palestinian consciousness,"[6] and they received their impetus when, in March 1959, Nasser's office issued the slogan "Palestinian entity" (Nasser's own objective was to revive Palestinian nationalism, which he hoped would serve him in his quest for pan-Arabism, which he would control). The group adopted the name Palestine National Liberation Movement, which remains its official title, but sought a more convenient and telling one. They therefore, at first, adopted the acronym, *hataf*, but subsequently decided on *fatah*, being simultaneously, acronym in reverse, and also an Arabic word which means "death from a lightning stroke."

The surfacing of *fatah* may be attributed to four main stimuli: the Israeli raid on Gaza; Nasser's coinage of the slogan "Palestinian entity;" the Algerian victory and Nasser's decline, which enhanced *fatah's* self-organization; and the atmosphere in the Arab world which resulted from the completion of the Israeli National Water Carrier, as well as the rift between Egypt and Syria. Concern over the Water Carrier led to the appointment, on September 10, 1963, of Ahmed Shukeiry as the respresentative of the "Palestinian people," with the declaration by the Arab League Council that, "The time has come for the Palestinian people to take the responsibility for the solution of its problem."[7] Subsequently, Shukeiry devoted his efforts to setting up the Palestine Liberation Organization (P.L.O.) and its Palestinian National Congress in Jerusalem, represented by a variety of Palestinian notables and representatives of the Arab nationalist and Ba'ath parties. From this congress came plans to establish branches, setting up headquarters (in Cairo), for establishing propaganda bureaus around the world, and for the financing of the P.L.O. and its P.L.A. Upon his election as Chairman, Shukeiri declared: "The phase of exile has come to an end. Now begins the phase of uniting and self-organization."[8]

From 1964 to 1966, *fatah* enjoyed the total support of the Syrian Ba'ath party, stemming largely from Ba'ath opposition to Nasser. Despite Arafat's personal absence from the third annual session of the Palestinian National Congress, *fatah's* influence was strong enough to elicit Shukeiry's complete support for guerrilla action against Israel (up to this time Shukeiry had strongly resisted sabotage activity), and, while the Congress ended with little agreement on other matters, it clearly decided to go the *fatah* route. This decision received the endorsement of Nasser in July 1966, not as the result of Nasser's concern with the Palestinian issue, but rather because of the stepped up tempo of the cold war with Jordan and Saudi Arabia brought on by Nasser's involvement in Yemen and his attempts to seize control in Southern Arabia following the British departure. A number of observers[9] maintain that had Israel reacted more vigorously against Syria in 1966, Nasser, Shukeiry, and the Arab nationalists might not have been driven into the arms of Syria and *fatah*.

Following the Six Day War, *fatah* emerged from the state of confusion by endorsing Arafat's stand that the doctrine of popular war of liberation might now be realized through the one million Palestinians under Israeli occupation. Despite the admiration which the West Bank and Israeli Arabs held for *fatah*, however, the extent of actual collaboration was negligible, and Arafat ultimately scrapped his hopes for the war to be fought by the occupied Palestinians.

Second to *fatah* in size and influence among the guerrilla organizations is the Popular Front for the Liberation of Palestine (PFLP), which owes its strength to the efforts of Dr. George Habash.[10] Born in Lydda in 1926, Habash studied medicine at the American University of Beirut, and it was there that he became active in politics. Soon after the first Arab-Israeli war, Habash emerged as a dominant figure in the Arab Nationalist Movement, which, while it gave voice to the call for justice in Palestine, emphasized the need for Arab unity. Habash's involvement in various aspects of Arab nationalism, in contrast to Arafat's distinctly Palestinian activity, is no doubt rooted in the fact that Habash is not a Muslim; his parents were Greek Orthodox.

Having developed close ties with both Egypt and Syria during the 1950s, Habash was expelled from Jordan in 1957 on suspicion of being an agent of Syrian intelligence, and he became one of the strongest supporters of the United Arab Republic and Nasser. When Syria broke from the UAR in 1961, Habash fled to Lebanon where he continued to advocate support for Nasser within the Arab nationalist movement. During the early 1960s the movement was wrought with internal strife between younger, more radical members and the moderates, among whom Habash was included. When the moderates also became disillusioned with Nasser in 1964, following his announcement that the Arabs were not ready to take military action against Israel and prevent the realization of the plans for the Israeli National Water Carrier, the radicals within the movement asserted themselves. They proclaimed the ideology of class struggle, and called for the overthrow of both Nasser and Syria by revolutionary regimes. The total defeat in the war of June 1967, marked the final step in the conversion of the initially non-ideological Arab Nationalist Movement into the Marxist-Leninist PFLP, and the even more rigidly Marxist-Leninist Popular Democratic Front for the Liberation of Palestine (PDFLP), which broke from the PFLP in February 1969 under the leadership of Nayef Hawatmeh. Hawatmeh and his PDFLP, the third largest guerrilla organization, are the strongest advocates of applying the revolutionary examples of Vietnam and Cuba to the Arab world. Among the guerrillas, there are probably more basically divisive issues than unifying ones. In fact, about the only issue upon which they all agree is that of hostility toward Zionism and the need for armed struggle to redress what they see as the unbearable injustice to Palestinians.[11] In addition to several conflicts between individual guerrilla leaders, there are the more basic questions of the relationship between Palestine and the Arab States, and the nature of the sought after Palestinian state. *Fatah* has attempted, for the most part, not to become involved with internal matters of individual Arab states, and to be as independent as possible. It sought to define Palestinian nationalism as neither right nor left, and thus not run the risk of antagonizing any of the Arab regimes. When it failed to accept limitations upon its independence, however, it was dealt a severe blow by Jordan in September 1970.

On the other hand, both the Habash (PFLP) and Hawatmeh (PDFLP) groups argue that the struggle in Palestine is inextricably linked with the basic social and political conditions in the Arab states. They both reject *fatah's* non-involvement in the internal matters of Arab states, and maintain that the overthrow of reactionary regimes (Jordan, Saudi Arabia and Lebanon) and revolution throughout the Arab world are prerequisites to the liberation of Palestine. PFLP and PDFLP in turn are at odds with each other as to the process for bringing about the revolution. PFLP maintains that armed conflict is the method by which to unite the masses, whereas the PDFLP appears to place initial emphasis on political and educational organization and only later on armed struggle.

A second ideological issue upon which there is no agreement is that of the nature of the Palestinian state. Although the P.L.O.'s National Convenant states the objective to be a democratic, non-sectarian Palestinian state, there have been many conflicting statements as to what that actually means. Even if (a big "if") any Israeli who so wished would be permitted to remain in that state, there seems to be a basic disagreement over the issue of national rights for Jews therein. Some *fatah* spokesmen have clearly indicated that the state would be an Arab state. PFLP spokesmen have stated unequivocally that it would recognize Judaism only as a religion but not as a nationality. PDFLP, in contrast, has made certain statements indicating the possibility even of a recognition of Jewish nationality, and has attempted to initiate discussions with like minded Israelis such as the extreme leftists in Matzpen.

Beginning with their clash with King Hussein's forces in September 1970 ("Black September"), the guerrillas steadily lost much of their prestige and support among the Arab governments and masses as well. Membership declined significantly, the leadership went into hiding, in fear of assassination and the contradictions grew larger with each passing day. Their refusal to accept a subordinate position with respect to any Arab regime, their refusal to accept both United Nations Security Council Resolution Number 242 and the Hussein Plan,[12] each of which promised Palestinians more than any guerrilla tactic had achieved, their impotence in the field in addition to their inability to arrive at any agreeable and realistic formulation of the nature of the dreamed for Palestinian state, were the major reasons for the decline of the fedayeen. Although there was appreciation for their having heightened Palestinian national consciousness, this feeling was part of an ambivalence which included many serious misgivings.

In addition to those actively involved with the guerrilla organizations, there are Palestinian intellectuals some of whom are on the faculty of the American University in Beirut, who serve as opinion leaders of Palestinian nationalism. The major outlet for many of their ideas is the Institute for Palestine Studies, "an independent non-profit Arab research organization not affiliated to any government, political party or group, devoted to a better understanding of the Palestine problem." The Institute publishes reprints of significant books espousing the Arab cause, in addition to many new anthologies, collections of documents and original works. One of the Institute's most impressive undertakings is its *Journal of Palestine Studies,* a quarterly consisting of articles, reviews, documents and translations from the Arabic press, and published as a quality and scholarly journal. Rather than simply harping on the evils of Zionism and Israel, as do most of the other publications of the Institute, the *Journal* also gives expression to critical analyses of Arab society, the "new left," and even the guerrilla organizations. [13] While all of the *Journal* pieces maintain a definite pro-Arab perspective, there is no rigid "party-line" and the authors are permitted a degree of latitude which is relatively refreshing when compared with the typically monotonous, broken-record type of material which the Arab propaganda organs unceasingly and unflinchingly grind out. Even this degree of latitude, however, is deceptive because, in the final analysis, there has yet to emerge from within the non-occupied Arab world any conciliatory voice, any call to concession and peaceful coexistence with Israel as she is or even as she would be. Above and beyond the differences as to tactics, there is unanimity in the objective of rectifying the injustice in Palestine through the elimination of Israel either by "voluntary de-Zionization" or by armed struggle.

On the West Bank, by contrast, the change in Palestinian attitudes has been striking. For the first two years of their occupation by Israel, the West Bankers looked forward to an imminent solution of their problem, and therefore adopted a position of negative *samoud* in their dealing with Israel (*samoud* is an Arabic term which means "hold your ground"). According to this position, any change suggested by the military government, such as the building of schools, hospitals, etc., was *ipso facto* opposed by the West Bankers. By the middle of 1969, however, there was a definite change from the position of negative to one of positive *samoud*, according to which the West Bankers would evaluate whether or not a particular suggestion of the military government is in their national interest. If the suggestion is deemed to be in their national interest then they will accept it, because they now make the distinction between cooperation and political collaboration.

This new approach enabled West Bankers to take advantage of development loans from the Israel Ministry of Finance and even to press the Military Government to get more funds, in contrast to the years 1967-1970 when the Military Government used less than half the funds available because there were no takers. This new approach has also resulted in a much more cordial relationship between the mayors on the West Bank and the Military Government, their businesslike meetings now preceded with coffee, fruit and informal conversation.

The new West Bank mayors, in particular, now feel that they have a new mandate. Thus, the mayors of Kalkiya and Hebron, the latter in the face of threats from Amman, now buy electricity for their towns from the Military Government, which in turn buys it from the Israel Electric Company. In the case of Hebron, the Mayor was faced with a challenge from the East Jerusalem Electric Company (an Arab company) which sought to prevent him from buying electricity "elsewhere," claiming that it had sole concession. The Mayor filed an *order nisi* with the Supreme Court of Israel to clarify the concession claim. That the Court ruled in favor of the Mayor is not as significant herein as is the fact that, in effect, West Bankers now recognize the decisions of the Supreme Court of Israel.

Whereas many West Bankers hold admiration and compassion for the guerrilla organizations, there is virtually no overt cooperation with them. West Bank officials have, on occasion, denounced the guerrillas publicly, even though the latter threatened them with assassination as collaborators. The officials responded that it is their duty to protect the West Bankers and they will do so at all cost.

Those West Bankers who are ideologically minded (the intellectuals, Ba'ath members, Communists, etc.) are finding it increasingly difficult to reconcile their ideologies with reality. This dilemma is clearly expressed in the writings of the noted Palestinian nationalist poetess, Fadwa Toukan. This poetess who, on the eve of the Six-Day War wrote about cutting out the livers of the Israelis and had consistently portrayed them as living demons, has undergone dramatic change. For a period after the war she found herself incapable of writing anything. Recently she began again to write poetry, and her poems reflect a different Fadwa Toukan. Her poem, "Planting a Tree," for example, tells of a beautiful tree planted and cared for in a kibbutz which is destroyed by Arab soldiers who have no conception of the tree's beauty. In another poem, "Etan Runs behind Barbed Wire," she pities a lovely Israeli boy who is going to grow up in a world of khaki uniforms and war, and expresses the hope that Etan will retain his humanity throughout this brutal experience. In sum, whereas prior to the Israeli occupation Toukan's poems portrayed Israel as the demon state, today Israel emerges not as a demon but as an enemy; an enemy with a face, flesh and blood, and as an enemy capable of being humane.

As to their future, there is anything but consensus among the occupied Palestinians as to how to resolve their plight. The idea of an independent Palestinian State which has been espoused by a number of sympathetic Israelis, is one which brings fear to most Palestinians. They fear the consequences of the inevitable wrath of the Arab countries toward such a State. The suggestion of a return to Hashemite rule is one which has more of a voice among West Bankers than among the Gaza population, and even on the West Bank it is undesirable to the majority. For the time being, it appears that with all their grievances, most of the Palestinians look upon their occupation by Israel as the lesser evil. Israel is the enemy, for sure, and the occupation is temporary, but they are willing to retain the status quo rather than risk casting their lot once again with their brethren in Cairo, Amman, Damascus and Beirut.

FOOTNOTES

1. Cf. Resolutions of the General Syrian Congress, Article 7, Damascus, July 2, 1919. The Resolutions appear as Appendix G in George Antonius: *The Arab Awakening*.

2. For a more complete analysis of Palestinian nationalism during this period, see the essay by Y. Ben Porat: "The Palestinian Arab Nationalist Movement," in this book.

3. *The Disinherited,* New York, Monthly Review Press, 1972.

4. Quoted in S. Teveth: *Moshe Dayan*, New York, Houghton Mifflin Company, 1973, p. 72. 72.

5. Biographical information on Arafat is sparse. One useful source is E. Yaari: *Strike Terror,* New York, Sabra Books, 1970.

6. Ibid., pp. 26-31.

7. Ibid., p. 45.

8. Ibid., p. 47.

9. Ibid., pp. 102-104.

10. W. B. Quandt, F. Jabber, and A. M. Lesch: *The Politics of Palestinian Nationalism,* Unviersity of California Press, 1973, pp. 84-86.

11. The early position papers of the major guerrilla groups appear in Leila S. Kadi: *Basic Political Documents of the Armed Palestinian Resistance*, Palestine Books No. 27, P. L. O. Research Center, Beirut, 1969.

12. The text of the Hussein Plan and the P. L. O. rejection of it appear in the *Journal of Palestine Studies*, Vol. 1, No. 4, Summer 1972, pp. 166-170. For the Israeli reaction to the Plan see *Jerusalem Post Weekly*, March 21, 1972, pp. 2, 3.

13. For example, the essay by Mirko Aksentijevic in the *Journal of Palestine Studies*, Vol. II, No. 1, 1972 and *Middle East Information Series*, Winter, 1973-74.

The Palestinian-Arab Nationalist Movement

By Yehoshua Porat

Arab nationalism is a relatively recent phenomenon which originated in the first and second decade of this century. In the beginning, this nationalism had two foci: the desire to protect the achievements of the Arab cultural and literary renaissance of the previous fifty years and the effort to obtain political rights for the Arab citizens of the Ottoman Empire. This latter effort was based on the Arabs' own awareness that they constituted a separate ethnic community—an awareness as old as the existence of the Arabs themselves.[1]

This movement encompassed the Fertile Crescent, including the numerically small educated elite of Damascus, Baghdad, Basra, Tripoli and Beirut. Palestine, at that time, was a relatively backward area; it hardly played any role in the movement. What is more, the leadership of Jerusalem enjoyed a considerable degree of autonomy and influence, consequently tending to support the Arab element that professed Ottoman patriotism.

During World War I, however, and primarily when the Ottoman Empire broke up at the end of that war, the nationalist trend among the Arabs overcame its two competitors, the Ottoman and the traditional Muslim, and gained widespread public support. In Palestine, the Arab political public was aware of an important change that was taking place among the Jews, beginning in the 1880s: Jews newly arrived in the country (_Hovevei Zion_—"Lovers of Zion") were trying to bring about fundamental changes in the Jewish community and in the country as a whole. The leaders of the Arab community quickly came to suspect that this change among the Jews had political purposes, aiming to restore Israel's ancient status. The heads of the Muslim and Christian communities in Jerusalem petitioned the

121

Sultan as early as 1891 to prohibit Jewish immigration to Palestine and the pur-
chase of land by Jews.[2] As the *Second Aliyah* ("wave of immigration") developed,
the newly established local Arab press *(al-Karmil,* and *Filastin)* came to express the
Palestinian political public's opposition to Zionism, beginning in 1908. The election campaigns for the Ottoman Parliament which took place in 1908, 1912 and
1914, also offered many opportunities for the expression of this public's anti-
Zionist position. In this manner, the nationalist movement of the Palestinian
Arabs possessed, from its very beginnings, a specific characteristic: the struggle
against a concrete enemy—Zionism.

This Zionist danger became much more important after the British conquest of
Palestine, between December 1917 (when Jerusalem was taken) and September
1918. Arabs and Jews alike took the Balfour Declaration to mean a promise that a
Jewish state would immediately be set up in Palestine. This resulted in very great
enthusiasm on the part of the Jews—and in equally great concern on the part of
the Arabs. In the course of 1918, the Arabs expressed this concern by founding
various societies, all of which had the purpose of opposing the Zionist danger.

At the end of 1918, the Palestinian Arabs faced a serious dilemma, the likes of
which they were to face many more times in the course of their history. In
Damascus a semi-independent Arab regime was being formed by Feisal, the son
of Hussein, king of Hedjaz: This the Arabs considered the seed of inclusive Arab
independence. In addition (on November 8, 1918) the governments of Great
Britain and France declared their recognition of the right of self-determination for
the inhabitants of Syria and Iraq.

Things were different in Palestine however. Here the Jews let their aspirations
be known. Far-reaching political demands were submitted to the Versailles Peace
Conference. In Palestine, the recently arrived official delegation of the World
Zionist Organization (The Zionist Commission) began to work for the realization
of the Jewish National Home and was even granted official recognition by the
British military occupation authorities. The combination of these circumstances
caused the Palestinian Arabs to resolve, at the first congress, held in Jerusalem in
January 1919,[3] that Palestine was nothing but "Southern Syria," and that the only
way to repel Zionism lay in unity with Damascus. True, the Jerusalem leadership
was not excessively enthusiastic about this decision, but the political considerations were held to be the decisive ones.

Until the summer of 1920, the Palestinian-Arab nationalist movement thus
supported the slogan of unification with Syria. However, nothing was left of this
dream of unity when Feisal was thrown out of Damascus in July 1920 and his
regime collapsed: "Southern Syria" disappeared, both as slogan and as the
appellation for the country, and "Filastin" was returned to the political scene.
From this point on the Palestinians' effort concentrated on the attempt to get the
British government's pro-Zionist policy revoked. They were prepared to accept
the British Mandate on condition that its Zionist elements be abrogated. They
were willing, in other words, to accept a regime that resembled what was coming
into existence in Iraq and Transjordan. This tendency found its expression at
their December 1920 Congress in Haifa, where an Executive Committee was
elected to serve as the organ of struggle against the British government's Zionist
policy.[4]

Not only did the slogans of Arab unity disappear, but, during the 1920s, the
Palestinian Arabs actually refused to cooperate, to any significant degree, with

the Syrian-Arab nationalist movement, which then attempted to continue its activity for Syrian independence and general unification with Lebanon, Palestine and Transjordan. That movement called its organization the "Syrian-Palestinian Congress," but it remained exclusively Syrian in composition—the Palestinians refused to participate in it—also, to a considerable extent, because of the Syrian leadership's moderate attitudes toward Zionism.[5]

However, the steadfast support of the essentials of Zionist policy on the part of the various British governments of that period left the Palestinian-Arabs with their frustration. The delegations they sent to London, the petitions they submitted and the demonstrations they organized all remained ineffective. Because of this, they refused to participate in any activity directed at the establishment of organs of self-government, and they rejected all the proposals made by the British to this effect in 1922 and 1923.

This failure resulted in the decline and split of the nationalist movement. Family rivalries again made their appearance. Some of them, headed by the Nashashibis, favored close cooperation with the Mandatory government. Others, led by the el-Hussaini family, entrenched themselves in the Supreme Muslim Council, of which al-Hajj Amin el-Hussaini, the Grand Mufti of Jerusalem, was president. The Supreme Muslim Council reinforced its president's status through its control over the Waqf properties and its supervision of the Muslim Shar'i courts.

From the very beginning, the Supreme Muslim Council tried to endow the anti-Zionist struggle with religious content. To this end, the two most important mosques of Jerusalem—el-Aqsa and the Dome of the Rock—were systematically developed. Contributions were collected throughout the Muslim world to finance restoration work, and Muslims everywhere were called upon to assist Palestine's Arabs in preserving Islam's holy places in Jerusalem. This policy inevitably came into conflict with the Jews' desire to obtain the right to pray at the Western Wall, which is part of *al-Haram al-Sharif,* the retaining wall that surrounds the Mosque compound. The result was the outbreak of riots in August 1929.

The 1929 riots marked the radicalization of the Arabs' struggle against Zionism. The former leadership, which had limited itself to legal methods, was replaced by the leadership of al-Hajj Amin el-Hussaini. The latter found support among a group of young radical leaders, who proposed that Zionism, and later also Britain, be opposed by violent means. They directly and indirectly criticized the Arab Executive Committee in their periodical, *al-Jami'a al-Arabiy-ya,* contributing to its ultimate dissolution in 1934, after the death of its aged president, Musa Kazim al-Husayni.

The Palestinian Arabs' movement's radicalization during the 1930s was part of more general processes which occurred in Palestine and throughout the Middle East. At that time it appeared that the Arab world was approaching independence, or even that it was about to achieve it. Ibn Saud established his United Kingdom in the Arab peninsula in 1927. Iraq became independent in 1930 and was admitted to the League of Nations in 1932; the Anglo-Egyptian Treaty was signed in 1936, while both Syria and Lebanon initialled similar agreements on their independence that same year.

In contrast to all this, the establishment of the Jewish National Home in Palestine gained momentum at a rate previously unknown. Nothing could represent this process better than the statistics on Jewish immigration during that period.[6]

Number of Jewish immigrants arriving in Palestine

Year	
1931	4,075
1932	12,553
1933	37,337
1934	45,267
1935	66,472
1936	29,595
1937	10,629
1938	14,675
1939	31,195

By 1939, the Jewish community already numbered about 450,000—some 30% of the country's entire population.

Under these circumstances, the Palestinian Arabs found themselves in a situation that resembled that of 1919: the Fertile Crescent appeared to be approaching independence while Zionism appeared to be approaching its realization in Palestine. This was the major factor that enabled al-Hajj Amin el-Hussaini to push the Palestinian Arabs to an increasingly extremist position, and it constituted the background of the armed Arab revolt in Palestine during 1936-1939. This revolt, for the first time ever, involved the participation of broader population groups, including the peasantry, Bedouin and villagers who had moved to the cities and became laborers. This explains the revolt's strength and persistence.

In military terms the revolt was defeated, but politically it was quite successful. The Palestinian Arab leadership did manage to exploit the impact that this revolt made in other Arab countries so as to make the Palestine problem the central political issue in nationalist circles in all the Arab countries. The Arab kings' intervention, in October 1936, in favor of ending the general strike, was the direct result of an appeal to them by the Palestinian-Arab leadership[7] This successful precedent had its impact on the British, who then also invited the participation of the representatives of the independent Arab states when they attempted, in the fall of 1938, to find a political solution to the revolt in addition to its military suppression. This involvement of the Arab states, and the British recognition thereof, finally led to the turning point in Britain's Palestine policy. A new policy was proclaimed by them in May 1939, after the London Conference.

The British considered the friendship of the Arab states to be of vital importance at a time when the world was approaching the brink of war. This belief led to the realization that this friendship could not be maintained while the Palestinian Arabs were in revolt and had to be suppressed and a change in British policy in Palestine became inevitable. This change did not satisfy the Arabs' demands, but it nevertheless constituted a real achievement for them. Jewish immigration and land acquisition were greatly reduced (although Palestinian independence was made conditional upon agreement between the Arabs and the Jews—a requirement that appeared bound to postpone that promised independence to the end of time).

Pan-Arab intervention in Palestinian affairs, which had its beginning at that time, was intensified after the end of World War II. Their revolt had left the Arabs of Palestine divided and in conflict with each other, and they consequently thought it best to let the Arab League—Britain's own creation—manage their struggle for them. With the massive support of the independent Arab states they would be able to oppose the growing Zionist pressure, the result of the Second World War's terrifying consequences for the Jews.

This dependence on the Arab states did not yield the results that the Palestinian Arabs had hoped for. It failed militarily in 1948, and it may even have weakened the Palestinian Arabs' will for self-sufficiency. The effect was to enable the half million Jews in Palestine to show that they had to struggle against the entire Arab world—against independent states with tens of millions of inhabitants and organized armies—a presentation that helped to gain a great deal of international sympathy for the Jewish cause. The 1948 war became a pan-Arab effort against the Jews of Palestine.

The process of "pan-Arabization" of the Arab struggle in Palestine was only intensified by the defeat of 1948 and the consequent fragmentation of the Palestinian Arab population into refugees in the Gaza Strip, into citizens of Israel, into refugees and permanent residents of the Kingdom of Jordan and refugees in Syria and Lebanon, etc.

The first independent Palestinian effort, made during the 1950s, to carry on with the struggle was also pan-Arab in character. This refers to the Movement of Arab Nationalists *(al-Qawmiy-yumi Al-Arab)*, which Dr. George Habash organized in Beirut at that time,[8] in order to achieve Arab unity at all costs, so that all the Arabs' resources could be used for the liberation of Palestine. This organization's slogan was "Unity, Freedom, Revenge"—a formula typical of its general approach. The *Fida'iyyun* (terrorists) of the mid 1950s were no more than one of the instruments used by the Egyptian army to strike at Israel.

During the early 1960s, however, the first indications of a turn toward self-dependence began to appear. In 1959, a small newspaper began to come out in Beirut under the name *Filastinana* ("Our Palestine"), preaching the liberation of Palestine by the effort of the Palestinians themselves. This paper claimed that the lesson of Algeria's struggle for national liberation must be learned. Its appearance was the first harbinger of *al-Fatah* on the political scene. The dissolution of the United Arab Republic in 1961—and, in particular, the failure of pan-Arab Nasserism during the 1960s—only strengthened the trends proposed by *al-Fatah*. *Al-Fatah* began troubling Israel in 1965 by sending terrorists across her borders on missions of sabotage and murder.

The same change also began to make its appearance in George Habash's own party. His organization, originally outspokenly Rightist, gradually came to adopt maximalist Leftist attitudes, stressing the need for "popular," rather than conventional, warfare. The order of priorities also came to be changed. Unity was no longer considered an essential precondition for the liberation of *Filastin* (Palestine); now a popular war for the liberation of *Filastin* was thought to be the way by which Arab unity would be realized. Taking its departure from this change, the Movement of Arab Nationalists established its own terrorist organization, which also began to cross Israel's borders in 1966 and to engage in sabotage and slaughter.[9]

This wave of terrorism—one of the important causal factors of the Six-Day War—intensified after June 1967, and the tendency toward Palestinian-Arab self-sufficiency appeared to be victorious. But this was only a temporary impression. In the first place, many Palestinian-Arabs came to doubt whether they were strong enough to act alone—after the defeats they suffered in Jordan in September 1970 and July 1971—and whether the first step, before the decisive battle with Israel, did not have to be a fundamental change in the Arab world itself. Secondly, even during the heyday of Palestinian independent action, these organizations still remained true to the ideology of all-inclusive Arab unity. The Palestinian National Charter (first formulated in 1964, amended in 1968 and since then ratified by all the National Congresses) defines *Filastin* as an integral part of the Arab homeland, while the people of *Filastin* constitutes an inseparable part of the Arab nation. Even *al-Fatah,* the most Palestine-oriented organization of them all, remained true to the ideology that proclaimed Arab unity. This is even more valid for the Popular Front for the Liberation of Palestine, founded by the Movement of Arab Nationalists, and for the Arab Liberation Front, a creation of the *Ba'ath.*

As in the past, the cultural and linguistic factor now also continues to be the most important element in the definition of the Arabs' national identity, including that of the Palestinians. It is true that political realities and practical considerations led to behavior at variance with such ideological beliefs—but in the ideological sphere, loyalty to the pan-Arab conception reigns supreme. This differentiation between ideology and reality is not the result of deceit. Quite the contrary: it reflects the basic fact that the process crystallizing the national identity of the Arabs, including that of the Palestinians, has not yet reached its conclusion. Common culture and language stand in conflict with factors of territory and local interest, and it is much too early to predict which will ultimately turn out to be decisive.

The Arab nationalist movement's radicalization has brought it to believe that the complete social revolution, as defined along Marxist-Leninist lines, constitutes an inseparable part of the struggle for national liberation. This the Palestinian-Arabs were not the first to advocate: the *Ba'ath* had preceded them in making socialism an essential part of its nationalist concept. However, when the Movement of Arab Nationalists and the Popular Front for the Liberation of Palestine (the Movement's affiliate) made this turn, the door was opened wide for the penetration of radical Leftist opinion into the Palestinian-Arab movement. In fact, such opinions also reached the other organizations through this opening. Until 1970 *al-Fatah* had considered itself as neutral with regard to the Arab world's different regimes, but since 1971 it too has begun to take a social stand in favor of the "progressive" Arab regimes and of the "Arab working class' struggle against the bourgeoisie and the reactionaries."

The Popular Front's drift to the Left did not satisfy its own Left-wing, which wanted complete identification with the international revolutionary movement. In February 1969 they split from the original organization to form the Popular Democratic Front for the Liberation of Palestine, under the leadership of Nayef Hawatmeh and Muhassan Ibrahim. At first this move was successful. Most of the members of the Popular Front's central committee joined the new organization, as did its organ "al-Hurriyya." However, this was soon followed by failure and weakness. This was, undoubtedly, due to their attitude to Israel.

Of all the terrorist organizations, it seems that the PDFLP was the only one that accepted, with any degree of seriousness, the slogan of a "Democratic Filastin." Certainly, they also registered their reservations, explaining that they did not mean a "bourgeois democracy" of "one man—one vote," but rather, a "popular democracy," but nevertheless, one cannot ignore the fact that they were the only ones who proposed to amend the National Charter in the spirit of a "Democratic Filastin." What is more, the Democratic Front's platform recognized that the

Israelis constitute not a religious community but rather one with a cultural identity of its own. In an article in *Le Monde* and *al-Hurriyya*, Nayef Hawatmeh even dared to propose that the solution to the Palestine problem might lie in a federative arrangement such as is to be found in Yugoslavia or in Czechoslovakia.

This organization also shows signs of deviation on the subject of Arab unity. In this context, they call for an Arab federation—a concept much less far-reaching than the call for complete unity. This has aroused many of their previous supporters against them, and these supporters have abandoned them in favor of the original Popular Front.

This development indicates that the general concept of unity on the basis of culture and language is accepted in the nationalist Palestinian-Arab camp while any suggestion that certain rights of Israel's Jews can be recognized is regarded by them as anathema.

FOOTNOTES

1. A Hourani, *Arabic Thought in the Liberal Age*, London, 1962.

2. This petition is quoted in *Ha'or*, 27 Nissan 5651.

3. Material on this Congress may be found in the Israel State Archives, Chief Secretary Files No. 156, and also in the Central Zionist Archives, L/4, File 276 IIB. For a description by an Arab eye witness, see Hala al-Sakakini (ed.) *Kadha Ana ya Dunya, Yamiyyat Khalil at Sakakini*, Jerusalem 1955, pp. 164-66.

4. A report on this meeting appeared in the newspaper *al-Karmil*, on December 16, 1920.

5. This problem is discussed at length in my book *The Emergence of the Palestinian-Arab National Movement*, London, 1973, Chapter 2.

6. *Statistical Abstract of Israel 1972*, No. 23, p. 127; these figures are somewhat higher than the official ones reported by the Mandate authorities, since they also include "illegal" immigrants.

7. Public Record Office, Colonial Office, 733/314/75528, parts II and III.

8. For further information on the Movement of Arab Nationalists, see also M. Suleiman, *Political Parties in Lebanon*, New York 1967, pp. 155-172.

9. The development of this organization is analyzed from the Marxist-Leninist point of view in the book *Liladha Munazzamat al-Ishtirakiyin* al-Lubnaniyin, Beirut, 1970.

The Emergence of
Yasser Arafat

By Joseph Neyer

The role of Yasser Arafat as the representative of the Palestinians at the proposed Geneva conference, where Israeli representatives will also be present (!) is a very recent turnabout in strategy, carried out under Soviet tutelage and under the influence of weighty Soviet material support. His followers in Fatah and in the P.L.O. need convincing—if they are to abandon a policy which he played an important role in urging upon them. The Palestine National Council, in its Congress in Cairo of July 1968 opposed strongly the idea of a Palestine state on the West Bank and resolved, under the heading, "The Dubious Calls for Creation of a Fraudulent Palestine Entity," that such a project "contradicts the right of the Palestine Arab people to the whole of its homeland of Palestine . . . Every Arab individual or group, Palestinian or non-Palestinian, calling for the vassal entity and international protection, or supporting it, is the enemy of the Palestinian Arab people and the Arab nation." The threat is clear, and the readiness to carry it out had been demonstrated. (Of course this was written before it would have occurred to anyone that Arafat might be "called" to preside over the arrangements for such a state in part of Palestine.)

The whole thrust of P.L.O. policy has been to oppose any kind of political agreements until all of Palestine has been conquered by force. Article IX of the Covenant of the P.L.O., as amended in 1968, states, "Armed struggle is the only way to liberate Palestine and is therefore a strategy and not tactics." The basis for this proposition is explained in the June 1968 issue of Fatah's monthly *Palestine Revolution* which, speaking in a philosophical mode, suggests that whereas in most wars the aim is to impose one's will upon the enemy, the present aim is "to extirpate him."

128

Not only is Arafat's present posture and role a new one for him, but the notion that the leader of Fatah is the appropriate statesman for representing the Palestinians in the international arena is a new one for much of the Arab world and also for the majority of Palestinian Arabs, to whom, it is fair to say, he is really not acceptable. He has been unable to establish a base of operations on the West Bank of over 600,000 Arab Palestinian inhabitants, where it was for a time his ambition to develop "another Viet Cong." As recently as the beginning of 1974, when the writer visited the West Bank, the majority of West Bankers with informed political convictions would have expressed themselves in somewhat the following manner: The occupation of the West Bank by Israel must come to an end, and the sooner the better; we have experienced some prosperity and a degree of freedom under Israel (especially freedom of expression), and we cannot return to the rule of King Hussein unless he has seriously changed; as for Arafat, let him represent the Palestinians outside the West Bank and Jordan, but we must send our own representatives to Geneva. A considerable number of West Bankers would, like Sheik Ali Ja'abari, the Mayor of Hebron, opt for the administration of an international (UN) authority for a period of at least five years in order to give the West Bank time to develop a genuine political consciousness.

What we should find as the expressed public opinion on the West Bank today it is difficult to say. For Arabs are not the only people in the world who are quick to join what may appear to be the wave of the future, especially when that wave is ridden by one whose ruthless methods appear to be supported by U.N. authority.

It should be recalled that as recently as September 1970, the forces of Arafat's Fatah and of other guerrilla groups suffered a crushing military defeat at the hands of the Jordanian army, with casualties estimated in the thousands. Over a hundred of the guerrillas fled over the border to the safety of Israeli prison camps, which they preferred to the dubious hospitality of the Jordanian forces. More than half of the Jordanian forces were Palestinian in every sense of that term.

Arafat's status has rarely been secure even in his own guerrilla group *al Fatah*, not to speak of the umbrella organization of most such groups, the P.L.O., which he has headed since 1969. As recently as January 1971, he was voted out of office during a meeting of Fatah's forty member "revolutionary council" in a secret ballot election, when he was challenged by the left wing of the group. Arafat recovered his authority be demanding an open vote. Perhaps some of the members who changed their vote had in mind the fate of some who had previously attempted to challenge his position.

For instance, after the revolution of 1966 in Syria (the sixteenth since 1948), the new regime was more ready to support an increase of sabotage against Israel, and it seemed at first that Fatah would flourish on Syrian soil. However, it soon became evident that the Syrians intended to take over Arafat's organization, and the job was assigned to a Palestinian officer in the Syrian Army, Captain Yussuf Urabi. When the captain informed all Fatah units that Arafat was dismissed, he was promptly murdered by one of Arafat's agents. Not long after this event, one of the units of the Syrian terrorist group Sa'iqa was named after Urabi. The Fatah-Syrian honeymoon was concluded by the imprisonment of the top Fatah leaders, including Arafat. These men came into their own again when, late in 1966, Nasser decided to use them in his campaign against the "reactionary" regimes of Jordan and Saudi Arabia, after his plans to seize Yemen and Southern Arabia went awry.

Arafat's imprisonment in Syria was not the first at the hands of his Arab "brothers." In 1956, he was incarcerated in Nasser's Egypt, probably as a consequence of his association with the Muslim Brothers, who had been largely destroyed by Nasser after they had made a number of attempts to assassinate him. As late as 1965, Nasser reacted to the Syrian-Fatah alliance and to the first sabotage operation of Fatah against Israel by referring to Arafat as "an agent of imperialism." (The Indian correspondent in Cairo saw Fatah as the brainchild of Pakistan!)

Arafat's associations with the Muslim Brotherhood, his family connections with the former Grand Mufti of Jerusalem, whose fascist proclivities and associations with Hitler are well-known, and Arafat's refusal today to commit himself on a social direction for Arab Palestine—all these serve to render him suspect among the more "progressive" elements of the guerrilla movement. At least until very recently, his impulse has been to secure the sanctification of the Muslim religious authorities for his movement, which would then be characterized as a *Jihad*, a holy war rather than a movement of socialist-democratic aspiration. Hence, the irony in the slogan of the Democratic State, which is offered for external consumption and taken seriously by few leaders within the P.L.O.—if one can judge by Arab newspaper reports of internal discussion of the slogan.

The former Grand Mufti of Jerusalem, Hajj Amin el Hussaini, to whom Arafat is related through both his father and his mother, lived in exile in Cairo during the late forties, and the Arafat family, also living in Cairo, maintained close contact with his following, among whom was Abd el-Kadar Hussaini, a veteran of the 1936-1939 hostilities in Palestine. Arafat claims to have been the secretary of el-Kadar and to have participated with him in the fighting in Palestine in 1947 at the age of eighteen. Now the hostilities inspired by the Mufti in Palestine during the twenties and thirties could hardly be regarded as part of a people's movement for democratic liberation. Their aim was, rather, to preserve the power of the effendi landlords and "religious" authorities, an establishment that was bound to disappear—with or without the example of social progress presented to the *fellahin* and to the town workers by the life of the Jews. Only in these terms can one understand the fact that during the 1936-1939 "disturbances" more Arabs were killed by Arabs than were Jews killed by Arabs.

In this respect (as well as in others), the P.L.O. and its disunited and splintered terrorist groups resemble today the movement of the Mufti of forty years ago. For more Arabs than Jews have been killed by these organizations. And far more terrorists have been killed in armed clashes between rival terrorist groups, and between regular Arab forces and terrorist groups, than by the Israeli defense forces.

In order to have a sense of the kind of matrix which has nourished the emergence of Arafat, it is important to take account of the uniqueness of the Arab guerrilla organizations. In fact it is questionable whether the word guerrilla is here appropriately applied. In the ordinary sense of the term guerrillas are "irregular" forces which work behind enemy lines, destroy enemy communications and supply depots, attack military installations by surprise and withdraw quickly into the hinterland where they receive the support of at least a solid sector of the local population. The Arab organizations, on the other hand, take pride in the slaughter of innocents, including women and children. The bases from which they come and to which they withdraw after attack are located behind the borders of the surrounding States, which provide supplies, weapons, and training; and due to the bizarre make-up of the United Nations, these surrounding states can with impunity applaud their actions while disclaiming responsibility—an unusual situation in the history of international relations.

However, the most important distinguishing fact about the Arab guerrilla groups is the enormous amounts of money that are at their disposal. It is no exaggeration to say that Fatah and most other Arab guerrilla groups have been, during much of their existence, primarily public relations and fund raising agencies. The energies devoted to sabotage activities have been secondary and have often been explicitly regarded as subordinate to the purpose of public relations. Thus, until relatively recently, several organizations would claim credit for the same exploit, often carried out by individuals hired especially for the performance of a single action.

Seen in this light, the guerrilla organizations have served as agencies which have provided the channel for the conservative regimes to buy off terrorism and secure their own governments against the "revolutionary" impulses of the Arab world. The kind of human material which previously was available for terrorism and subversion directed against the oil-rich heads of state was redirected into the struggle against Israel.

The leadership of the guerrilla organizations have been the very well paid agents in this siphoning off of "revolutionary" energies. They have developed their professional vested interests, their style of life, their modes of funding their establishment and of playing off one Arab state against another. And they have learned to sponsor their own poets and intellectuals (or "ideologists") many educated in the West, who appear to have mastered the techniques of presenting the "Arab case" in terms that make effective contact with the political, moral, and rhetorical styles of the non-Arab world.

This very well endowed "information" apparatus has succeeded, in the short time since the war of 1967, in changing the international perception of the conflict so that what at one time appeared as the consequence of the effort of sixty million Arabs to drive the three million Israelis into the sea is now perceived as the struggle of a displaced Palestinian "nation" to recover its homeland. This is not the place to discuss the complex theme of the late emergence on the scene of the Palestinian "entity", a term which was first invoked at Arab League meetings in 1959. At that time the Arab concern was not to secure the "legitimate national rights of the Palestinians," but rather to mitigate the struggles among the Arab states themselves in their projected dismemberment of what had previously been Palestine. It is no accident that the celebrated Resolution 242 of 1967 refers to the "refugee problem," rather than to "Palestinian national rights." As recently as the General Assembly resolution of November 5, 1972, the United Nations, as well as the Arabs themselves, were split, because the resolution referred to "the Palestinians" as "an indispensable element" of any resolution of the conflict.

The phrase "recognition of the legitimate national rights of the Palestinian people" has recently served the purposes of convenient ambiguity. When the Arab states have invoked this phrase in order to state the conditions of any peace settlement, the question was at least left open as to whether this condition was compatible with the continued existence of the state of Israel. Now that the P.L.O. (Yasser Arafat) is declared to be the "sole legitimate representative" of the Palestinians, can we say that there is no longer any doubt as to the meaning of the phrase?

The aim in this article has been to communicate some sense of the quality of life from which Yasser Arafat has emerged to appear on the global stage. Anyone writing about the Middle East runs the risk of being outdated in a very short time. Perhaps some of this background material will become irrelevant, should great and unanticipated changes occur. What qualitative transformations will emerge from the quantitative differences entailed in the newly available Arab oil moneys? From the enormous military support apparently to be made available to the P.L.O. by the Soviet Union? Will Arafat learn to play a new role under the tutelage of the Soviet Union, which has apparently decided to make the projected Arab Palestine State a very important instrument of its policy in the Middle East?

Insufferable Silence

By Muhammad Watad

There are times when a man, any man, feels helpless and he can usually find any number of excuses for the feeling. But it's hard to excuse a man who chooses to be silent when he ought to speak. And, if it is wrong in one man, it becomes insufferable in a community of men whose strength lies in the clarity of their thought and their power of expression.

Here we are, confronted with a hideous crime in Ma'alot.* We're not blind, we're not deaf. And here, day follows day but our writers are still. They seem helpless, their excuses are legion and their silence is stifling.

I can feel with the Hebrew writers who, one after the other, filled the Hebrew press with obituaries for the Palestinian entity and the Palestinian right to self-determination, against the background of the slaughter at Kiryat Shmona and Ma'alot. What makes these writers special is that, until now, most of them were fervent supporters of the Palestinian cause. For them, it is not a political idea-game, nor a matter of tit for tat. But, in our reality it's difficult to follow in the steps of Jesus. The other cheek is, in fact, not a cheek but life—the life of the Jews in Israel.

Israeli writers and intellectuals cried out ardently against every "violation of law" committed by the institutions of their State. Their protests drew us closer to them, if only verbally. Ultimately, it was not we who demonstrated; we were not

*The terrorist massacre of Israeli school children of May 15, 1974.

The above was addressed to the PLO National Council convening in Cairo on June 11, 1974.

prepared to go to jail. They did. They understood that this was a way to protect the spirit of their people, their moral and human substance. And here, between "violations" and "exile," we are splashed in the bloodshed planned by the agents of our people—the murder of children on an innocent outing. We answer with silence. They, the Jewish writers, are bitterly disappointed: are they growing "wiser?" I am tormented by their anguish.

As Arabs, as Palestinians, we have failed many tests. In this test we have failed twofold: we have failed because we have produced murderers of the Ma'alot kind; and we have failed because we let our adversaries defeat us morally, by our own lack of concern for human life. A man sensitive to the cornfields of Kfar Akraba must be sensitive to human life—he must raise his voice against the destruction of life in general, and young life in particular. This failure is not a feature of ours as Arabs, provided that we return to the sources of our human culture and the origins of our tradition. People who hallow the lives of their children cannot raise them to kill the children of others.

I must sound a warning against the "philosophy" of excuses, spreading among the common people and intellectuals alike seeking to justify the carnage at Kiryat Shmona, at Avivim before that, and later at Ma'alot. They tell us: "The Israeli government is responsible for what happened . . ." They mean all the governments of Israel, from Ben Gurion's time until today. But I want them to look at what the governments of Israel, for all their faults, have built and developed. Above all, they built the Jewish individual, the creative individual. Why do we never, not once, hear Palestinians saying: "Some of us will build and some of us will fight?" What kind of war is this? Is butchery to be called war? And where are the constructive efforts, the development? And why don't we, Palestinians, learn the object lessons of history?

Many states, many nations even, have disappeared without a trace because they didn't build moral values around human life, and didn't develop values meant to sanctify human life. We claim the right of our continued existence. How can we secure it before we break the conspiracy of silence, break the barrier of fear in the face of all those who wave whips and swords?

Look at ancient history, at Sparta and Athens. Look how wretched seems Sparta, which existed by virtue of her sons' strength, compared to Athens which evolved a whole system of culture and development. And in modern history, remember Japan of the "Rising Sun"? Germany of the "superior race"? The Japanese suicide fighters didn't save the Rising Sun's empire, but they may have helped to bring about the disasters of Hiroshima and Nagasaki. And Hitler's Gestapo didn't give the Aryan race dominion over the world, but left in its wake a scorched, defeated, wounded Germany. Japan and Germany are now two industrial powers. It is the philosophy of building, in place of racism on the one hand and megalomania on the other, that safeguards the future of the two countries; this, despite the continued presence of conquering armies—NATO and the Warsaw Pact—on their soil.

I have heard the specious argument that the Germans and the Japanese had at least ruins left to build on —what is left to the Palestinians? And I say: with Ma'alot to haunt us, that is a secondary question. First we must define what it is we want, what is our strategy. "A democratic secular State" which would wreck what exists to erect X, Y, Z? That thought starts with destruction, not building.

Just when public opinion was beginning to swing toward the Palestinian cause, you—the representatives forced upon the Palestinians—demonstrated the malignant thinking that guides you. As a result, public sympathy vanished, and so did the trust that had begun to grow. The refugee camps are bombed in retaliation, and the world is silent . . .

Israel's secret weapons are her values, and her dedication to those values. Despite her sundry "violations," she embraced a philosophy of building, of adding another house and another tree. She almost lost the day when she began to block wells and uproot trees in Rafiah, instead of digging wells and planting trees as she used to. But she made an about-face quickly enough. Those writers and intellectuals, that labor movement—they're a kind of insurance policy for the Israeli society. Ben Gurion's governments didn't 'hang' any of those who demonstrated against the military rule and expropriation of land. Israel guaranteed a fair trial to the perpetrators of the Kfar-Kassem massacre; the Israeli public revolted against the murders, though they were not planned and bear no resemblance to the blood-bath of Ma'alot. Golda Meir's government didn't execute any of those who rose against the "violation" at Kfar Akraba. Nothing could be better for Israel than such an insurance policy. Where is our insurance policy, as Arabs? Where is our insurance policy, as Palestinians?

. . . the Palestinian entity was not buried at Ma'alot. True that our values were dealt a death-blow, but our human substance was not destroyed. And our substance is Palestinian.

IV

The Palestinian Organizations and Terrorism

The Palestinian Organizations, Their Leaders and Ideologies

Palestine Liberation Organization (PLO)
Chairman:
  1964-1967: Ahmed Shukeiry
  1967-1970: Yahya Hammouda
  1970-   : Yasser Arafat

Founded in 1964 at the first Palestinian National Congress and endorsed by all the Arab States, the PLO is the umbrella organization for all the other groups. At its head is the *Palestine National Council*. The PLO *Central Committee*, the *Palestine Liberation Army* (PLA), the *Palestine National Fund*, the *Palestine Planning Board* and the *Palestine Research Center* are part of the framework. PLO has offices in all the Arab states, in the U.S., China, Yugoslavia, Switzerland.

The *Palestine National Council*, with 151 members, meets twice annually, generally in Cairo. All organizations, PLO bodies, trade unions and students are represented in the Council. The *Executive Committee* is elected by the Council and runs the PLO between Council meetings.

Yasser Arafat is Chairman of the Council and Commander-in-Chief of the Palestine Liberation Army.

A *Central Committee of the Palestine Resistance Movement,* created in 1970, represents all the Palestinian organizations. The most important of these are: *el Fatah; Popular Front for the Liberation of Palestine; Saiqa; Popular Democratic Front for the Liberation of Palestine; Popular Front-General Command; Arab Liberation Front.*

El Fatah

Leaders: Yasser Arafat and *Salah Khalaf*

The oldest of the organizations, *Fatah* is larger than all the others combined, numbering some 10,000, including terrorists and members of the "Peoples' Militia." Two-thirds are based in the refugee camps in southern Lebanon and along the coast. The rest are in training and supply bases in Syria.

Fatah's founders run the organization as a collective leadership, with Yasser Arafat as "first among equals." They are mainly Palestinian intellectuals with conservative backgrounds who stem from the extremist Conservative *Muslim Brotherhood*. Their average age is about 40. Syria is *fatah's* chief patron.

Fatah's first cell was formed in the early 1950s, in Cairo. Its leaders have worked in the Persian Gulf states. With the exception of a small group of ex-Ba'athists and leftists (like Abu Iyad and Abu Lutef), its leaders believe in concentrating on the "military struggle" (i.e., terrorist activity) to the exclusion of attention to social and economic problems. *Fatah* has set the tone for all the terrorist groups and has carried out the bulk of terrorist operations.

Arafat, aged 45, unmarried, has seniority in leadership. A Cairo-educated engineer trained by the Egyptian army, he was an affluent contractor in Kuwait for some time. Although he tries to conceal it, he is related to the powerful Hussaini clan, who have always greatly influenced Arab politics. Temperamental, given to angry outbursts, he was hostile to Nasser and is still suspicious of Egypt. He now concentrates on political activity but occasionally still helps plan terrorist operations. His top aide, Halil al-Wazin (Abu Iyad) who shrinks from publicity, runs the organization.

Arafat has set policy since the terrorist groups' emergence as a political factor. He defined the PLO's principles and solidified its *Palestinian National Charter*, to which all terrorists swear allegiance. His "long range" program is the destruction of Israel, but his new policy, formulated after the October 1973 war, is to attain an interim goal: the establishment of an "independent fighting Palestinian national regime" in all the territories to be evacuated by Israel—i.e., the creation of a Palestinian state under PLO hegemony. As stated in the political program of the *Palestine National Council*, however, all the principles of the previous platform still hold. The interim goal does not include recognition of Israel but implies that the PLO could participate in the Geneva Conference—on condition that such participation is based on recognition of the Palestinian problem as a national problem and not solely as a refugee problem (as stated in U.N. Resolution 242). This interim goal, *Fatah* has said, will enable the organization to survive and to maintain Egypt's good will until it becomes clear that no peace arrangement is possible. The proposed new state would serve as a base for continued war against Israel and preparation for war against Jordan. Terrorism would not be halted at any stage. The West Bank must come to realize that its future can only lie with the PLO.

Popular Front for the Liberation of Palestine (PFLP)

Leader: Dr. George Habash

This organization stems from the Arab Nationalist Movement and first made its appearance in November, 1967. It is Marxist-Leninist in ideology and receives the bulk of its financial and operational support from Egypt. Its bases are in Syria and Lebanon and its headquarters are in Beirut. Terrorism is its almost exclusive activity.

Habash, its leader, is a Lydda born physician who headed a subversive political movement in the Arab states in the 1950s and 1960s which had strong ties with President Nasser of Egypt. PFLP's military force is small but its main strength is in terrorist activity and in propaganda. PFLP condemns the idea of a Palestinian state as an unrealistic goal, and considers Arafat's "interim goal" as dangerous, since it would ultimately lead to the abandonment of the long-range goal—the destruction of Israel. Habash also attacks Arafat's contacts with Moscow, viewing these as preparations by the PLO to go to Geneva, a move he rejects.

The organization's program is to "devise tactics to shake, upset and financially eradicate from human history" Israel's "economic establishment, which is harnessed in the service of imperialism" and "the Israeli military establishment" and the "world Zionist movement." (*Al-Hadaf,* Beirut, Nov. 26-Dec. 19,1970). Habash reiterates the goal of "a single Palestinian State in the whole territory of Palestine" and a "popular war until victory." (*El Moudjahid,* Algiers, July 12, 1973.) A simultaneous objective is the destruction of the "imperialist agent" regime in Jordan.

Saiqa

Leader: Zahir Mukhsan

This Syrian terrorist organization was created in 1968 by the Syrian Ba'ath party, to act as the terrorist arm of the Syrian army and under its command. It is now the second largest group after *fatah,* numbering about 4,000 (including drafted officers and men from the Syrian army). Its main bases are in the Damascus-Darra region of Syria, with a branch in Southern Lebanon.

Saiqa's political platform exactly parallels that of the Syrian Ba'ath regime. It emphasizes the need to consolidate an alternative program that would unite Syria, Egypt, the Soviet Union and the PLO against the U.S., Jordan and Israel.

Zahir Mukhsan, 43, is a Palestinian from Lebanon and a permanent resident of Beirut, where he serves as *Saiqa's* spokesman. He is also head of the PLO's Military Department.

Mukhsan was appointed to his position by President Assad of Syria, who had dismissed *Saiqa's* previous head. The real power is, however, wielded in Damascus, by Sami el Attari.

Popular Democratic Front for the Liberation of Palestine (PDFLP)

Leader: Nayef Hawatmeh

PDFLP is a small group which broke away from the PFLP in 1969. It sees itself as the focal point of the Palestinian Left and defines itself and its program in neo-Marxist terminology. It has some 500 members and organizes terrorist activities, but its major importance comes from its provision of an ideological cover for Arafat's programmatic approach.

Hawatmeh, 39, is not a Palestinian but a Jordanian. Like Habash, he is also a Christian. He accepts the term "Israeli nation" and advocates the creation of a Palestinian state in an anti-imperialist context, stressing the struggle against the Palestinian (and Arab) bourgeoisie. His goal remains the annihilation of Israel (and of Jordan).

Popular Front—General Command (PF-GC)

Leader: Ahmed Jebril

This small but comparatively effective terrorist group is Syrian and Libyan supported. Its bases and headquarters are in Lebanon. PF-GC was formed when its leaders split away from the PFLP, for ideological reasons, in 1968.

Jebril, a former Syrian army officer, is regarded as the most effective terrorist organizer. He is opposed to any development which constitutes a deviation or even a supplement to the Palestinian National Covenant and also to any cooling of the Lebanese-Israeli border. He never appears in public and does not personally participate in meetings of the PLO leadership.

PF-GC's goal is "to renew the fedayeen spirit and carry out suicide missions." *(MENA,* Damascus, April 12, 1974.)

Arab Liberation Front (ALF)

Leader: Dr. Abd el Wahab el Hiyali

ALF is the Iraqi equivalent of the Syrian *Saiqa.* Its position is identical to that of Baghdad, which opposes any political arrangement. Formed in 1968 to counter the other organizations, its membership is Iraqi and its aim is to conduct terrorist activity inside Israel and the occupied territories in order to foment a "war of national liberation."

Palestine National Front

This group was formed prior to the October 1973 war and began operations when the war ended. It is only active on the West Bank.

Basically a partnership between the Jordanian Communist Party and *fatah,* it also includes the Arab Nationalists, among others. Practically liquidated by Israel in early 1974, its leaders were deported and its overwhelmingly Communist activists jailed. Abd el Mukhsan Abu Mazer, an East Jerusalem lawyer and a veteran Ba'athist, is one of their leaders and serves as spokesman for the PLO Executive Committee. He supports the concept of a Palestinian state and advocates that the Palestinian movement follow the Zionist model.

The Palestinian National Covenant

By Yehoshefat Harkabi

The Palestinian National Covenant is perhaps the most important document of this stage of the Israel-Arab conflict, especially with regard to the Arab side. It represents a summation of the official position of the Palestinian organizations in the conflict.

The previous version of the Covenant was adopted by the First Palestinian Congress, which convened in Jerusalem in May, 1964 at the time of the establishment of the Palestine Liberation Organization. In the official English translation of the previous version it was called "Covenant" and not "Charter," in order to emphasize its national sanctity, and the introductory words to the Covenant conclude with an oath to implement it. The Congress stipulated that a Palestinian National Council, the highest institution of the Palestinian organizations, would meet periodically, and that a two-thirds majority of the Council members would be required to amend the Covenant. As a result of the changes which came about in the Palestine Liberation Organization after the Six Day War the Palestinian National Council convened in Cairo for its fourth session on July 10-17, 1968 and amended the Covenant. It should be noted that representatives of almost all the Palestinian organizations existing in Arab countries participated in this session, including all the fedayeen organizations. Fatah and the fedayeen organizations under its influence had thirty-seven representatives in the National Council of one hundred members and the Popular Front had ten. Fatah's style is recognizable in the new Covenant. This amended version was certainly not formulated casually; it represents a position that was seriously considered and weighed. The amended version is here presented. In order to highlight the changes we shall compare this version with its predecessor.

143

The main principles which were set down in the Covenant are:

In the Palestinian State only Jews who lived in Palestine before 1917 will be recognized as citizens (Article 6).

Only the Palestinian Arabs possess the right of self-determination, and the entire country belongs to them (Articles 3 and 21).

Any solution that does not involve total liberation of the country is rejected. This aim cannot be achieved politically; it can only be accomplished militarily (Articles 9 and 21).

Warfare against Israel is legal, whereas Israel's self-defense is illegal (Article 18).

For the sake of completeness the Covenant is presented here in its entirety.

The body of the document is translated from the Arabic original.

The Palestinian National Covenant

This Covenant will be called "The Palestinian National Covenant (Al-Mithaq Al-Watani Al-Filastini).

In the previous version of the Covenant of May, 1964 the adjective "national" was rendered by *qawmi*, the usual meaning of which in modern Arabic is pan-Arab and ethnic nationalism, whereas here they use the adjective *watani*, which signifies nationalism in its narrow, territorialistic sense as patriotism toward a specific country. This change intends to stress Palestinian patriotism.

Articles of the Covenant

Article 1) Palestine is the homeland of the Palestinian Arab people and an integral part of the great Arab homeland, and the people of Palestine is a part of the Arab nation.

In most Arab constitutions it is simply stipulated that the people of that country constitutes an integral part of the Arab nation. Here, because of the special problem of territory, it is also stressed that the land is an integral part of the general Arab homeland. The previous version in the Covenant of 1964 was more vague: "Palestine is an Arab homeland bound by strong Arab national ties to the rest of the Arab countries which together form the Great Arab Homeland." The combination "the Palestinian Arab people" recurs often in the Covenant and is also intended to stress the special status of the Palestinians, though as Arabs.

Article 2) Palestine with its boundaries that existed at the time of the British mandate is an integral regional unit.

The same formulation as in the previous version. It is implied that Palestine should not be divided into a Jewish and an Arab state. Although it is an accepted tenet of Arab nationalism that existing boundaries should be abolished, since they were artificially delineated by the imperialist powers, here they are sanctified. The expression "that existed at the time of the British Mandate" is vague. The article is subject to two interpretations: 1) The Palestinian State includes also Jordan and thus supercedes it; 2) The West Bank is detached from Jordan.

Article 3) The Palestinian Arab people possesses the legal right to its homeland, and when the liberation of its homeland is completed it will exercise self-determination solely according to its own will and choice.

The decision concerning the problem of the internal regime is deferred until after the liberation. The crux of this article is to postpone the decision concerning the relation to the Kingdom of Jordan and Hashemite rule. There is also the emphasis here that only the Palestinian Arabs possess a national legal right, excluding of course the Jews, to whom a special article is devoted below.

Article 4) The Palestinian personality is an innate, persistent characteristic that does not disappear, and it is transferred from fathers to sons. The Zionist occupation, and the dispersal of the Palestinian Arab people as result of the disasters which came over it, do not deprive it of its Palestinian personality and affiliation and do not nullify them.

The Palestinian, therefore, cannot cease being a Palestinian. Palestinianism is not citizenship but an eternal characteristic that comes from birth. The Jew is a Jew through the maternal line, and the Palestinian a Palestinian through the paternal line. The Palestinians, consequently, cannot be assimilated. This Article implies that Palestinian citizenship follows from the Palestinian characteristic. This is the Palestinian counterpart to Israel's Law of Return.

Article 5) The Palestinians are the Arab citizens who were living permanently in Palestine until 1947, whether they were expelled from there or remained. Whoever is born to a Palestinian Arab father after this date, within Palestine or outside it, is a Palestinian.

A reinforcement of the previous article. This definition refers solely to the Arabs. With reference to the Jews the matter is different. This is because being Palestinian is basically equivalent to being Arab.

Article 6) Jews who were living permanently in Palestine until the beginning of the Zionist invasion will be considered Palestinians.

In the section on Resolutions of the Congress, in the chapter entitled "The International Palestinian Struggle" (p. 51), it is stated: "Likewise, the National Council affirms that the aggression against the Arab nation and its land began with the Zionist invasion of Palestine in 1917. Therefore, the meaning of "removal of the traces of the aggression" must be removal of the traces of the aggression which came into effect from the beginning of the Zionist invasion and not from the war of June, 1967. . . ."

"The beginning of the Zionist invasion" is therefore at the time of the Balfour Declaration. This conception is current in Arab political literature. In the 1964 version the corresponding Article was: "Jews of Palestinian origin will be considered Palestinians if they are willing to endeavor to live in loyalty and peace in Palestine." The expression "of Palestinian origin" is vague, for the Article does not specify which Jews are to be considered of Palestinian origin. Since in the previous Article (5 in the new version, 6 in the old) the date which determines being Palestinian is set at 1947, the implication could be that this applies also to the Jews. Since the aim is the return of the Arab Palestinians, it is necessary to make room for them. However, in the meantime, Jews have taken up residence in Arab dwelling-places, especially those Jews who immigrated after 1947; hence also from a practical aspect it is necessary to remove these Jews in particular.

The Jews who will not be recognized as Palestinians are therefore aliens who have no right of residence and must leave.

The National Covenant is a public document intended for general distribution. The Executive Committee of the Palestine Liberation Organization specified in its introduction to the official report of the proceedings of the Congress as follows: "In view of the importance of the resolutions of the Palestinian National Council in its session convened in Cairo from July 10 to 17, 1968, we publish them in this booklet so that the Palestinians in every place may read them and find in them a policy and a program. . . ." (pp. 17-18).

One might expect that those hundred members of the National Council would have recoiled from adopting such an extreme position which could serve as a weapon against the Palestinians. The fact that they did not is itself of great significance and testifies to the severity of the Palestinian Arab position.

Several years have elapsed since the Covenant was amended, sufficient time to raise criticism against this manifestation of extremism. However, until now no Arab body, including the Popular Front for the Liberation of Palestine, which is usually critical of the Palestine Liberation Organization and Fatah, has dissociated itself from the position presented in this Article. To the best of my knowledge, no article has been published in an Arab newspaper that raises criticism against it. This silence is also highly significant.

The amended version of this Article points to a radicalization of the Palestinian Arab position. It contains decisive evidence as to the nature of the slogan Arab leaders brandish concerning a "pluralistic, democratic state." Pluralism that is expressed in the elimination of two million four hundred thousand Israeli Jews is nothing but throwing dust in the eyes.

Arab spokesmen add that the aim is for the Palestinian state to be secular, as opposed to Israel, which they condemn as an anachronistic state founded upon a religious principle. It should be noted, however, that in all the constitutions of the Arab states (except Lebanon) Islam is explicitly established as the state religion. The Syrian constitution of 1964 stipulates that the president of the state must be a Muslim. In most of the constitutions it is also emphasized that the *Shari'a* (Islamic Law) is the source of the laws of the state. Fatah appealed to a congress held in al-Azhar University in September, 1968 to consider contributions to the fedayeen *Zakat* (a religious alms tax) and warfare against Israel, *Jihad*. Thus they wage a religious war in order to establish a secular state. The crown of democracy, with which Palestinian spokesmen adorn the Palestinian state, also arouses skepticism in view of the Arabs' failure to set up democratic regimes.

Even if the Palestinians, realizing how this Article damages their cause, amend it, such an amendment would be tactical and reactive, a response to foreign criticism, while the 1968 version reflects the more spontaneous mood.

Article 7) The Palestinian affiliation and the material, spiritual and historical tie with Palestine are permanent realities. The upbringing of the Palestinian individual in an Arab and revolutionary fashion, the undertaking of all means of forging consciousness and training the Palestinian, in order to acquaint him profoundly with his homeland, spiritually and materially, and preparing him for the conflict and the armed struggle, as well as for the sacrifice of his property and his life to restore his homeland, until the liberation—all this is a national duty.

The second part, the preparation for the struggle, is new and was formulated under the influence of the special place that is now given to fedayeenism.

Article 8) The phase in which the people of Palestine is living is that of the national (Watani) struggle for the liberation of Palestine. Therefore, the contradictions among the Palestinian national forces are of a secondary order which must be suspended in the interest of the fundamental contradiction between Zionism and Colonialism on the one side and the Palestinian Arab people on the other. On this basis, the Palestinian masses, whether in the homeland or in places of exile (Mahajir), organizations and individuals, comprise one national front which acts to restore Palestine and liberate it through armed struggle.

It is necessary to postpone internal disputes and concentrate on warfare against Israel. The style of "secondary contradictions" and "fundamental contradictions" is influenced by the language of Fatah and the younger circles. In the previous corresponding Article it is stated: "Doctrines, whether political, social or economic, shall not divert the people of Palestine from their primary duty of liberating their homeland. . . ."

Article 9) Armed struggle is the only way to liberate Palestine and is therefore a strategy and not tactics. The Palestinian Arab people affirms its absolute resolution and abiding determination to pursue the armed struggle and to march forward toward the armed popular revolution, to liberate its homeland and return it [to maintain] its right to a natural life in it, and to exercise its right of self-determination in it and sovereignty over it.

The expression "a strategy and not tactics" is from the lexicon of Fatah expressions (see Y. Harkabi, *Fedayeen Action and Arab Strategy* [Adelphi Papers, No. 53, The Institute for Strategic Studies, London, 1968], p. 8). They use it with reference to fedayeen activities: they are not a support weapon but the essence of the war. "The armed struggle" is a broader concept, but here too stress is placed on action of the fedayeen variety. "The armed popular revolution" signifies the participation of the entire people in the war against Israel. It is depicted as a stage that will be reached by means of broadening the activity of the fedayeen. They are merely the vanguard whose role is to produce a "detonation" of the revolution until it embraces all levels of the people.

The radicalism in the aim of annihilation of the State of Israel and the "liberation" of all its territory eliminates the possibility of a political solution, which is by nature a compromise settlement. Such is the reasoning in this article and in Article 21. There remains only the way of violence.

Article 10) Fedayeen action forms the nucleus of the popular Palestinian War of Liberation. This demands its promotion, extension and protection, and the mobilization of all the mass and scientific capacities of the Palestinians, their organization and involvement in the armed Palestinian revolution, and cohesion in the national (Watani) struggle among the various groups of the people of Palestine, and between them and the Arab masses, to guarantee the continuation of the revolution, its advancement and victory.

This Article is new. It describes the "alchemy" of fedayeenism, how its activity broadens and eventually sweeps the entire people. The masses in Arab countries are described in the language of Fatah as constituting "the supportive Arab front," the role of which is not only to offer aid but to assure that the Arab states will not deviate, on account of local interests and pressures, from their obligation to support the Palestinian revolution.

Article 11) The Palestinians will have three mottoes: National (Wataniyya) unity, national (Qawmiyya) mobilization and liberation.

Here there is no change. These mottoes are inscribed above the publications of the Palestine Liberation Organization.

Article 12) The Palestinian Arab people believes in Arab unity. In order to fulfill its role in realizing this, it must preserve, in this phase of its national (Watani) struggle, its Palestinian personality and the constituents thereof, increase consciousness of its existence and resist any plan that tends to disintegrate or weaken it.

The idea of Arab unity requires giving priority to the pan-Arab character over the local character. From the aspect of a consistent doctrine of unity, stressing local character or distinctiveness is divisive because it strengthens difference, whereas unity rests on what is common and uniform. The issue of the relation between local distinctiveness and pan-Arab unity has much preoccupied the ideologues of Arab nationalism. The conservative circles tend to stress the need for preserving local character even after unity has been achieved. By this means Arab unity will be enriched through variegation. The revolutionary circles, on the other hand, stress unity and homogeneity. This is based either on a practical consideration, that internal consolidation will be reinforced in proportion to the reduction of distinctive factors, or on the view that the local character is part of the heritage they wish to change. The controversy between distinctiveness and unity is also reflected in the conception of the structure of unity. Those who seek to preserve distinctiveness deem it necessary to conserve the existing political frameworks in a loosely confederated unified structure. Those who stress unity tend to try and obliterate the existing political frameworks, along with their boundaries, which were merely the adjunct of a colonial system, with the object of achieving a more consolidated political structure. This controversy may be represented as an antinomy in which Arab nationalism is caught: Unity which tries to suppress the distinctive character of its parts will arouse local opposition; unity which conserves the local distinctive character may abet divisive tendencies.

This Article intends to answer the charge that stressing Palestinian distinctiveness is an objective that conflicts with Arab unity (in the language of Arab nationalism, the sin of *Shu-ûbiyya* or *Iglimiyya*). This charge was heard, for example, from within circles of the Qawmiyyû al-'Arab movement, who were dedicated to the idea of Arab unity. Previous to the Six Day War this charge also had a practical aspect, namely, the assessment that excessive stress on the Palestinianism of the struggle against Israel diminished the role of the Arab states as direct participants in this confrontation. The response to this charge is, therefore, that preservation of Palestinian distinctiveness is merely a temporary necessity, to be transcended in favor of Arab unity. There is, however, a contradiction between this contention and the previous assertion of the eternity of the Palestinian personality.

Article 13) Arab unity and the Liberation of Palestine are two complementary aims. Each one paves the way for realization of the other. Arab unity leads to the Liberation of Palestine, and the Liberation of Palestine leads to Arab unity. Working for both goes hand in hand.

This again is an antinomy. Victory over Israel requires concentration of all Arab forces upon the struggle, a concentration made possible only by the establishment of a supra-state authority to control all these forces, that is, a common government. Nasser repeatedly warned that unity is a precondition for initiating war against Israel. But attaining unity is a long-range affair. Consequently, war against Israel is deferred until a remote time, because undertaking a war without unity would only lead to defeat. On the other hand, unity can be attained only by the detonation of a spectacular event, like victory over Israel. The ideologues of Fatah were much preoccupied with this issue (see *Fedayeen Action and Arab Strategy,* p. 9). Their response is contained in their slogan: "The liberation of Palestine is the road to unity, and this is the right substitute for the slogan, 'unity is the road to the liberation of Palestine.' " Actually, this Article offers a verbal solution, circumventing the problem of priority by characterizing both events as contemporary, just as in the previous version of the Covenant.

Article 14) The destiny of the Arab nation, indeed the very Arab existence, depends upon the destiny of the Palestine issue. The endeavor and effort of the Arab nation to liberate

Palestine follows from this connection. The people of Palestine assumes its vanguard role in realizing this sacred national (Qawmi) aim.

This is a common notion in the Arab position. It is often stated in Arab political literature that the Palestine issue is *fateful* for the very Arab existence. It is maintained that the existence of Israel prevents the Arabs from achieving their national goal. Furthermore, the existence of Israel necessarily leads to its expansion and the liquidation of the Arabness of additional Arab lands. The Palestinians have an interest in stressing the fatefulness of the struggle against Israel and its centrality for the whole Arab world. They thus spur on the others to take an active role in the struggle against Israel. It may be that there is also hidden here the intention to lend symmetry to the conflict. Thus, both sides threaten each other with extinction, and the Arabs are not alone in this. A formula for division of labor is also presented here. The Palestinians will be the vanguard marching before the Arab camp.

Article 15) The liberation of Palestine, from an Arab viewpoint, is a national (Qawmi) duty to repulse the Zionist, Imperialist invasion from the great Arab homeland and to purge the Zionist presence from Palestine. Its full responsibilities fall upon the Arab nation, peoples and governments, with the Palestinian Arab people at their head.

The goal is, therefore, twofold: defense of the rest of the Arab countries and removal of Zionism from Palestine.

For this purpose, the Arab nation must mobilize all its military, human, material and spiritual capacities to participate actively with the people of Palestine in the liberation of Palestine. They must, especially in the present stage of armed Palestinian revolution, grant and offer the people of Palestine all possible help and every material and human support, and afford it every sure means and opportunity enabling it to continue to assume its vanguard role in pursuing its armed revolution until the liberation of its homeland.

There is the implied concern lest, without the support of the Arab states, the drive of "the Palestinian revolution" will dissipate. The distinction of this version as compared with its predecessor, is mainly in the accentuation of "the active participation" of the Arab states and the issue of "the armed Palestinian revolution," which is certainly to be attributed to Fatah's ideological influence upon the Palestine Liberation Organization.

Article 16) The liberation of Palestine, from a spiritual viewpoint, will prepare an atmosphere of tranquillity and peace for the Holy Land, in the shade of which all the holy places will be safeguarded, and freedom of worship and visitation to all will be guaranteed, without distinction or discrimination of race, color, language or religion. For this reason, the people of Palestine looks to the support of all the spiritual forces in the world.

Article 17) The liberation of Palestine, from a human viewpoint, will restore to the Palestinian man his dignity, glory and freedom. For this, the Palestinian Arab people looks to the support of those in the world who believe in the dignity and freedom of man.

The very existence of Israel and the lack of a Palestinian homeland create alienation in the Palestinian, for these deprive him of his dignity and bring him to a state of subservience. As long as Israel exists the Palestinian's personality is flawed. This is an addition in the spirit of Fatah which was not in the previous version, and it is probably influenced by recent revolutionary literature, such as the teaching of Franz Fanon.

Article 18) The liberation of Palestine, from an international viewpoint, is a defensive act necessitated by the requirements of self-defense. For this reason, the people of Palestine, desiring to befriend all peoples, looks to the support of the states which love freedom, justice and peace in restoring the legal situation to Palestine, establishing security and peace in its territory, and enabling its people to exercise national (Wataniyya) *sovereignty and national* (Qawmiyya) *freedom.*

As in the previous version, the existence of Israel is illegal; therefore war against it is legal. In Palestinian literature there is a frequent claim that the fedayeen assaults against Israel are legal, while the self-defense and reactions of Israel are illegal, for their aim is to perpetuate the state which embodies aggression in its very establishment and existence. To the foreign observer this distinction between the legality of attacking Israel and the illegality of the response may appear as sham innocence that is indeed even ludicrous. Nevertheless, it may be assumed that there are Arabs for whom this is not only a matter of formal argument but a belief.

Ibrahim al-'Abid, in an article entitled "The Reasons for the Latest Israeli Aggression" (The Six Day War), writes: "Fedayeen action is a right of the people of Palestine because the right of national liberation is an extension of the right of peoples to self-defense, and it is the right which the United Nations Charter affirmed as an original natural right" (Anis Sayegh, ed., *Filastiniyyât*, PLO Center for Research, Beirut, 1968, p. 107).

Article 19) The partitioning of Palestine in 1947 and the establishment of Israel is fundamentally null and void, whatever time has elapsed, because it was contrary to the wish of the people of Palestine and its natural right to its homeland, and contradicts the principles embodied in the Charter of the United Nations, the first of which is the right of self-determination.

It is often found in Arab literature that the Mandate and the Partition Resolution, though accepted by the League of Nations and the United Nations Organization, have no legal force. They represent an aberration and not a norm of international law. The reason for this is that they contradicted the fundamental principle of the right of self-determination. This Article is copied from the previous version.

Article 20) The Balfour Declaration, the mandate document, and what has been based upon them are considered null and void. The claim of a historical or spiritual tie between Jews and Palestine does not tally with historical realities nor with the constituents of statehood in their true sense. Judaism, in its character as a religion of revelation, is not a nationality with an independent existence. Likewise, the Jews are not one people with an independent personality. They are rather citizens of the states to which they belong.

Again an identical formulation. This Article incorporates the principal claims concerning historical right: The Jews lived in Palestine for only a brief time; their sovereignty over it was not exclusive; the Arabs did not conquer it from them and need not restore it to them; and the Arabs remained in the country longer than the Jews. Moreover, a state embodies a national, not a religious, principle. The Jews, as having merely religious distinctiveness, do not need a state at all, and a Jewish state that makes of Judaism a nationalism is a historical and political aberration. Therefore, Zionism, as a manifestation of Jewish nationalism, distorts Judaism.

Since the State of Israel is not based on a true nationalism, it is very often described in Arabic as "an artificial entity." This is also brought as proof that Israel can be destroyed. This conception is also at the basis of fedayeen theory: since the Jews have no real nationalism, terror will cause their disintegration to the point that they will consent to relinquish Jewish statehood.

The conception that the Jews do not constitute a national entity is a vital principle for the Arab position. For if the Israelis are a nation, then they have the right of self-determination, and the claim that only the Palestinian Arabs have the right of self-determination, and that only they must decide the national character of the country, is not valid. Moreover, the Arab claim for exclusive national self-determination appears in all its starkness as chauvinism that demands everything for itself while denying any right to the other.

Article 21) The Palestinian Arab people, in expressing itself through the armed Palestinian Revolution, rejects every solution that is a substitute for a complete liberation of Palestine and rejects all plans that aim at the settlement of the Palestine issue or its internationalization.

This rejection of any compromise settlement is an addition to the previous version. In the resolutions of the fourth session of the Palestinian National Council a long and detailed section is devoted to the rejection of the Security Council Resolution of November 22, 1967 and any peaceful solution, with insistence upon the intention to undermine any attempt in this direction.

Article 22) Zionism is a political movement organically related to world imperialism and hostile to all movements of liberation and progress in the world. It is a racist and fanatical movement in its formation; aggressive, expansionist and colonialist in its aims; and Fascist and Nazi in its means. Israel is the tool of the Zionist movement and a human and geographical base for world imperialism. It is a concentration and jumping-off point for imperialism in the heart of the Arab homeland, to strike at the hopes of the Arab nation for liberation, unity and progress.

In this new version there is an accentuation of Israel's relation to world imperialism and intensification of its denunciation. This is in the spirit of the Leftist sentiments that prevail among the up-and-coming Arab generation. The claim that the hostility of Zionism is directed, not only against the Arabs, but against all that is good in the world, is also an addition. Thus, warfare against Israel is elevated from an Arab interest to a universal humanistic mission.

Israel is a constant threat to peace in the Middle East and the entire world. Since the liberation of Palestine will liquidate the Zionist and Imperialist presence and bring about the stabilization of peace in the Middle East, the people of Palestine looks to the support of all liberal men of the world and all the forces of good, progress and peace; and implores all of them, regardless of their different leanings and orientations, to offer all help and support to the people of Palestine in its just and legal struggle to liberate its homeland.

Article 23) The demands of security and peace and the requirements of truth and justice oblige all states that preserve friendly relations among peoples and maintain the loyalty of citizens to their homelands to consider Zionism an illegitimate movement and to prohibit its existence and activity.

The attachment of Jews to Israel expressed in Zionism creates dual-nationality and political chaos. Arabs apparently do not sense the contradiction in this claim. Despite the prevalence of supranational tendencies among circles in the progressive world, with which the Palestinians claim to have an affinity, a narrow, formal nationalistic approach is stressed here, which maintains that a man cannot cherish a loyal attachment to any factor apart from his own state.

Article 24) The Palestinian Arab people believes in the principles of justice, freedom, sovereignty, self-determination, human dignity and the right of peoples to exercise them.

Article 25) To realize the aims of this covenant and its principles the Palestine liberation organization will undertake its full role in liberating Palestine.

This Article (with the omission of the conclusion, "in accordance with the fundamental law of this organization") is identical to the previous version. In this and the next Article the Palestine Liberation Organization is presented as the umbrella organization bearing the general responsibility for the struggle of all the Palestinians against Israel.

Article 26) The Palestine Liberation Organization, which represents the forces of the Palestinian revolution, is responsible for the movement of the Palestinian Arab people in its struggle to restore its homeland, liberate it, return to it and exercise the right of self-determination in it. This responsibility extends to all military, political and financial matters, and all else that the Palestine issue requires in the Arab and international spheres.

The addition here, as compared with the previous version, is that the organization assumes also the role of bringing into effect the regime it prefers after the victory.

Article 27) The Palestine Liberation Organization will cooperate with all Arab states, each according to its capacities, and will maintain neutrality in their mutual relations in the light of and on the basis of, the requirements of the Battle of Liberation, and will not interfere in the internal affairs of any Arab State.

The obligation of neutrality, therefore, is not absolute but is qualified by the requirements of the battle of liberation.

Article 28) The Palestinian Arab people insists upon the originality and independence of its national (Wataniyya) *revolution and rejects every manner of interference, guardianship and subordination.*

The Palestinian movement is not the tool for any Arab state and does not accept orders from any outside authority.

Article 29) The Palestinian Arab people possesses the prior and original right in liberating and restoring its homeland and will define its position with reference to all states and powers on the basis of their positions with reference to the issue [of Palestine] and the extent of their support for [the Palestinian Arab people] in its revolution to realize its aims.

This is a new Article, which includes a threat that the friendship of any state toward Israel will entail the enmity of the organization. A similar principle was established in the First Arab Summit Conference.

Article 30) The fighters and bearers of arms in the Battle of Liberation are the nucleus of the Popular Army, which will be the protecting arm of the gains of the Palestinian Arab people.

In other words, there is a future in the fedayeen or military career.

Article 31) This organization shall have a flag, oath and anthem, all of which will be determined in accordance with a special system.

Article 32) To this covenant is attached a law known as the fundamental law of the Palestine Liberation Organization, in which is determined the manner of the organization's formation, its committees, institutions, the special functions of every one of them and all the requisite duties associated with them in accordance with this covenant.

Article 33) This Covenant cannot be amended except by a two-thirds majority of all the members of the National Council of the Palestine Liberation Organization in a special session called for this purpose.

A Palestinian Democratic State as the Political Goal of the Palestinians

By Yehoshefat Harkabi

Historical Background

According to a Palestine Liberation Organization publication, the slogan of the Palestinian Democratic State was first launched by the Fatah at the Second International Conference for Support of the Arab Peoples in Cairo (January 25-28, 1969). It was subsequently discussed and expounded in three articles in the "Fatah", the English-language periodical (November 10, 1969—January 1, 1970—January 19, 1970).

This slogan was apparently designed to counter the impression that the Arab attitude toward the Israelis was extremist, aimed at their liquidation, as well as to refute the contention that the 1968 Covenant was worse than its 1964 predecessor as far as the Israelis were concerned and belied the claims of the Arabs that their position had become more moderate (this refers especially to Article 6, which implied that only Jews who lived in the country before 1917 are to be recognized as Palestinians in a liberated Palestine).

At the Sixth Palestinian National Assembly (Cairo, September 1969), the Democratic Front demanded that the goal of a Democratic State, in which all citizens, Christians, Muslims and Jews, will have equal rights and duties, should be enacted as a *principle* and the Palestinian Covenant be amended accordingly. This demand was *rejected*, although all the groups represented at the Congress agreed that the slogan should continue to be flaunted as a public-relations device.

Article 5 of the Agreement, of May 6, 1970, signed by all the terrorist organizations, provides: "The object of the Palestinian struggle is the liberation of the whole of Palestine in which all citizens will coexist with equal rights and obligations, within the framework of the aspirations of the Arab nation to unity and progress."

154

The Seventh National Assembly (Cairo, May 30—June 4, 1970) directed that the subject of the Democratic State should be studied by the Executive Committee of PLO and the conclusions submitted to the next Assembly.

At the Eighth National Assembly (February 28—March 5, 1971), the goal of the Democratic State was defined for the first time by an Assembly resolution: "The Palestinian armed struggle is neither a racial nor a religious struggle against the Jews. That is why the future State in the Palestine liberated from Zionist colonialism will be the Democratic Palestinian State, where those wishing to live peacefully in it would enjoy equal rights and obligations within the framework of the aspirations of the Arab nation for national *(qawmi)* liberation and complete unity, with emphasis on the unity of the people on both banks of the River Jordan" (the closing phrase refers to the declaration of May 6, 1970, that Jordanians and Palestinians are one people, a conception inconsistent with a distinctive Palestinian identity). The resolutions of the Assembly bind all the organizations affiliated to the PLO.

Details

The following emerges from the discussion of the Democratic State by the Palestinian organizations:

1. The Palestinian Democratic State is to be *Arab*, although its citizens are to enjoy equal rights irrespective of creed. Its Arab character is to be further strengthened by affiliation to an Arab federation. The Jews in it must constitute only a minority.

2. It is to be established after the destruction of the Zionist State and to take its place.

3. It is not to be a binational State; Matzpen's (the extremist Israeli left, anti-Zionist splinter group) demand for a binational State is described by the Democratic Front as not sufficiently progressive. While, in its ethnic respect, the State is to be *Arab*, its Jewish citizens are to be given "democratic" rights, including cultural autonomy, but their ethnicity is to be the same as that of the State, viz. Palestinian Arab; they are only to be different as regards their religion.

4. The State is to be non-sectarian. This means that posts in the public service are not to be alloted on a denominational quota basis as in Lebanon. Its President may be a Jew. Non-sectarianism is sometimes described as secularism, especially in writings intended for foreigners. This is too an insinuation aimed against Israel as an allegedly clericalist State.

5. The Jews as individuals are to have full rights, but the Jews as a group are to have no corporate political rights or, at best, the rights of a cultural minority (according to the Democratic Front, which is "moderate"). The Jews are thus not to qualify for political, but at most for cultural, self-determination, since they are to be regarded not as an ethnic but only as a religious group, which, as such, needs no State of its own.

6. The Jews who will be permitted to remain in the Palestinian State are to be required to declare that they completely renounce Zionist ideas.

7. The Jews have until now fought desperately because they believed that, if their State was destroyed, so would they be. To ensure the existence of the State of Israel seemed to them an existential imperative. The slogan of the Democratic State confronts them with a third choice. This slogan, therefore, will benefit the Arab struggle against Israel by weakening the Jewish fighting spirit and perseverance.

The Reduction of the Number of Jews

Since the Democratic State must be Palestinian Arab *(inter alia,* in order to be able to merge with the other Arab States and not to constitute an anomaly among them), the question arises how the Jewish population is to be reduced. This question has been much discussed by the Palestinians. The following emerges from these discussions:

1. The Palestinians tend to magnify their numbers throughout the world (3.27 million according to a PLO publication) and to assume that most of this "diaspora" will return to the homeland, thus giving a Palestinian Arab character to the State.

2. Some expect that many Jews will not wish to live in the "liberated" Arab State. The European Jews will prefer to return to their countries of origin. Many of the Oriental Jews will be glad to return to the Arab countries. Still the majority of those remaining will also be Oriental Jews, who will actually be Arabs of the Jewish faith.

3. As against this assumption, apprehensions have been aimed that the number of native-born Israelis is increasing and that they have not ties with the countries from which their parents came and thus have nowhere to return.

4. There are those who maintain that there is no need, at this stage, to discuss the establishment of the Democratic State, and that its problems will be solved by the struggle against Israel. It is advisable, they say, to refrain from discussing long-range aims and to concentrate on the objectives of the present stage which are: the demands for the implementation of the right of the Palestinian people to return to its home-land and exercise self-determination there. The reduction of the Jewish population will be brought about by the struggle, as was that of the French population in Algeria. (This seems to be the prevalent view today, whence the diminution, in recent years, of discussions concerning the Democratic State.)

5. The new State shall protect the interests of those who fought with the Palestinian Revolution, that is to say, help them to recover landed property on which Jews have settled (Resolution of the Political Committee of the Tenth Palestinian National Assembly in April, 1972). In this way, the establishment of the Palestinian State will involve a mass eviction of Jews from property that belonged to Arabs. The resulting confusion will compel to emigrate. The Jews must be evicted for practical reasons, viz., to make room for returning Palestinians (this aspect is not given prominence in Arab discussions. It should be noted that it conflicts with the principle of equality of rights).

The Positions of the Organizations

There are sharp differences regarding the slogan of the Democratic State as a political objective. Here are the positions of some of the main organizations:

The Democratic Front

This is the only organization that views the Democratic State as a *principle, i.e.,* an ideological tenet. The Democratic State, it argues, is an appropriate compromise solution in which both sides give up chauvinistic aims: the Arabs renounce the objective of throwing the Jews into the sea, and the Jews renounce their State. The democracy in the Palestinian State is not to be a parliamentary regime of parties in the Western sense, but a people's democracy as in the Communist countries.

Fatah

The Democratic State is a *strategic* objective, *i.e.*, the principal aim of the struggle.

The Popular Front (Dr. Habash)

The slogan of the Democratic State is a *tactical* objective. Its idea is nothing new; it has always been the Palestinian position. The revolutionary organizations are not responsible for the utterances of extremists like Shukeiri who created an impression that the Palestinians must now try to correct, nor should they seek shelter behind dazzling slogans. Democracy does not mean equality between communities but a people's democracy and the dictatorship of the proletariat. In the liberal version "Democracy" means oppression of the worker. The Palestinian State must not differ from the other Arab States, for, if it were, it would be a foreign body. Nor does the revolutionary movement need a democratic solution, and democracy does not mean equality of the oppressors and the oppressed. Jews and Arabs must, therefore, not be treated on the same footing. There are no democratic solutions for capitalists, let alone Nazis. The democratic solution of the Jewish problem consists in the assimilation of the Jews in their respective countries.

The Arab Liberation Front

It is strongly opposed to the whole idea. In its view, the establishment of a separate Palestinian State is an anti-national act since it will increase the number of Arab States. A tactical step, it argues, must be subordinated to the general strategy, whereas here it conflicts with it. Even as a tactic, the Democratic State slogan is not acceptable because it is not sincere, because there is no intention to implement it. The hope that it will induce leftist Israeli circles to cooperate with the Arabs is illusory as there can be no real Israeli leftists. Moreover, the Jews will be more numerous in Palestine than the Palestinians, even if all of the latter return, it is the Jews who will determine the character of the Palestinian State, and even if Israeli government institutions are destroyed, there will still be Jewish social and economic institutions, which will prevail as there will be no corresponding Arab institutions. For all these reasons, the Democratic State slogan should be rejected. Democratic rights should be granted to the Jews within the framework of an Arab General Unity.

The Democratic State and Article 6

It should be noted that, in spite of the adoption of the Democratic State formula, Article 6 of the Covenant has not been amended by any of the nine sessions of the Palestinian National Assembly since held. In fact, the resolution concerning the Democratic State says only that all the Jewish citizens of that State will enjoy equal rights, but does not say who, and how many, these Jews will be. The adoption of the goal of a Democratic State, therefore, does not contradict the limitation or reduction of the number of Jews. The resolution merely says that those Jews who will remain in the liberated land will be given equal rights. Moreover, the reduction of the number of Jews and the democratic principle are bound up with each other, since only by reducing that number will it be possible to grant equal rights to those remaining whilst preserving the Arab character of the State.

Sources

Dr. Mohammad Rasheed, *Towards a Democratic State in Palestine,* PLO Research Center, Beirut, November 1970. (Summary of the positions of Fatah)

Leila S. Kadi, *Basic Political Documents of the Armed Palestinian Resistance Movement,* PLO Research Center, Beirut, December 1969.

Summaries of the positions of the different *fedayeen* organizations are contained in the following:

Ghazi Khurshid, *Dalil harakat al-muqawama al-filastiniyya* Beirut, *Markaz al-abhath,* March 1971;

Nahwa hall dimurgrati (The Popular Front);

Harakat al-muqawama al-filastiniyya fi waqi'iha al-rahin, Dar al-Tali'a, Beirut, 1969 (The Democratic Front);

Al-tariq al-qawmi li-tahrir Filastin, Dar al-Tali'a, Beirut, 1970, the chapter on the slogan of the Democratic State, pp. 107-132 (The Arab Liberation Front);

Zuhayr Muhsin, *Al-thawra al-filastiniyya bayn al-fakhr wal mumasara,* Damascus, August 1972, pp. 29-40 *(Al-Sa'iqa).*

Y. Harkabi, "Three articles on the slogan of the Democratic State", a booklet in English translated from *Ma'ariv,* April 3, 1970—April 17, 1970—and June 10, 1970 (Hebrew). French and German translations in the author's *Palestine et Israël* and *Palästina und Israel.*

Y. Harkabi, *Yesodot be-sikhsukh Yisrael 'Arav,* Publishing Service of the Ministry of Defense, 1971, the chapter on the slogan of the United Democratic State, pp. 65-71.

The Debate at the 12th Palestinian National Council

By Yehoshefat Harkabi

In 1967, following the Six-Day War, the Palestine Liberation Organization (PLO) and its affiliates rejected a political solution to the Arab-Israel conflict and the establishment of a Palestinian state limited to the West Bank. In the wake of the War of October 1973 and the initiation of agreements between Israel and Egypt (and later Syria) on the disengagement of forces, these organizations were confronted with the problem of what their stand should be on the Geneva negotiations.

Two basic schools of thought emerged. One took a positive view, supporting participation in the negotiations, and the other a negative view. The question was a public and political one, and the debate and controversy received wide coverage in their publications; it became, among other things, a revealing symposium between the heads of the Palestinian organizations.

This paper contains a summary of the arguments raised by both sides. It adheres closely to the original Arabic text and also includes additional material.

The Arguments for Participation in the Geneva Conference

• The PLO's refusal to participate in the Geneva negotiations will leave the field open to Jordan as the sole Arab claimant to the West Bank and the Gaza Strip, areas which may come under Jordanian sovereignty if a settlement is in fact attained.

Jordan will use force to liquidate the *fedayeen* organizations in these areas, as it did on the East Bank. Lebanon will thus become their last refuge. In the wake of a settlement Lebanon, too, might tighten its control and prevent the *fedayeen* from acting against Israel. In the absence of military action against Israel the *fedayeens'*

159

raison d'etre will cease to exist, as will eventually the organizations themselves. Taking measures to prevent the West Bank from falling into Jordanian hands is therefore a vital imperative for the *fedayeen* and the PLO.

● By its refusal to participate in the negotiations, the Palestinian position reverts to its traditional one of intransigence. The history of the Palestinian movement teaches the lesson that extremist positions have courted misfortune. Proposals which were at first rejected subsequently became keenly sought after objectives. Negotiations would facilitate consolidation of the gains resulting from the October War. Failure to exploit them would constitute a major default. Should the Israel Defense Forces withdraw from some areas, the Palestinians would take their share in the resultant profits. Revolutionary wisdom demands that no achievement, however small and problematical, should be turned down so long as it involves a weakening of the adversary and a strengthening of the revolutionary's position. The objective is to be attained in stages. The first stage will be the establishment of a "national authority" in every area from which Israel withdraws, provided no commitment is given—or circumstance develop—to prevent the continuation of the struggle toward the final objective: the destruction of Israel and the establishment of a Palestinian state. Thus it is considered worthwhile to make some effort to achieve even limited gains within this longer-term perspective.

● Israel will undoubtedly demand a settlement which will safeguard its security and involve an Arab commitment to end the conflict. This should not cause undue concern. The continued struggle against Israel will· be nurtured by the realities, such as the resultant change in the balance of power, rather than by any formal settlements. The blow to Israel's status entailed in its withdrawal to the 1967 lines, and even more so to the Israelis' self-confidence, will be such as to shake its very foundations. Israel's image as a success will be shattered. Jews will, as a result, cease to immigrate to the country and to invest their money there. Signs of this development have already become evident in Israel's present situation. The country's expansion during the 1967 war has become a hindrance to it as in the Arab saying, "When God wishes an ant to die, He causes her to sprout wings." The wings which Israel sprouted during the Six-Day War will lead to its downfall. Israel's relinquishment of the far-flung borders to which it has grown accustomed will undermine the Israeli population's confidence in a secure future. In addition, even if Israel does withdraw to the 1967 lines, the Arabs will still be able to claim that the Palestinian issue is not yet settled. They will be able to maintain their demand that Israel must withdraw to the borders of the 1947 U.N. Palestine Partition Resolution and that all the Palestinians formerly residing within the area must be allowed to return and to get back their property. Thus a settlement will not terminate the conflict.

● The tenuous hold of the PLO on the West Bank has hitherto been a point of weakness. The inhabitants of the West Bank undoubtedly rejoiced at the achievements of the *fedayeen* and wished them luck but, in the PLO's concept of war against Israel to the bitter end, it is conceivable that the inhabitants of the West Bank will remain under Israel's rule until the final victory is attained. The West Bank's inhabitants have found it difficult to reconcile themselves to this idea. Thus the only other possibility open to them has been to hope that the West Bank will revert to Jordan and thus relieve them of Israeli rule. Jordan, therefore, has many adherents among the West Bank population. Moreover, the pejorative PLO allusions to a Palestinian state on the West Bank, such as "statelet," "Palestinian" or "the emaciated entity" (*al-khian al-hazil*) imply contempt of its inhabitants. Accepting a Palestinian authority on the West Bank would close the gap between the PLO and West Bank population. This policy would attract the population to the PLO, which would come to be regarded as the peoples' representative. [1]

• It is important that the Palestinians be integrated into the mainstream of Arab nationalism, as represented by Egypt, even if they are forced to pay for it by going to Geneva. They must not refuse Egypt's calls for a positive response on participation in the negotiations. Even though differences of opinion may exist between the Palestinians and the Egyptians as to the most suitable methods, there is unanimity on the final objective, as has been asserted more than once by Egyptian leaders. Adoption, by the Palestinians, of a separate political line would only weaken them as well as the entire Arab front. Such a trend must be rejected, unless there is absolutely no other alternative and it becomes clear that the Arab states have, in fact, betrayed the Palestinian cause. This is not the case at present.

• The Palestinians and the other Arabs should have no fear at all of expressing their readiness to reach a settlement with Israel. Such a settlement is, in actual fact, impossible, since Israel will not agree to withdraw to the pre-1967 boundaries, will not concede the Golan Heights and will not relinquish its rule over Jerusalem—or at least, not over the newly constructed Jewish quarters. Egypt and Syria have definitely committed themselves never to agree to any territorial concessions. Resolution 242 will support them, as will the world powers, which have promised that they too would demand an Israeli withdrawal. Moreover, the Arab condition for a settlement also includes the realization of "the legitimate rights of the Palestinians," i.e., fulfillment of UN resolutions, which includes reversion to the 1947 partition boundaries, and permission for every Palestinian who lived in the area of the present Israel to return and to get back his property, in accordance with the UN Assembly Resolution of September 11, 1948. Fulfillment of this resolution involves the eviction of Jewish residents from cities and large areas of Israel, so that a large homeless Jewish population would be created. This would bring about the economic, social and political collapse of Israel without necessitating any acts of violence on the part of the Arabs. The UN resolutions are the instrument by which Israel will be annihilated, and the Arabs should not spoil their chances by refusing to abide by Resolution 242 and by continuing to demand the elimination of Israel in the crudest terms.

In brief, Israel cannot possibly fulfill the demands of the Arabs and the UN resolutions, even if it is governed by the purest of those calling themselves doves. Since even the doves in Israel cannot agree to the Arab demands, including the implementation of UN resolutions, they are nothing but hawks, unaware of their own hawkishness! However, the internal Israeli controversy itself and the illusion cherished by the doves that a settlement could be reached on their terms benefit the Arabs, since they serve to aggravate internal tension in Israel and give Israel a reputation for extremism and recalcitrance. The negotiations will eventually come to an explosive end and the "immobility" which developed in Israel before 1973 and for which the Israelis are now reproaching themselves, will reappear. It is desirable, however, for the negotiations to break off owing to Israel's intransigence. A Palestinian refusal to go to Geneva will prejudice Palestinian interests. The Palestinians must try to appear reasonable in their demands, anxious to attain a righteous settlement, based on the UN resolutions, and to realize their rights. It would be best not to specify now what these rights are and to reveal them only when the time is ripe.

• The Arab side can create difficulties for Israel by demanding an end to Jewish immigration, since it is this which creates Israel's need for expansion. Such a demand will be based on the grounds that it safeguards the security of the Arab states and constitutes a proof of Israel's non-expansionist intentions. In order to compound Israel's difficulties its agreement to Arab demands must be couched in terms which contradict the Zionist ideal and the very foundations of Israel's existence. Israel will refuse this demand and thus facilitate the continuation of the Arab struggle.

• The Palestinian National Council does not need to formulate an unequivocal resolution favoring participation at Geneva. The PLO has yet to be formally invited to the talks, and any decision on the matter would be premature. Moreover, such a resolution may splinter the organizations and lead to internal strife. It is thus preferable to use a formula which, on the one hand, does not seal off the possibility of participation at Geneva while being, on the other hand, ambiguous enough to gain the approval of all factions. Opponents of participation at Geneva may be placated by the addition of a clause to the effect that if the talks reach a concrete stage a new Palestinian National Council will be convened to make a decision. (Even the Israel government has declared that there will be a general election when the decision about the future of the West Bank is at hand.)

• It is true that Resolution 242 refers to the Palestinians as refugees rather than as a people with national rights. It is true that Resolution 242 provides a basis for Jordan's claim that the West Bank should revert to its rule. However, the problem is merely legalistic. This situation can be rectified by the demand for recognition of the corporate national rights of the Palestinians.

• The Soviet position recognizes Israel's existence while adhering to the demand for fulfillment of the UN resolutions, including Israel's return to the 1947 partition boundaries.[2] Although this position contradicts the Palestinian standpoint of obliterating Israel's very existence it does, for the moment, facilitate a considerable amount of joint action, until Israel's withdrawal to the 1947 boundaries is achieved. As long as this demand is not met—even if Israel withdraws to the 1967 boundary lines—there are sufficient grounds for our refusal to recognize Israel and to become reconciled to its existence. Even if the U.S.S.R. were to recognize an Israel within the proposed 1947 borders, the Kremlin cannot ensure the viability of so truncated a state.

The Arguments Against Participation in the Geneva Conference

• The Geneva negotiations will be based on Resolution 242 of the U.N. Security Council. It is true that the amendment to the resolution, to make it refer to the Palestinians as a nation rather than as refugees will be an achievement, but the actual passing of such an amendment is far from certain. Resolution 242 also constitutes a legal basis for Jordan's claim to the West Bank. Israel and Jordan will therefore jointly oppose any change which would have an adverse effect on them both.

• Resolution 242, although it does not refer to peace or recognition, states that belligerency must cease, and Israel will demand that physical and legal arrangements be made, as well as guarantees given, and that there be demilitarization and supervisory measures. Even if the Palestinians are given authority over the

West Bank, they will either be forced or unwillingly ensnared into a commitment in the course of the negotiations; a commitment that they will cease their military struggle against Israel. Any talk of continuing the war, using a Palestinian state on the West Bank as a base, can only be self-deception.

• Participation in the Geneva conference and agreement to a political settlement, even a temporary one, is a denial of all the resolutions adopted by no less than ten of the recent Palestinian National Councils (nine regular sessions and one extraordinary session) and makes a mockery of the Arab ideology in the conflict. The very act of deviation and change in the Arab position and the willingness to agree to a small Palestinian state will invalidate the national Palestinian vision of a Palestinian state in the whole area west of the Jordan river. This inconsistency will undermine the people's faith in the PLO's course of action. It should be borne in mind that a proposal for a political settlement was made in the past and that the PLO and the *fedayeen* organizations did not then hesitate to reject it flatly. What has changed? Why the faint heartedness? The results of the October 1973 war do not at all justify such a change.

• A Palestinian state on the West Bank would provide a solution for the local population since they would be rid of the Israeli presence. However, it provides no solution whatsoever to the real Palestinian problem, since the masses of Palestinians abroad will not be able to settle there. An abyss will open between the two sections of the Palestinian people—those living on the West Bank, for the most part in rural settlements, and the Palestinian refugees abroad, the only ones who embody the Palestinian problem in all its gravity. The solution to the Palestinian problem can only be the establishment of a Palestinian state in the whole area west of the Jordan River, particularly after the Jewish withdrawal from all Arab land (including structures built on the land). The returning Palestinians will then come into a rich inheritance as compensation for their suffering. The establishment of a Palestinian state on the West Bank, on the other hand, will make possible the claim that the Palestinian demands have been fulfilled, and the Palestinian masses abroad will be condemned to eternal exile. The Palestinian struggle would thus come to grief.

• The PLO can exist only in an atmosphere of continued warfare between the Arabs and the Jews. Any political arrangement between the Arab states and Israel which might be supported by the Palestinians contradicts this prerequisite and would deprive the confrontation of its urgency. Even a settlement which is regarded as a tactical step may become firmly rooted and achieve permanency.

• A Palestinian state on the West Bank will be caught between Israel and Jordan. Its existence will be enmeshed in a contradiction, since, while it will be established with the aim of undermining both Israel and Jordan, it will depend on the goodwill of both these countries for the right of its citizens to cross through Jordan to the Arab countries and to pass through Israel to the Gaza Strip. A landlocked Palestinian state cannot be viable without these two outlets, and the granting of these rights will enable Jordan and Israel to exert pressure on it. Jordan, in particular, will be able to threaten to cut off the Palestinian state from the Palestinian population still in Jordan and so from the Palestinian communities scattered throughout the Arab countries.

Such a situation of dependency on Jordan and Israel would condemn the state to the service of two masters: it would be a satellite obsequious toward both. Geographical reality therefore dooms such a state to misery. It would certainly be in no position to serve as a base for a campaign to defeat either Jordan or Israel. This is a vicious circle from which it would not be able to extricate itself. Practically, as well as legally, the notion that a Palestinian state on the West Bank may be a base to continue the struggle against Israel may prove an illusion. The existence of such a state, in the face of the pressure exerted by both neighbors, is questionable. Internal problems and disputes within the Palestinian state would facilitate the intervention of these neighbors, to the point of annexation. This is especially true of Jordan. Internal malaise of the Palestinian state may even force its citizens to request annexation by Jordan.

• The idea of agreeing to a settlement with Israel (and Jordan) with the intention of later undermining their existence is self-contradictory, since it is presented solely as a tactical step aimed at the attainment of a contradictory strategic goal—peace with Israel in order to wage war against it; acceptance of its existence in order later to repudiate it. Tactics are valid only if they form a cohesive part of the strategy they are meant to serve. In this case there is a contradiction, and therefore the entire program is flawed from the outset.

• The Palestinians should not fear a settlement which the Arab states may reach behind their backs with Israel through the pressure and inducements of the United States. They should not even fear a confrontation with Egypt, despite its present prestige, which has arisen because of the achievements of the recent war. The Palestinians are not alone and can find aid and support in countries such as Iraq and Libya. Furthermore, PLO threats of personal vengeance against deviants carry considerable weight and influence. The Palestinians are more powerful than they believe, and can change the trend favoring an agreement with Israel, even if this trend is supported by the Arab states. Moreover, deviant states which participate in a settlement with Israel will only hasten their own internal revolutionary processes. No regime will be able to withstand internal resentment at such treason. The Palestinians will find aid and allies among the opposition within these states.

• There is no need to fear that the existence and struggle of the Palestinian organizations will die away after a political settlement which would place the West Bank under Jordanian rule. Salvation will come through the Arab social revolution and efforts must be made to achieve this revolution. This is especially true of Jordan, where the regime should be overthrown. A social revolution is bound to come throughout the Arab world and it will hand over both Jordan and the West Bank to the Palestinian organizations, facilitating the development of the struggle against Israel into an all-Arab war of national liberation. The successes of the regular Arab armies do not render less valid the central idea, enshrined in the Palestinian National Covenant, that the struggle against Israel should develop into a protracted people's war.

The Purpose of the Resolution at the
Twelfth Session of the Palestinian National Council

Above and beyond the differences of opinion, the leaders of the Palestinian organizations were aware that the opening of a rift between them would be catastrophic for all. They were conscious of the need to act with restraint and seek for an agreement, since all concede that the final objective is the elimination of Israel and the establishment of an Arab Palestinian state in its place. After prolonged discussions the Council, which convened in Cairo June 1-9, 1974, adopted a resolution which approved the summary of a compromise reached earlier between the leaders of the organizations. This summary is a masterpiece of wizardry. It contains something to please every party.

It includes agreement, in principle, to participate in the Geneva negotiations while stating that any settlement reached must provide the possibility of continuing the struggle against Israel (and Jordan). It rejects Resolution 242 on the ground that the resolution does not refer to the Palestinians as a nation. This gives the impression that Resolution 242 suffers from only a slight blemish which should be corrected, while in fact the 12th National Council also rejects all other sections of Resolution 242 as well, such as cessation of belligerency and recognition of the sovereignty and the right of the states to live within secure boundaries. Moreover, the Council's resolution pledges allegiance to the Palestinian Convention and the Political Program of the PLO, approved by the 11th National Council (January 1973). These two documents vehemently reject any political settlement, including Resolution 242. The Council's resolution also implies agreement to establish "national rule" in any area from which Israel withdraws, so that it may serve as a base for the continuing struggle. On the other hand, a challenge is posed to the Jordanian regime and the intention to topple it is clearly stressed.

This vague moderation and explicit extremism runs through the whole Council resolution. The contents of the resolution are more a public relations stratagem, meant for internal as well as external consumption. The Council thus attained its objective, since any faction, internal or external, Arab or foreign, can find a phrase to suit it in the resolution and can disregard the rest.

FOOTNOTES

1. Practical expression of this trend can be found in the appointment of four people who had been deported from the West Bank to the PLO Executive Committee, which was reconstituted at the 12th Palestinian National Council (June 1-9, 1974). This also emphasized, to West Bank leaders, that the political future is reserved for PLO supporters only.

2. This position was apparently made clear to the organizations through their contacts with Soviet officials.

The Position of the Palestinian Organizations on the Establishment of a Palestinian State and on Peace

From: *Palestinian Leaders Discuss the New Challenges for the Resistance,* Beirut; Palestine Research Center, April 1974.

Zahir Mukhsan (PLO and Saiqa)

Before the last war our thoughts about the struggle against Zionism were romantic. We never specified what we wanted . . . We wanted war for its own sake, to instil in us the spirit of fighting rather than to seek crystal-clear goals by stages. Feelings of impotence dominated all of our actions and thinking.

After the last war, inner changes began to take place. It was no longer acceptable for the Arab nation and the Palestinian national movement to remain prisoners of romantic notions. Both had to specify, for the first time, what they wanted within realistic limits. Possibly, this is why we fought and won for the first time.[1]

Now that we have proven to ourselves and to the world our military capabilities and economic prowess,[2] we can specify clearly what we want because we are not only facing ourselves but the world at large. We have emerged from the stage of despair and romantic struggle into that of clear and specific programs. Even opting for a new war, which in my opinion should be at the top of any list of future plans, entails specifying immediate goals — for what the Zionist entity has achieved over decades and in a number of wars cannot be wiped out in a single day.

It will take other wars and a number of years to liberate Palestine completely . . . This is the real situation, not as we imagine it in our dreams . . .

Before the October war, U.N. Resolution 242 was the maximum limit for realizing Arab aspirations in any settlement. At present, this Resolution can no longer play the same role. Concessions which we were ready to grant before the war in

166

order to implement Resolution 242 can no longer be considered because the balance of power has changed and we are not more capable of continuing the struggle, particularly armed struggle . . . The American-Israeli-Hashemite scheme . . . which aims at implementing a settlement consistent with pre-war conditions, can only be foiled by establishing a counterfront composed of the U.S.S.R., Egypt, Syria, and the PLO. It should draw up a minimalist program which would realize our provisional demands on the Arab and Palestinian levels. It should also decide on the maximal concessions that the Arab nation can afford. Without the solid commitment of the members of this opposing front, it will not be easy to block attempts at bilateral settlements and the high political costs of submissive solutions. Solidarity is required to prevent the giving up of fundamental concessions for secondary acquisitions and to safeguard a solid patriotic position in the face of those attempts which seek to restore the region to the *status quo ante*.

It is the duty, therefore, of the patriotic forces to concentrate at this stage on halting Egypt's participation in the proceedings of the Geneva Conference because in the absence of an agreed-upon strategy that would unify our friends in a front, Egypt's continuation alone will lead it into the trap of bilateral settlements and fundamental concessions . . . I believe that any Arab participation in the Geneva Conference must be delayed until after the determination of a minimal program to which all parties could commit themselves in a unified manner, without allowing any one of them to negotiate separately.

One cannot reject or accept any form of political activity absolutely. Rejection or acceptance is based on an assessment of its capability to realize tangible results for our specified, immediate programs . . . Even if we were given three-fourths of Palestine, we would have considered any form of acceptance as a form of liquidation and defeatism. If the leadership had agreed to these offers, then it would have found itself in a critical position. Since the war, a new feeling has emerged characterized by a more realistic determination to continue the struggle and realize successive achievements.

I do not think that the fundamental problem that the Palestinian Revolution is facing, albeit a significant one, is that of King Hussein. The fundamental issue is the likehood that the state of belligerency between the Arab states and Israel may terminate with the conclusion of a settlement. Under the new circumstances, our movement will not be able to continue its struggle . . .

In the early sixties, Arab officialdom, especially Nasser, became convinced that the defeat of Israel was not possible. They sought, however, to keep the Palestinian problem alive. Thus, the idea of reviving the Palestinian entity emerged. It was first discussed in a conference in Chtaura, Lebanon, in 1960 . . . The idea came to fruition in 1964 with the creation of the Palestine Liberation Organization designed to serve as a Palestinian political entity and to juxtapose the Israeli existence with a Palestinian one. It should be noted that the ultimate Arab aspiration at that time was to secure the implementation of U.N. resolutions concerning Palestine, including the 1947 Partition Plan.

The June [1967] war and its aftermath strengthened already existing tendencies, such as the call for a people's liberation war and armed popular struggle as an alternative to the incompetence of the conventional armies. The PLO thus acquired content; whereas before it had simply been a political instrument. In the years following the June war, the PLO became a symbol of the resilience of the Palestinian people and the continuity of their struggle for the liberation of Palestine[3] . . .

The PLO has been able to undertake its struggle in the context of the continuing state of belligerency between the Arabs and Israel. However, if this situation ends, the PLO will not survive as it is. Therefore, we must find a new formula whereby the PLO can continue to function in the likelihood of such an eventuality. It should guarantee the continuation of the Palestine question, prevent the dispersion of the Palestinian people, and guard them from falling prey, once again, to feelings of despair and incompetence. It will also help to avoid the repetition of the experiences of the All-Palestine Government and the Arab Higher Committee, which were lifeless. I am compelled, therefore, to call for the formulation of a clear program which can give rise to an Arab commitment that would oppose the termination of the state of belligerency or that would provide those minimal conditions enabling the Palestinian people to preserve their existence, fighting identity, ability to protect their case, and continuation of their struggle.

The fundamental tactical goal at present should be to prevent the Arab states from ending the state of belligerency in order that it may not obstruct the Palestinian people from persevering in their national cause.

George Habash (P.F.L.P.)

Before the war, the Eleventh National Palestinian Congress . . . formulated a specific political program focusing on the continuation of the struggle of the Palestinian Revolution. Soon after, the war broke out. Regardless of what Sadat wanted from the war, it created new conditions . . .

The June war questioned thereafter the plausibility of the destruction of the State of Israel . . . Of course the Palestinian Resistance redressed this image to a certain extent.[4] But the masses remained skeptical of the resistance movements' abilities to attain the goal of liberating all of Palestine . . .

The October war has created new beliefs in the ranks of the Palestinian and Arab masses. It has brought about Palestinian and Arab unity in a firm way through the state of highest conflict itself; namely, armed combat . . .

The most important change on the international level is the adoption by imperialism, and especially American imperialism, of a new approach to the Arab-Israeli conflict — to a limited extent of course . . . After the war, it observed that the balance of power had undergone limited changes and felt compelled to apply relative pressure on Israel to make concessions in a manner which would secure all of its interests and which would also guarantee the survival of the Zionist entity.

If we consider the Soviet point of view which believes, out of friendship, that Resolution 242 serves the purposes of the Palestinian and Arab liberation movement, as well as the positions of the European, non-aligned, and African states, we can see that the international community believes that it is in the interest of all of its members to end the tension in the region. Conflict does not serve their interests, not the interest of international detente, nor the orientation of international politics at this time. The fact that all these international powers are pushing in the direction of a political settlement must not be underestimated . . . if the U.S. and U.S.S.R. agree on a detailed settlement and the full implementation of Resolution 242 . . . the U.S. will put pressure on Israel which will in turn give in . . . The same thing applies to Arab official leadership . . . As long as this leadership conceives of the struggle in terms of MIG-21s and MIG-23s, it will not be able to freely move in the international setting . . .

The danger of this settlement exceeds the danger of any other we have faced so far since June 5, 1967 . . .

The regional and international changes after the October war constitute a proper vantage point from which events can clearly be seen . . .

What is the effect of these international transformations on Palestinian strategy and tactics? They have shown that the goal of the Palestinian Revolution is not merely a just and legitimate one but an attainable one. We have not been living in a dream-world because we have been specifying a sound political line, establishing a revolutionary organization and mobilizing the Arab and Palestinian masses for the realization of our goal . . .[5]

What will determine the outcome of the Geneva Conference? In Geneva, Israel will present its position. The Americans and Jordanians will do likewise. The three points of view will be very close to one another and it is possible to say that the Conference will witness an imperialist-Zionist-Hashemite point of view.

Of course the Egyptians and Soviets will present theirs, too. We may safely assume that there will be a unified Egyptian-Soviet stand. It is possible to say that there will even be an Egyptian-Syrian-Arab-Soviet position with agreement on all issues. What will be the consequences? . . . Assuming that the outcome of the Geneva Conference will be determined by the discussions that will take place among the participants, we can say that it may lead to all possibilities and may end with completely differing results. Let us explore these contingencies . . .

Let us assume for the sake of argument that the Geneva Conference ends with the triumph of the Soviet viewpoint. What does it entail? The Soviets are friends, and their friendship is of concern, but . . . we must not allow our concern for this friendship to subject the interests of the Revolution to those of any ally. Much as I want to emphasize the importance of our mutual friendship and our genuine gratitude, we, and not the Soviets, must determine our own program, for the very survival of the Revolution is at stake. We and our masses must realize that important differences may arise, ones which we should not ignore. Our Soviet friends have their own interpretation of Resolution 242. Will the present balance of power and the Soviet viewpoint enable us — as some comrades imagine — to realize the goal of a national democratic Palestinian authority and the withdrawal of Israeli forces from occupied Arab territories without the concomitant recognition, conciliation, secure borders, demilitarized zones, and international forces? My answer is no, because the Soviet position, which represents the maximum extent to which a favorable result for the Arabs can be attained at the Geneva Conference, has maintained (unless changed by the Arab and Palestinian Revolution) that a just settlement includes the continued existence of the State of Israel. Its stand should be made clear for our masses, as the Soviets have for our delegation in Moscow. Our position on Israel and its secure borders thus differs from that of the Soviet Union. Issues must be debated in a way which do not harm our mutual friendship. The Soviets ask us to take our own position; they have theirs and are not prepared to compromise.

Some of our brothers in the Resistance movement conceive of a democratic national authority[6] without realizing what it entails: recognition, reconciliation with, and the diplomatic exchange with Israel as the maximum demands that will be asked of us. Can our position — and I am not talking about our historical rights — be realized in the context of the existing balance of power and in the absence of an altered political, economic, and military program following the October war?

I have a clear answer to this question — it is not possible. Those who think otherwise are gravely mistaken. It will only lead us astray. Matters should be seen and explained to the masses . . . We are not talking about a democratic national authority in five or ten years' time, but are discussing it in the context of the 1974 Geneva Conference which is being held within the framework of Resolution 242. This resolution has two parts. We cannot simply achieve one part and leave the Conference. For this reason I deem it necessary that the Revolution say no to Geneva . . .

Salah Khalaf (Abu Iyad) (fatah)

The greatest mistake a revolutionary movement can commit is the inability to measure its magnitude. I want to criticize myself first, as a member of a movement. We consider ourselves as the vanguard of the Arab liberation movement, if not a vanguard of the world liberation movement. Actually we should be less modest and say we are a part of both movements.

. . . Despite the changes brought about by the October war, the existing situation does not radically differ from that prevailing after the 1948 war, except for some features, such as the international situation and the fact that our Arab brethren have for the first time bravely fought in a way that has had its effects on Zionist society . . .

. . . I would agree that the Geneva Conference has not realized any of what we are looking for. I do not believe that any person in the Resistance hopes to set up a national authority as a result of deliberations in Geneva, for that would amount to asking Kissinger and Abba Eban for their blessings. Our only demand is the establishment of a national authority on Palestinian territory which would be consistent with our struggle. If this demand is considered difficult, how much more would the struggle of liberation be! If we in the PLO can agree on a minimum of demands that express the attitudes of the masses, including those of the patriotic Arab regimes, then we can embarass those that are proceeding with concessions.

We do not think that a national authority can be obtained through the Geneva Conference, or that any patriotic forces would acquire a mandate over any part of Palestine. To imagine so would be visionary. We can realize our goals at this stage only by a joint struggle that would mobilize the masses.

. . . Let us survey our options and see whether we can implement them or not. None of the Resistance organizations have opted for settlement, for it would have been inconsistent with our fundamental principles . . . The decision to launch the October war was not ours, and it was definitely a limited war, not a people's war, which would have been different. The political consequences of the October war were calculated. Arab assessments of the Geneva Conference and the possibilities of settlement may differ, but the Palestinian Revolution would make a grave mistake if it misses any opportunity to establish an anti-settlement — a fighting front stronger than the pro-settlement front. The basic condition is that the members of the anti-settlement front agree with each other. The question facing us now cannot be found in our literature. We should think of how to face what may be imposed on us. Naturally, we cannot accept a submissive settlement. Therefore, there must be a program that will guide us in our struggle, and provide answers to our present and long-term problems on the basis of our historical right. If we had such a program at this stage, the question would not be one of going to Geneva or not, but whether we should ever consider the very idea of a peace conference. Of course, there is the possibility that such a program may entail going to Geneva and of appointing someone to speak on our behalf.

However, we all agree that discussion would not lead to a return of any Palestinian territory. Yet the voice of the Palestinian people should be heard. Otherwise, others — who have been responsible for the perpetuation of the Palestine tragedy, who have shackled them in order to prevent them from acting and from expressing themselves — will speak on their behalf.[7]

Nayef Hawatmeh (Popular Democratic Front for the Liberation of Palestine)

From an interview published in the *Deutsche Zeitung,* April 19, 1974

. . . The central question now facing us—one with which we are profoundly concerned—is how to reach a formulation of our position which will safeguard our people against the danger of an American solution. The position of the Popular Democratic Front for the Liberation of Palestine on that issue is plain and simple . . . We are striving at this moment to get the other organizations, together with us and our people, to fight for the expulsion of the Israeli occupier, to shield our people in the occupied areas from a return of the rule of King Hussein, to guarantee our self-determination, and to gain the right to an independent and sovereign State within these regions. Our main task at present is to see to it that the PLO, as the exclusive and authorized representative of the Palestinian people, formulates these aims as its fixed and clear program and call upon the entire nation to fight for the realization of these concrete, self-understood and realizable objectives. We are aware that the posture of the United States, Israel and the Hashemite Kingdom of Jordan is unreservedly hostile to the legitimate rights of the Palestinian people, and their only fear is that the PLO will be ready to transform those rights into actuality.

There are, however, others in the resistance movement, such as the members of George Habash's Popular Front for the Liberation of Palestine, who think that the main problem is saying No to the Geneva talks. In this, they merely reveal their tactical nihilism. They betray the interests of our people, who are fighting the occupation and the Hashemite Government alike. The nihilism of these others finds expression in the slogan: 'All or nothing.' This is not revolutionary policy, for it gives the Egyptians freedom to maneuver at our expense and, furthermore, also serves the imperialist policy.

. . . The United States and its allies would react joyfully if the PLO were to proclaim that what is discussed in the negotiations in Geneva and other places is none of our business. We must not give the American imperialists and their allies a chance to determine the fate of our nation.

This is a decisive tactical question. Aside from this, we do not consider that the conference will limit the possibilities of the struggle of the revolutionary movements or—God forbid!—entail the end of the struggle. Conferences have never led to perpetual situations—as can be seen from the example of Europe during the last seventy years.

. . . Our purpose is a democratic State in the whole of Palestine. We will establish our State and at the same time remain loyal to the strategic aim of our revolution. We will advance step by step toward our objective and not be deterred. A State in the occupied areas will not constitute an obstacle. The contrary is true—it will be a point of departure.

. . . This State will be the backbone of our struggle against Israel.

FOOTNOTES

1. The allusion appears to be to the general Arab contention that the war of October, 1973 was won, militarily, by Egypt and Syria (Eds).

2. The reference is, presumably, to Arab oil power (Eds).

3. When its terrorist groups turned to violence and sky-jacking on an international scale (Eds).

4. Presumably, via terrorist acts (Eds).

5. This statement appears to suggest that the Palestinian Arabs were mobilized through the activities of the small terrorist bands (Eds).

6. On the West Bank (Eds).

7. The reference is to King Hussein of Jordan (Eds).

V

Israeli Views on the Palestinian Problem

On The Palestinian Problem

Yitzhak Rabin

From an interview given by the Israel Prime Minister, Mr. Yitzhak Rabin to *Yediot Ahronot,* Tel Aviv Daily, July 26, 1974.

Question: . . . are you prepared to spell out what is your own concept regarding [the Jordanian-Palestinian] issue?
Mr. Rabin: . . . the Palestinian issue is not, as others describe it, the focal point of the Israel-Arab conflict. To my mind, the central issue in the Israel-Arab conflict is the system of relations between the Arab States and Israel. They have the strength, they have the ability, and they also possess the capacity to achieve political settlements and eventually also a peace agreement. They also possess the ability to decide on a different direction—that of war.

In other words, first let us place the Palestinian issue in the right frame. As I see it, it is not the central issue. It may possibly have been so twenty or thirty years ago. At present it is not so. I am now dealing with the entire complex of the Israel-Arab problem, and the Palestinian issue to my mind is therefore secondary in the system of Israel-Arab relations. At the same time, this is one of the issues which require solving and which must determine our approach to the entire complex—and that is how we see it. The fact of the Israel Government having dealt with the Palestinian issue just now stems from its topicality and not from its relative importance in the scale of priorities within the complex of Israel-Arab relations.

My approach to the Palestinian issue is based principally on three points: the first is that solution of the Palestinian issue must be included within the framework of the system of relations between Israel and Jordan. That is to say,

175

should you ask me who is the negotiating partner with whom a solution must be worked out for the issues referred to as Palestinian, the answer is Jordan.

A second point: I see no room for a third state between Israel and Jordan. Since a separate state for the Palestinians—fundamentally and by its very nature —would strive for the destruction of Israel, its very establishment would imply a priori acceptance that one is setting up an element that is bound to strive for a clash with one—the inference being both in Israel and in Jordan.

And this leads me to the third conclusion: if the first two assumptions are correct, I see no point to political talk of a political solution with a Palestinian body, and it is pointless to say that I am seeking Palestinians who are prepared to talk with me (assuming such exist at all) if I have reached the conclusion that I oppose the establishment of a separate Palestinian State. In fact, we are in daily dialogue with the Palestinians, or with Arabs residing in Judaea and Samaria and with the visitors to the country from other Arab countries. But a distinction must be made between this dialogue and political negotiation with them as an independent political entity.

This is my fundamental approach. Moreover: even if we were to state today that we were prepared for political dialogue with a Palestinian body, it would be illusory to assume that we would be allowed to determine who that body was to be. As aforementioned, however, to me this is a secondary issue, since my point of departure is that there is no room for a separate Palestinian State.

It should be recalled that Jordan is the only Arab State in which the Palestinians became fully integrated before and after the Six-Day War. Nowadays, the Palestinians constitute an integral part—one which is well-nigh inseparable from the life texture—of the Kingdom of Jordan. To the best of my recollection, seven of the eleven members of the Jordanian delegation which arrived in Geneva were Palestinians. But they appeared as a Jordanian delegation. This is the fundamental point of departure I mentioned of importance to me: there is no separate Palestinian State, and there is therefore no point to separate Palestinian representation and separate political negotiations.

Question: Certain people claim that there is a substantial difference of wording between your Knesset appearance on June 3 [1974] and your statements in the Cabinet. We have heard it stated that whereas in the Knesset you laid strong emphasis on the impossibility of a third Arab state, when the vote was held in the Cabinet your position was defeated and you remained in a minority. Is this true?

Mr. Rabin: There was not a single Cabinet member expressing himself in favor of a third state. The question was how to word it—whether in a positive or a negative manner. But there were no differences of opinion in the Cabinet on this point, that there is no room for a separate Palestinian state between Israel and Jordan. In this there was absolute consensus among all Cabinet members who had anything to say on the matter.

Question: The Government's statement on the Jordanian-Palestinian question says, inter alia, "The Government of Israel will work toward negotiations with Jordan." Is this to be interpreted as meaning that Israel will take special steps toward dialogue with Jordan?

Mr. Rabin: The initiative, to my mind, is important and should always be examined in a most sober fashion. I do not think that there is a change in . . . [the] . . . Cabinet decision on the Jordanian-Palestinian issue. That is to say, there is greater emphasis on readiness, since the impression has been created—rightly or wrongly—as though Israel does not want negotiations with Jordan. We are prepared to talk with Jordan. The separation-of-forces agreement with Egypt notes that this is a first step toward lasting peace in the Middle East. The Government therefore deemed it appropriate to stress that although there is no agreement on separation of forces with Jordan, she, too, is a serious candidate for Israeli peace initiative.

Question: When referring to talks with Jordan, is the implication talks without a separation of forces or concurrently with a separation of forces?

Mr. Rabin: At present, the reference is (to talks) with Jordan in the direction of a political settlement, and what are the possibilities? The Jordanian proposal with which we are acquainted via the United States, deals with a geographical separation of forces. Such a separation of forces with Jordan does not appear feasible to us: as may be recalled, it was published that Hussein proposed an Israeli withdrawal to a depth of 8-10 kilometers west of the Jordan. Such a proposal for a separation of forces does not appear feasible to us. On the other hand, other proposals may conceivably be raised. If there are any, we shall examine them on their own merits.

Question: Does Israel have proposals of her own for negotiations with Jordan?

Mr. Rabin: There have been ideas which were raised every now and again concerning a functional rather than a geographic separation of forces—namely, that the Israel Defense Forces remain in Judaea and Samaria, the Jewish settlement remains extant, and certain civilian spheres of operation are implemented by Jordan. Such proposals have been raised in the past, and may possibly be raised in future. I doubt Jordan's readiness to discuss an overall peace agreement with us at this stage. We have no knowledge of Jordan's readiness to enter at this stage into negotiations on an overall peace agreement.

Question: Is there at present any pressure being exerted on Israel by the U.S. with regard to the Jordanian-Palestinian problem?

Mr. Rabin: I don't hold with the use of the term 'pressure.' How do you define pressure? From my experience in the United States I realize that the United States may state: our evaluation is this and that.

If there will be no move, no political activity, this will lead to a freeze which in turn may deteriorate into war. I do not consider this pressure. This may be the correct presentation of the circumstances in which we find ourselves—in which case Israel must make her own assessment. But I would not want us to create an image of American pressure on Israel. I cannot say that American readiness to aid Israel is not now and again influenced by certain conditions, although, fundamentally, the U.S. is interested in a strong Israel.

Question: Mr. Rabin—the former Cabinet, as well as your own, have declared that prior to any agreement with Jordan the matter would 'be taken to the people.' Would you hold elections, or a referendum, on this specific issue alone? And, to follow up this question: at what point, do you believe, the people should be consulted—prior to the opening of negotiations with Jordan, or before signing an agreement?

Mr. Rabin: As I see it, the former Government, as well as the present one, have felt free to conduct negotiations with Jordan should a suitable occasion arise. As for consulting the people, and I refer to elections—I repeat: elections, and not a referendum—this will be only if and when the Government will have something to put before the people. There is no point in holding elections over an idea. The time for that is when the Government will have succeeded in reaching a negotiated agreement with Jordan on an arrangement acceptable to the Government. Only, prior to the final signature, the people must be consulted.

Question: There is some concern that the public may one day be facing accomplished facts in the Jordanian-Palestinian question.

Mr. Rabin: I can see no possible reason for such concern. I should be happy if we achieved peace with Jordan. I do not believe that there are members of the Government who are not guided by concern for our security. Fundamentally, the Government is bound to explore and decide on ways that may lead to peace pacts. As for Judaea and Samaria—there exists a definite undertaking on the part of the Government not to conclude any agreement without first holding elections. It follows that there are no grounds for concern over the possibility of accomplished facts. At present, my main concern is that, in case Jordan should consider Israel's position toward her too extreme, this might push Jordan toward Syria. To my mind, this concern is far more serious than the 'concern' over possible peace with Jordan.

Question: Minister Bar-Lev stated . . . that Israel was prepared to return most of the West Bank to Jordan. Is this also your position?

Mr. Rabin: I don't believe that now, before negotiations have started, is the time for drawing geographical lines. As far as any political subject is concerned, every Minister represents a political party. The Alignment has a platform on which it went to the electorate. This platform states clearly that Israel is prepared for territorial concessions against a true peace. I personally cannot see any point in defining now the extent of these concessions, their geographical and other details.

Question: Have you lately noted a certain erosion in the American stance on the Palestinian question?

Mr. Rabin: This is the situation on the main confrontation fronts in the Israel-Arab conflict: the main sectors of confrontation—Egypt, Syria and Jordan—are quiet. Such acts of hostility as are committed against Israel at present are carried out by the terrorist organizations. The result is the optical illusion of terrorist activity as the central problem. I have no evidence of an erosion in the American stance on the Jordanian-Palestinian question. I also believe that the U.S. feels concern about Jordan because of the affinity that exists between both nations, and I am certain that the U.S. does not wish to undermine the foundations of one of the friendly regimes in the Middle East.

Question: Mr. Prime Minister, without committing yourself—would you say there are fair prospects for reaching any kind of agreement with Jordan?

Mr. Rabin: My experience in the army and the Foreign Service, as well as my brief experience in my present office have driven me to the conclusion that one should not engage in prophecies. I prefer to seek ways to progress in directions I consider worthwhile.

Question: Do you believe that Egypt genuinely and sincerely wants some sort of settlement with Israel?

Mr. Rabin: As far as I know Egypt is willing to arrive at a settlement with Israel on the basis of a complete Israeli withdrawal to the lines of June 4, 1967 and the creation of a Palestinian State in Judaea, Samaria and the Gaza Strip. Now, if you ask me—won't such an arrangement bring peace and permit Israel's survival?—My answer is clearly no. If you ask me—isn't Egypt today prepared to arrive at a settlement with Israel, one which will give us peace and security—my answer is again no. Therefore the course which we are seeking is to ascertain the extent to which there is a prospect of bringing about a change in the Egyptians' position, in their attitude to an overall settlement, and to what extent it will be possible to advance toward an overall settlement which we could accept in stages.

On a Palestinian Identity

Yigal Allon

Excerpted from an Address by Mr. Yigal Allon, Minister for Foreign Affairs of Israel in the General Assembly of the U.N., October 3, 1974.

Mr. President,

Israel is cognizant of the existence of the question of Palestinian identity. It holds that it can and should be solved, in the context of the settlement of the dispute with her neighbor to the east. It is there, on both sides of the Jordan, that the great majority of the Palestinian population is concentrated. Moreover, most of the citizens of Jordan are Palestinians and most of the Palestinians are Jordanian citizens. It is also a fact that the area east of the Jordan is an integral part of the historic Land of Israel or Palestine and that it is already the national home of the Palestinians. If there is any ethnic significance to the Palestinian concept it applies equally to the peasant, to the townsman and to the Bedoui east of the Jordan as it does to the peasant, townsman and Bedoui to its west. It is in the light of these considerations that the Israel Government on 21 July 1974 resolved that:

> . . . "The Government will work toward negotiations for a peace agreement with Jordan.
>
> "The peace will be founded on the existence of two independent States only—Israel, with united Jerusalem as its capital, and a Jordanian-Palestinian Arab State, east of Israel, within borders to be determined in negotiations between Israel and Jordan. In this State, the independent identity of the Jordanian and Palestinian Arabs can find expression in peace and good-neighborliness with Israel."

However, the Palestine community in general must in no way be equated with the terrorist organizations. From my own personal acquaintance with this community I refuse to identify it, or at least its great majority, with the terrorist grouping known as the PLO, which is not a national liberation movement but the roof organization of disunited and splintered terrorist groups whose pretensions and support do not spring from the broad masses of the Palestinian population. It is a fact that more Arabs than Israelis have been killed by these organizations. It is also a fact that more terrorists have been killed in the armed clashes between regular Arab forces and the terror gangs, and between the rival terror gangs themselves, than by the Israeli security forces.

These facts are obvious to anybody who cares to examine them. We refuse to recognize the PLO and we will not recognize it, because of its doctrines and of its deeds alike. The Palestine Charter which embodies the political ideology of the PLO stands in direct contradiction to the Charter of the United Nations. It denies absolutely the right of Israel to exist and postulates its destruction as a principal objective.

This ideology is accompanied by the criminal methods of warfare used by the organizations which make up the PLO, such as indiscriminate terror and deliberate murder of women and children, pupils and teachers, athletes at the Olympic Games, passengers on a Swiss airliner, chance visitors and Jewish and Christian pilgrims at airports, Arab women workers in Galilee. In reality the situation here is not that of a subject people trying to liberate itself with its own underground forces, but of gangs of desperadoes imposing themselves on a people and attempting to form and dominate it by means of the destruction of another people: this at a time when there is ample room for two states, Jewish and Arab, to co-exist in peace in the historic Land of Israel or Palestine on both sides of the Jordan, their common border being determined by negotiations.
Mr. President,

It is of course no secret that with the parliamentary situation existing in this General Assembly, the preconceived ideas held by a great number of those taking part here, and the irrelevant considerations which guide many delegations, a majority might concede the PLO demands. A resolution that would concede such demands will be regarded by Israel as an arbitrary resolution impinging on its fundamental rights, as illegal and not binding in any way. Every delegate here would reject a negative resolution which strikes at the foundation of his country's being. One cannot ask of any nation to agree to its own elimination or to commit suicide.

Understanding for the needs of the Palestinians—certainly; satisfaction of the demands of arch-murderers who appoint themselves as saviors—decidedly not!

I regret that many members of the United Nations do not delve into this problem thoroughly, with the consequence that, either deliberately or through misunderstanding, they reward these murderers and in so doing stoke the fires in the Middle East. Israel will not submit to violence and terror. Terrorism is an infectious disease which knows no national frontiers. Many states have already paid the price of submission to terrorism and I am afraid that the last word has not been said on the subject. Following the latest terrorist attacks in Paris and at the Hague, President Valery Giscard D'Estaing said: "Violence, which is sometimes presented and justified as an avant garde act is nothing but the rise to the surface of those depths of barbarism and primitive cruelty of which humanity has devoted all its efforts to rid itself." These are trenchant words, but there is need for action and for courageous co-operation in order to put an end to manifestations of terror before further disasters occur. The essence of the PLO is terror. It is no coincidence that whenever a concrete proposal for a political solution is put forward, the PLO leadership rises up against any such peace initiative. Their insistence on inscribing the question of Palestine on the agenda of this General Assembly is designed above all to destroy the prospects of the political efforts at the very beginning. A debate on this matter cannot fail to poison the international atmosphere. Acceptance of PLO demands may well condemn the prospects of the negotiating process to failure—just when the first ray of light has been glimpsed on the horizon.

Palestinians who wish to give constructive expression to their independent identity can be helped to do so in the context of the negotiations with Jordan. Moreover, I would not agree to a general settlement without including in it satisfaction of the needs of the Palestinians. It is after all not Israel which has prevented the crystallization of what is known as "Palestinian identity." To the extent that such a desire existed among the Palestinians it is the Arab states that have frustrated it during all these years. If not, how can one explain the fact the during 19 years of Arab rule in the Gaza Strip and on the West Bank, this identity never achieved any definite form or full expression?

The joint communique by Egypt, Syria and the PLO in Cairo on September 21, 1974, also deals a blow to the prospects of a constructive solution to the issue of Palestine identity. In the same way that the PLO bends all its efforts to prevent political progress in the area, certain Arab states are whittling down the hopes for a solution of the Palestinian question by granting the terrorist organizations the monopoly of representation of the Palestinians, when they know perfectly well that these organizations are not able to be a party to negotiations because of what they are.

Mr. President,

There is no sadder example of the heartless attitude of the Arab governments than the freeze which they have imposed on the status of the 1948 refugees. It is true that many of them have been absorbed in the economies of the Arab states in which they now live, but there has been a deliberate policy to prevent a constructive solution to this sore problem in order to exploit human suffering for political and propaganda ends. If the problem in itself were not so sad I would say that there is nothing more ludicrous than the annual fund raising efforts of UNRWA to make up the deficit in its budget—at a time when the Arab oil states command the biggest monetary reserves in the world.

Israel did not adopt this course: not toward the 600,000 Jewish refugees who fled the Arab states stripped of all their possessions, and not toward the survivors of the millions of Jews destroyed by the Nazis, with the blessing of the Mufti Hajj Amin el Hussaini who found refuge among his own kind in Nazi Berlin and fascist Rome. All of these were fully absorbed in Israel economically, socially and culturally.

In the light of the vast economic opportunities which now exist in the Middle East, the refugee problem must, and can, be solved. Far more difficult refugee situations in other parts of the world have been solved long ago. Given good will, without which no problem can be resolved, the question of compensation for both Arab and Jewish refugees can be settled. Israel is contributing, and will continue to contribute, its share in the solution of this painful human problem.

Palestinian Nationalism: An Established Fact

By Amnon Rubinstein

Sometimes there is a relation between a name and a fate: Had King Abdullah chosen the name of Palestinian Kingdom instead of the Hashemite Kingdom of Jordan, the Palestinian issue would not have had such powerful international resonance. If Israel shared its border with the Palestinian Kingdom, in which the majority of the population were Palestinian Arabs, the nature of the issue would be clearer to side spectators. The question would, in this case, have had the proper clarification: In the Arab Palestinian country, east of Israel, there are differences of opinion regarding the regime, and an internal struggle for the right of representation of the population's majority.

But King Abdullah did not name his kingdom Palestine and this marginal fact, together with other decisive political facts, gave rise to what is now known the world over as "the Palestinian problem."

The decisive political facts are: a constant conflict between sectors of the Palestinian population and the regime that is sustained by the Bedouin loyalty; a radicalization of Palestinian factors, with regard to Israel or to the Hashemite's pro-West policy; and Israel's continuing domination of the populated Palestinian territories. To this it should be added, of course, the extremist influence of the terrorist organizations which, as it were, brought the Palestinian message to the world's consciousness through abominable murders; these acts gave rise, along with the revulsion and the shock, to an adjustment to the horror and an understanding of what brought it about.

Of course, it is possible to rightly and most convincingly argue against overstating the Palestinian case: after all, even if there is Palestinian discontent, it cannot be compared to the suffering that is the lot of other peoples in our times. The

183

Palestinians are among their brethren, whose riches grow astronomically. They are not doomed to destruction by man or heaven. Their refugees, who were kept in their camps by the Arab countries, are afforded impressive and continued aid by the international community, the same that disregards famine and death in Africa and southeast Asia. When we compare the Palestinian suffering to that of others—and this while overlooking what the Jewish people have been through —one can sadly ponder upon the international hysteria over the Palestinian tragedy.

We know that when the terrorist organizations speak of this tragedy, they do not have in mind the human suffering of their brethren, but Israel's very existence here. The legitimate rights of the Palestinians, according to their formula, means the destruction of Israel.

But even if we argue, time and again, against the exaggeration of the question, even if we write self-convincing articles in our newspapers—the favorite sport of rightists—there still are facts we cannot eliminate. The first fact is the existence of Arab power. The Palestinian problem is now on the agenda of the international community first and foremost due to the Arab countries' enormous political and economic bargaining power. The Bangladesh refugees and the famished in Biafra, the Asians in East Africa and the Latvians in the Soviet empire have stronger arguments, both from the moral and the juridical point of view. But contrary to the Palestinians, they have no political support. For this reason, too, of the world's refugees, only the Arabs attained an extraordinary position, the refugees' descendants being given continuing aid to the end of time, regardless of their economic situation. It is possible and necessary to argue against this unfair order of priorities—and the writer of these lines has more than once done so in the foreign press—but the Arab power is a fact of life and no moralization in an Israel newspaper will ever reduce it.

Another fact is the strong Palestinian nationalistic feelings. Were it not for Arab power, this nationalism would never have become as strong as it has, but no power would have been able to create this nationalism if it did not exist. In fact, every observer knows that the Palestinian nationalism is a fact and finds its expression in a hundred and one ways: in writing and speech, in actions and wishes, in overt expression and disguised feelings. Again, it is not important how this national feeling arises and whether it has an "historic justification"; it is not important if the rights of this new nationalism are equal to those of Israel's; and none of this has bearing on whether it deserves the world's attention. The determining fact is that this nationalism is now a reality—and the fact that it thrives mainly on our very existence and on its opposition to Zionism, does not in the least detract from its own existence. So, in the background of Palestinian nationalism and Arab power, the Palestinian problem arose and made itself felt everywhere. Everywhere—except for Israel. Here, in the atmosphere of imaginary-power intoxication that existed before Yom Kippur, the political administration decided to disregard it altogether. In a proud world—again, unjustly, but no matter—the Palestinian wave and the consciousness of the new nationalism slowly penetrated until it reached formal declarations by countries friendly to us. More than one hundred—yes, this is no printing error—recognized the Palestinian Liberation Organization and in other countries its offices are opened as a matter of routine. From many aspects this murderous terrorist organization is given the same position the Jewish Agency held before the establishment of the State of Israel.

The recognition of the Palestinian problem spread beyond the New Left and liberal circles and even penetrated Jewish circles in the Diaspora. Even before President Nixon—who yesterday was the hero of the Israel right wing—spoke about the Palestinians' interests, it was clear that the day was not far when no politician in the world would disregard this combination of power, nationalism, and propaganda. Except for the Israel politician.

In fact, when the Palestinian wave swelled the world over, Israel's captains decided to determine—once and for all—that the problem itself does not exist, that there is no Palestinian nationalism, there is absolutely nothing.

Today this sounds strange and it's hard to remember that Prime Minister Golda Meir rejected the very concept of "Palestinian" and the use of this word was almost taboo at government meetings. Moshe Dayan went even further, and, in a series of appearances and speeches in June 1973, determined that there is no entity called "Palestinian." In his speech to Technion graduates, the then Minister of Defense declared that "politically, Palestine is finished." In those far off days — i.e., in 1973 — Mr. Dayan would repeatedly explain to his admiring followers the principles of his wonderful doctrine: there is no danger of war, there is no danger of invasion, there are no Palestinians, there is absolutely nothing.

It would be possible, somehow, to understand the governmental policy if the disregard of the Palestinian nationalism led to an agreement with the King of Jordan—i.e., to the known Hashemite solution." It would be possible to understand the disregard of the Arab power factor through the attempt to solve it by means of another power factor. But Mr. Dayan—who in fact shaped the policy of Meir's government—did not want this solution either. When he rejected the Palestinians' national existence, he advised King Hussein not to accept Israel's offer. He admitted that a "Hashemite solution" was possible, and even a peace agreement with Hussein was possible. But he strongly opposed any solution of this sort that was suggested. After rejecting the Palestinians and the possibility of an agreement with Jordan, he proposed his well known solution, by which Israel would have sovereignty over Judaea and Samaria whereas "sovereignty" over the population would be held by Jordan. This vision of an eternal Israel military rule over more than a million Arabs stemmed from Mr. Dayan's intoxication with his successes in the administration of the occupied territories. For lack of historic feeling and political understanding, the former Minister of Defense thought that it would be possible to change long-ranged political problems into an enlightened policy of conquest.

Today, so it seems, there is no room for a policy of absolutely nothing, which avoids both Israel's eastern border problems and the nature of the understanding that must be reached with Jordan and the Arab people on both sides of the river. Rabin's government is willing, contrary to its predecessor, to mention the forbidden name "Palestinian" and at least to discuss the subject. This means that there is an initial readiness to confront the question. This confrontation does not imply, to my mind, acceptance of the creation of a Palestinian entity or a separate Palestinian country in Judaea and Samaria, or negotiations with the organizations of terror and murder. What is implied is that Israel must consider the overall problems the Palestinian challenge faces Israelis with. There is no need for Israel to be—overtly or as a rule—the defenders of a certain regime. There is no need to become involved in the consolidation of political conceptions regarding Judaea and Samaria by forbidding political activity, as long as it does not deal with terror and sabotage; Israel must declare and inform the whole world that the Arab people on both sides of the Jordan has the right to define the nature of its regime and rule, as long as these do not go counter to Israel's security and peace. This is an apparently internal question of a neighboring country but for long-range political interests and for the immediate benefit of Israel's public image, she must recognize this right of the world living east of Israel.

Israelis must not be the only ones to deny the interest of the legitimate rights of the Palestinians, when the whole world recognizes them. On the contrary, we must join those who acknowledge these interests and define them in such a way that it may serve Israel's interest for security and peace. It should not apppear as if we are trying to prevent political organization in the occupied territories by means of administrative authorities. On the contrary, we must advise the territories' population to choose their representation as a part of the political power tactics inside Jordan. We must not determine beforehand who represents whom but on the contrary, we must put the cart before the horse and demand that the people on both sides of the river themselves determine the link between east and west Jordan. Of course, there is no assurance that this policy will bear good results. It may also be argued that Israel missed the precious opportunities that were lost during the period of imaginary power intoxication. But it is difficult to see how a realistic policy, which recognizes the Palestinian nationalism and considers it part of a Palestinian Jordanian country, could damage Israel more than a policy of blindness and sleight of hand.

The Palestinian Option

By Uri Avneri

Many years ago, I heard a major radio address by the late Egyptian President Nasser. The President, then at the beginning of his career, went far afield with his usual flowery rhetoric, encompassing the entire world in his speech. Suddenly his utterance was disrupted by a voice from the crowd: "Falasteen, Ya Gamal!"

Abdel Nasser broke off in the middle, abandoned the topic of his address, and devoted the rest of the speech to an emotional pledge of loyalty to the Palestinian people.

Ever since then this exclamation has been echoing in my brain, literally, so that every time I listen to a speech by an Arab leader, I know that as soon as this call is sounded: "Falasteen, Ya Arab!" everything else will be forgotten, and the Arab world will turn to deal with this open wound.

I am absolutely convinced that no genuine peace will emerge, between Israel and the Arab world, if no solution is found to the Palestinian problem.

And I am prepared to say that the converse is true: I am convinced that using the Palestinian option open to us is the best and most effective way of achieving the peace goals of the State of Israel.

Getting on the Map

Actually, what are the "peace goals" of the State of Israel? Or, in other words, what are our "war goals"?

We have been in a state of war with the Arab nations for three generations. What is it that we seek to achieve through this warfare?

The matter has never been defined, and therefore Israel does not have a clear and consistent policy. At most, we are using nebulous expressions, such as "genuine peace," "security," and such. Except for a small minority in our midst, we are not interested in additional territory; we do not want "a kingdom of Israel from the Nile to the Euphrates"; we do not believe that we can conquer or subjugate the Arab world. If so, what are our interests?

187

I would define our goals in terms of a picture. At this moment, in half a million classrooms throughout the Arab world there are maps where the area of the State of Israel is marked as "Conquered Palestine." Millions of Arab children from Marrakesh to Mosul, are taught every day that the State of Israel does not actually exist, and that its physical being is an illegal fact which must be put to an end.

All we want is that all these maps carry the word "Israel."

Our goal is to exchange the present warfare for peace, in which the Arab world would reconcile itself, in fact and deed, to Israel's existence as a legitimate and permanent fact. This recognition of the legitimacy of Israel's existence in the heart of the Arab expanse is the cornerstone of peace and security. No substitute—"military superiority," "defensible borders," "nuclear balance of fear"—can replace this basic recognition. No new status will hold fast, if so focal a factor as the Palestinians denies its legitimacy.

Actually this is the consummation of the fundamental Zionist program, as adopted at Basel. The establishment of the Jewish National Home, assured in the open council of nations, is not fully attainable until the State of Israel is recognized in the open council of the Arab peoples.

Hamlet's Father

When Israel was established, its founders believed that this could be achieved by wiping the name "Palestine" from the map and by the disappearance of the Palestinian people as a national-political entity. This concept was based on two elements: the optimistic hope that the Palestine problem would gradually disappear, in time, and the pessimistic expectation that the Palestinian people would never make peace with the usurpation of part of its historical homeland by a foreign people. This expectation was set forth in a most pointed fashion by Moshe Dayan: "In front of their (the Palestinian refugees') eyes, we are taking possession of the land and the villages in which they and their forebears have dwelled . . . Let us not draw back at the sight of the burning hatred which fills the lives of the hundreds of thousands of Arabs surrounding us . . . this is the destiny of our generation" (from the eulogy for Roy Rothenberg)[1].

This hope evaporated. The Palestinian people did not vanish in due course; to the contrary, it has become consolidated, strengthened, and has emerged as a top-ranking international factor. Like the ghost of Hamlet's father, it has kept reappearing on the stage. Today the Palestinian people is about to achieve that which Herzl demanded for the Jews—recognition of their right to a national home, guaranteed in the open council of nations.

Also dissipated is the hope that the Arab world would gradually abandon the Palestine problem. The Arab regimes have more than once betrayed the Palestinians, exploiting them for their own purposes. Twenty-six years of experience, however, show that there is no regime in the Arab world capable of coming to terms with Israel while disregarding the issue of the Palestinian people. Without authorized approval by a trustworthy Palestinian representation, any Arab-Israel arrangement will be in the nature of a provisional armistice, as was the original armistice of 1949.

The question is whether the pessimistic expectation has also been vindicated, to the effect that there can be no peace of any kind between Israel and the Palestinians. Are we indeed "doomed" to live forever between terror and warfare, between the horrors of nuclear dread? Or can we set up formats for the peaceful coexistence of two peoples in this land, regarded by both as their native land?

This question is both fateful and practical—so fateful that we must harness our full intellectual powers for an objective evaluation, in order to obtain a truthful answer.

A Palestinian "Return to Zion"

The national tragedy of the Palestinian people has led to its dispersion and fragmentation. Half of it dwelt in Palestine (according to the Arabs, this is the area between Jordan and the sea) and half outside its borders. Part of it lived under a tyrannical and hostile regime (Trans-Jordan), and another part under the rule of the Fedayeen (in Lebanon), and the rest in a worldwide dispersion, similar to that of the Jews. Some are now living in urban and rural centers under the Israel occupation regime, others are in subhuman refugee camps, and still others have gained standing and status in countries like Kuwait. As one who has met with hundreds of Palestinians in the last twenty years, of all categories, I can testify to the tremendous variegation of their fabric—but also to their impressive national unity.

It is senseless to deceive ourselves. There isn't a single Palestinian who doesn't believe that the Palestinian people has prior right to this country. There is none among them who doesn't feel that Zionism and its confederates have done the Palestinians wrong, historically. Not a single one loves Israel, or would not be happy to see it disappear. One and all, they would like to see a "return to Zion" and an "ingathering of the exiles," Palestinian-style.

Opinions are split, however, as to how these goals are to be achieved, under present historical circumstances.

It may be said that the Palestinian people resembles a trailing column, at one end of which is the traditional approach of "everything or nothing" and, at the other, "be satisfied with what you can get."

There are Palestinians, whose numbers and strength should not be minimized, who adhere to the opinions that no compromise is acceptable and that Israel is not to be recognized, come what may, even if this would lead to the final destruction of the Palestinian people or to a two hundred-year war (as was the war between the Muslims and the Crusaders). On the other hand, there are many Palestinians of considerable standing who have now arrived at the point which many Zionists reached in the early forties, namely, that a national state should be established in part of the country, because the matter of attaining national sovereignty is more important than the size of the territory. These Palestinians are aware that this is possible only if an arrangement is reached with Israel, based on cooperation.

Between these two segments—the vanguard and the rear guard—are all the other factions. Some are content with a "small" Palestinian state on the West Bank and in the Gaza Strip, with the nebulous hope that, at some future time, this state would become federated with Israel, and the land would revert to its full entity. Others are willing to accept a "small" state so as to convert it into a military base of operations against Israel.

An Arab "Biltmore Program"

The fragmentation is natural. For the Palestinians, abandonment of the idea of an "undivided Palestine" is an historical, difficult, and painful revolution, accompanied with feelings of guilt for having abandoned the original goal. This revolution beats in the heart of every Palestinian. Some digest it in one fell swoop, courageously, in cognizance of the inevitable results (the creation of a legitimate and practical status of Israel-Palestinian coexistence). Others take the step with hesitation, clinging to the ideological alibi ("this is just a passing stage") to look right to themselves and others. Others are not prepared to take the step at all.

To put it in brief schematics, most of the inhabitants of the administered areas are willing to see the establishment of a Palestinian state on the West Bank and in the Strip (with or without Jordan's approval). The camp which negates the very idea includes the more extreme groups of the Fedayeen (Habash's 'Front' and Jebril's 'Command'). The idea of a state-for-war is being espoused by the doctrinaire handful gathered about Nayef Hawatmeh. The central group of the Fatah and the Palestine Liberation Organization (PLO) headed by Yasser Arafat, actually supports an immediate establishment of the state, while paying lip service to the "final goal" of an indivisible Palestine.

At the twelfth conference of the Palestinian Council, held at the beginning of June of this year in Cairo, Arafat prevented a final confrontation among these concepts. Since the Israel Government was against all of these ideas, he was not forced to bring the matter to a head. As an astute politician, he tried to get a unanimous wall-to-wall consensus. The closing document of the conference indeed shows him burning the candle at both ends: he demands Palestinian rule over the areas to be evacuated by the Israel army but repeats the "final goal" of a whole Palestine. While the second point is but a routine continuation of the old line, the first point has a decisive innovation as in the Zionist Biltmore program of 1943, which gave authorization for the partition of the country.

"A Zionist Trap"

I must refer to a matter which involves me, so as to prove that anyone who agreed to the contents of this document was aware of its far-reaching implications.

In May of 1971, the PLO published a book in Beirut, in Arabic, titled *Uri Avneri, or the New Zionism*. After a basic (and rather fair) analysis of my opinions, the book comes to the following summation: the proposal to establish a Palestine state on the West Bank and in the Gaza Strip, which the Arabs ascribe to me, is a Zionist plot far worse than the schemes of Golda [Meir] and [Menahem] Begin. Implementation of this proposal would necessarily terminate the "Palestine revolution" and would lead to a final Arab reconciliation with the existence of sovereign Israel.

The same persons who wrote and published this book (similar pamphlets were also published in Europe) now adopted a resolution with exactly the same meaning, although they tried to trim it with faded ideologies. The significance of the act is quite known to them.

The historic drive of the Palestinian people toward compromise and reconciliation is not over. It is at its high point. Its continuation and speed depend largely on the stand taken by the State of Israel. It is in our power to accelerate it and to propel it toward its historical destiny, which is also our destiny, or to halt it and even derail it.

A Political Solution

Israel now has an option open to it—the Palestinian option. How can it be utilized? How does it affect the terror warfare? What risks confront it from the political and military standpoints?

Amos Kenan once wrote a story about a boy who saw a corpse lying in the yard, covered with flies. When he went into the house to inform the occupants, he found them all engaged in killing flies. They wouldn't let him open his mouth because they were so busy.

For the past twenty-five years I have been feeling like that boy. In our courtyard lies a corpse—the Palestinian problem. However, the Israel Government is not of a mind to think about it because it is immersed in killing flies—in retaliation acts against brutal acts, from Ma'ale Akrabim to Ma'alot.

We have been busy killing flies ever since the founding of Israel, and the flies are not diminishing in number; they are increasing. This is called the "pragmatic" approach. It may be termed in words less complimentary.

In the twentieth century there hasn't been a single instance of a military victory over a terror setup. This is a simple fact.

This era has known many terrorist formations (every terrorist calls himself a "freedom fighter," and every freedom fighter is called "terrorist" by his opponents. For the sake of clarity, I intend to keep away from qualifying terms). To mention some of the more prominent examples: Ireland in the last days of World War I and Northern Ireland of today, Kenya's Mau-Mau and the Malayan guerrillas, the Hebrew underground in the Land of Israel and the FLN in Algeria, the Giapp guerrillas in Northern Vietnam, and the struggle in Portuguese Guinea, now terminating.

All these formations, and many others, have a common denominator; they were not overcome by military means. No "retaliatory action," "raids of the murderers' nests," or "amputation of the criminal arm" were of any use.

Some of the greatest military commanders of the twentieth century met defeat in such contests. None achieved anything more than temporary victory, which soon faded.

Whenever such a terrorist formation was liquidated, it was done through a political solution which satisfied the basic demand of the terrorists. This came about in one of two ways: talks with the terrorists themselves and a coming to terms, as in Algeria, or talks with a moderate national leadership which put an end to the terror by itself, as in Malaya.

The reason for it is simple enough:

Terrorist action (or a war of liberation) cannot achieve strength without drawing on wide public support. Terror organizations must have a broad popular base, a constant stream of volunteers, and moral and material support. All this is possible only if the terrorists are giving voice to a basic desire on the part of a large segment of the population within which they function.

One of the greatest guerrilla fighters of our times, Mao Tse-tung, once compared the fighters to fish in the water. The water is the civilian public. The fish cannot live and grow except in water.

This means that the only effective way of liquidating the terror is to get the fish out of the water—that is, to detach the terrorism from the sources of its nourishment and to exclude the terrorists from the community in whose name they are acting. This can be done in one way: to satisfy the basic demand of that community.

The only way to terminate the Palestine terror is, therefore, to find a solution acceptable to the decisive majority of the Palestinian people.

1967 Proposal

This solution must satisfy its yearning for a national identity, for the establishment of a national home which will carry the name Palestine and fly the Palestinian flag. The most reasonable way to satisfy this yearning is to establish a national Palestinian state, free and sovereign, on the West Bank and in the Gaza Strip, alongside and in accordance with an arrangement with the State of Israel.

As for the terrorists, the question immediately suggests itself: How do we know that this solution will satisfy the terrorists? How can we be sure that the terrorists will not seize control of the new state and turn it into a military base against Israel?

Many enlightened Israelis will no doubt form their opinion of the Palestine option in the light of the answer to this question.

On the fifth day of the Six Day War—immediately after the fall of the West Bank and the Gaza Strip—I sent a letter to the late Prime Minister Levi Eshkol, which was published on the same day. I asked him to make an immediate proposal to the Palestinian people regarding the possibility of setting up a state of its own in the areas we had just taken, and to put through a referendum on the subject in those areas.

We were then at the peak of our strength and prestige. The Arab forces had been routed. The Fedayeen organizations were at low ebb. The Palestinian people was freed of the guardianship of the Arab states. I have not the slightest doubt that, had a referendum been conducted in 1967, most of the dwellers of Palestine would have voted for the establishment of a state via an arrangement with Israel.

The idea behind my proposal was that conditions were ripe for the creation of a national Palestinian leadership from among the public figures in the occupied territories. This leadership would necessarily have a moderate cast, interested in living in peace, at long last. This political reality would have neutralized the Fedayeen organizations, and would have led to orderly transfer of rule in the territories, to a new and stable force, without leaving a vacuum.

The proposal was not accepted, as is known. Worse than that, for seven years, to this day, the Military Government has forcibly prevented any political activity from taking place in the territories. Many dignitaries who were expressly in favor of Israel-Palestine coexistence were arrested or expelled. Half the Palestinian people—and the more moderate half at that—was doomed to political muteness. Israel handed the monopoly of representing the Palestinian issue to the Fedayeen, on a silver platter. Moshe Dayan was Yasser Arafat's devoted aide, in Arafat's efforts to have himself and the PLO regarded as the exclusive spokesmen of the Palestinian people. Should the PLO set itself up tomorrow as a provisional Palestinian government, he would at once receive recognition from more than a hundred states.

"Middle East Cuba"

This does not mean that it is too late to allow the West Bank community to organize itself, to be expressive and to wield influence. If we allow this community to act on behalf of peace, and if we announce our readiness to negotiate earnestly regarding the future of the occupied areas, a leadership will spring up in the territories very quickly.

I do not believe, however, that in 1974, it is still possible to have a Palestinian leadership which could ignore the existence of the PLO. Under present conditions, I would expect a broad coalition of the leadership in the territories and the moderate elements of the PLO and Fatah. This coalition would rule the Palestinian state, when it arises.

What leads us to think that this leadership would want to halt the terror?

The question is not whether "the Arabs can be trusted." I do not trust Arab politicians any more than I trust Soviet, American, or Israel politicians. But I do believe in the force of life.

Once a Palestinian state comes into being, it will have to man its governing apparatus. It will require thousands of ministers, officials, officers, ambassadors. Each of these will have a vital interest in maintaining the new status. Any threat to this status will be a threat to his own position. It won't be worth while to be a Fedayee.

We have seen this process in other countries, Israel among them: yesterday's terrorist is today's conservative and tomorrow's reactionary. Is there a more outstanding legitimist than Menahem Begin? This, too, is an expression of the power of the legitimate status quo.

A new state means a new living pattern. The ties between Hebron and Gaza would require open borders and a free flow of men and commodities. The position of the new state as a transit-state between the Arab countries and the west and Israel would make it a second Lebanon. The tremendous undertaking of ingathering and rehabilitating the refugees, with the generous support of the international community, would engage the Palestinian state, from the viewpoint of economics, for a long time.

The new reality will be the directing force behind the new Palestinian regime—be its composition what it may—toward channels of peace. The night-mare of Palestine's becoming the "Cuba of the Middle East" is groundless. The entire historical experience points in an opposite direction (I doubt that Cuba would have taken the course it did, had the United States not behaved toward it as it did).

The Soviet Union is now supporting the establishment of a Palestinian state just as at one time it supported the creation of the State of Israel—and for the same astute reasons. However, the new state, if it comes into being by arrangement, will not be pro-Soviet, just as Israel did not turn pro-Soviet. It will probably be pro-Egyptian. Peace with Palestine and peace with Egypt, I believe, are inter-twined.

This does not mean that the Palestinian terror will cease at once.

It is probable that a segment of the Fedayeen movement will object to partition, just as part of the Jewish underground opposed it, at one time. I believe that this would be an insignificant segment, since the vast majority of the Palestinian people will welcome the establishment of its national state with the same joyous enthusiasm that the bulk of the Jewish community greeted the founding of Israel, in a small area of the country. After continued tragedy stretching over three generations, this people is yearning for peace and for the rebuilding of its ruins.

A minority will remain, determined to fight on. What then?

We must understand that, should this situation arise, the threat would not be to the State of Israel but to the new Palestinian state and its rulers. Should there be a struggle, it would be a civil war, and the new regime would be interested in working with Israel to eradicate the evil. The same Palestinian community which is now adoring the Fedayeen and is praying for their success would regard them as disturbers of the peace, separatists and detructionists.

In brief, only the Palestinians themselves are capable of removing the Palesti-nian terror. This is the entire issue in a nutshell.

FOOTNOTE

1. Head of security on a kibbutz, killed by Arabs in a border dispute.

A Palestinian State–Where?

By Moshe Maoz

The Arab-Palestinian sense of identity is a relatively new phenomenon—about half a century old—which came about in large measure as a result of the (artificial) "Palestine—Land of Israel" framework set up by the British Mandate authorities at the close of World War I. This feeling grew and expanded during the Mandate era, due to its conflict with and imitation of the national Jewish movement in the Land of Israel, but it receded and shriveled following the establishment of the State of Israel and annexation of the West Bank to Jordan after the 1948 war. In the mid-sixties, this feeling resurged, with the founding of the Palestine Liberation Organization (PLO) and the Palestine Liberation Movement (al Fatah), and has been gaining strength, encompassing large segments of the Arab community of Palestinian origin living east of the Jordan, in the Gaza Strip, in Israel, in the Persian Gulf emirates and outside the Middle East.

This national Palestinian identity has short roots and is certainly not as comprehensive or consolidated as is the Jewish-Zionist or the Arab-Egyptian entity. It does exist, however, and it is no weaker than other national Arab feelings—such as the Syrian, Iraqi, Jordanian or Lebanese. The Jewish community in Israel must reconcile itself to this fact, even if its larger segment is not happy about it.

Another fact which we must recognize is that the Palestinian problem constitutes one of the fundamental elements of the Arab-Israel conflict, both because of the emotional involvement and ideological obligation on the part of the Arab states towards the issue, and because of the military and political use of the Palestinians by the Arab states in their struggle against Israel.

The conclusion emerging from the foregoing is that solving the Palestinian problem may not only fulfill the national aspirations of the one Arab people which

194

has not as yet enjoyed the privilege of self-determination, but also may help settle the conflict between the Arab states and the State of Israel.

The focal question is how the national aspirations of the Palestinian Arabs may be realized, under present conditions and at this historic juncture.

On the surface it would seem that the most reasonable solution would be to establish a Palestinian state in the section of the western portion of the Land of Israel alongside the State of Israel—an arrangement favored by the larger segment of the Jewish community on the eve of Israel's founding. Contemporary circumstances, however, are far different from pre-1948 conditions and such an arrangement cannot be implemented without seriously endangering Israel's security and perhaps its very existence.

Unlike the Mandate period, in which practically the entire Arab Palestinian community was living in Palestine—Land of Israel, today only about half of the Palestinian people lives on the West Bank and in the Gaza Strip; the other half lives on the East Bank (Jordan) where it comprises slightly more than half the population. A Palestinian state west of the Jordan, not including the Palestinians east of it, would not realize the aspirations of the entire Palestinian people; on the other hand, such a state, of limited size, would not be able to take in all the Palestinians who might wish to live there, and it would therefore strive to expand at the expense of its neighbor, Israel.

It may of course be argued that in light of Israel's power, this Palestinian state would not wish, or would not be able to spread westward, and might expand to the east—across the Jordan. The answer to this contention is that, aside from the economic considerations of pushing westward (such as an outlet to the Mediterranean), the Palestinian Arabs view the State of Israel as their "usurped" land, and they are determined not to renounce it, under any circumstances.

This stand is particularly characteristic of the hundred of thousands of refugee camp inmates east of the Jordan, in Syria and in Lebanon, who abandoned their land inside Israel during the 1948 fighting, and are now yearning to go back to it. This group, perhaps unlike many residents of the West Bank, refused to recognize Israel's existence, and it serves as the main reservoir of manpower and the foremost source of ideological-moral inspiration for the Palestinian terror organizations, whose goal is the annihilation of Israel.

These terrorist organizations, organized for the most part in the PLO, are the ones who have been recognized by the Palestinian community, the Arab states, and by more than one hundred countries as the sole representatives of the Arab Palestinian people; there is no doubt that if and when they take over the rule in a sovereign Palestinian state, they would turn it into a base of operations against Israel. It may be assumed that the members of these organizations would become the Establishment in this new state and be engaged in setting up and manning its institutions. But this is no assurance that they will not build the state establishments—especially the military machine—in such a way as to enable them to continue the struggle for the areas just immediately beyond their own borders.

It is quite possible that the Palestinian war machine set up to fight Israel—or presumably to protect itself against Israel—will be based on massive aid from the Soviet Union and various Arab countries and become a kind of North Vietnam of the Middle East, or perhaps a version of the Sudetan district in Czechoslovakia, after the Munich Pact.

The risk for Israel in the establishment of the Palestinian state on the West Bank is far too great in view of the chances for peaceful settlement of the Arab-Israel conflict resulting from this move.

Israel would be assuming quite a risk by even agreeing to a Jordan-Palestine solution, namely, the return of the West Bank and the Gaza Strip to Jordanian rule, in view of the possibility that the Palestinian element in this united state, accounting for two-thirds of its population, might assume control of the country and turn it into an extremist anti-Israel entity. This is a remote possibility, however, in view of the power of the Jordanian regime, and even if it should materialize, it would be possible to counteract the threat in time.

On the other hand, the Jordan-Palestine solution does have good prospects for settling the Palestine issue. Such a setup, which would take in the great majority of the Palestinians, would allow this people to find an outlet for its national-political aspirations, along with Jordan's residents with whom it has linguistic-cultural, economic, and historical ties. The establishment of a Jordan-Palestine entity, with its center east of the Jordan, could transfer the core of the Palestinian issue from the western part of the Land of Israel eastward, and thus contribute to its gradual settlement.

VI

General

Palestinian Nationalism: Its Development and Goal

By Marie Syrkin

I

Its Development

Have we been witnessing the synthetic creation of a Palestinian identity? In the total evaluation of Arab Jewish rights this question looms large. The Palestinian Arab nationalist, whether in costume or true guise, is a new factor in the Arab-Jewish conflict; and one treated respectfully by commentators many of whom argue that the origin of Palestinian nationalism is irrelevant to the issue. Supposing it did spring belatedly out of the head of Arab nationalism merely as a hostile response to Israel? The lad is alive and kicking and calling him bastard will not exorcise him. But by the same token Israel is also there; if its ouster is demanded on the grounds of illegitimacy then the counterclaims must be examined. Can the newcomer be fed only at the expense of the Jewish state or is there room elsewhere in the family domain for his natural development?

The question of origins is not merely academic. The terrorist justifies his act on the grounds that the first Zionist Congress took place in Switzerland in 1897 so ushering in the "horror" of Zionism to the world scene. Commentators of all shades of the political spectrum seek to determine future policy according to their view of what actually took place in the last fifty years. Obviously, if the British sponsorship of the Zionist endeavor was a bad business to begin with, at best an error of judgment as Dean Acheson discreetly indicates in his memoirs, or at worst, a gross injustice as Toynbee would have it, then the possible accommodations of the present must be made with such history in mind. Even those who believe that truth is best served by granting the clash of two wrongs or two rights will fit their prescription to their diagnosis of the cause of the trouble. Any view of what should be done now to achieve a peaceful settlement between Arab and Jew

199

is bound to be practically affected by a determination of the extent of the injury. A dispossessed Palestinian people, able to flourish only within the area of the Jewish state, would require compromises from Israel other than those to be made for the same number of dislocated refugees. For this reason a discussion of Palestinian nationalism is not a futile semantic exercise. There is little hope of devising a satisfactory territorial solution if the existence of Israel is really predicated on the ruthless dispossession of a people from its homeland—something radically different from the dislocation or resettlement of individuals as an aftermath of war, a familiar process in the Europe and Asia of the twentieth century.

The characterization of Palestinian nationalism as "artificial" does not come from Zionist adversaries but from classic Arab sources. In the period before and after the issuance of the Balfour Declaration Arab nationalists consistently protested the use of the name "Palestine" or the adjective "Palestinian" to demark them from other Arabs in the region. All the declarations of the nascent Arab nationalist movement from 1880 on concentrated on "the unity of Syria" with no references to Palestine as other than "south Syria." Nothing could be more explicit than the statement of the General Syrian Congress in 1919: "We ask that there should be no separation of the southern part of Syria, known as Palestine, nor of the littoral western zone which includes Lebanon, from the Syrian country. We desire that the unity of the country should be guaranteed against partition under whatever circumstances."

The Arab Congress meeting in Jerusalem in 1919 formulated an Arab Covenant whose first clause read: "The Arab lands are a complete and indivisible whole, and the divisions of whatever nature to which they have been subjected are not approved nor recognized by the Arab nation." George Antonius, the Arab historian, makes sure that there will be no misunderstanding on this score. In *The Arab Awakening* (1939) he writes: "Except where otherwise specified the term Syria will be used to denote the whole of the country of that name which is now split up into mandated territories of (French) Syria and the Lebanon, and (British) Palestine and Transjordan."

The extremist Mufti of Jerusalem originally opposed the Palestine Mandate on the grounds that it separated Palestine from Syria; he emphasized that there was no difference between Palestinian and Syrian Arabs in national characteristics or group life. As late as May, 1947, Arab representatives reminded the United Nations in a formal statement that "Palestine was . . . part of the Province of Syria . . . Politically, the Arabs of Palestine were not independent in the sense of forming a separate political entity."

Before the creation of the Jewish state the whole thrust of Arab nationalism was directed against what its proponents viewed as the dismemberment of an ideal unitary Arab state. Even the setting up of several independent Arab states was viewed as a subtle thwarting of Arab nationalism, not its fulfillment. Nor was there a change after the establishment of Israel. In 1952, Charles Malik, the Lebanese scholar and statesman described the process dourly (Foreign Affairs): "greater Syria was dismembered, the southern and northern parts being put under different administrations." The Arab Ba'ath Party, which describes itself as a "national, popular revolutionary movement fighting for Arab Unity, Freedom and Socialism," declared in its constitution (1951): "The Arabs form one nation. This nation has the natural right to live in a single state and to be free to direct its own destiny," and equated the battle against colonialism with the "struggle to gather all the Arabs in a single, independent Arab state." Ahmed Shukeiry had no hesitation, while head of the Palestine Liberation Organization, in announcing to the Security Council that "it is common knowledge that Palestine is nothing but southern Syria." (May 31, 1956.)

For Arabs "Palestine" was merely an inaccurate name for a sector of the Middle East whose separate designation was the result of imperialist plotting against Arab independence. Unlike its role in Jewish history and tradition, in Arab eyes Palestine was neither the cradle of a nation nor a holy land. Arab national passion was engaged by the concept of a greater Syria or an even larger united Arab state. In the lexicon of Arab nationalism the independent existence of a Palestine state, like the existence of an independent Lebanon, represented a violation of the Arab national will.

The concept of Palestine as a separate national entity arose among Arabs as a purely negative reaction to Zionism after the Balfour Declaration. It is worth noting in this connection that those Arab spokesmen who originally welcomed the setting up of a Jewish homeland in a small portion of the territories freed from Ottoman rule made no pretense that they viewed the abstraction of Palestine from the total area assigned to the Arabs other than the loss of a given number of square kilometers. Emir Faisal signed his celebrated agreement with Dr. Weizmann (January, 1919) in behalf of the "Arab Kingdom of Hedjaz," and in his letter to Felix Frankfurter, then a member of the Zionist Delegation to the Peace Conference, the Emir wrote a few months later (March 1, 1919) "We are working together for a revived Near East, and our two movements complete one another. The Jewish movement is national and not imperialist. Our movement is national and not imperialist, and there is room in Syria for us both."

The Arab organizations who justify their demand for bases in Lebanon as in Jordan and Syria with the argument that the Arabs are one nation and therefore have the right to use each others territories interchangeably, operate completely within the tradition of orthodox Arab nationalism. Some sophisticated Arab spokesmen have become aware of the pitfalls presented by Arab avowals that they are all one people with no difference between Jordanian, Palestinian or Syrian. The editor of the Amman weekly, *Amman al Masa* warned that such reasoning might make the notion of the resettlement of Arab refugees "respectable," since its advocates could justly claim that the refugees were merely being moved to another part of their Arab fatherland, whatever its name. Such considerations, however, trouble neither the terrorists who move freely across the borders of the Arab states as citizens of the Arab nation, nor their sponsors.

Contemporary polemics maintain the fiction that the British and the Jews proceeded with a total disregard of an Arab presence in Palestine. The many pages devoted to analyzing the Sykes-Picot Agreement, the McMahon Letter or the recommendation of the King-Crane Commission—all pre-Mandate documents—indicate that however proponents varied in the solutions or interpretations they offered, every aspect of the Arab case was weighed and considered; it did not go by default as rewriters of history like to pretend. The King-Crane Commission, appointed by President Wilson to study the question of the Palestine Mandate, brought in an outspokenly hostile report; it urged the abandonment of a Jewish National Home and proposed instead that Palestine be included "in a united Syria state" for which the United States should hold the Mandate. The very nature of the anti-Zionist opposition—American, British and Arab—its indifference to Palestine except as part of an Arab whole, made the reasoning of pro-Zionists like Lord Balfour plausible. Their psychology may have been faulty; the Arabs did and do "grudge" the "little notch," but nothing could be more irresponsible than to foster the myth that Arab national feelings were ignored by the promulgators of the Balfour Declaration.

The same holds true for the Zionists. They were thoroughly aware that Palestine, though denuded and sparsely inhabited, had a native population. They came prepared with agricultural studies and demographic charts demonstrating that soil reclamation in Palestine would make room for more Arabs as well as Jews and would provide a better life for both. Weizmann declared unequivocally that the Zionists assumed that the "national sentiments of the Palestinian Arabs would center in Baghdad, Mecca and Damascus, and find their natural and complete satisfaction in the Arab kingdoms which resulted from the Peace Treaty settlement in the Near East." If peaceful Jewish colonization beginning at the turn of the century had resulted in the dispossession of the local population this would have been a more serious indictment of Zionist policy than the subsequent flight of refugees in later war. No such dispossession took place. Since the current indictments of Israel include not only the urgent troubles of the present, but the "historic wrong" done the Arabs through their dispossession by Jewish settlers, this must be clearly established. Instead of diminishing, the Arab population increased spectacularly in the three decades after the Balfour Declaration.

The British Secretary of State for the Colonies declared in the House of Commons (November 24, 1938): "The Arabs cannot say that the Jews are driving them out of the country. If not a single Jew had come to Palestine after 1918, I believe the Arab population of Palestine would still have been around 600,000 at which it had been stable under Turkish rule. . . . It is not only the Jews who have benefited from the Balfour Declaration. They can deny it as much as they like, but materially the Arabs have benefited very greatly from the Balfour Declaration."

In 1948, the Jewish State created through partition in one-sixth of the territory originally envisaged by the Balfour Declaration emerged without dispossessing a single Arab. Had the account between Arabs and Jews been closed in 1948 with the acceptance by the Arabs of the compromise represented by the Partition Resolution, it would have been difficult to place the Arabs in the loser's column.

Where six independent Arab states had emerged to enjoy sovereignty over a million and a quarter square miles, the Jewish state was ready to dwell in peace with its neighbors within its 8,000 square miles. But this balance could not be struck. Arab calculations were different and the attack of the Arab states on newly declared Israel, with all that followed in its wake, changed the bookkeeping.

Now there were to be dispossessed Arabs who would continue to multiply but without flourishing, while the Jewish state would expend on war and defense the energy and tenacity that had formerly been expended on the desert. From this point on the drama unfolds with the fatality of a self-fulfilling prophecy. The Arabs, who in the thirties had raised the false spectre of dispossessed Arabs, created the reality of the Arab refugees.

All kinds of reasons have been offered for the flight of the Arabs from Israel in 1948 when hostilities started; none makes adequate allowance for the swiftness and readiness with which the flight took place. Part of the speed was due to irrational panic, part to the assurance of return after the victory, but it was undoubtedly abetted by the subconscious or conscious feeling that flight to a village on the West Bank or across the Jordan was no exile, and that any differences between a man and his neighbors were due to local antagonisms not national alienation. The West Bank which had been Palestine till its seizure by

Abdullah in 1948, Jordan which had been Palestine till 1922, offered the familiar landscape, language and kin of the abandoned village. No tragic uprooting such as befell the Jews in Europe lucky enough to survive, or the countless millions shuffled around in World War II by the victors, particularly by the Soviet Union, took place.

Only in the case of the Arabs has village-patriotism been raised to a sacred cause. Even in June 1967 the comparatively small number who crossed into Jordan did so in the inner assurance that both banks of the Jordan were home regardless of the physical privations endured as a result of the war. The mobility of the Arabs as refugees or terrorists, within Jordan, Lebanon and Syria indicates strikingly the strength of Arab nationalism and the tenuous character of the Palestinian attachment except as a political tactic against Israel.

II

Its goal: A Palestinian State?

It is now quite clear that the question of "Palestinian rights" as distinct from problems of peace in the Middle East or of the Arab refugees will for the first time appear as a separate item on the agenda of the forthcoming General Assembly. With Yasser Arafat, chairman of the Palestine Liberation Organization—the umbrella organization which includes the various terrorist groups—as the recognized spokesman of the Palestinian Arabs, the issue will center on the establishment of a Palestinian state on the West Bank and Gaza. The bloody agitation of the terrorists will so receive a legitimacy not previously accorded to a movement openly dedicated to the destruction of a member state of the United Nations—one brought into being by that body. Despite this paradox the issue will probably be joined at the world forum in which the Arab states, the Soviet bloc and the so-called non-aligned countries of the Third World enjoy a majority.

Israel's firm opposition to the establishment of a third state within the borders of historic Palestine is familiar. Israeli government spokesmen have repeatedly declared that there is room for only two states, one Jewish and one Arab, within the territory originally encompassed by the Balfour Declaration—an area which includes Jordan. This opposition to a minuscule Palestinian state on the West Bank and Gaza is not motivated by a mulish insensitiveness to the national aspirations of Palestinian Arabs but by grave misgivings which cannot be dismissed out-of-hand. In the first place no Israeli government can be expected to ignore the objective of such a state as formulated by its proponents. The chief Palestinian spokesmen have made no secret of their purpose.

The supposedly moderate Nayef Hawatmeh, leader of the Marxist Popular Democratic Front for the Liberation of Palestine, (Hawatmeh, it should be noted, claimed the glory for perpetrating the massacre at Ma'alot) put the matter candidly. When asked by an interviewer (*Deutsche Zeitung*, April 19, 1974) whether after the establishment of a Palestinian state on the West Bank of the Jordan and the Gaza Strip his organization would remain unwavering in its aim to destroy Israel, he did not bother with subterfuge:

"Yes, we will not abandon it, for our purpose is a democratic state in the whole of Palestine. We will establish our state and at the same time remain loyal to the strategic aim of our revolution. We will advance step by step towards our objective and not be deterred. A state in the occupied areas will not constitute an obstacle. The contrary is true—it will be a point of departure."

Hawatmeh was equally explicit as to the ability of such a state, once established, to flout any agreements or controls in regard to armaments. On the basis of experience Hawatmeh expressed his confidence that "no supervisory system of the kind that may be set up by the UN will prevent us from exploiting every opportunity to transform the entire country into an arsenal." The record of the UN in the Middle East richly supports his estimate.

While the moderation of Hawatmeh may have become suspect, Yasser Arafat, chief of Fatah, is still viewed by determined optimists as less obdurate in his dedication to the destruction of Israel. However, even if we choose to discount past declarations of Arafat on the theory that he has lately suffered a change of heart and is readier for compromise, the decisions of the Palestine National Council, during its meeting in Cairo on June 9, 1974, leave no room for illusion. The political program adopted emphasizes that the Palestine Liberation Organization, headed by Arafat, will seek to establish a "national, independent, and *combatant* [my emphasis] authority" on any portion of liberated Palestinian territory, but that such a state would be "only a step toward the realization of its strategic objective, namely the establishment of a democratic Palestinian state in conformity with the previous resolutions of preceding sessions of the Palestine Council."

In view of Arafat's leading role in the PLO, applause for his restraint seems premature. By this time it is hardly necessary to reiterate that a "democratic Palestinian state" is not a euphemism for the destruction of Israel but a straightforward program for its obliteration. The Palestinian nationalists, unlike some of their interpreters, are plain-spoken and direct. They do not resort to euphemisms. For this reason a world that has still not assimilated the lesson taught by Hitler prefers to dismiss their pronouncements as "rhetoric."

Nor has the era of negotiation inaugurated after the October War altered Arafat's basic policy. His Fatah aide, Abu Iyad, speaking three months after the cessation of hostilities (*Al-Balagh*, Beirut, December 24, 1973) made clear that the gains of the October War would not result in the abandonment of "our [Arab] historical right to the whole of Palestine—the historical right of the Palestine people to establish the democratic state of Palestine and to liquidate the Zionist entity."

So there we have it. More extreme Palestinian groups, such as George Habash's Popular Front (PFLP), reject even the temporary establishment of a mini-state on the West Bank as a sell-out, while the supposed moderates make no secret of their intention to exploit such a state as "a point of departure," an "arsenal" and a convenient first stage toward the fulfillment of their stated goal. The debates at the Cairo meeting reveal how astutely the protagonists of a temporary mini-state on the West Bank propose to use its establishment to achieve their unflagging purpose. There was no nonsense about genuine peace with Israel. If we recall how effectively the Arab states parleyed the exodus of 600,000 refugees after the Arab attack in 1948 into a major national cause, Israel has good reason to be wary of a tactical maneuver frankly designed to abet Arab long-term strategy for the annihilation of the Jewish state.

In addition, the issue is bedevilled by disputes not only among the PLO, but also among the Arab states. Jordan, for one, opposes a PLO authority on the West Bank and insists that its agreement to the presence of a PLO delegation at the forthcoming Geneva talks is predicated on the assumption that the discussion will center on "the Palestinian people's rights which go beyond the June 5, 1967 lines." Recently (Amman radio, June 12, 1974) Jordan's Premier, Zaid el-Rifai, stated that the Palestine question could not be solved by the establishment of a Palestinian state on the West Bank and Gaza: "If the rights of the Palestinian people are merely the establishment of a Palestinian state on the West Bank and the Gaza Strip, then what did we fight for as an Arab nation in June, 1967?"

While such declarations obviously spring not from Jordanian maximalism, but from an understandable reluctance to surrender to the PLO what Jordan considers its lawful territory, there is no unanimity even among the Arab notables of the West Bank in regard to the desirability of the proposed state. Even declared opponents of Hashemite rule fear that the mini-state would weaken Arab unity. At the other extreme, some Syrian enthusiasts will envision a "greater Syria" which would eventually absorb a "democratic Palestine" plus Jordan, so achieving the dreamed-of unified Arab state without the fragmentation brought about by "artificial" creations such as Israel, Jordan or Lebanon. Iraq and Libya predictably fulminate against a West Bank "statelet" as a retreat from the Arab right to all of Palestine.

On the other hand, Egypt, while somewhat ambiguously conceding Hussein's right to speak for the Palestinians now living in Jordan, supports the political aims of the PLO, adheres to the principle of not returning the West Bank to Jordan, and has reaffirmed its opposition to Hussein's project for a federal union of the West and East Banks. The old rivalries, not ideological but territorial, are in full swing. At the same time, Sadat, judging from the joint communiqué published by Sadat and Hussein on July 18, 1974 appears to seek some accommodation with Jordan.

Amid these cross-currents the Soviet Union is following its usual blunt course. Having lost ground in Egypt, Russia, not content with rearming Syria at a deadly tempo, has seen fit to espouse the Palestinian terrorists more formally and openly than ever before. Arafat has been received in Moscow where he was promised not only the moral support of which he had long been the recipient but sophisticated weapons and other forms of aid "it would not be expedient to specify," according to Palestinian publications. Soviet approval of the PLO program extends to the establishment of a mini-state under the PLO aegis. That such an interim Palestinian state should enjoy Russian support is to be expected. It would provide an ideal base for operations against either Israel or Jordan. More important, such a state, ideologically aligned with Soviet aims in the Middle East, dependent like Syria upon its patron for armaments, could prove a valuable focus for the extension of Russian influence and the Russian presence in the entire region. Above all, such a state, irredentist and "combatant," could be relied on to maintain the local tensions Russia considers useful for its larger purposes. Like the terrorists it supports, Russia, too, embraces a Palestine state on the West Bank primarily as a "point of departure."

Another question mark is the economic viability of a land-locked Palestine state. The area under consideration is less than 6000 square kilometers, some of it desert. Its present population of one million Arabs, if cut off from Israel on the one hand, and Jordan on the other, would lack the agricultural and industrial resources for self-sufficiency, nor could the area possibly absorb Palestinians now living in Jordan, Lebanon, Syria or Egypt should these seek to migrate to the new state. In Jordan alone 600,000 Palestinians dwell as citizens and occupy leading positions in the government.

Without pretending to purely humanitarian concerns Israel would have good reason to be disturbed by the prospect of an enclave of economically depressed Arabs, concentrated on its eastern flank. Such a state would inevitably become the breeding ground for the kind of unrest the PLO vows to foster. The present comparative prosperity of the West Bank is largely due to the employment opportunities provided by Israel. Upwards of 70,000 Arabs from the West Bank and Gaza work in Israel at the higher wage rates there current. How an arrangement for the free entrance of Arab workers into Israel could be continued in the hostile climate promised by Arafat is difficult to visualize. Lacking a viable economy the mini-state would carry within itself the seeds of its own demise and of the perpetuation of the very ills it was supposed to cure, so posing a constant threat to Israel and to the stability of the region—which is precisely what Arafat and his fellows desire.

But arguments against a Palestinian entity on the West Bank do not dispose of the demands of Palestinian nationalism or the requirements for its legitimate expression. The fact that Palestinian, as distinct from Arab, nationalism is a development that post-dates the birth of Israel does not nullify its present reality. Most Israelis understand that the Palestinian movement cannot be exorcised by appeals to logic, history or the admirable statistical evidence which refutes Palestinian accusations. Whatever the genealogy the child is alive and kicking. The question, therefore, is how it can thrive without fatal injury to its neighbors.

Contrary to a popular myth, Israel has come to recognize the new nationalism on its doorstep, not only as a perpetrator of hideous terrorist outrages but also as an exponent of intense national desires. The old Zionist faith that Arab nationalism would be amply gratified in the Arab states established in the territories liberated from the Turks by the Allies, and that the Arabs would not grudge the "small notch" reserved for the Jewish state, has reluctantly given way to the realization that, however inequitable the distribution of lands and resources between Jew and Arab, the Palestinian demand can no longer be ignored. How can it be met without suicidal concessions?

It should be noted that even Israelis most sensitive to the rights and wrongs of the Palestinians, such as Arie Lova Eliav, do not favor the establishment of a ministate. In his much publicized book, *Land of the Hart,* Eliav writes:

> Here it must be stressed that partition as a possible solution of the problem of the Israel and the Palestinian Arabs does not mean dividing Eretz Yisrael [historic Palestine] into more than two states. In other words, I do not have in mind a Palestinian state in the administered areas separate from the state of Jordan; I am speaking of one Arab state which will contain the majority of the Palestinians.

Curiously, the dovish Eliav is not too far removed from the official Israeli position as stated previously by spokesmen of the Meir government, including the supposedly hawkish Mrs. Meir herself, and more recently in pronouncements of the Rabin Cabinet. The consensus in Israel appears to favor a Palestinian-Jordanian state. The form of the state—union or federation—as well as its name would be a matter for the Arabs to determine. Disagreement remains, however, as to how far Israel should withdraw from occupied territory and what safeguards it should demand. The parties of the political Right and of religious orthodoxy stridently insist on the retention of Judaea and Samaria as Israel's historic patrimony; the extreme Left urges total withdrawal to the June 1967 borders. The majority, however, seems to be reconciled to the return of the West Bank with some border rectifications and the retention of control-points on the Jordan River to prevent the passage of Arab military forces across the Jordan. The exact terms of withdrawal would presumably be determined at the Geneva talks, to be then ratified by an Israeli plebiscite so that no element of the population could claim that it had been betrayed by pusillanimous negotiators yielding to Arab threats or American pressure.

Zionist opponents of Israeli withdrawal from the West Bank (Judaea and Samaria) point out that from 1920 to 1946 the territories on both banks of the Jordan River were integral parts of Palestine, and that in 1946 Great Britain arbitrarily established the kingdom of Transjordan (later renamed Jordan) on 80% of the original territory of Palestine. Consequently the partition of Palestine into a Jewish and an Arab state has already taken place, with over three quarters of the land going to the Arabs: Jordan is Arab Palestine. No further truncation of the remainder should be allowed and Israel should not be called on to make further sacrifices of the small area it commands.

It is hard to argue with either the history or justice of this contention. However, one uncomfortable fact is glossed over. Judaea, Samaria plus Gaza have an indigenous Arab population of a million. The historic claim and contemporary demography are here at odds. Furthermore, Israel already has a sizable minority of 400,000 Arab citizens. Those who did not join the Arab exodus in 1948 and their descendants at present constitute over 12% of the population. In view of the high rate of natural increase of Israeli Arabs—one of the highest in the world—and the low Israeli Jewish birth rate, the numerical balance between Arab and Jew may steadily shift in Arab favor. The incorporation of an additional million Arabs into Israel would threaten its identity as a Jewish state, so obliterating the Zionist dream as effectively as an Arab military victory. Nor is there any reason to assume that the West Bank Arabs, despite the economic advantages they now enjoy, would prefer Israel to an accommodation with Hussein. The problems of indefinitely administering a reluctant citizenry would not enhance Israel's moral posture or physical safety.

On the other hand, both demography and geography suggest that the legitimate interests of Palestinian Arabs would best be served through the union or federation of that portion of the West Bank from which Israel withdraws with Jordan. Whatever the nomenclature, there is no blinking the fact that the territory in question is Palestine, and that some 70% of the Palestinian Arabs live on the West and East Banks of the Jordan. (Incidentally, these figures indicate that the overwhelming majority of the Arab refugees, though they fled from native villages, never left their "homeland.") The subsequent political structure of a Palestine-Jordan and the relationship of its constituents to the Hashemite dynasty would be determined by its citizens. Of course, substantial roadblocks lie in the way of such a proposal. Intra-Arab enmities and Great Power ambitions for dominance of the Middle East can be trusted to offer formidable obstacles. But a favorable outcome would at least hold promise of a rational solution to the most acute conflict of the region—that between the Arabs and Israel.

Nothing except a brief and spurious respite, if that, will be achieved by handing over the minuscule area between Israel and Jordan to the PLO. Israel's refusal to negotiate with terrorists whose murderous exploits demonstrate what the perpetrators have in mind for the Jewish state should they gain power and be ensconced on its border is self-explanatory. Certainly peace in the Middle East will not be furthered by carving out another piece of Palestine for an entity whose proponents assure us beforehand that it will be "combatant" and an "arsenal." Prime

Minister Rabin has aptly described such a creation as a "time-bomb." Since time-bombs are designed by their contrivers not to defuse tensions but to explode in disaster, all who accept PLO declarations at face-value are likely to share Israel's reservations. Only an economically viable state, adequate in size and peaceful in intent, can further a just settlement of the Arab-Israel conflict and satisfy the aspirations of Palestinian nationalism within the boundaries of historic Palestine without cannibalizing Israel, as Arafat and his sponsors urge. In the bargaining about to ensue at the Geneva Talks and elsewhere, we must trust that the agile diplomats of the West, particularly the representatives of the United States, though floundering in Arab oil, will not lose sight of what should be a realistic objective even for accomplished practitioners of *Realpolitik:* a stable and equitable peace.

On Israel's East

By David Pryce-Jones

Palestine. Capital, Jerusalem. Population, one million. This state comprising the so-called West Bank formerly incorporated into the Kingdom of Jordan, together with the Gaza Strip, was created in 1975, after resolutions to that effect had been passed unanimously by the delegations attending the Geneva Conference. Principal exports, agricultural products. Official currency . . .

Well, would the Palestinian currency be the Israeli pound or the Jordanian dinar, or both, or the Arafat ruble? Will there be a national airline and a central bank, those prime status symbols of new countries? Will there be members of a parliament meeting perhaps in the Crusader hall of the Haram as-Sharif, a police force, a permanent delegation to the United Nations, ambassadors?

A world that has witnessed such contrivances as the Polish corridor or divided Berlin—not to mention such fresher examples as independent Noumea—may be prepared to believe that a state of Palestine on the West Bank is another proof of human ingenuity in a tight corner. Where there's a will there's a way. And after all the United Nations *did* vote for such a thing in 1947. Since the Six Day War it has become an article of faith among the kind of intellectuals who like to order other people's lives for them that such a state, a whole state, and nothing but such a state, can satisfy the legitimate rights of the Palestinians.

In their view Israel has no claim to the West Bank. Jordan's claim was in the first place gained, and later lost, by force of arms. Properly Palestinians, the West Bankers are being granted no more than the home they possess already. Expressed like this, the idea of some sort of independent Palestinian entity has the advantage of tidiness, which is perhaps why so many professors have committed their names, if not their reputations, to its sponsorship.

Resistance to the proposal is to be found among the Palestinians now living in

209

Jordan who are at least as numerous as those on the West Bank, and constitute more than half of Jordan—Jordan being of course also part of historic Palestine. But in contemporary theory, a national home not in Jordan is the essential prerequisite to a decent life for these people. Perhaps as many as 200,000 of them have a genuine right to be allowed back immediately to the West Bank or to the Gaza Strip, if only to the refugee camps from which they fled so wretchedly in 1967. They could then indeed become citizens of a diminutive Palestine. The majority of the Palestinians in Jordan, though, are either refugees from what has become Israel, or more likely now, their children and grandchildren.

Their hopes still lie with King Hussein who alone among Arab rulers integrated refugees into his country. These Palestinians supported him and not the guerrillas in the civil war of 1970, as they do now. Nor have the guerrillas forgotten that fact, which explains why they no longer go through the motions of recruiting a mass movement, but cast about instead in any foreign capital willing to receive a delegation. Generating power spontaneously is not the same as being handed it on a plate.

The West Bankers themselves might have been expected to show more enthusiasm for becoming masters in their own house. They are in the disagreeably unique position of being able to compare life under a Jordanian military governor to life under an Israeli military governor. The thought occurs that life under a Palestinian military governor appointed by the Palestine Liberation Organization (PLO) will prove no happier. Better the king you know than the commissar you don't.

Critics of the Israelis interject at this point that it has been a deliberate political act on the part of the present occupying authorities to deport from the West Bank any person of consequence who might have led an opposition movement, thus short-sightedly stifling the few progressive elements that are now needed for cooperation. In his time King Hussein had had trouble from the Dr. Dallals and Rushdi Shahins of the Communist party who were among the first to be expelled by the Israelis. To their number has lately been added the mayor of El-Birch, Abdul Jawad Salah, and Dr. Walid Kamhawi (to be appointed, significantly, to the Palestine Liberation Organization National Executive as one of three West Bank representatives) and the lawyer Mohsin Abu Mazer—a clean sweep by the Israelis, in short, of Communists, Socialists and radical Ba'athists of every stripe.

Whether all or some of these men were in league with guerrilla organizations in Beirut, or whether they were agitators or careerists or idealists, is a matter not to be settled without more facts being available. What is beyond dispute is the firmness with which the traditional Palestinian establishment on the West Bank sits in the saddle, thanks partly—but only partly—to the Israelis. Nothing within the West Bank now challenges the position of the old ruling groups, the Tuqan and Abdul Hadi and El-Alami families, the Nusseibehs and Khalidis. Under the British Mandate a certain number of *nouveaux-riches* rose through the bureaucracy or through business, and their social and financial hold has been stabilized as never before.

In the age-old approved manner, notables of this kind have done themselves a good turn while they could, holding onto their civic offices as mayors and profiting from the local economic boom, which has nothing to do with being a quisling or a collaborator. They have always suspected that behind their backs King Hussein and Israel might do a deal, and they would therefore wake up one morning and find that the King was driving in triumph back across the Allenby

Bridge. To try to hunt with the hounds and run with the hare has been brought to a very fine and necessary art on the West Bank. The penalties of making a mistake might be very severe, and indefinitely delayed, which is just as bad. The practical effect is that no popular basis for asserting national rights exists. Leadership, personal initiative, the qualities that might allow a sudden development of public life, are lacking.

I have been present on more than one occasion when Sheik Ali Ja'abari, mayor of Hebron, and the leading local despot with the superb style of a storybook Islamic grandee, has been asked if he favors a Palestinian entity of any sort on the West Bank. His usual answer is obscure and couched in metaphors, but his long, hooded stare expresses an amazement that Allah in His wisdom permits so many pestering fools to come to Hebron. And how much more true is this in Gaza, where there is no public life at all, not so much as a marketing cooperative or a football team, nothing between the leading families and the potentially explosive mob in the *souks* or the camps.

Whoever is to rule on the West Bank has to come to terms with the dignitaries, with Sheik Ali Ja'abari and his kind, including his son-in-law Anwar Khattib, once governor of Jerusalem and still King Hussein's representative there. It may be argued that *force majeure* at Geneva will oblige King Hussein to drop those who have remained loyal to him. By the same token the Israelis may be pressured into more disengagement, to use the euphemism for pulling out. In which case we shall see a power struggle directly between the conservative establishment actually on the West Bank and the scarcely more representative PLO that will at last be rushing in for the available spoils, or if diplomatic language is to be observed, for their legitimate rights.

Put to this horrible test, the old ruling classes might vanish. Perhaps nobody would be persuaded to take up the struggle on their behalf, and they themselves might simply prefer to seek shelter in the comfortable villas of Lebanon, which the PLO leaders would have just vacated. If Yasser Arafat and the PLO were to succeed in eliminating this opposition on their right, they would still have to deal with the hardier ideologists on their left, the Popular Front of George Habash, and the splinter groups under Nayef Hawatmeh and Ahmed Jebril. Since these rivals already shoot each other over possession of landrovers and sentry posts in Beirut, how much further will they go when the entire West Bank and Gaza is at stake?

Before formal talks have begun, the Israeli government has made clear it will not be prepared to withdraw at all if the West Bank is to become a base for two-way irredenta, against Jordan and Israel alike. One state and one state only is to be countenanced to the east of Israel, and it is referred to as Jordanian-Palestinian, a convenient shorthand. The Arabs may work the meaning of that out for themselves, so long as fighting on the score takes place a good way off. However vague, this solution at least does not perpetuate the artificial division of the Palestinian Arabs in two countries over both sides of the Jordan River. American policy apparently is in agreement, for the time being at any rate.

No other solution takes account of the security of Israel and Jordan. In the last resort a Palestinian state on the West Bank, a little nut between two light crackers, would, moreover, be a standing temptation to outside interference. The divergent interests of the main separate blocs of Palestinians—the PLO, the West Bankers and the East Bankers—are too easily played off against one another in the classic ploys of divide-and-rule.

Suppose for a moment that the fantasy of the opening paragraph has come true and Palestinians *are* ruling in Jerusalem. If this administration consists exclusively of West Bankers, then the PLO will use all available methods to overthrow it. Terrorism has led both Israel and Jordan in the past to resort to arms. Neither country wants to have a permanent police problem with the Palestinian organization, any more than the disgruntled Lebanese do. An external government alone can give the PLO the requisite leverage in arms and finance to move it toward its aims. This means Russia.

Until lately the main Palestinian organizations had shown skill at avoiding subordination to Russia, and the Russians had seen larger fish in the sea. Dr. Kissinger's extraordinary successes in Egypt and Syria have more than ever isolated Palestinian extremists. They have virtually no expectations from Arab backers; they have nowhere to turn but inward against themselves, or to Moscow, whose larger fish are in other waters. If the Russians and the PLO together go for their version of Palestinian statehood, then nothing will be salvaged at Geneva, and ordinary Palestinians will be helpless to help themselves, as usual.

Israel and The Palestinian Question

By Terence Prittie

In its present form, that of a burgeoning national movement, the Palestinian Question is of recent origin. There are several reasons for this:

1. There has never, in the whole history of the area known today as Palestine, been a Palestinian Arab state. Palestine, between the river Jordan and the Mediterranean, has been ruled, since the Arab invasion in the seventh century, by Bedouin, Christian Crusaders, Mamelukes, Turks, and finally, from 1919 to 1948, by the British. The area has generally been an outlying province, as during the four and a half centuries of Turkish rule which preceded the British Mandate. Historical Palestine included an area east of the river Jordan, which has been part of the Emirate, and later Kingdom of Jordan, since 1921. It could be argued that this is the only Palestinian Arab "state" which has ever existed.

2. Because there has never been any other Palestinian state, there has not until very recently been a well-defined Palestinian national identity. The Palestinians can hardly be blamed for this; they have been subjected to continual invasion and alien rule. In addition, they were a very small community, probably less than 600,000 in all, up to the time of the British Mandate. The area in which they lived was conventionally regarded by other Arabs as "southern Syria".

3. The principal failure of the Palestinian Arabs to create a well-developed sense of national identity occurred during the period of the British Mandate. The Jewish community established its own institutions and its own instinct for nationhood during this period. The Palestinian Arabs did not, although they roughly doubled in numbers—thanks to Jewish immigration and increased material prosperity under British rule.

213

4. The 1947 United Nations Partition Plan gave the Palestinian Arabs a state of their own. Not only did they reject the U.N. Plan, but after joining in a war waged against Israel by the armies of five outside Arab countries, they made no attempt to set up a state of their own when the fighting ended. The Arabs of the West Bank accepted occupation and annexation by the Kingdom of Jordan, while the Arabs of the Gaza Strip were placed under Egyptian military occupation. Significantly, it is precisely in these areas that it is now proposed to set up a Palestinian "mini-state".

5. Between 1949, when armistice agreements were signed between Israel and her Arab neighbors, and 1967, when the West Bank and the Gaza Strip fell into Israeli hands, neither Jordan nor Egypt made any serious attempt to encourage a Palestinian national identity or to give the Palestinians even the kernel of a state of their own. Not a word was said about the Palestinian right of self-determination, save in so far as it concerned the right claimed by Palestinian refugees to return to their old homes.

6. The existing Arab states, equally, have made no serious attempt to set up or sponsor a Palestinian government-in-exile. This could have been done at any time after 1949, and it could have developed a political philosophy and an understanding of governmental aims, methods and institutions.

To sum up, one can say that the Palestinians showed little ability to evolve a full and normal national consciousness, and the outside Arab world showed singularly little interest in them and no desire to give them the help and advice which they needed so badly. This failure of the Arab world to look after "its own" had nothing to do whatever with the Israelis. It was a projection of the previous history of the Palestinians within the Arab world, and of a basic lack of Arab unity.

Israel and the Palestinian Arabs

It has become conventional to accuse Israel of being the sole instigator of the injustices inflicted on the Palestinian Arabs, although they had lived for long centuries as a chronically neglected and periodically oppressed community in a part of the world where there was generally only a small Jewish minority. Jews and Palestinian Arabs, indeed, were co-sufferers in an area which was allowed to remain poor and backward and with no status of its own.

It has become conventional, again, to blame Britain and the 1917 Balfour Declaration for the Jewish-Arab dispute and the resulting sufferings of the Palestinian Arabs. In fact, the Balfour Declaration provided for the creation of a Jewish "National Home", on a basis of internal autonomy and free immigration, and not for a Jewish state. It provided, too, that "nothing shall be done which may prejudice the civil and religious rights of existing non-Jewish communities in Palestine". It has been constantly asserted that the two parts of the Declaration were mutually incompatible. This need not have been the case; Britain was prepared to safeguard the *civil* and *religious* rights of the Palestinian Arabs. Given cooperation between the Jewish and Arab communities, this was in no way impossible. Instead of cooperation, the Jewish community in Mandatory Palestine was confronted by a series of negative developments:

• Whereas the Jewish community sought to live in peace in the area, Palestinian extremism, as exemplified by the Grand Mufti of Jerusalem and his followers, resulted in attacks on Jewish settlements, riots and murders. These occurred in particular in 1922, 1923, 1929, 1933 and from 1936 onwards.

• When the Arab refusal to live in peace with the Jewish community had become irrevocable, different plans to partition the area were at once and totally rejected by the Arab side (thus the "Peel Plan" of 1937).

• The U.N. Partition Plan of 1947 was the signal for the organization of irregular warfare directed against the Jewish community by the Palestinian Arabs, and for the declaration by the eight states of the Arab League of a program for the occupation of the whole of Palestine by their armies and the prevention by force of the creation of a Jewish state.

• The termination of the British Mandate in May 1948 brought the invasion of Israel by Arab armies, and out of this war and the earlier hostilities was born the Palestinian refugee problem—comprising at the outset between 550,000 and 600,000 Palestinians who fled or were driven from their homes.

• The refugee problem has been treated as evidence of Israeli hard-heartedness towards the Palestinians, even of an alleged "campaign of genocide" against them. U.N. resolutions, however, which have called for the repatriation of Palestinian refugees, have at the same time laid down that they should be prepared to live in peace with the inhabitants of the state of Israel, within the framework of an overall peace settlement. From 1949 to the present day Israel was denied a peace settlement and, up to the end of 1973, any prospect of peace talks of any kind.

• Palestinian refugee claims were maintained to the full by Israel's Arab enemies, and "refugee status" was extended to the children, grandchildren and even great-grandchildren of original refugees. Thus a mistily all-embracing "refugee community" of between one and a half and two million Palestinians has been created, extending over the whole Arab world and even outside it, including several hundred thousand people still in refugee camps but countless others who have been fully integrated into the economies of "host" countries. The sufferings of the weaker members of this "greater Palestinian" refugee community are very real. They could have been alleviated, or even eliminated.

Israel, it has been argued, could at least have done much more than she has done to have helped over this. The facts about what she did either propose or do have been stated often enough before:

1. Israel allowed the immediate repatriation of Palestinians, who had fled from their homes but decided to return of their own accord. They probably comprised nearly half of the 150,000 Palestinian Arabs left in Israel early in 1949. Many more could have returned.

2. Israel offered to make the refugee question the first item on the agenda in negotiations for a peace settlement. The Arab states, however, flatly refused to negotiate and declared themselves to be in a state of permanent war with Israel.

3. In 1950 Israel offered to repatriate 100,000 Palestinians as an integral part of a peace settlement. The offer was rejected at once.

4. Israel repeatedly expressed willingness to negotiate the compensation of refugees who did not return to their homes. Such offers were ignored.

5. In 1953 Israel approved, but the Arab states rejected, the American plan for the utilization of the headwaters of the Jordan. One of its primary aims was the resettlement of nearly a quarter of a million Palestinian refugees.

6. As her own, automatic contribution to the Palestinian community, Israel raised the living standards of the Arabs living within her borders and gradually restored their full civil and political rights. In a quarter of a century of Israeli rule, the Arab community has increased from 150,000 to 400,000 and become the most prosperous such community outside one or two of the immensely rich oil-sheikdoms.

A second main accusation against Israel has been that, by refusing to allow the further repatriation of Palestinian Arabs after 1949, she deliberately contravened U.N. resolutions on the subject. The operative U.N. resolutions, however, all laid down that Palestinians whose right to return to their homes was implemented should be prepared to live in peace there with their Israeli neighbors. With some justice, Israelis point out that their Arab neighbors engineered a situation which made it unlikely, or even impossible for Palestinians to carry out this condition. The permanent state of war maintained against Israel was reinforced by a total blockade of her frontiers and by an economic boycott which sought to disrupt Israel's trading relations with countries outside the Middle East. Israeli ships were prevented from using the international waterway of the Suez Canal and a maritime blockade was imposed on Israel's Red Sea coast. By 1951 organized guerrilla warfare was being waged against Israel, and up to the end of 1956 there were 11,650 armed clashes with the Palestinian and mercenary "fedayeen" bands which attacked Israeli settlements and killed 434 people, most of them non-combatants. Fedayeen raids were a principal cause of the 1956 war between Israel and Egypt, and it is highly significant that Egypt thereafter never again allowed Palestinian guerrillas to raid out of her territory into Israel.

Under all these circumstances, Israel felt amply justified in taking no further steps on her own to solve the Palestinian refugee problem. In addition, she had a refugee problem of her own, of relatively far greater proportions than those of neighboring Arab states with their quotas of Palestinian refugees. During the two decades following the birth of the State of Israel, around three quarters of a million Jews left their homes in Arab countries, partly as a result of intermittent and often bitter persecution, partly because they were treated traditionally as second-class citizens, and partly because of increased hostility arising from the Middle East dispute. Whereas Arab countries, largely for political reasons, generally resettled only a proportion of their quotas of Palestinian refugees, Israel sought to integrate all Jews arriving from Arab countries. Three things should be said about this:

1. The three quarters of a million refugees from Arab countries all arrived virtually penniless. Their land, goods and property were taken from them.

2. By the early 1970's these refugees, with their children, constituted more than half the total population of Israel. Their absorption was an immensely greater task than that faced by any Arab country.

3. It is conventionally supposed that, after Israel's ready acceptance of this huge influx of refugees from Arab countries, that was the end of the matter—Israel is always expected to work miracles. In reality, the influx landed Israel with by far her biggest, and still persisting social problem. The great majority of the immigrants from Arab countries were under-educated and had been under-privileged; they automatically became the more backward half of the community. They cannot be enabled to "catch up" in a single generation, probably not in under fifty years.

Bitterness is increased by the treatment of the Jewish minorities in Arab countries—which has been in stark contrast to the treatment of the Arab minority in Israel. The sufferings of these Jewish minorities continue to be a factor in Israeli-Arab relations.

The Growth of Palestinian Nationalism

Just as it has been popularly supposed that there has been only one Middle East refugee problem, that of the Palestinian Arabs, so the belief has grown up that Palestinian nationalism grew contemporaneously with Jewish-Zionist nationalism, or even pre-dated it. This was not the case. The Zionist philosophy of a mass return to Palestine, to reinforce the Jewish community which had maintained a continuous presence there throughout history, was born in the middle of the last century. The spontaneous return of Jews to what they regarded as their historical home was well under way before the Balfour Declaration of 1917. By 1948 the Jews of Palestine had fully prepared themselves for the statehood granted them under the U.N. Partition Plan.

In contrast to all this, the following points should be noted about Palestinian nationalism, or the lack of it:

• Since no Palestinian Arab state had ever existed in history, the Arab world regarded Palestine as "southern Syria"—a phrase still in use even after the Second World War. This made it difficult for Palestinians to develop a sense of national identity.

• In the First World War, when the Jews of Palestine threw in their lot with Britain, joining the British Army and establishing an intelligence network behind the Turkish lines, the Palestinian Arabs did not lift a finger to win their independence from Turkish overlordship; they were freed from it solely by Britain.

• Under the British Mandate, as already mentioned, the Palestinians did not protest when the eastern half of their "patrimony" was detached by Britain's unilateral action in setting up an independent Emirate of Transjordan in 1921.

• Although comparatively few Palestinians sold their land to Jewish settlers, the Palestinians did not "own the land" of the country. Arab propagandists maintain that they owned 95% of it. In reality, 70% of the land in what became Israel had been the property of the Turkish Government and passed to the British Mandatory Power. This land would automatically have been vested in the Jewish and Arab states foreseen under the terms of the U.N. Partition Plan.

• In 1947, the Palestinian Arabs refused to accept the state offered to them under the U.N. Partition Plan. This may have been understandable, since they considered the plan unfair. More significant, perhaps, is that they made no protest when the West Bank was occupied by Jordan and the Gaza Strip by Egypt, so destroying the chance of setting up any Palestinian state whatever. One should recall that the Jordanian occupation of the West Bank was condemned by virtually the whole world, including the Arab League states, and was initially recognized by only Britain and Pakistan.

Admittedly, leading Palestinians refused to recognize the State of Israel, since this would have meant the end of their claim to the whole area of Palestine. But for the best part of two decades after the 1948 war the Palestinians failed to make any attempt to establish a "government in exile" of any kind—which would have been, far more, a shadow government on Palestinian soil. For, including Transjordan, four-fifths of the area originally designated as the British Mandate of Palestine lay outside Israel's borders and remained in Arab hands.

Some Israelis have concluded that a Palestinian identity had to be synthetically created, as an answer to and accusation against the intensely self-aware, self-reliant State of Israel. Palestinian nationalism was in some degree a reflex action triggered by the Jewish example in successful self-determination. But the contention that the Palestinian Arabs would in any event have won their way to independence at some future date is of doubtful validity. A Palestinian people which had shown so little volition could have fallen an easy prey to Arab neighbor-states. Paradoxically, it has been the success of Israel as an independent state which has fired the Palestinian imagination.

Much quoted by friends of the Palestinian cause has been a passage from a book, *Return Ticket,* by Nasir an Nashashibi. It reads:

"Every year I shall say to my little son: We shall return my son, and you will be with me. We shall return to our land and walk there barefoot. We shall remove our shoes so that we may feel the holiness of the ground beneath us. We shall blend our souls with its air and earth. We shall walk until we come to the orange trees . . . feel the sand and water . . . kiss seed and fruit. We shall sleep in the shade of the first tree that we meet; pay homage to the first martyr's grave that we come across.

"We shall turn here and there to trace our lives. Where are they? Here with this village square, with this mosque's minaret, with the beloved field, the desolate wall, with the remains of a tottering fence and a building whose traces have been erased. Here are our lives. Each grain of sand teaches us about our life. Do you not remember Jaffa with its delightful shore, Haifa and its lofty mountain, Beth Shean and the fields of crops and fruit, Nazareth and the Christians' bells, Acre and the memories of Al-Jazzar, Ibrahim Pasha, Napoleon and the fortress, the streets of Jerusalem, my dear Jerusalem, Tiberias and its peaceful shore with the golden waves, Majdal and the remnants of my kin in its land?"

This is a passage full of evocative charm. It deserves to be quoted. But equally worth reading is what Nashashibi writes on the very next page of his book, describing the effect of his words on his "little son":

"I shall see the hatred in the eyes of my son and your sons. I shall see how they take revenge. If they do not know how to take revenge, I shall teach them. And if they agree to a truce or peace, I shall fight against them as I fight against my enemy and theirs. I want them to be callous, to be ruthless, to take revenge. I want them to wash away the disaster of 1948 with the blood of those who prevent them from entering their land. Their homeland is dear to them, but revenge is dearer. We'll enter their lairs in Tel Aviv. We'll smash Tel Aviv with axes, guns, hands, fingernails and teeth. . . . We shall sing the hymns of the triumphant, avenging return."

This passage is never quoted by friends of the Palestinians.

Perhaps the first operative step toward creating it was the formulation, at the First Palestinian Congress in 1964, of a "Palestinian National Covenant," revised and reissued by the Palestine National Council in Cairo in July 1968. The basic thesis of the Covenant was the destruction of the State of Israel, and the creation, in its place and in the rest of Palestine west of the river Jordan, of a "secular, bi-national, democratic" state of Palestine. Since 1968, the Covenant has neither been revoked nor revised—although some Arab spokesmen have hinted that it could be quietly shelved. Key clauses of the Covenant include:

1. Article 2 lays down that Palestine's boundaries should be those "which existed at the time of the British Mandate." Whether or not this implies inclusion of what became Transjordan, it clearly means the inclusion of all of Israel in the Palestinian state.

2. Article 5 provides that Palestinians, who alone have an inalienable right to live in the state of Palestine, are Arab citizens who were living in the area until 1947, and their descendants.

3. According to Article 6 only those Jews who were living permanently in Palestine "until the beginning of the Zionist invasion" can be considered Palesti-

nians, with a consequent right to live there today. The Palestine National Council has defined the "Zionist invasion", as taking place in 1917. This means that perhaps over 80% of the present population of Israel would not qualify for Palestinian citizenship.

4. Article 9 lays down that "Armed struggle is the only way to liberate Palestine"—which is hardly encouraging for all those protagonists of the Palestinians who urge the Israelis to negotiate with them.

5. The same can be said of Article 15, which establishes it as a "national duty" to "purge the Zionist presence from Palestine."

6. Articles 19 and 20 declare the Balfour Declaration, British Mandatory enactments, and the U.N. partition of Palestine all to be null and void.

7. Article 21 is of particular relevance today. It states: "The Palestinian Arab People, in expressing itself through the armed Palestinian Revolution, rejects every solution that is a substitute for a complete liberation of Palestine, and rejects all plans that aim at a settlement of the Palestinian issue or its internationalization." This clause effectively takes care of U.N. Resolution 242 and all other U.N. pronouncements favoring a negotiated settlement of the Middle East dispute.

8. The final Article 33 provides that the Covenant cannot be amended save by a two-thirds majority of all members of the Palestine Liberation Organization, meeting in special session for this purpose. A subsequent interpretation of the Covenant, published in the "Middle East International" of May 1974, states that "All Palestinians, no matter what their political beliefs, belong to the P.L.O."—surely the most striking arrogation in history of power by a single, non-elected and utterly unrepresentative "liberation organization."

The 1968 Covenant has not been amended. Indeed, from 1968 onwards there have been repeated statements confirming its basic aim, the "continuation of the struggle for the liberation of the entire territory of the Palestinian homeland and the setting up of the Palestinian democratic society." A "tacit" amendment of the Covenant—for instance, by re-defining aims which might be short-term rather than fundamental—is ruled out by Article 33. For no Palestine National Congress or Council has been summoned with the express purpose of amending the Covenant.

The claim of the P.L.O. to represent the whole Palestinian people rests, in the first place, on its creation in 1964 and the part which it played in drawing up the Covenant in its earliest form. Its "fighting arm," the "el Fatah," was formed in the same year and began active operations against Israel in January 1965—although the Fatah remained nominally independent of the P.L.O. By 1971 the P.L.O. was "accredited" to most Arab governments and it had begun to open offices in the outside world, at the U.N., Peking, East Berlin, Santiago, Paris, Geneva, Belgrade, Rome, Hanoi, New Delhi. The question whether there was or was not a P.L.O. office in London was debatable; P.L.O. publications claimed that it existed.

By 1973 the P.L.O. had taken a very important step. It had already been recognized at the Arab "Summit" in Algiers as the "sole legitimate representative of the Palestinian people." The P.L.O. proceeded to give concrete force to this recognition by appointing an Executive Committee of eight, which included representatives not only of the Fatah but of other main "activist" groups ostensibly totally independent of the Fatah and of one another. These included the Syrian-based "Saiqa," the leftwing terrorist Popular and Popular Democratic Fronts for the Liberation of Palestine, and the even more militant "General

Command" of the Popular Front. The P.L.O. pattern has now been extended to the Palestine National Council; its 14-man executive likewise represents all activist groups of importance. Activists, with a high proportion of terrorist leaders who are committed to the destruction of long-established Arab regimes, dominate the General Assembly of the National Council, which has 150 members and which purports to be representative of the Arabs of Jordan, the West Bank and Gaza, as well as the military-organized terrorists in Syria and the Lebanon.

A Footnote on Palestinian Terror

Israel is today confronted by a Palestinian nationalist movement which is spearheaded by the P.L.O., in turn the self-admitted representative of Palestinian terrorism. Much has already been written about Palestinian terrorism, and these are only its salient features:

• Since 1965 terrorist attacks on Israel have been directed essentially against the civilian population, and increasingly, against women and children. In this year's peculiarly brutal raids, schools were deliberately selected as targets.

• Equally deliberately, the Palestinian terrorists have placed their headquarters in refugee camps in Lebanon and Syria. Their reasoning has been sound; the Israelis could hesitate to attack targets when innocent civilians might be killed, but better still, should the Israelis attack and kill civilians, this could escalate the conflict.

• Terrorism, again, has been directed against the non-combatants of countries outside the Middle East. Here, too, is a dual purpose; the people of these countries, sickened by slaughter, might lose patience with Israel as the object of controversy, and the support of other terrorist revolutionaries could be enlisted.

• Terrorist leaders like George Habash (PFLP) and Nayef Hawatmeh (PDFLP) readily admit that their underlying aim is to destroy established society in the Middle East—groups like theirs played a key role in bringing the Fatah and other so called "moderates" into open conflict with King Hussein's regime in Jordan in 1970. Habash and Hawatmeh are ready to make allies of subversive forces in all parts of the world, in order to destroy the western way of life and substitute a new "revolutionary-Maoist" world-order in its place.

• Increasingly dominant in the P.L.O. are "professional revolutionaries" who have a vested interest in terrorism. It gives them a living and is at the same time their way of life. Any compromise peace settlement with Israel is, of course, totally unacceptable to them. Even the creation of the "secular, bi-national, democratic" Palestinian state would only be a means to an end, that of fomenting revolution throughout the Middle East and spreading it, like a forest fire, to every corner of the globe. They have no other occupation than revolutionary violence.

• Palestinian terrorism, finally, is not wanted in Arab countries, which support it in order to keep its attentions focussed on Israel. This is why terrorist organizations can site their headquarters in Beirut, why Syria, Egypt and other Arab states have supplied arms and instructors, why "reactionary" regimes like those of Saudi Arabia and the far-off Gulf Sheikdoms have subscribed huge sums of money. Palestinian terrorism is kept alive by Arabs who cannot afford to have it as an enemy but are far indeed from being its friends.

The fact that the P.L.O. is now the ostensible leader of the Palestinian nationalist movement, and that revolutionary terrorists are firmly entrenched within the P.L.O., is a main contributory factor toward Israel's quandary over the "Palestinian Question." Israelis, and their governments, have always believed that an "atmosphere of peace" needs to be created in the Middle East, if there is ever to be the full, final and lasting settlement which the area needs so badly. Obviously, one way of helping to create such an "atmosphere of peace" would be to end the state of incipient or chronic warfare and tension on Israel's borders. Since the "Yom Kippur War" of October 1973, disengagement agreements between Israel on the one hand, and Egypt and Syria on the other, have at least relaxed tension to some extent and made it possible for both sides to contemplate peace negotiations—without feeling the need to strike a more powerful military blow, or counter-stroke, than the other side. These arrangements, admittedly of a temporary nature, have covered two out of Israel's four common frontiers with neighboring Arab states. The third, with Lebanon, has been kept in a state of ferment by the Fatah. Yet this frontier has assumed an air of permanency. Israeli raids across it, intended to destroy terrorist bases and drive the terrorists away from the frontier itself, have never been followed up by an Israeli occupation of Lebanese territory—although the southern Lebanon would be a valuable prize for Israel. It includes the Litani River, with twice the flow of the Jordan. Israel needs more water, and will need it increasingly.

Israel's fourth common frontier is with Jordan; it is by far her longest. For two decades Jordan has been ruled by King Hussein, whose remarkable courage and virtuosity have compensated for his kingdom's lack of material wealth and power. There have been a dozen attempts on King Hussein's life, all by Arabs, and at least three major efforts to overthrow his régime by armed force. In 1970-71 King Hussein had to fight a bloody war against the Palestinian terrorists. Today, he is acutely aware of the fact that all revolutionary elements within the Palestinian national movement earnestly desire the destruction of himself, his state and the way of life which has been created in it. All this is recognized by Israel.

Israel and the Kingdom of Jordan

Critics of Israel who have advocated a policy of Israeli-Palestinian rapprochement have failed to take the very real and continuing existence of the Kingdom of Jordan into account. In spite of the experience of the last twenty years, it has been assumed that the Palestinians are now the "people that matter" in the area and that Israel would be well-advised to do business with them. For Israel, however, the following considerations are important:

1. King Hussein's personal powers of survival are as great as ever. His younger brother, Hassan Talal, is equally tough and resolute, a fact which may have much to do with the tailing-off of Arab attempts to murder the King. Because of the singular endurance of the Hashemite family, the Kingdom of Jordan cannot simply be written off.

2. King Hussein has displayed qualities of statesmanship and political moderation which place him apart from the rulers of other Arab states in the area. He has made Palestinian refugees citizens of his country. He has condemned bestial acts of Arab terrorism. He has subscribed to the policy of "open bridges" across the river Jordan, which has made a degree of economic and social normalization possible in Palestine's heartland. Apart from allowing himself to be dragged into the 1967 war, he has avoided direct conflict with Israel. He has advocated the settlement of the Middle East dispute by peaceful means. He has remained the friend of the western world.

3. He has created, long ago, the nucleus of a mainly Palestinian state. Before the Second World War, Transjordan—as it then was—had a population of between

300,000 and 400,000, a third of it nomadic. In 1948 the West Bank was annexed during the course of the war against the infant state of Israel, and Jordan's population was increased to 1,200,000. In 1967 it was about two million, including a substantial majority of the Palestinian people. Inevitably, a measure of "Palestinization" has taken place in Jordan. Thus, in mid-1974 twelve out of twenty Jordanian Ministers were Palestinians; so were seven out of twelve Jordanian delegates to the preliminary Geneva peace talks in December 1973. From all of this, it is easy to understand the Israeli predilection for regarding Jordan as already being "the Palestinian state".

4. King Hussein has produced what, up to the present, emerges as the most feasible plan for creating a Palestinian "entity". In March 1972 he proposed giving the Palestinians of the West Bank autonomy, following its reunion with Jordan, with only defense and foreign policy continuing to be determined by his government in Amman. The Gaza Strip, with its 400,000 Palestinian inhabitants, could be linked with the West Bank, and democratic government could be introduced into this potential tripartite Jordanian "federation". Only the timing of King Hussein's announcement was unfortunate; it immediately preceded the holding of municipal elections, under Israeli aegis, on the West Bank. Israel's Prime Minister, Mrs. Meir, believed that this had been done in order to sabotage these elections, and her initial reaction to the "Hussein Plan" was negative.

5. To Israel, the views of the U.S. administration are of the utmost significance and, up to the time of writing, it has shown a very clear preference for dealing with Jordan rather than with a Palestinian national movement lacking a broadly-based and truly representative leadership. American thinking is purely pragmatic; there is a state of Jordan in being, it contained the majority of Palestinians, and it has shown a genuine readiness to negotiate, albeit toughly. It is, again, axiomatic that the Soviet Union—intent on having a finger in the Middle East pie—has readily supported the idea of a "mini-Palestine" consisting of the West Bank and Gaza, which it wants to link up with revolutionary "liberation" movements, especially in the area of the Persian Gulf. This support of a mini-Palestine is the very opposite of a recommendation for it, for Soviet policies in the Middle East have been persistently mischievous or dangerous.

King Hussein has had a very difficult diplomatic role to play. He has had to demonstrate a degree of solidarity with other Arab states, although two of them—Syria and Egypt—have been intimately concerned with efforts to overthrow his régime. He has had to try, from a distance, to stimulate support for the Kingdom of Jordan among the people of the West Bank—hence his discreet measures, announced in July of this year, to reestablish administrative and governmental connections with that area. He has had, at least superficially, to come to terms with Palestinian nationalism. In his interview with the American journal "Newsweek", published on June 17, 1974, he made it plain that Jordan alone was in a position to negotiate the return of the West Bank by Israel. This was a logical first step, and the second would be the decision of the Palestinian people where they belonged—in his Kingdom, in a federal state, or as a separate entity. He gave it as his opinion that a mini-Palestine was not viable, and he added: "Since we all belong to one family, I am sure we will all come together again on a much better basis than existed before the 1967 war." As for the P.L.O., "We cannot ignore 24 years of unity and tell half our people that the P.L.O. will now represent them. The P.L.O. has a representative role to play, but they are not alone."

Hussein even held out some hope of a compromise over Jerusalem. He told "Newsweek" that he did "not visualize a return to the conditions that existed before the June 1967 war". From 1948 to 1967 the city of Jerusalem was divided, by a miniature Berlin Wall, and all access to Jewish Holy Places in East Jerusalem was denied to the Israelis. Jerusalem, according to the King, should become a "city of peace", and Arab sovereignty should be restored to the "Arab part of the city" This, at least, was a much more hopeful formulation than that of the P.L.O., which demands a new division of Jerusalem as an interim measure and its eventual reunification under Palestinian jurisdiction.

Israel and the Palestinians

It is clear that Israel can visualize a peace settlement with Jordan, based on territorial compromise, providing that the question of Jerusalem can be solved. What, then, of the chances of an accommodation with the Palestinians?

There is no unified Israeli view about the desirability of negotiating with the Palestinians. Among young Israelis and leaders in the intellectual world, there is an increasingly strong feeling that the Palestinians cannot be left out of the picture—because they have suffered most from the Middle East dispute and because they "belong" in the area, in the fullest sense of the word. Official Israeli thinking, of course, is more concerned with practical possibilities and with the popular fallacies about the Palestinians, particularly the following:

• "The Palestinians are a nation of refugees."

In fact, the U.N. relief organization issues about 1.6 million ration-cards, but only about half a million Palestinians are still in refugee camps. Is a Palestinian still a refugee, when he has a home, a job and, quite possibly, citizenship in an Arab country?

• "The Palestinians were driven out of their country."

According to the P.L.O. Research Center in Beirut, there are something over three million Palestinians in the world. Of these, 2.4 million live either in Jordan or in that part of Palestine occupied at present by Israel; they live, in fact, in what has historically been Palestine. Of the remainder, over 400,000 live in Syria or Lebanon, on the borders of Palestine. Although the Palestinians have suffered injustices, they are mostly living among their own kith and kin.

• "The only representatives of the Palestinian people are the P.L.O."

The P.L.O. leadership has never been democratically elected and has no links with the great majority of Palestinians. It consists of members of terrorist groups which have shown themselves to be the enemies of ordered society. A West Bank leader like Sheik Ja'abari, the Mayor of Hebron, has stressed that if the P.L.O. is to send "observers" to peace talks in Geneva, the people of the West Bank and Gaza should be entitled to choose their own delegates.

• "The P.L.O. are desperate men who fight on because there is no alternative."

It is arguable that they are, instead, an "establishment" with a material interest in perpetuating itself.

• "P.L.O. policies are accepted by the masses of the Palestinian people."

The one million Palestinians living under Israeli military administration and the 400,000 Arabs of "Israel proper" have shown no desire to espouse the P.L.O. creed of violence or take any part in the P.L.O. campaign of armed conflict with Israel. During the 1967 and 1973 wars they remained absolutely quiet—as one Israeli spokesman put it "If they had even spat at us, it would have made us think." The Palestinians of Jordan have remained equally uninterested in the P.L.O.

• "The P.L.O. are moderates, ready to accept a compromise peace."

The informed Israeli view is that there are only two trends of thought within the P.L.O. The first favors the immediate destruction of Israel, the second is prepared to contemplate its destruction by stages. There is no difference of opinion about basic aims, but only about tactics in attaining them.

• "The Palestinians are utterly distinct from the Jordanians, and so require a separate existence."

Once again, one must point out that two-thirds of the Palestinians were either born as Jordanian citizens or were given Jordanian citizenship. Today, less than one-third of the population of even Jordan east of the river Jordan are Bedouin, who might claim to be non-Palestinian.

From these considerations a clear-cut line of official thought has emerged in Israel. A mini-Palestine, consisting of the West Bank (or most of it) and the Gaza Strip, is too small to form a completely independent entity. Lacking natural resources and an industrial infrastructure, it would—on its own—be economically unviable. Unless it maintained the economic links established with Israel since 1967, the area would experience a sharp economic decline—for 70,000 Palestinians, representing perhaps 250,000 in all, work in Israel today and earn three or four times as much as they could before 1967. More important the "wild men" of the P.L.O. would move into the new mini-state and take it over. They have the organization and the brute force to do so. They would launch guerrilla warfare across Israel's borders, and maintain it indefinitely. The upshot would be a chronic state of instability, in which the terrorists in control of the mini-state would seek to provoke Israeli reprisal raids, escalate the conflict and force Jordan, Egypt and Syria into a new war with Israel.

The Government of Israel has not dreamt up thoughts like these; on the contrary, they seem the likely and logical consequences of creating an unviable state which would fall an easy prey to Palestinian extremists. It follows that Israel's leaders must remain acutely skeptical about negotiating with people committed to the obliteration, by force or diplomacy, of the State of Israel.

What the Palestinian Activists Say about Themselves

A ray of hope was decried early in April, when the London representative of the P.L.O., Mr. Said Hammami, told the "Jewish Chronicle" that his organization was now prepared to settle for a small Palestinian state which would "draw out the poison between us." Such a state would be entirely independent of Jordan, for "Jordan committed a crime against the Palestinians" and "We don't trust Hussein." The creation of the Palestinian state could be discussed in face-to-face talks with the Israelis, and it would mean that "terrorism would come to an end".

Hammami's statement was greeted by sections of the British and international press as a big step forward, as it suggested that the P.L.O. now limited its aims to what could be attainable. Very little notice, however, was paid to the reaction of P.L.O. headquarters in Beirut, which at once stated that Hammami's remarks "do not reflect P.L.O. views," adding that "The strategic aim sought by the P.L.O. is the establishment of a democratic Palestinian state on all Palestinian territory, where Muslims, Christians and Jews can coexist in equality, justice and brotherhood." Hammami, doubtless under orders from Beirut, claimed that he had been misquoted by the "Jewish Chronicle." Significantly, he denied that Arafat, titular head of both the P.L.O. and the Fatah, had said that he was "prepared to live in harmony with the State of Israel." So much for the possibility of what a "Guardian" editorial called "A dialogue worth pursuing".

A second ray of hope was equally quickly extinguished. On July 12 the Israeli Minister of Information, Aharon Yariv, said in a radio interview that talks with the P.L.O. were possible, if it was ready to recognize the State of Israel and terminate terrorist action against it. The Palestinian news agency in Beirut, WAFA, at once rejected the proposal—the armed struggle against Israel would be carried on until all Palestinian aims were realized. Three revolutionary groups, all of them components of the P.L.O., equally summarily dismissed Yariv's statement, as "arrogant and aggressive imperialist claim to part of Palestine". At the same time, they rejected all idea of cooperation between the Palestinian leadership and the Jordanian regime—the phrase was used "Reconciliation with the Jordanian regime is a step toward the liquidation of the Palestinian revolution". Jordan, indeed, was regarded as almost as great an enemy as Israel. The leader of the PFLP, Dr. George Habash, even rejected Palestinian participation at peace talks in Geneva. The same view was taken by the leader of the "General Command", Ahmed Jebril.

Between April and July a number of statements were made by spokesmen of member groups in the P.L.O., which were indicative of Palestinian intransigence:

• In April the leading member of the Fatah, Salah Khalaf, stated that the establishment of Palestinian authority over any part of Palestine would never justify the abandonment of the historic right to the whole of Palestine. In his radio interview, given in Cairo, he called for an escalation of armed struggle.

• In April the head of the PDFLP, Nayef Hawatmeh, told a West German newspaper, the "Deutsche Zeitung", that there could be one end only to the struggle for liberation, the establishment of a "democratic" state in the whole of Palestine. In this struggle, the enemies of the Palestinians were Israel, Jordan and the United States.

• Speaking in Kuwait in April the head of the General Command, Ahmed Jebril, said: "The struggle between us and Israel is one of existence. It is either we or they. There is no third solution." He added: "We will not allow American or Soviet Jews to remain in Palestine. And we will scatter anew the Jews who came there from Arab lands." Moreover, "Recognizing U.N. Resolution 242 means recognizing the Zionist enemy".

• In May Hawatmeh welcomed the massacre of Israeli schoolchildren at Ma'alot, since it could disrupt Dr. Henry Kissinger's efforts to secure a military disengagement agreement between Israel and Syria—"We are fighting for the destruction of Kissinger's mission."

• In June the Palestine National Council, meeting in Cairo, decided to step up military operations against Israel by every possible means. In theory, the P.L.O would be entitled to join in peace negotiations. But extremist groups succeeded in having a clause added, to the effect that a mini-Palestinian state would be acceptable only if it were used as a base for continued armed action against both Israel and Jordan. The so-called "moderates" led by Arafat accepted this clause in order to avoid a show down.

• In July the chief adviser to the P.L.O. Research Center in Beirut, Asad Abdul-Rahman, told an American interviewer that a mini-Palestine which left Israel intact within her pre-1967 frontiers would "not be *the* solution, but a temporary solution". The P.L.O. would not underwrite a temporary solution nor be bound by its terms in any way; and until all legitimate Palestinian aims were realized, "violence will gather momentum, rather than diminish".

• In July Cairo radio announced the unanimous approval of the Arab Interstate Information Committee for an all-out propaganda campaign against Israel. Its aims included the propagation of armed struggle, the prevention of Israeli counteraction, and the demonstration of the "Nazi nature" of the State of Israel.

• At the P.L.O. "emergency conference" in Beirut in July it was decided unanimously that "There can be no just and durable peace in the area, without the restoration of the full national rights of the Palestinian people, in particular the right to repatriation and self-determination on the whole of their national soil". It was further agreed that the winning of total sovereignty, over the whole of Palestine, could be in stages—the "moderate" London representative of the P.L.O., Hammami, pops up again with an admonition to remember what Israel's own leader, David Ben-Gurion, had said in 1946, that the Jews could accept a part of Palestine without foregoing their claim to the whole of it.

Conclusions

Unlike the bulk of the press of the outside world, Israelis have taken careful note of statements like these. They have drawn certain inescapable conclusions:

1. The P.L.O.'s claim to represent the whole Palestinian people is utterly unjustified. At least four-fifths of the Palestinians have had no contact with it, know next to nothing about it, and have shown no desire to have anything to do with it. But the P.L.O. has sought to "represent" all activist groups, and these are all represented in the hierarchy of the P.L.O. When the P.L.O. dissociates itself from the revolting murders perpetrated by, for instance, "Black September", this means nothing at all. "Black September", like the "RASD" and other murder gangs, is recruited to "do the dirty work" from the ranks of Fatah and other groups. It is merely a convenience to claim no official connection with it.

2. The P.L.O., however, is not truly united. In June rival factions fought a number of pitched battles on the outskirts of Beirut and elsewhere in the Lebanon, the main center of P.L.O. activity. Apart from rivalry between factions, the seeds of decay are within all of them; there is a growing gap between the rank and file and the leadership, and soft living is having its effects on the latter.

3. The P.L.O. wants all of Palestine for the Palestinians, and the consequent destruction of the State of Israel. There is no cleavage over this between "radicals" and "moderates", as is fondly but foolishly imagined by a section of so-called "informed" opinion in the outside world. All sections of the P.L.O., again, are committed to the use of force to achieve basic aims.

4. It follows that the creation of a mini-Palestine, under the control of the P.L.O., would be a menace to the existence of Israel, as well as to the peace of the Middle East and the stability of Arab régimes such as those of Jordan, Lebanon, Saudi Arabia, Iran and the Gulf Sheikdoms. It would, in the longer-term, be a menace to the traditional Arab way of life, and to religious ethic and religious institutions, Christian as well as Muslim. Some observers have suggested that a "P.L.O. state" would be the nearest equivalent to the medieval, sub-Syrian dominion of the Assassins. Such a state would, by natural volition, turn to the Soviet Union and Communist China, as well as to international terrorist organizations, for aid and inspiration.

It is hardly surprising that the Israelis have shown the utmost reluctance to treat with the P.L.O. or contemplate the creation of a mini-Palestine under its control. The U.S. administration shares the doubts of the Israelis, believing that a mini-Palestine would become communist-orientated, would be a security risk for the whole region and would impede an Israeli-Jordanian settlement. Yet the predicament of the Palestinian people remains a real one. A proportion of them is living in miserable conditions; they are developing a national consciousness without the prospect of acquiring full national identity; they remain, to some extent, scattered, living in different states none of which they feel they can call their own. What, then, can be done for them? Here, at least, are some suggestions:

1. A "refugee claims conference", perhaps under international auspices, can examine the question of compensation for refugees who have lost land and property, and make appropriate recommendations.

2. A "Palestinian national conference", with delegates representing the sections of the Palestinian people in strict proportion to their numbers, should debate the question of Palestinian aims and policies.

3. A "little Arab summit", of states in the area with a real stake in the future of Palestine, should consider plans like that of King Hussein for a Jordanian-Palestinian federation.

Only through concrete steps of this kind can a feasible future be worked out for the Palestinian people, a future which can then be profitably discussed at a Geneva peace conference. Until such steps are taken, Israel can only be expected to regard with the gravest suspicion the grandiose plans of terrorist organizations pledged to Israel's own destruction.

Moscow and the Palestinians
A New Tool of Soviet Policy
in the Middle East

By Augustus R. Norton

I Introduction

The purpose of this paper is to call attention to a development in Society policy toward the Middle East that may have highly significant implications for Moscow's intentions regarding either a temporary or lasting settlement in that troubled region as an aftermath to the costly war of October, 1973.

The development in question is a marked shift in the Soviet position vis-à-vis the Palestinians, indicating a growing Soviet interest in the utility of the Palestinian issue as an instrument of policy in the Middle East. At the same time, the closer Soviet identification with, and support of, the Palestinians and of the Palestine Liberation Organization (PLO) has been facilitated by indications of, in at least overt terms, a less extremist stance by the latter on immediate objectives and strategies.

The possible significance of this development has been underscored by a number of official Washington pronouncements as to the weight the US is attaching to actual Soviet conduct respecting efforts to achieve a new order of stability in the Middle East. Thus, Secretary of State Henry Kissinger stated at a press conference on December 27, 1973 that the US "would have to judge the Soviet sincerity in seeking across-the-board relaxation of tension by its behavior in all negotiations in which we are engaged with it, including the Middle East." There are, the Secretary added, "two schools of thought" about future Soviet objectives in the Middle East: one holds that the Soviet Union has an interest in maintaining tension "because this will guarantee permanent Arab hostility to the United States and enhance the possibilities of Soviet influence." The other holds

228

that after three costly and inconclusive wars and the realization that conflicts in the Middle East "can bring the superpowers into a position of potential confrontation," the Soviet Union possibly "now has an interest" in cooperating with the US in achieving a "stabilization of the situation."

So far the Soviet leadership has given little reason for suppositions that it has shifted its goals in the Middle East. Moscow appears in fact determined to continue to pursue a line aimed at eroding US influence while strengthening that of the Soviet Union, and to this end at undermining the progress toward a peaceful settlement achieved by Secretary Kissinger's diplomatic initiatives in the wake of the October War.[1] Indeed, Radio Moscow warned on March 21, 1974 that "a settlement cannot be attained without the Soviet Union, and more so, against its interests," while an authoritative Soviet spokesmen, I. Beliaev, a foreign news editor of Pravda and Deputy Director of the African Institute of the USSR Academy of Sciences, had earlier candidly declared in a speech in Beirut, Lebanon that "we need a peace that will contribute to the improvement of our [Soviet] relations with the Arab countries and with all the peoples of the Near East."

Soviet efforts to recapture the initiative in the political negotiations for a settlement of the Middle East problem and to counteract improvements in US relations with, and influence among Arab states, have included:

- Denigration of the significance of the disengagement agreements and of US suggestions for compromise solutions, which Brezhnev personally denounced on April 11, 1974 as "ersatz" plans and a US-Israeli plot to deny the Arabs a "just" political solution.
- Urging the continuing use by the Arabs of the "oil weapon" against the US and the West, and the renewal of the oil embargo against the US should the US fail to secure a settlement in accord with maximum Arab demands.
- Suggesting that Israel and "those who support it," i.e., the US, should pay the Arabs compensation for damages suffered since the 1967 Arab-Israeli war.
- Encouraging the Arabs to avoid all compromises and to insist on their maximum territorial demands on the basis of UN Security Council Resolution 242.
- Calling for an early convening of the Geneva negotiations, seeing in them a means for enhancing Moscow's role and initiatives, and for disrupting efforts at negotiating separate agreements between Israel and some of its Arab neighbors, notably Egypt.
- Gaining a position for influencing by obtaining formal assurances by the Arabs that the Soviet Union will be included in all aspects and all working bodies of the Geneva negotiations, and that they will closely coordinate their policies with Moscow.

While these particular maneuvers by the Soviet authorities might be explained on grounds of an understandable desire of Moscow simply to redress the shift in the balance of US as against Soviet influence in the Middle East in consequence of the war and subsequent US successes in improving its relations with Egypt and its position among the Arabs generally, other Soviet moves are suggestive of more far-reaching purposes. Moscow, for example, has underway a massive effort to rearm Syria to a level well above that of its military capability on the eve of the 1973 war, including particularly offensive weapons. It has sought to strengthen its overall position in Syria, as well as in Iraq, the People's Democratic Republic of Yemen, and Somalia, and to improve its relations with Libya by taking advantage of its growing hostility to Egypt's President Sadat, and to exacerbate Israeli-Lebanese differences by offering arms aid to Lebanon.

It is in the context of these latter moves, more than in that of efforts to secure a key role for the Soviet Union in still pending negotiations, that Moscow's shift in policy toward the Palestinians must be closely examined and weighed.

The Palestinians have been called the "conscience" of the Arabs, a characterization which was brought home to President Nixon during his tour of the Middle East in June 1974 by the emphasis which every Arab leader he met placed on the solution of their problem. Moscow has fully endorsed the Arab position arguing that no lasting peace settlement in the Middle East is possible "unless the legitimate rights" of the Palestinians are taken into account and satisfied, and has taken credit for persuading President Nixon at the Washington Summit in June 1973, and the Moscow Summit in July 1974, to include references to these "legitimate rights" in the communiqués issued on those occasions. More important, however, is that the Soviet Union gives clear evidence of a calculation that precisely because of the complexities of the Palestinian issue and the enormous difficulties of finding a solution, it can become an excellent tool for Moscow to influence the policies of the Arab states and the course of the peace negotiations, and depending on the outcome of the latter, either to expand Soviet influence in the Middle East or to keep the region in turmoil indefinitely.

It may well be, consequently, that what we have in progress is an extension of Soviet operations in the Middle East into a new, and perhaps more dangerous, dimension. The point is not only that the Soviets plan to use the Palestinian issue as an important bargaining counter to influence negotiations at Geneva, if these ever actually take place, but also as a means of obstructing conclusion of separate agreements between various Arab states and Israel. The critical point is that Moscow appears to be laying foundations for the use of the Palestinians as an added instrument of policy in the Middle East over the long run. Although leaving its options open for movement in some other direction, Moscow appears to be preparing the groundwork for either of two alternatives.

First, to press for the establishment of an independent Palestinian state with the intention of making the Soviet Union its indispensable patron as against Israel and the US on the one hand, and moderate Arab states on the other.

Second, if the establishment of a Palestinian state proves unfeasible, to accord the Palestinians, and more particularly the Palestine Liberation Organization, the status of a "national liberation movement" in their own right and to give it sufficient military and other assistance not only to keep the Middle East in turmoil indefinitely but also to bring to bear increasing pressures, including terrorist pressures, on both "progressive" and conservative Arab regimes to step up their "anti-imperialist" policies and activities against the US and Israel.

II Origins of the Palestinian Problem

The "Palestinian problem" which came into being with the establishment of the State of Israel in 1948 and the flight of some 700,000 Palestinian Arab refugees to neighboring countries, has become over the years an increasingly important political factor in the Middle East. First used by the Arab states as an instrument of harrassment against Israel and as a justification for their continued opposition to and non-recognition of the right to existence of the State of Israel, as established by the United Nations, the Palestinians, especially their guerrilla movement, became in time an independent political force in the region. It became a force capable of threatening not only Israel and any settlement between it and its Arab neighbors but also the security of the latter and the survival of individual Arab leaders and regimes. In recent years, Palestinian terrorism has also posed a growing problem for countries outside the Middle East.

Israeli successes in the 1967 war further complicated and aggravated the Palestinian problem by bringing some 200,000 additional members of the Palestinian-Arab population into a refugee status. Today, refugee camps in Gaza, on the East and West banks of the Jordan River, and in Lebanon and Syria, house some 650,000 of the estimated three million Palestinians who are scattered throughout the Middle East, North Africa and beyond, including some 340,000 who live in the pre-1967 boundaries of Israel and hold Israeli citizenship.[2] These conditions have spawned the emergence and increasing activism of the Palestinian guerrillas, or *fedayeen* (literally, those who sacrifice). The Palestinians have developed many *fedayeen* organizations reflecting various political views and leadership personalities, each of which has courted the support of the Palestinian people and of sympathetic Arab states as well as of public opinion and governments outside the area.

As a result of an Arab League Council decision to "affirm a Palestinian entity and place the cause of liberation in the hands of the Palestinians," the Palestine Liberation Organization (PLO) was founded at the meeting of the first Palestinian National Congress in 1964 to serve as an umbrella organization and executive for the various *fedayeen* groups, and a Palestinian Liberation Army was established to serve as the military wing of the PLO. The first chairman of the PLO, Ahmed Shukeiry, whose promise to "drive the Jews into the sea" did little to lend credibility or respectability to the organization, was replaced in 1969 by Yasser Arafat, the leader of the largest and most influenitial of the *fedayeen* groups—*al-Fatah*.[3]

The other organizations in the PLO include the Popular Front for the Liberation of Palestine (PFLP) led by George Habash; the Popular Democratic Front for the Liberation of Palestine (PDFLP), led by Nayef Hawatmeh; *al Saiqa,* an organization sponsored by Syrian military intelligence, led by Zahir Mukhsan; and most recently the Popular Front for the Liberation of Palestine: General Command. A Palestine National Front, which claims to have been established in January 1973 and to be based in the Israeli occupied areas, also asserts that it regards the PLO as the sole authority. Although a number of other splinter groups are not formally members of the PLO, they do pay a degree of allegiance to that organization and partially heed its decisions. While no accurate membership figures for these groups are available, their total is estimated at some 14,000, while the strength of the Palestinian Liberation Army is believed to be of the order of 4,000 to 6,000. The actual fighting strength of these organizations is probably considerably smaller, having suffered severe losses since 1970 in a number of bloody clashes with Jordanian and Lebanese armed forces.

For political reasons, terrorist attacks have usually been conducted by *ad hoc* groups masquerading under various names in order to avoid making their parent organizations targets for Israeli retaliation and international criticism. For example, the Black September group which took responsibility for a number of terrorist attacks outside the Middle East was led by Salah Khalaf, Arafat's deputy in *al-Fatah*, and several other leaders of the latter organization.

Prior to 1967, except for Communist China, the PLO was paid scant attention and given little support even by the Arab states which purported to be its sponsors. Its efforts to coordinate the activities of its member groups, or to develop a joint political position failed, while its guerrilla activities were largely ineffectual. However, after the defeat of the Arabs in the 1967 Six Day War and the Israeli occupation of the West Bank and Gaza, the Palestinian issue gained new importance and with it came greater interest and support not only from the Arab states but also from the Soviet Union.

Because of the wide ideological divergences between the Palestinian organizations, it is not possible to synthesize a *"fedayeen* position," and whatever agreements exist within the movement tend to be based on the lowest common denominator. However, in view of the strength and importance of *al-Fatah* and of its leader Arafat, the positions held by them can serve as a sort of guide to the predominant objectives of the Palestinian movement. There have been some shifts in the public formulation of these aims as the Palestinians have debated the realism of some of their more extreme ambitions and have come to realize that the more radical *fedayeen* positions tended to alienate world opinion and deprive the Palestinians of the latter's support for their cause.

The basic objective of the Palestinians has been the "total liberation of the Palestinian homeland" through armed struggle and includes, therefore, total irreconcilability to the existence of the State of Israel. In the aftermath of Israel's crushing victory over the Arabs in the 1967 Six Day War, which demonstrated the unreality of Shukeiry's extreme position on the complete expulsion of the Jews, Arafat has been publicly claiming that the PLO is merely opposed to Zionism and Israeli "imperialism" and that it seeks the creation of a "democratic, non-sectarian state of Palestine" for all Palestinians and a hazily defined number of Jews. Nevertheless, the PLO has so far shown no real willingness to compromise its basic position or to give up "armed struggle" in favor of a political solution.

While most recently the creation of some sort of Palestinian state made up of the West Bank and Gaza has not been entirely precluded by the PLO, at least as an interim step toward the total liberation of Palestine, the organization has been adamant in rejecting proposals that such a state would be, in one form or another, tied to Jordan. Various *fedayeen* groups oppose even the concept of such an interim Palestinian state, fearing that its creation would undermine their struggle to attain their total objective. This has led to internal disputes and tensions within the PLO over the issue of what it can realistically expect to achieve as against the perpetuation of an uncompromising armed struggle for the liquidation of the State of Israel.

III The Pre-1973 Soviet Position on the Palestinians

Prior to the 1967 Arab-Israeli war, the Soviet Union evidently saw little profit in supporting the *fedayeen*, who were more often than not making brash and inflammatory threats against Israel, with little potential for effectuating such threats. Soviet distaste for the rhetoric of the *fedayeen*, coupled with the Soviet preference for conducting relations in the Middle East on a state-to-state basis, a deep suspicion of the political and social makeup of the *fedayeen*, and a general aversion to terrorism, served to block Soviet interest. However, Moscow at first avoided a public position. Thus, when *al-Fatah* carried out its first act of sabotage in Israel in January 1965, the Russian media simply ignored the action. There was, however, a brief flirtation with the Palestinians in early 1966 as a result of the

Soviets' desire to satisfy the neo-Ba'ath, the ruling group which had come to power in Syria. But Moscow soon adopted a line which explicitly denied the existence of the *fedayeen*. For example, the Soviet government organ, *Izvestia*, on May 8, 1966 referred to alleged *fedayeen* actions as the "activity of mythical diversionary groups." Shortly thereafter the combined organ of the RSFSR Government and CPSU Central Committee, *Sovetskaia Rossiia*, insisted that the *fedayeen* were mythical inventions of Israel which served to justify Israeli aggression against Syria. Later that year, a Soviet note to the Israeli Government, while acknowledging the existence of the *fedayeen*, argued that they were creatures of Western intelligence agencies "for provocation purposes." The Soviet Government meanwhile showed a marked distaste for Shuqairy's leadership of the PLO, characterizing him as "an extremist of extremists" and as an "unscrupulous politician" who did not warrant Soviet consideration or support, and in the 1967 power struggle between the PLO and *al-Fatah*, Moscow publicly sided with the latter. With Shuqairy's removal and indications of growing *fedayeen* strength, positive Soviet statements of support for them became more common, and Moscow tried to maintain contact with the PLO, using the Jordanian Communist Party as intermediary. In January 1969, Soviet commentators began to speak of the Palestinian struggle as a "lawful and just struggle," and as an act of "self-defense" against Israeli "aggression," and even to equate the movement with the activities of the resistance against the Nazis in World War II.

Subsequently, Aleksandr Shelepin, a member of the Soviet Politburo, made clear that a new line had been given official sanction. Speaking in Budapest on October 20, 1969, he pointed to the similarity between the *fedayeen* and the anti-Nazi resistance movement and then added:

> We consider the struggle of Palestinian patriots for the liquidation of the consequences of Israeli aggression [i.e., the recovery of occupied territory and the restoration of the Palestinian peoples' rights] as a just anti-imperialist struggle and we support it.[4]

The same line was repeated by Premier Kosygin in December in a speech to a visiting Egyptian delegation, as well as by other official Soviet spokesmen. Thus, the authoritative journal of the Soviet Communist Party Central Committee, *Kommunist*, asserted in its November 1969 issue that

> . . . all the world's progressive and democratic forces are supporting the Palestinian resistance movement directed at eliminating the consequences of Israeli aggression, regarding this movement as a *just, anti-imperialist, national liberation struggle.* [Emphasis added.]

However, when such statements are juxtaposed to Soviet actions at the time, there is little evidence of anything more than rhetorical support. The Soviets seemed primarily concerned with appearances. The Palestinian cause clearly had great emotional appeal within the Arab world, and by pledging support to the Palestinians the Soviet Union symbolized an anti-Israeli position even if unwilling to move beyond symbolism. The issue, in other words, was far too sensitive to continue to be simply ignored by the Soviet Union. The Kremlin perceived that its relationships with the Arab world required at least lip service to pro-Palestinian words and phrases. Furthermore, Moscow did not want to leave this field entirely unchallenged to the Chinese who had endorsed the PLO from the beginning and were supplying it with some arms.

There were a number of reasons for the persistent Soviet caution in their support of the Palestinians and in becoming too closely associated with the PLO.

The Issue of Existence of the State of Israel

Despite Moscow's alignment with the "progressive" Arab states (i.e., Syria, Iraq, Egypt and Algeria), the Soviets have never publicly called for or supported calls for the destruction of the State of Israel. Not only had the Soviet Union supported the UN resolution establishing Israel but it has consistently argued that a Middle East settlement must guarantee the existence of all states in the region, including Israel. It is on this issue that the *fedayeen* have most frequently been extremist and adamant and thus divergent from the Soviet position.

Soviet criticism of the *fedayeen* objectives vis-à-vis Israel, however, has not been based so much on moral grounds or grounds of a Soviet commitment to the existence of a State of Israel, as on practical considerations. For example, even while expressing new support for the Palestinian struggle, Soviet commentators and their Arab Communist spokesmen criticized the *fedayeen* for their "extremist ideas" and "unrealistic" aims. Thus, an article in the April 15, 1969 issue of the RSFSR newspaper *Sovetskaia Rossiia* said that

It is clear the the aims which *al-Fatah* and some other organizations have set for themselves, which amount to the liquidation of the State of Israel and the creation of a "Palestinian democratic state" are not realistic. . . . The liberation struggle in occupied territories awakens the deep sympathies of the whole progressive public. It is all the more to be regretted that some of its leaders do not take into account the present situation in the Arab East and the relation of forces in the world arena.

At the same time, Soviet leaders were opposed to a renewal of the war by the Arabs against Israel, which Moscow expected the Arabs to lose, and which could involve it in a dangerous confrontation with the US. Consequently, it believed the *fedayeen*'s call for a new armed struggle to be not only unrealistic but dangerous, all the more so as the Palestinians lacked the strength to attain their stated aims. These and other factors at play were candidly discussed in a rather remarkable document published by the Beirut newspaper *al-Rayah*.[5] This was a critique by Soviet officials and ideologues of the proposed 1970 Syrian Communist Party program. The Soviet representatives argued that

The presence of Israel is a reality and eliminating Israel as a means to achieve the Palestinian people's right to self-determination are two things which cancel one another. This can only be done through a world war.

You [the Syrian Communist Party] should not imagine that you will enter Israel with bayonets and establish a Palestinian state. This is unrealistic, this would cause a third world war.

They asserted, furthermore, that it was "Zionism," and not the State of Israel, which had to be destroyed.

The way is in the two peoples' struggle against imperialism. This is to say that the Israeli people should turn against Zionism. It is in liquidating the Zionist inclination in the Israeli state. These are the starting points for establishing a Palestinian state.

Thus, the correct slogan, according to these representatives, was that the "struggle against Zionism should be stepped up and strengthened." The right of the Israeli state to exist was said to be an established fact, for "Israel is a reality."

It is clear that there was no Jewish nation or Jewish nationalism before. But now an Israeli nation is coming into being. This is a current process. I do not wish to justify this historically, but let us start from the present reality.

The slogan of eliminating Israel is wrong, not only tactically, but also as a matter of principle. . . .

Look at the possibility of realizing the slogan. It is a slogan which is impossible to *achieve*. The Arab leaders understand this. . . . As for the logic of struggle: Under the slogan of eliminating Israel and of liberating the usurped homeland, the Arabs will not win the support of world opinion, or of the Soviet Union or of the world communist movement. . . . Of course, after eliminating the consequences of the Israeli aggression [i.e., the 1967 War], the struggle must continue and must be directed against Zionism.

Aside from the question of the practicality of *fedayeen* aims, the Soviet position on the issue was also influenced by its view that the conflict in the Middle East was essentially a part of the global class struggle between the forces of Western imperialism and those of national liberation, and not merely a clash between two nationalisms—Arab and Jewish. Thus, according to an article in the October 15, 1970 issue of *Pravda*:

The Soviet Union regards the Middle East crisis not as a clash of national interests [between Israel and the Arab states], but as an attempt by world imperialism with the aid of the Israeli elite . . . to strike a blow against the national liberation movement of the Arab countries.

The problem, as Moscow saw it, is not to eliminate the State of Israel after it gives up the territories it has gained through its "aggressions," but to bring about its abandonment of Zionism, its willingness to act as an "agent" of US imperialism and to promote its joining the "anti-imperialist" struggle in concert with the "progressive" Arab regimes and the Soviet Union.

Palestinian Disunity and Separation

At the time of the formation of the PLO in 1964, Moscow apparently had hoped that it would become a unified organization whose policies and actions the Soviets could influence. However, it was unable to effectively unify or control all the Palestinian organizations and the Palestinian movement remained fragmented and subject to strong, and at times violent, internal competition and disputes. Furthermore, the Soviet Union and the Arab Communists remained uneasy because, as a Jordanian Communist go-between reported in 1968, "some leaders, especially in *al-Fatah*, come from the reactionary Muslim Brotherhood and are still under its influence."[6]

In an unusually blunt article in *Sovetskaia Rossiia* of October 25, 1972 the Soviets provided clear explanations of their concern over the lack of Palestinian unity and the failure of the Palestinians to work within the Arab "front," and why this affected Soviet support. The numerous organizations of the *fedayeen* were said to be united only formally in the PLO, which "does not have clear political and ideological aims." The multifarious groups all proclaim "their aim to be the struggle to liberate the occupied territories and return home," but do not agree on "ways and methods to achieve that aim," due to their "motley" social composition and "political heterogeneity."

> . . . Advancing nationalist and religious slogans to the forefront some of the Palestinian organizations even strove to isolate the Palestinians' actions from the all-Arab front of the struggle. . . .
> Disunity among the numerous groups of Palestinians has had an adverse effect on the Palestinians' struggle for their rights. . . . [Extremist Palestinians] failed to master the political methods of waging the struggle among the population of the occupied regions.

Thus, the Soviets were seeming to encourage the unification of the Palestinians, and in doing so, to make the movement socially conscious; i.e., a movement recognizing the identity of their interests with those of other Arabs, and the need for cooperation with the Soviet Union. For in the Middle East, "there are only two sides, that of the backers of an Israeli-American solution of the crisis, and that of the supporters of an Arab solution."

> Objectively, then, there is no room for a third approach. The weakness of the second camp . . . stems from the division which prevails within it and the Resistance movement can play an essential role in this realm. . . .[7]

Any "just solution of the Palestinian problem," Soviet spokesmen contended, "can be achieved only within the framework of the joint liberation struggle of the Arab peoples and in close cooperation with the progressive Arab regimes and the countries of the socialist comity."[8] In this respect the Soviets appeared to continue to be disturbed by the lack of homogeneity of the PLO in terms of its class composition and by the fact that "alongside the forces oriented towards progressive development . . . there are also reactionaries and extremists" who do not appreciate the real correlation of forces in the area or choose the correct tactics, i.e., who do not follow Soviet advice and threaten to cause difficulties for Soviet policy.[9]

"Leftist Adventurism"

Many of the "Marxist" *fedayeen* organizations, such as the PDFLP and the PFLP, have espoused a doctrine of total revolution in the Arab world which, of course, would entail the destruction of several regimes which the Soviets support actively, and others which they seek to bring under their influence. In addition, while countries such as Egypt have tacitly accepted the concept of a peaceful solution of the Arab-Israeli conflict, albeit on their own terms, many of the *fedayeen* have deemed such acceptance as justification for overthrowing their government.

The Soviet strategy was to encourage the *fedayeen* to recognize their struggle as only one segment of the greater "liberation struggle" of all the Arab people. Thus, on September 26, 1968 *Pravda* carried a statement by pro-Moscow Arab Communist parties denouncing the "romantic and reckless course advocated by progressive national patriotic elements of the petty bourgeoisie." The commentary continued:

> The call of the exponents of this reckless trend to separate the Palestine issue from the Arab nationalist-liberation movement is entirely incorrect and, consequently, so is the slogan that Palestinians should fight their battle alone on the same pretext that Palestinian movements are "independent" and need no "patronage."

The Soviets were well aware that "independent" movements in the Middle East can work against their established interests as well as those of the United States. Thus, during the 1970 crisis in Jordan, when Hussein decisively defeated the Palestinians, the Soviets reacted publicly with a striking even-handedness. Perhaps more than any Arab country, Jordan was identified with the United States, yet the Soviet response was that any split in Arab unity helped the "imperialists" and Israel and that the Soviet Communist Party and people "attach great importance" to a unified Arab struggle against "Israeli aggression." Indeed, *Pravda* of October 17, 1970 went so far as to place part of the blame for the war in Jordan on "crazy extremists among the *fedayeen* governed by the slogan 'the worse it is, the better it is.' " In the same vein, Soviet commentators condemned the May 1973 armed clash between the *fedayeen* and the Lebanese Armed Forces as only serving the interests of the "enemies" of the Arabs.

Terrorism

The use of terrorism by the *fedayeen* has been endemic. The spokesmen for the Palestinians justify terrorism as a means of maintaining visibility for the plight of the Palestinians and as a means of resisting attempts to "liquidate" the struggle of the Palestinian people. The Soviet reaction to such tactics has been condemnatory. The line has been to link the "forces of reaction" in the Arab world with Israel as the elements which "cause" the resort to terroristic methods by the *fedayeen*, and harm "their relations with the Arab masses and deprive them of international support." Thus, after the tragedy at the Olympics in Munich, *Pravda* stated on September 10, 1972:

> Arab reactionaries and Israeli agents are deliberately pushing the Palestinians toward extremism in order to create in the international public the idea that the Arab partisans are only fanatical terrorists. This is precisely what is happening now, when reactionary circles are trying to use the events at the Olympic Games as a pretext for intensifying military provocations against the Arab countries.

Similarly, Moscow condemned the hijacking of civilian planes by Palestinian terrorists and the mailing of explosive parcels and letters to prominent Jewish or pro-Israeli persons in and outside Israel, noting that such activities "arouse universal indignation," and claiming that they are condemned by "the progressive Arab public" as harmful to the "common struggle of the Arab peoples." At times Soviet propaganda even sought to suggest that the terrorists "are being directed by agents of the Tel-Aviv secret service."

After nearly every incident of terrorism attributed to the Palestinians, the Soviet press and radio uniformly noted the denial of involvement that the Palestine Liberation Organization regularly issued following each incident. Such demands have been particularly handy to the Soviets since they make possible claims of steadfast support for the PLO on the one hand, and condemnation of extremism on the other. When an incident proved especially sensitive, the Soviet ploy was usually to ignore it or at least to play it down. For example, after the Qiryat Shemona raid in April 1974 in which 18 Israelis and three *fedayeen* died, the Soviet news agency TASS issued only a four-sentence report. All later mention of Qiryat Shemona was tied to condemnations of Israeli retaliatory attacks on Palestinian refugee camps in Lebanon, and with PLO and Lebanese statements being cited to the effect that the guerrillas originated from within Israel. In this way, the Soviets sought to maintain the myth that only a small segment of the Palestine resistance movement engages in "ideologically immature" acts which merely serve to distract world public attention from Israeli "acts of aggression," play into the hands of Arab "reactionaries," and disrupt efforts to improve relations between the Palestinian resistance movement and the Middle East states.

This did not mean, however, that the Soviet Union was opposed to the use of armed struggle by the Palestinians as a matter of principle. Thus, while criticizing the tactics and aims of the PLO, a Jordanian Communist spokesman wrote in the October-November 1968 issue of the Soviet sponsored journal, *Problems of Peace and Socialism*, that "we do not write off armed struggle," which may be "entirely justified, depending on the scale and scope of the general movement in the occupied areas and on the readiness of the masses to repulse the [Israeli] aggression." In line with this statement, Soviet spokesmen have also drawn a clear distinction between the use of terrorism and the use of violence to further the struggle of the national liberation movements in general, and the armed struggle of the Palestinians in the occupied areas in particular. Recent Soviet statements have been especially candid concerning this issue. For example, an article in the March 1974 issue of *New Times* asserted that "international terrorism has nothing in common with the revolutionary movement of the masses" since the former can at best provide only "limited results," while the latter seeks to "bring about radical changes in society."

> However, one must draw a clear-cut moral and political dividing line between acts of international terrorism and the use of force in struggle for national liberation, such as that waged by the Palestinian patriots on territory unlawfully occupied by Israel. The Soviet Union is opposed as a matter of principle to the question of international terrorism being used to damage this struggle, the justice and legitimacy of which has been recognized also in official U.N. decisions. [10]

Similarly, a "political observer" of *Izvestia*, writing in that paper's July 30, 1974 issue, condemned terrorism, but noted with obvious approval as a "correct" and more "effective" form of struggle, that the "Palestinian partisans have intensified their actions against the aggressor: They have blown up military supply depots, attacked the occupiers' bases and attacked Israeli military ports." [11]

Soviet statements thus indicate that notwithstanding their talk of a "moral" dividing line between terrorism and armed struggle, the basis for a distinction between proper and improper use of force is the determination of its effects in, and especially beyond, the area of its application. Moscow's line has been aimed at encouraging the *fedayeen* to employ violence not as a means in itself, but as a part of, and in coordination with, the overall "Arab national liberation struggle," and as a means to the latter's success. Where violence does not contribute to the attainment of this end, Soviet spokesmen argue that it should be avoided.

The Palestinian Attitude Toward Political Settlement

Although the Soviets have not been reluctant to support and encourage the Arabs to take up arms against Israel, as evidenced by their involvement in the wars of 1967 and 1973, they have argued that military means cannot be relied upon to achieve a total solution of the Arab-Israeli conflict, but serve to enhance negotiating positions and make the adversary more willing to seek pacific solution. The Soviets have been free in their criticism of the *fedayeen* for believing "that a solution to the problem can be found by exclusively military means." They describe such views to be "unrealistic," and as held by "rightists and extreme leftists, circles which fail, as a rule, to take account of the strategic tasks of the Arab peoples' anti-imperialist struggle" and are, therefore, wrong both strategically and tactically. The Soviets insist that, given favorable conditions, a peaceful solution of the Palestinian problem is possible on the basis of the U.N. Security Council Resolution 242 of November 22, 1967, which requires Israel to relinquish all territories occupied by it in the Six-Day War. At the same time, the Palestinians have been warned that they "cannot make headway without . . . the sustained backing of freedom-loving forces of the world, especially the socialist countries."[12]

Thus, according to Moscow, the *fedayeen* must recognize that a solution to the plight of their people requires the backing of the Soviet Union and that backing is unlikely to be forthcoming unless they are willing to accept Soviet guidance. Since Resolution 242 says nothing of an independent Palestinian state, but speaks only of the "rights of refugees," the *fedayeen* have refused to accept the document as the basis for settlement. Moscow, in contrast, has seen the Resolution as a highly useful instrument for legitimatizing its support of the Arabs, and until recently has been unwilling to support Arab positions going beyond it. This issue, therefore, had been a persistent bone of contention between the Soviet Union and the *fedayeen*.

IV The Beginning of a Shift in Soviet Policy

On March 19, 1973, I. Beliaev, the Deputy Director of the African Institute of the USSR Academy of Sciences and Foreign News Editor of *Pravda*, said in a lecture in Beirut: "Our relations with the Palestinian liberation organizations have recently improved." The cited reasons for this were the improvements in "these historic circumstances" of the "social aspects" of the *fedayeen* movement and the possibility that "in the process of transforming it into a social revolution, the Palestinian revolution is called upon to play an important role in the Arab national liberation struggle." However, while Moscow claimed to discover the potential of the Palestinians as "one of the units" of the Arab-liberation struggle, the heart of the matter was that the Soviet leadership was coming to see in them a new opportunity for influencing political developments in the Middle East.

The Soviet Union and the "National Rights" of the Palestinians

While the Palestinians have consistently claimed the right to establish a "secular, democratic state of Palestine" to replace the present State of Israel and in the Arab territories it presently controls, the Soviet Union in the past had been unwilling to recognize such "national rights" and instead had proclaimed its support for undefined "legitimate rights" or "interests" of the Palestinian people. This formula was included, at Soviet urging, in the Washington and Moscow Summits' joint US-Soviet communiqués in 1973 and 1974, respectively.

However, hints of possible Soviet support for the Palestinians' "national rights," i.e., the right to form some sort of Palestinian state, became apparent in early 1973. Thus, Beliaev in his speech in Lebanon in March 1973, spoke of Soviet support for the struggle of the "Palestinian resistance movement . . . for the recognition of the legitimate national rights" of the Palestinians. On June 22, Radio Moscow in a broadcast to the Middle East, repeated this formula as a part of "a just settlement of the Middle East crisis." The first high-level Soviet endorsement occurred in the communiqué issued on November 15, 1973 on the occasion of Yugoslavia's President Tito's meeting with Brezhnev in Moscow. However, in his major speech on October 26, 1973 to the World Conference of Peace-loving Forces, Brezhnev only mentioned the "legitimate rights" of the Palestinians and this remained also true throughout the year for the speeches of other Soviet leaders.

Arafat's "Unofficial" Visits to Moscow

Even while the Soviet leadership appeared to be testing the water of endorsement of the Palestinians' demands for recognition of their "national rights," contacts between the PLO leadership and the Soviet Union were expanding. Arafat had first visited the Soviet Union in February 1970 at the invitation of the Soviet Committee on Afro-Asian Solidarity, ostensibly an "unofficial" Soviet organization. According to Soviet reports, discussions held at that time dealt with questions of cooperation between the Committee and the PLO "in the common struggle to remove the imperialist-Zionist-Israeli aggression and for the defense of the just and legitimate demands of the Palestinian Arab people." Arafat visited Moscow again in July 1972, still without meeting any high level Soviet officials and, according to reports, discovered that the Soviets were more interested in the ideological orientation of the PLO than in granting it practical support. Whatever Arafat's disappointment, he repaid the Soviets by publicly praising Soviet support for the Arab cause.

The frequency of PLO contacts increased during 1973. In August of that year, Arafat visited the Soviet Union "at the invitation of the Organizing Committee of the World University Athletic Games," but was also "received" by the Soviet Committee on Afro-Asian Solidarity. This visit, like the preceding ones, still bore an "unofficial" character and appears to have produced little beyond condemnations of "wicked Israeli aggression" and expressions of Soviet support of Arab demands for Israeli withdrawal from the occupied territories and affirmation of "solidarity" with the Palestinians. In October 1973, a PLO delegation attended the World Conference of Peace-loving Forces in Moscow and heard Brezhnev call for the "guarantee of the legitimate rights" of the Palestinians as one of the fundamental principles for a peace settlement in the Middle East.

When Arafat arrived in Moscow during the second half of November, 1973, following the October War, Soviet statements regarding the Palestinians were markedly less perfunctory than for previous visits. Although the visit was once again sponsored by the Soviet Committee for Afro-Asian Solidarity, thus avoiding any direct identification of the Soviet Government with the PLO, the talks were characterized by one knowledgeable participant as a "marked development in the Soviet policy on the Palestinian issue."[13] Arafat was reported to have met with "Soviet officials dealing with the Middle East issue." On this occasion the visit ended with an "official communique" being issued in Moscow and carried by the Soviet news agency TASS and *Pravda*, which stated that the objectives of the PLO included, among others, "satisfaction of the legitimate national rights" of the Palestinians and that the "Soviet side" was determined "to continue assistance and support to the struggle of the Arab people of Palestine for its legitimate national rights."[14]

In return for such Soviet endorsement, Arafat included in this communiqué a reference to the PLO's cooperation with all Arab countries which advocate "a political settlement" of the Middle East conflict and the satisfaction of the Palestinians' "lawful national rights." The possible acceptance of a "political settlement" (i.e., partial settlement) by the principal *fedayeen* leader constituted a major departure from the position previously held by the PLO and suggested that Moscow and at least some of the PLO leadership, notably Arafat, had arrived at some sort of understanding on this sensitive issue. As was noted, previously the Soviet Union had been pressing the *fedayeen* to adopt more "realistic" aims and attitudes on the territorial question and the liquidation of the State of Israel. PLO spokesmen have acknowledged the leverage and influence of the Soviet Union, and have presented at least the appearance of a willingness to acquiesce to Soviet demands. Thus, an official spokesman for *al-Fatah* asserted in Novemebr 1973 that "there are in the world forces which are friendly to our revolution; these must in no way be opposed." No doubt Arafat also recognized the danger of the Palestinians becoming isolated not only from the Soviet Union but also from Arab support as the Arab-Israeli conflict moved from armed struggle to negotiation. Indications of a shift by Arafat to a more "moderate" position were probably a precondition for the Soviet endorsement, albeit still cautiously so, of the Palestinian state concept in November.

V Toward a New Soviet-PLO Relationship

The first month of 1974 revealed a weakening of Soviet influence on events in the Middle East and a corresponding determination on Moscow's part to recapture the initiative from the US. The October War and the Arab oil embargo had significantly altered the power relationships and political environment in the Middle East, and the positions of the Soviet Union and the US therein. Despite massive Soviet aid to the Arabs prior to and during the war, the US had gained increasing influence in the negotiatory phase as a result of its special ability to mediate between Israel and its Arab neighbors and, more particularly, its leverage on Israeli policies. Furthermore, despite Soviet protests, the Arab oil-producing countries lifted their embargo on oil deliveries to the US. These adverse developments, from Moscow's point of view, inevitably tended to enhance the importance of the Palestinian problem not only as one of the critical issues at the scheduled Geneva Conference, or lacking this in bilateral negotiations between particular Arab states and Israel, but as a continuing factor in Middle East relationships. Consequently, Moscow has come to increasingly see in the Palestinians an opportunity to manipulate and influence future developments, embarrass the US and complicate its relations with Israel and the Arabs, pressure the conservative Arab regimes, and help recapture for the Soviet Union its image as the sole "reliable" friend and supporter of the Arabs, and as a dynamic force in the Middle East.

The Recognition of the PLO and Its Participation in the Geneva Negotiations

The Arab States' Conference in Algiers on November 26-28, 1973 had officially recognized the PLO as the "sole representative" of the Arab people of Palestine, but this had not been followed by a similar recognition from Moscow. In his opening statement at the first session of the Geneva Peace Conference on the Middle East on December 21, 1973, Soviet Foreign Minister Gromyko had called for the "participation of representatives of the Arab people of Palestine" as essential to a solution to this problem, without, however, identifying the PLO as the sole representative.

Even so, the development of closer relations between the Soviet Union and the PLO became increasingly apparent in the course of 1974. Thus, during Gromyko's trip to the Middle East (February 27-March 7, 1974) he met twice with Arafat. This was the first time that a Soviet leader of Gromyko's stature had publicly met with the head of the PLO, thus underscoring the growing Soviet interest in the Palestinians and the PLO. According to Soviet reports of these meetings, the discussions dealt with the issue of "restoration of the legitimate national rights" of the Palestinians. On March 6 a Radio Moscow commentary on the meetings described them as "a brilliant confirmation of the steadfastness of the Soviet Union's stand of comprehensive support for the just struggle of the Palestinian Arab people for their legitimate national rights."

Even so, neither Gromyko nor Arafat gave any indication that the Soviet Union had recognized the PLO as the sole representative of the Palestinian cause. However, during March, a series of Soviet articles and broadcasts appeared to be laying the foundation for a formal Soviet recognition of the PLO. For example, they reported that the Palestinian National Front, which was said to include "communists and non-party people, Ba'ath Party members and other patriots" had recognized the PLO as the sole representative of the entire Palestinian people. Radio Moscow on March 23 also reported Arafat's claim that "103 countries have recognized the PLO as the legitimate sole representative" of the Palestinians, and went on to say that "the support expressed by the Arab countries, the Soviet Union and other socialist countries adds to the PLO's high esteem in the international arena." In April, an article in the *World Marxist Review* asserted that "despite its flaws and errors," the PLO "which enjoys the comprehensive support of the Arab Palestinian people is doing its best to become their legitimate representative," and that "all progressive forces and anti-colonialist forces which belong to the Arab front sympathize with the PLO."

On May 28, 1974 Gromyko again met with Arafat in Damascus. Soviet commentaries on that meeting underscored the consistent Soviet support for the Palestinians and asserted that the latter "were deeply angered" by the reports that the United States had doubts about the participation of the Palestinian Arabs in the Geneva Conference. By contrast, Moscow had continued to support the concept of such participation on equal terms with the other countries' delegations and had affirmed this in the joint communiqué issued in January on the occasion of Egypt's Foreign Minister, Isma'el Fahmi's visit to Moscow.

On July 30, 1974, a high level Palestinian delegation, headed by Arafat, arrived in Moscow. The delegation also included non-*fedayeen* members of the Palestinian National Council as well as a member of the Central Committee of the Jordanian Communist Party. Unlike on previous occasions, this visit bore an "official" character and was on the invitation of the Soviet government and the Secretariat of the Central Committee of the Soviet Communist Party. The delegates met with

B. Ponomarev, a candidate member of the Politburo and head of the Central Committee's International Section, R. A. Ul'yanovskiy, the Deputy Chief of that section, V.L. Kudriavtsev, a First Deputy Minister of Foreign Affairs, and various lesser officials. The tone of the meeting was set by a lengthy article in *Izvestia* on July 30, dealing with the Palestinians and the PLO, which asserted that "now almost all the Palestinian organizations occupy more realistic positions," and that the main *fedayeen* leaders "speak of the Soviet Union as a force without which the Palestinian resistance movement could not exist." The article called on the Palestinians to develop "clearly defined tactical aims" which must include a "program which would combine with international [i.e., Soviet] efforts to achieve a just settlement of the Near East conflict." At the same time, the article noted that it is "essential" to take account of the non-homogeneous class character of the Palestinian movement and that "alongside the forces oriented towards progressive development," who were said to form the movement's nucleus, there were also reactionaries and extremists "who do not know how to choose the correct tactics."

This hedge may explain why the joint communiqué issued on August 4 contained only an oblique Soviet recognition of the PLO. In the communique "both sides noted with satisfaction" the various decisions taken by Arab governments and Moslem states to recognize the PLO as the sole legitimate representative of the Palestinians, and it was announced that the Soviet Union had agreed to allow the PLO to open an office for permanent representation in Moscow. As far as it went this constituted a sort of Soviet *de facto* rather than *de jure* recognition of the PLO as representative of the Palestinians. Furthermore, the communique reiterated that the Soviet Union supported the PLO's participation in the Geneva negotiations, but did not specify that it would be necessarily the sole Palestinian group to do so. The PLO representatives in their turn were reported to have called for the "further consolidation of friendship and cooperation with the Soviet Union."

Moscow's failure to become fully and formally identified with the PLO indicated not only a desire to retain political flexibility on the Palestinian problem, but also uncertainty about the extent to which the PLO would actually accept Soviet guidance and control. While noting the greater "realism" among important segments of the *fedayeen*, and movement toward unity, the Soviets seemed to remain disturbed by the indications that such a unity "has not yet been forged," and by the continuing resort to terrorism by various Palestinian groups. Moscow was disappointed that the meeting of the Palestinian National Council in June failed to achieve complete unity and discipline among the *fedayeen*, or to develop a clear program on the Palestinian national state issue or on the question of the PLO's participation in the Geneva negotiations. The meeting did agree on the establishment of a Palestinian national authority on any Palestinian land relinquished by Israel, but on the question of the participation in the Geneva negotiations, the more radical groups, notably the PFLP, feared that this could lead to a compromise of their objective of replacing Israel with a Palestinian state and thus result in a "liquidation" of their struggle. Consequently, the "moderates" chose to avoid taking a firm stand on this issue, all the more so as no invitation for participation in the negotiations had been officially extended to the PLO and, as one leader said, "we know that Israel, the United States and Jordan, and possibly other powers as well, don't want us."

Furthermore, Moscow may have been disturbed by *al-Fatah's* announcement taking responsibility for the June 25 terrorist attack on the Israeli settlement of Nahariya. Previously, *al-Fatah* had avoided taking public responsibility for such acts of terrorism, and since October 1973 had maintained the fiction that all *fedayeen* raids were conducted by units of the Palestinian resistance movement inside Israel. The flamboyant statement issued by *al-Fatah* on the occasion of the Nahariya attack, that "our conflict with the invading enemy will be decided only through armed popular struggle," did not help matters, all the more as the attack came on the heels of the bloody terrorist raids on Qiryat Shemona and Maalot, which had caused widespread public revulsion in the West. Moscow chose to pass over the Nahariya attack in silence and to concentrate instead on denouncing Israel's retaliatory air raids on *fedayeen* bases and camps in Lebanon. Radio Moscow, however, indirectly criticized the Palestinians by warning that those who adopt Mao Tse-tung's "harmful" doctrine of reliance on violence risk isolating the movement "from the moderate elements that call for a peaceful political settlement of the Middle East crisis," and place "certain sections of the population in the host countries [i.e., Lebanon] in opposition to the Palestinians." Even so, Radio Moscow affirmed the Soviet Union's full support for "the efforts of the Arabs to organize a collective and decisive reply to the aggressive attacks of Israel against Lebanon and the Palestinians," and backed this with an offer of arms to Lebanon.

The Soviet leaders were and undoubtedly continue to be disturbed by the indications that even the moderate forces in *al-Fatah* are not fully capable of controlling or resisting the pressures from the more radical elements. Nor can Moscow expect that its exhortations concerning terrorism will prevail among the *fedayeen,* as is evident from the recent interceptions by the Israelis of terrorist teams attempting to cross into Israel from Lebanon. The Soviet Union also has been sensitive to the public criticism of its "struggle for a peace settlement" by the leader of the PFLP, George Habash, a member of the PLO, who has claimed that this "has weakened the socialist movement in the Arab world."[15]

While rejecting such "Maoist demagogy," Soviet spokesmen nevertheless continue to express the hope that other elements of the PLO approach the process of the Palestinian movement's development "if not from Marxist-Leninist positions, then at any rate from positions of revolutionary democracy" and, consequently, that the movement "is one of the potential revolutionary phenomena" in the Arab world and could become a "leading unit" of the Arab anti-imperialist national liberation movement.

Moscow's Views on a Palestinian National State

While in 1973 the Soviet Union gave indications of considering endorsing the concept of the creation of some sort of Palestinian state, in 1974 Moscow moved to a position of outright support for the need to satisfy the Palestinians' "national rights" as a part of the Middle East settlement. Beginning in February, the inclusion of this formula became a nearly regular feature in the agreements and joint communiques issued on the occasion of meetings between high level representatives of the Soviet and Arab governments. This has been true also for various messages sent by Brezhnev and other Soviet leaders to a number of Arab heads of state, and for the statement on the Middle East problem adopted on April 19 by the Political Consultations Committee of the Warsaw Pact. Although Soviet spokesmen and media have also continued on various occasions to refer to the "legitimate rights" of the Palestinians, this is no longer used in juxtaposition to the concept of "national rights," but appears instead to be employed interchangeably, the Soviet Government being officially committed to the latter formula.

While the Soviet Union has not made it clear how far it is willing to go to implement the "national rights" of the Palestinians, Soviet discussions of this issue appear to favor the establishment of an independent Palestinian State on the territory to be relinquished by Israel under the UN Security Council Resolution 242, i.e., the West Bank and Gaza. Moscow has indicated approval of the decision of the Palestinian National Council to establish a "Palestinian national authority" on any portion of Palestinian territory relinquished by Israel. At the same time, it has expressed opposition to the Jordanian proposals to create some sort of autonomous Palestinian region under Jordanian control, or to exclude the Palestinian population of the West Bank and in Jordan from being represented by the PLO, as King Hussein and President Sadat had agreed on in July 1974. *Izvestia* of July 30 warned against plans being "nurtured" by Arab reactionary forces "to take the Palestinian state 'in hand' if it emerges" and "in particular, on how to implement so-called Palestinian autonomy within the framework of the Kingdom of Jordan," in order to prevent such a state from becoming a part of the "progressive forces in the Arab world." The Soviets also publicly identified such schemes with Israel's efforts to prevent the establishment of an independent Palestinian state and its refusal to give up Jerusalem or to negotiate directly with the PLO.

The Soviet Union appears to see in the establishment of an independent Palestinian state an opportunity for bringing it under Soviet influence and thereby strengthening Moscow's position in the Middle East, all the more so as such a state would have difficulties being politically or economically viable and, therefore, could be made dependent on the Soviet Union for political, economic and military support. Thus, a member of the Central Committee of the Jordanian Communist Party wrote in the April 1974 issue of *World Marxist Review* that the establishment of a Palestinian state:

> . . . would lead to bitter resistance on the part of imperialist and Zionist quarters and the Arab reactionaries of neighboring countries [i.e., Jordan]. This would objectively encourage the choice of an orientation towards progressive Palestine national forces—the Arab liberation movement and the progressive regimes of the area on the regional scale, and the world socialist system, primarily the Soviet Union, on the international scale. This state should become the exponent of the revolutionary aspirations of the Palestinian masses.

Subsequently, as was noted, *Izvestia* foresaw the possibility of the Palestinian movement adopting the position of "revolutionary democracy" and called for struggle against efforts of reactionary forces to "extinguish the revolutionary spirit of the Palestinians" and to "place at the head of the future state, when it is created, a bourgeoisie which would cooperate closely with Arab reaction, imperialism and the regimes following a pro-imperialist [i.e., Western] course in the Middle East."

Even so, the Soviet Union has avoided publicly pressing the Palestinians to accept any specific formula for settlement, or clearly defining its views on what the "national rights" of the Palestinians entail. Consequently, Moscow is not tied to specific proposals and formats, and retains a great deal of flexibility vis-à-vis the *fedayeen* and in forthcoming negotiations at Geneva or otherwise. Such a flexible position is advantageous in view of the continuing uncertainties of Palestinian politics, and of the policies of the various Arab governments on the question of the solution of the Palestinian problem, as well as of the attitudes of Israel and the US on this issue. Having endorsed the concept of the "National rights" of the Palestinians, the Soviet Union remains free to accept any formula which provides for the return of some of the Palestinian land by Israel, and thus can choose whether to cooperate in or hinder the attainment of a comprehensive negotiated settlement.

VI Conclusions

The Soviet Union's position on the Palestinian question has been essentially pragmatic and unencumbered by any moral concern for the plight of the Palestinians. The record of Moscow's policies indicates that these have been dictated primarily by considerations of the utility of the Palestinians to the attainment of Soviet objectives. So long as the *fedayeen* complicated, rather than complimented, Soviet relations with Arab client states and could be an embarrassment to Moscow's prestige and image in the world, they presented problems which Soviet strategists preferred to keep at arm's length.

The dynamic aspect of Soviet policy vis-à-vis the Palestinian question has been due to a shift, particularly since the 1973 war, in Soviet appreciation of the utility of the Palestinian question and of the PLO for Soviet policy, as well as to presumed changes in the policies of important elements within the *fedayeen*. Concerning this change, the *fedayeen* have recently tended to adopt positions which seem to signal greater realism and a recognition of the true correlation of forces in the Middle East. For the present, the PLO, under Arafat's leadership and control, has drifted to a position which tacitly accepts the concept of a partial, though admittedly interim, solution to the Palestinian problem and increased readiness to participate in the Geneva negotiations if invited to do so. Under these conditions, it has become more likely that the PLO will establish some sort of Palestinian national authority, either in exile or on whatever Palestinian territory that may be relinquished by Israel. However, the metamorphosis of the *fedayeen* is by no means complete and the unity of the PLO is far from being assured. Thus, while the *fedayeen* movement appears to have moved closer to the Soviet concept of a national liberation movement and has been publicly identified as such by Soviet spokesmen, the complexities of the Middle East situation and the instability of the PLO have led Moscow to hesitate in formally recognizing the latter as the sole representative of the Palestinians or to embrace any specific solution to their problem.

The growing Soviet interest in the Palestinians, as is evident from Soviet pronouncements and contacts of high-level Soviet officials with Arafat, has been heavily influenced by the seeming deterioration in the Soviet position in the Middle East. This development, which began with Sadat's expulsion of a major portion of Soviet advisors from Egypt in July 1972, became more pronounced after the October 1973 War as a result of the Egyptian-US rapprochement, the capture by the US of the predominant role in the negotiatons, and President Nixon's tour of the Middle East. These circumstances, in turn, have enhanced the potential of the Palestinians as an element in Soviet policy in the Middle East, all the more so as the PLO leadership tends to look to Moscow as a friend and supporter of the Palestinian cause.

In the short run, the Palestinians can be a valuable tool of Soviet policy in connection with the Geneva negotiations. By supporting the participation of the Palestinians in the negotiations and their "national rights" as a prerequisite for a "comprehensive settlement" of the Middle East problem, a position which is shared by many Arab states, the Soviet Union would be able to exploit Israel's opposition to this position, to appeal to the conscience of the Arab World and isolate the more moderate regimes, to greatly complicate US negotiatory efforts, and possibly to scuttle the negotiations by supporting maximum Arab demands on the Palestinian as well as territorial issues. Thus, the Soviet Union could use the Palestinian cause in its efforts to capture the initiative and a major role for itself in the Geneva negotiations.

Of course, the Palestinian issue is a type of insurance policy for the Soviet Union, which it may or may not try to collect, depending on its perception of the cost-benefits of its policy options in that respect. The Soviet position on the recognition of the PLO and on the specific meaning of the "national rights" concept is sufficiently flexible to leave Moscow with a great deal of room for maneuver and for adjusting its position to the conditions and opportunities which may arise in the course of the negotiations, as well as to the developments which may take place within the PLO and in its policies. In this manner, the Soviet Union can minimize the risks of its involvement in the Palestinian problem while reaping considerable political and psychological advantages.

Whether a Palestinian state is ever created is perhaps a matter of conjecture. However, should one be established, the Soviet Union assuredly would attempt to exploit it to promote its interests. In such an event, Moscow could have considerable leverage in the new state as a result of its record of support of the "national rights" of the Palestinians, and more particularly, as a source of aid which the Palestinians are likely to seek to develop a viable economy, and in order to remain independent from their Arab neighbors. Unless the Soviets are pre-empted by Arab oil money, their exercise of leverage in such a direction seems probable. The extent to which the Palestinians will regard the creation of a state merely as an interim solution and persist in acts of terrorism against Israel will pose both problems and opportunities for the Soviet Union, depending on the attitudes of Egypt, Syria and Jordan, and on Soviet interest in stabilizing the Middle East situation, or in maintaining tensions in that region. No doubt the Soviet Union could become the main supplier of arms to the Palestinians, unless precluded by the settlement, but even so, it would have the opportunity, if it so chose, to pose as the main protector of a Palestinian state against Israel and in that role remain in juxtaposition to the US, still committed to the support of Israel.

By identifying itself with the Palestinians and supporting their cause, the Soviet Union has attained a position where without foreclosing any of its options, it stands to gain from a failure of a settlement of the Palestinian problem as well as from its solution.

FOOTNOTES

1. For a detailed discussion of Soviet policy, see F. D. Kohler, L. Gouré and M. L. Harvey, *The Soviet Union and the October 1973 Middle East War: The Implications for Detente*, Monographs in International Affairs. (Coral Gables, Fla.: Center for Advanced International Studies, University of Miami, 1974).

2. At the time of the partition of Palestine and the establishment of the State of Israel in 1948, some 860,000 Palestinian Arabs lived on the territory of the Palestinian Mandate.

3. Variously estimated as having from 3,000 to 10,000 active members.

4. *Trud*, October 21, 1969.

5. "The Observations and Views of Soviet Statesmen and Scientists on the Draft Political Program of the Syrian Communist Party," *FBIS-Daily Report–Soviet Union*, Supp. 21, July 14, 1972, pp. 14-15, 23.

6. Fahmi Salfiti, in *Problemy Mira i Sotsializma*, Nos. 10-11, October-November, 1968, pp. 92-98.

7. Unidentified Soviet official cited in Semir Franjiyah, "The Resistance Faced with Peace," *L'Orient-Le Jour*, Beirut, April 4, 1973.

8. V. Aleksandrov, commentary, Radio Moscow, January 21, 1973.

9. L. Tolkunov, "A Grave Fate," *Izvestia*, July 30, 1974.

10. V. Terekhov, "International Terrorism and the Fight Against It," *New Times*, No. 11, March 1974, p. 20.

11. Tolkunov, *Izvestia*, July 30, 1974.

12. Naim Ashab, "To Overcome Crises of Palestinian Resistance Movement," *World Marxist Review*, May 1972, p. 72.

13. Statement by Nayef Hawatmeh, leader of the PDFLP, Iraq News Agency, November 24, 1973.

14. Moscow, Tass, November 26, 1973; *Pravda*, November 27, 1973.

15. M. Maksimov, "Prejudice or Ignorance," *Literaturnaia Gazeta*, August 14, 1974.

VII

Appendices

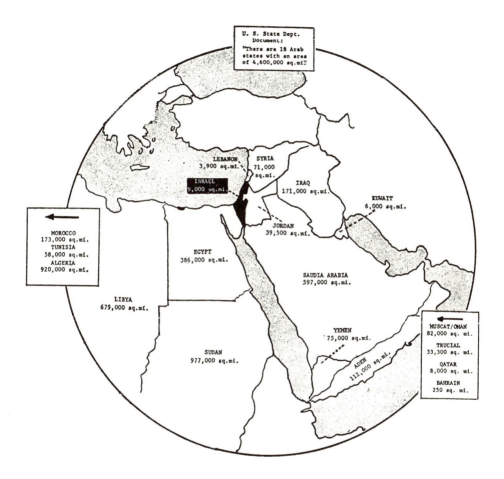

U. S. State Dept.
Document:
"There are 18 Arab
states with an area
of 4,600,000 sq.mi."

LEBANON
3,900 sq.mi.

SYRIA
71,000
sq.mi.

ISRAEL
9,000 sq.mi.

IRAQ
171,000 sq.mi.

KUWAIT
6,000 sq.mi.

JORDAN
39,500 sq.mi.

MOROCCO
173,000 sq.mi.
TUNISIA
58,000 sq.mi.
ALGERIA
920,000 sq.mi.

EGYPT
386,000 sq.mi.

SAUDIA ARABIA
597,000 sq.mi.

LIBYA
679,000 sq.mi.

YEMEN
75,000 sq.mi.

MUSCAT/OMAN
82,000 sq. mi.
TRUCIAL
33,300 sq. mi.
QATAR
8,000 sq. mi.
BAHRAIN
250 sq. mi.

SUDAN
977,000 sq.mi.

ADEN
112,000 sq.mi.

ISRAEL AND THE ARAB WORLD

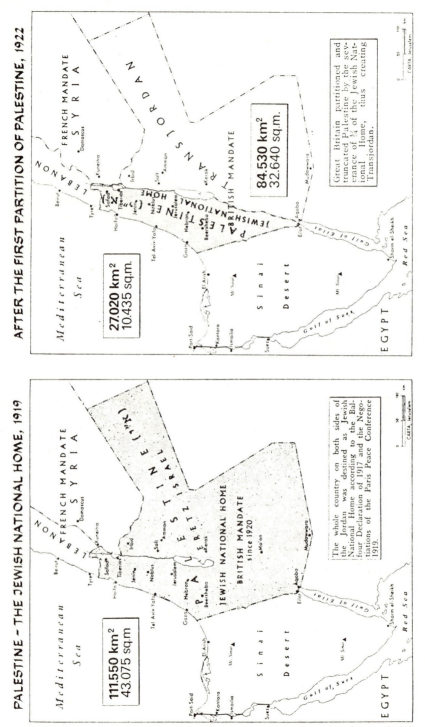

AFTER THE FIRST PARTITION OF PALESTINE, 1922

FRENCH MANDATE
S Y R I A

Damascus

LEBANON

Beirut

Tyre

Safed
Tiberias

Haifa

Kuneitra

Irbid

Salt

Amman

Merah

TRANSJORDAN

BRITISH MANDATE

Jenin

Nablus

Tel Aviv Yafo

Jerusalem

Gaza

Hebron

Beersheba

PALESTINE
{ "EY" }
JEWISH NATIONAL HOME

*Mediterranean
Sea*

27.020 km²
10.435 sq.m.

El Arish

Port Said

Kantara

Ismailia

Suez

Mt. Yenni

Mt. Sinai

S i n a i

D e s e r t

Gulf of Suez

E G Y P T

Eilat
Aqaba

Gulf of Eilat

Sharm el Sheikh

Red Sea

Mudawwara

84.530 km²
32.640 sq.m.

Great Britain partitioned and truncated Palestine by the severance of ¾ of the Jewish National Home, thus creating Transjordan.

0   50   100 km
CARTA, Jerusalem

PALESTINE – THE JEWISH NATIONAL HOME, 1919

FRENCH MANDATE
S Y R I A

Damascus

LEBANON

Beirut

Tyre

Safed
Tiberias

Haifa

Kuneitra

Irbid

Salt

Amman

Merah

Mudawwara

ERETZ ISRAEL ("EY")

P A L E S T I N E

Jenin

Nablus

Jerusalem

Hebron

Beersheba

Gaza

Tel Aviv Yafo

JEWISH NATIONAL HOME

BRITISH MANDATE
since 1920

*Mediterranean
Sea*

111.550 km²
43.075 sq.m.

El Arish

Port Said

Kantara

Ismailia

Suez

Mt. Yenni

Mt. Sinai

S i n a i

D e s e r t

Gulf of Suez

E G Y P T

Eilat
Aqaba

Gulf of Eilat

Sharm el Sheikh

Red Sea

The whole country on both sides of the Jordan was destined as Jewish National Home according to the Balfour Declaration of 1917 and the Negotiations of the Paris Peace Conference 1919.

0   50   90 km
CARTA, Jerusalem

Note: The area south of the Dead Sea was part of the Kingdom of Hedjaz until 1925.

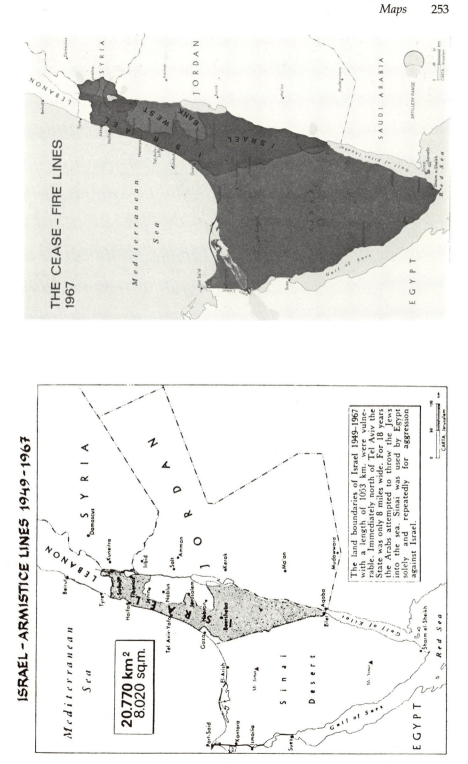

THE CEASE-FIRE LINES
1967

ISRAEL – ARMISTICE LINES 1949-1967

20.770 km²
8.020 sq.m.

The land boundaries of Israel 1949-1967 with a length of 1053 km. were vulnerable. Immediately north of Tel Aviv the State was only 8 miles wide. For 18 years the Arabs attempted to throw the Jews into the sea. Sinai was used by Egypt solely and repeatedly for aggression against Israel.

Palestinian Arab Terrorist Acts Against International Civil Aviation: 1968-1973

The Special Assembly of the International Civil Aviation Organization (ICAO) meeting in Rome on Aug. 30, 1973, passed a Resolution which:

1. *Strongly condemns* Israel for violating Lebanon's sovereignty and for the forcible diversion and seizure of a Lebanese civil aircraft and for violating the Chicago Convention;

2. *Urgently calls* upon Israel to desist from committing acts of unlawful interference with international civil air transport and airports and other facilities serving such transport;

3. *Solemnly warns* Israel that if it continues committing such acts the Assembly will take further measures against Israel to protect international civil aviation.

The Resolution followed Israel's forcing down of a Lebanese plane on August 10, 1973.*

●

The countries sponsoring the Resolution included:

Algeria — which in 1968 held an El Al plane which, with its crew and passengers, had been hijacked to an Algerian airport. The hijackers have not been brought to trial. Algeria actively supports the Palestinian terrorist organizations.

●

Egypt — which permitted a hijacked American jumbo plane to land at Cairo airport, September 1970, where it was blown up. The hijackers were never brought to trial.

The plane, crew and passengers were released several hours later. Israel's argument, for the incident, was that a group of terrorists responsible for a large number of terrorist acts were suspected to be on board the plane. It was later revealed, in Beirut, that the group had in fact planned to be on board but had cancelled their reservations at the last moment.

Egypt's prime minister congratulated the Japanese terrorists guilty of mass murder at Lod airport in May 1972.

Egypt has openly and actively supported the terrorist organizations.

Egypt has consistently backed the *Popular Front for the Liberation of Palestine* (PFLP), which was responsible for many acts of air terrorism, and has provided it, and *el-Fatah*, with practical aid in carrying out terrorist acts. It has supplied both organizations with passports, and allowed them to use the diplomatic pouch.

●

Lebanon — which is the terrorists' permanent base.

●

Libya — which permitted a Lufthansa plane, carrying the Munich terrorists set free by the West German authorities, to be flown to a Libyan airport, October 1972, and also a Japanese Jumbo plane, July 1973. The Libyan authorities have not brought a single hijacker to trial. Financial and operational assistance is provided by Libya to terrorist activities, including air terrorism. A BOAC plane was forced down by the Libyan air force onto the airfield at Benghazi, July 1971. Two Sudanese officers on board were seized and handed over to the Government of the Sudan to be shot.

●

South Yemen — which permitted a Lufthansa plane, hijacked in February 1972, to land in an airfield in South Yemen. The authorities there split the ransom money with the members of the PFLP who had done the hijacking. Those authorities make a practice of furnishing logistic aid to the terrorist organizations to carry out acts of violence overseas and to engage in air terrorism.

●

Saudi Arabia, Kuwait and the Union of Arab Emirates — All these countries regularly underwrite the costs of terrorism, including, in particular, terrorism against international civil aviation.

Of the thirty members of ICAO sponsoring the Resolution of August 30, 1973, fifteen were Arab States.

INCIDENTS

*23 July 1968. El Al plane hijacked in flight from Rome to Lod. Plane forced to land at Algiers. Twenty-one Israeli and eleven other passengers, and ten crew members, kept in detention for five weeks. Two Palestinians, one Syrian. Detained by Algerian authorities, but quickly set free. Departure point of perpetrators: Lebanon. Organization responsible: PFLP. Base: Beirut. Resolution of ICAO: None.

26 Dec. 1968. Gunfire attack on El Al plane at Athens airport. Israeli passenger killed stewardess wounded. Two Palestinians. Sentenced to 17 and 14 years imprisonment, respectively. Freed after the hijacking of an Olympic Airways plane to Beirut on 22 July 1970. Departure point of perpetrators: Lebanon. Organization responsible: PFLP. Base: Beirut. Resolution of ICAO: None

18 Feb. 1969. Gunfire attack on El Al plane at Zurich airport. Co-pilot killed, pilot wounded. Five Palestinians. One killed, others sentenced to varying terms of imprisonment, but freed after the Zerqa affair in September 1970. Departure point of perpetrators: Lebanon. Organization responsible: PFLP. Base: Beirut. Resolution of ICAO: None.

29 Aug. 1969. TWA plane hijacked from Los Angeles, forced to land at Damascus and there sabotaged. Six Israeli passengers detained, and two of them kept in detention until 5 December 1969. Two Palestinians. Not brought to trial. Departure point of perpetrators: Lebanon. Organization responsible: PFLP. Base: Beirut. Resolution of ICAO: None.

8 Sept. 1969. Hand-grenade attack on El Al offices in Brussels. Damage to building. Two Arab boys, one of them 13 years old. One boy took refuge in the Iraqi Embassy, which helped him to escape across the border. Departure point of perpetrators: Jordan. Organization responsible: Boys recruited by Al-Fatah. Base: Jordan. Resolution of ICAO: None.

27 Nov. 1969. Hand-grenade attack on El Al office in Athens. Greek child killed, 13 persons wounded. Two Jordanian terrorists. Sentenced to 11 and 8 years imprisonment, respectively, but freed after the hijacking of an Olympic Airways plane on 22 July 1970. Departure point of perpetrators: Lebanon. Organization responsible: PFLP. Base: Beirut. Resolution of ICAO: None.

12 Dec. 1969. Bomb planted in El Al office in Berlin. Abortive. Unknown. Departure point of perpetrators: Unknown. Organization responsible: Unknown. Base: Unknown. Resolution of ICAO: None.

17 Dec. 1969: Conspiracy to blow up an El Al plane at Heathrow airport, London. Abortive. Two British nationals. One sentenced to 12 years imprisonment, the other turned 'King's evidence'. Departure point of perpetrators: Unknown. Organization responsible: Contacts with Military Attaché of Egyptian Embassy in London. Base: Cairo. Resolution of ICAO: None.

21 December 1969. Attempt to hijack a TWA plane in Athens. Abortive. Three Lebanese. Detained, but freed after the hijacking of an Olympic Airways plane to Beirut on 22 July 1970. Departure point of perpetrators: Lebanon. Organization responsible: Unknown. Base: Unknown. Resolution of ICAO: None.

9 Jan. 1970. TWA plane hijacked to Beirut from Paris. Unknown. Frenchman. Freed after a few days' detention. Departure point of perpetrators: Paris. Organization responsible: Unknown. Base: Unknown. Resolution of ICAO: None

10 Feb. 1970. Attack on El Al plane at Munich airport. Israeli passenger killed, eight other passengers wounded. Two Jordanians, one Egyptian. Murderers set free after Zerqa affair in September 1970. Departure point of perpetrators: Lebanon. Organization responsible: PFLP. Base: Beirut. Resolution of ICAO: None.

21 Feb. 1970. Swissair plane explodes in mid-air over Switzerland. Forty-seven passengers and crew members killed, fifteen of the passengers Israelis. Jebril, a former colonel in the Syrian army, declares responsibility of the general Headquarters of PFLP. Departure point of perpetrators: Lebanon. Organization responsible: General Headquarters of PFLP. Base: Beirut. Resolution of ICAO: A special assembly of ICAO called to discuss stronger security. General debate. No Resolution passed.

21 Feb. 1970. Bomb planted in Air Austria plane in flight from Frankfurt to Vienna. Slight damage to plane. Jebril again declares responsibility of the General Headquarters of PFLP. Departure point of perpetrators: Lebanon. Organization responsible: General Headquarters of PFLP. Base: Beirut. Resolution of ICAO: None.

22 July 1970. Olympic Airlines plane hijacked to Beirut from Athens. Under that blackmail, seven sentenced terrorists were set free by the Greek authorities. Six members of PPSF (Palestine Popular Struggle Front—later joined Al-Fatah). None was brought to justice. Departure point of perpetrators: Lebanon. Organization responsible: PPSF. Base: Beirut. Resolution of ICAO: None.

6 Sept. 1970. Three planes, Pan-Am, TWA and Swissair, with a total of 400 passengers, hijacked on flights from Amsterdam, Frankfurt, Zurich, respectively, to New York. The TWA and Swissair planes were forced to land at Zerqa in Jordan, the Pan-Am plane in Cairo. All three were blown up. Members of PFLP. None of them was brought to justice. On the contrary, seven Arab terrorists imprisoned in other countries for acts of air terrorism were freed under terrorist blackmail in the context of the Zerqa affair. Departure point of perpetrators: Lebanon. Organization responsible: PFLP. Base: Beirut. Resolution of ICAO: None.

6 Sept. 1970. Attempt to hijack El Al plane from Amsterdam to New York. Abortive, but El Al steward wounded. Of the hijackers, Leila Khaled wounded and a second terrorist killed. Two members of PFLP. British authorities freed Leila Khaled on the ground that the crime was not committed on British soil or in British air-space. Departure point of perpetrators: Lebanon. Organization responsible: PFLP. Base: Beirut. Resolution of ICAO: No Resolution was passed by ICAO concerning this specific terrorist operation. At the instance of the United States, ICAO resolved to draft a convention which would allow States to take coordinated action to stop all flights to and from a State which did not free aircraft hijacked to its territory, together with all the passengers and crew members of the aircraft, as well as a State which failed to punish hijackers in accordance with the Hague Convention.

9 Sept. 1970. BOAC plane hijacked on flight from Bombay to Rome and forced to land on the airfield of Zerqa in Jordan. Plane blown up on the airfield. Members of PFLP. Not one of them was brought to justice. Departure point of perpetrators: Unknown. Organization responsible: PFLP. Base: Unknown. Resolution of ICAO: None.

17 Dec. 1970. Five terrorists planned to sabotage an El Al plane, but were arrested on board a Yugoslav plane during a stop-over in Munich. Unknown. Sentenced to three months' imprisonment. Departure point of perpetrators: Unknown. Organization responsible: PFLP. Base: Unknown. Resolution of ICAO: No Resolution was passed concerning this specific terrorist act. A Resolution was passed to convene a special 'consultation' which would discuss the imposition of sanctions.

28 July 1971. Attempt to blow up El Al plane in flight from Rome to Lod by device of explosive suitcase. Abortive. Suitcase taken on to plane by Dutch girl, to whom it had been given by an Arab acquaintance. She did not know that it was booby-trapped. Departure point of perpetrators: Unknown. Organization responsible: Unknown. Base: Unknown, Resolution of ICAO: None.

1 Sept. 1971. Attempt to blow up El Al plane in flight from London to Lod, again by device of explosive suitcase. Abortive. Suitcase taken on to the plane by a Peruvian girl, to whom it had been given by an Arab acquaintance. She did not know that it was booby-trapped. Departure point of perpetrators: Unknown. Organization responsible: Unknown. Base: Unknown. Resolution of ICAO: None.

22 Feb. 1972. Lufthansa plane hijacked in flight from New Delhi to Beirut. Plane forced to land in Aden. Hijackers were paid $5 million for its release. The ransom money was divided between them and the Government of South Yemen. Unknown. Departure point of perpetrators: Unknown. Organization responsible: PFLP, under the cover-name of 'Organization of Victims of Zionist Occupation'. Base: Unknown. Resolution of ICAO: None.

8 May 1972. Sabena plane hijacked in flight from Brussels and forced to land at Lod. Unknown. Four Palestinian terrorists, two of them girls. The two men terrorists were killed by Israeli security personnel. The two girls were sentenced by an Israeli court to life imprisonment. Departure point of perpetrators: Lebanon. Organization responsible: Al-Fatah, under the cover-name of 'Black September'. Base: Beirut. Resolution of ICAO: None.

30 May 1972. Three Japanese terrorists machine-gun pilgrims and other passengers at Lod airport. Twenty-seven persons killed, eighty wounded. Most of the victims were Puerto Rican pilgrims. Japanese members of the Red Army, despatched by PFLP. Departure point of perpetrators: Lebanon. Organization responsible: PFLP. Base: Beirut. Resolution of ICAO: None.

16 Aug. 1972. Booby-trapped gramophone in El Al plane in flight from Rome to Lod. Explosion in luggage compartment, causing slight damage. Two British girls, unaware that the gramophone given to them by two Arab acquaintances was booby-trapped. The two Arabs were freed by the Italian authorities after a short period of detention. Departure point of perpetrators: Italy. Organization responsible: Probably the Jebril group (see incidents listed 21 Feb. above), but now under the cover-name of 'National Youth Group for the Liberation of Palestine'. Base: Lebanon. Resolution of ICAO: None.

29 Oct. 1972. Lufthansa plane in flight from Beirut to Ankara hijacked to Zagreb. Plane released after the Arab terrorists who had murdered eleven Israeli sportsmen at the Olympic Games in Munich had been let go by the West German authorities. Members of Al-Fatah acting under the cover-name of 'National Youth Group for the Liberation of Palestine'. Not one of them was brought to justice. Departure point of perpetrators: Unknown. Organization responsible: Al-Fatah. Base: Beirut. Resolution of ICAO: None.

4 April 1973. Attempt to attack passengers of El Al plane in Rome airport. Abortive. Two Arabs, who were arrested at the airport. They carried forged Iranian passports. They were set free and sent back to Lebanon. Departure point of perpetrators: Unknown. Organization responsible: Unknown. Base: Unknown. Resolution of ICAO: None.

9 April 1973. Attempt to attack Arkia plane in Nicosia airport. Abortive, thanks to intervention of Cypriot police. Four Arabs, carrying forged Saudi Arabian and Oman passports. They were sentenced to 7 years imprisonment. Departure point of perpetrators: Lebanon. Organization responsible: PFLP, under the cover-name of 'National Youth Group for the Liberation of Palestine' (see incident 29 Oct. above). Base: Beirut. Resolution of ICAO: None.

27 April 1973. Murder of an Italian clerk of the El Al office in Rome. Unknown. The murderer, a Palestinian Arab, is still under arrest, and has not been brought to trial. Departure point of perpetrators: Lebanon. Organization responsible: PFLP. Base: Beirut. Resolution of ICAO: None.

19 July 1973. Attack on El Al office in Athens. Abortive. Terrorist took two hostages in adjoining hotel, but released them after negotiations with police. Palestinian. Departure point of perpetrators: Lebanon. Organization responsible: PFLP. Base: Beirut. Resolution of ICAO: None.

20 July 1973. Japanese Jumbo plane hijacked in flight from Amsterdam to Tokyo. Plane blown up at the airport of Tripoli in Libya. Five terrorists. One of them, apparently the leader, an Arab girl, was killed by a grenade that she carried. Another was a Japanese. The terrorists have not been brought to trial. Departure point of perpetrators: Lebanon. Organization responsible: PFLP. Base: Beirut. Resolution of ICAO: None.

5 Aug. 1973. Machine-gunning of passengers in lounge of Athens airport. Four dead, fifty-five wounded. Two Arab terrorists, who are still under arrest. Departure point of perpetrators: Lebanon, by way of Libya. Organization responsible: PFLP. Base: Beirut. Resolution of ICAO: None.

5 Sept. 1973. Five terrorists, who had planned to shoot down an El Al plane over Rome airport by Soviet ground-air rockets supplied by the Soviet Union to the air forces of Egypt, Iraq and Syria, were arrested in Rome. Plan forestalled. Palestinians, carrying presumably forged passports of various countries. Resolution of ICAO: Although the incident took place while the special assembly of ICAO was actually in progress in Rome, the assembly did not see fit to discuss it.

*The above lists the date, outcome and terrorists responsible for the terrorist acts cited.

Palestinian Arab Terrorist Acts – 1968-1974

4 October 1974

Excellency,

On instructions of my Government, and further to the statement made yesterday, 3 October 1974, by Mr. Yigal Allon, the Foreign Minister of Israel, I have the honour to draw your attention to the following:

1. The aims of the so-called P.L.O. are in flagrant violation of the Charter of the United Nations. The "Palestine National Covenant" adopted in 1964 by the "Palestinian National Council" (the highest institution of the P.L.O.) makes it clear beyond any doubt that the objective of that organization is the destruction by armed force of a member state of the United Nations.

Article 19 of the Covenant states:

"The establishment of Israel is fundamentally null and void . . .."

Article 9 provides:

"Armed struggle is the only way to liberate Palestine and is therefore a strategy and not tactics . . ."

Many other provisions of that Covenant call for Israel's destruction and for the uprooting of its inhabitants by armed force.

The P.L.O., which is the umbrella organization of the Arab terrorist groupings, strives, therefore, to deprive a state member of the United Nations of its national existence, and thus of its independence and sovereign equality with other states, and to deny to the Jewish people of Israel its inalienable rights to self-determination and liberty. These objectives, contrary to the fundamental principles and provisions of the United

Nations Charter, place the P.L.O. in a category totally different from that of national liberation movements, the aims of which are, not the destruction of states, but the liberation of subject peoples from colonial rule. Thus the extension of any invitation by the General Assembly to the P.L.O. to participate in the deliberations of the Assembly would be a travesty of the United Nations Charter.

2. Such an invitation would also be a violation of the Rules of Procedure of the General Assembly. Chapter II of the United Nations Charter, which refers to Membership, and Chapter IV which deals with the General Assembly, as well as the Rules of Procedure, make no provision for inviting an organization such as the P.L.O. to attend the Assembly.

On the other hand, Chapter X of the Charter, dealing with the Economic and Social Council, contains a provision, namely, Art. 71, which permits the Council to make suitable arrangements for consultation with non-governmental organizations. Art. 71 and Rule 83 of the Rules of Procedure of the Economic and Social Council provide that certain categories of non-governmental organizations may designate authorized representatives to attend as observers public meetings of the Council and of its committees. Had it been intended to permit such arrangements within the framework of the General Assembly, a provision similar to that contained in Chapter X would have been inserted in the Charter.

Consequently, even if the P.L.O's declared criminal objectives, contrary to the United Nations Charter, were to be disregarded and any invitation were to be extended by the General Assembly to the P.L.O. an amendment of both the Charter of the United Nations and of the Rules of Procedure of the General Assembly would be indispensable.

It is, therefore, evident that an invitation by the General Assembly to the P.L.O. would be contrary to the Charter and to the Rules of Procedure, and thus illegal and not binding.

I am enclosing a list of the principal crimes perpetrated by the P.L.O. in pursuance of its nefarious goals.

I have the honour to request that this letter and its enclosure be circulated as an official document of the General Assembly and the Security Council.

Please accept, Excellency, the assurances of my highest consideration.

Yosef Tekoah
Permanent Representative of Israel
to the United Nations

His Excellency
Dr. Kurt Waldheim
The Secretary-General

---

23 July 1968. El Al plane hijacked on its way from Rome to Lod by three Arab terrorists and forced to land in Algeria. 21 Israeli passengers and 11 crew members held for five weeks. The terrorists were subsequently freed. PFLP—General Command officially accepted responsibility.

26. Dec. 1968. Israeli passenger killed (Mr. Leon Shirdan-50-Haifa engineer) and a stewardess wounded in an attack on an El Al plane at Athens airport by two terrorists. They were caught and sentenced to 17 & 14 years and released on 22.7.70. PFLP—General Command officially accepted responsibility.

18 Feb. 1969. In an attack on an El Al plane at Zurich airport, crew member (co-pilot Yoram Peres) killed and the pilot wounded. The attack was carried out by 5 Palestinians. One terrorist was killed by security guards, the other four, including a woman, were arrested. The woman was released and the three men were sentenced to 12 years hard labor. They were released soon afterwards on 22.7.70. PFLP—General Command officially accepted responsibility.

29 Aug. 1969. TWA plane, on its way from Los Angeles—Lod, hijacked by two Arab terrorists and forced to land in Damascus. Six Israeli passengers were detained, two of whom were held until 5 December 1969.

27 Nov. 1969. One Greek child was killed (George Nasos 2½ years old) and two civilians injured by a grenade thrown at the El Al office in Athens. Two Arab terrorists arrested and sentenced to 8 and 11 years. They were released on 22.7.70.

5 Dec. 1969. In course of preparations for an attack on El Al aircraft at London Airport, four British nationals, recruited by PLO agents arrested. One was sentenced to 10 years imprisonment.

21 Dec. 1969. Attempt made to hijack a TWA plan in Athens. The attempt was thwarted. Three Lebanese PLO terrorists were arrested, and subsequently released on 22.7.70

9 Jan. 1970. TWA plane hijacked in flight from Beirut to Paris by French mercenary of the PLO who was subsequently released in Beirut.

10 Feb. 1970. One Israeli was killed and eight others wounded in an attack on El Al passengers at Munich Airport. Two Jordanian and one Egyptian agents of the PLO were arrested and released in September 1970.

17 Feb. 1970. Three PLO terrorists, one Jordanian and two Iraqis were arrested at Munich Airport and charged with conspiring to hijack an El Al aircraft. They were sentenced to three months in jail. (They had flown in on a Yugoslav plane).

21 Feb. 1970. 47 passengers and crew, including Israelis, Germans, Swiss and other nationals, perished in an explosion of a Swissair plane, leaving Kloten Airport in Zurich. PFLP—General Command officially accepted responsibility.

25 April 1970. Explosion in an El Al office in Istanbul caused by PLO agents.

4 May 1970. Wife of member of Israel Embassy in Asuncion (Paraguay) killed and woman employee wounded by two Arab gunmen of the Popular Front.

22 July 1970. Olympic Airways aircraft hijacked in attempt to bring about release of seven PLO terrorists detained in Greek jails. The plane was on a Beirut-Athens flight. The hijacking was carried out by six agents of the "Palestine Popular Struggle Front".

6 Sept. 1970. Three airplanes of Pan Am, TWA and BOAC, carrying some 400 passengers, were hijacked by members of the PFLP. The Pan Am plane landed in Cairo and was blown up there. The other two aircraft were flown to Zerqa, a desert airfield in Jordan and blown up.

6 Sept. 1970. Attempt to hijack an El Al plane in flight from Amsterdam to New York was thwarted. Leila Khaled, woman terrorist, and a PLO agent, was caught and subsequently released by British authorities, while another terrorist was killed during the attempted hijacking.

8 Sept. 1970. An attempt to blow up an El Al office in Athens was thwarted. Two

PLO terrorists arrested and released the same month following the massive hijackings of several civil aircraft to Jordan.

9 Sept. 1970. A second BOAC plane was hijacked enroute from Bahrain to London. The plane was brought to Zerqa and was blown up there by PLO agents, together with the other three aircraft. (see above).

6 Oct. 1970. Two parcels containing grenades, addressed to the Israeli Embassy in London and the El Al office in London, were found in a locker at Heathrow Airport.

20 July 1971. Three "Molotov cocktails" placed by PLO agents exploded in the Alia office in Rome (Alia is the Royal Jordanian Airline).

23 July 1971. One PLO agent was arrested in an attempt to attack Jordanian targets in Paris. On the same day, "Molotov cocktails" were thrown by PLO terrorists at the Jordanian Embassy in Rome.

24 July 1971. An attempt to blow up an Alia plane by PLO agents was thwarted on the runway at Madrid. The plane was damaged.

28 July 1971. Attempt to blow up an El Al plane by a Dutch woman who carried explosives in a suitcase was thwarted. Responsibility assumed by PFLP—General Command.

5 Sept. 1971. Two attempts to blow up El Al planes on their way from New York to Israel were thwarted. Explosive charges smuggled by women terrorists, one from Peru, the other from the Netherlands were discovered. Both women were arrested on arrival at Lod, but later released as they had been unwittingly used by two Arab terrorists. PFLP—General Command officially accepted responsibility.

8 Sept. 1971. Alia plane hijacked by PLO terrorist to Libya. The hijacker was released by the Libyan authorities.

16 Sept. 1971. PLO attempt to hijack an Alia plane on its way from Beirut to Cairo failed.

28 Nov. 1971. Wasfi Tal, Prime Minister of Jordan, assassinated in Cairo by members of "Black September" (el-Fatah).

15 Dec. 1971. Attempt to assassinate the Jordanian Ambassador in London by PLO agents.

6 Feb. 1972. Oil tanks set on fire in the Netherlands by members of "Black September."

19 Feb. 1972. Attempt to hijack a Jordanian plane flying from Cairo to Amman failed. One PLO agent arrested.

22 Feb. 1972. Lufthansa aircraft hijacked en route from India to Beirut and forced to land in Aden by PLO agents. The hijackers received 5 million dollars from West Germany.

22 Feb. 1972. Oil pipeline damage near Hamburg by agents of "Black September."

9 May 1972. Sabena plane on Brussels-Vienna-Lod route hijacked and landed at Lod Airport. One passenger killed and five injured in the course of an Israeli action which freed the remaining passengers. Two terrorists killed and two others (women) captured. All four were PLO agents. The two women captured are now serving life sentences in Israel.

30 May 1972. Three Japanese mercenaries of the PFLP who came to Lod in an Air France plane, massacred civilians in the passenger terminal at Lod, killing 26 and wounding 80. Two o the terrorists were killed and the third, Kuzo Okamato, is now serving a life sentence.

5 Aug. 1972. Oil tanks blown up in Trieste by Black September agents.

16 Aug. 1972. Explosion in the cargo compartment of an El Al aircraft en route from Rome to Lod. Explosive charge was hidden in a tape-recorder given by PFLP agents to two British girls who were afterwards arrested in Rome. Two Arab suspects were released on 14.2.73.

5 Sept. 1972. Murder of members of Israel's Olympic team in Munich by Black September terrorists. Two sportsmen killed in their living quarters and nine at the Munich Airport.

10 Sept. 1972. A member of the Israel Embassy in Brussels shot by Black September agent.

19 Sept. 1972. Booby-trapped envelopes sent out by P.L.O. agents to addresses in Israel and abroad. One of them killed Dr. Ari Shechori, Agricultural Counsellor, at the Israel Embassy in London.

13 Oct. 1972. Bomb planted by PLO terrorists at El Al office in Paris, discovered and dismantled.

17 Oct. 1972. Bomb discovered at the entrance to a Rotterdam office building, housing the agency of Zim Israel Shipping Lines.

23 Oct. 1972. Hijacking of a Lufthansa aircraft en route from Beirut to Frankfurt. Subsequently, German authorities released three terrorists who participated in the Munich murder of Israel Olympic athletes. The three were flown to Libya. The hijacked plane landed in Yugoslavia. A deal was arranged there, whereby the terrorists, members of el-Fatah, were released.

25 Nov. 1972. Four suitcases with explosives, belonging to a PLO agent, were discovered at Rome Airport.

December 1972. Arab terrorist group discovered in Greece. Planned to proceed by ship to Haifa on a murder and sabotage mission. The terrorists, were PLO agents who had come from Lebanon.

20 Dec. 1972. A booby-trapped motor car left the el-Fatah base Nahar al Bared in Lebanon and arrived in Europe for the purpose of sabotaging an Israeli Embassy.

24 Dec. 1972. A PLO agent arriving from Beirut arrested in London in possession of weapons and explosives which he planned to use against an Israeli Embassy in Scandinavia.

28 Dec. 1972. Six members of the Israeli Embassy in Bangkok seized and held as hostages by PLO agents. They were released after 19 hours. The terrorists were flown to Cairo.

9 Jan. 1973. Bomb planted by PLO exploded in front of Jewish Agency building in Paris.

12 Jan. 1973. PLO terrorist group arrived in Cyprus by ship which was on way to Haifa. Their plan was to carry out sabotage acts in Haifa. The terrorists were discovered and flown from Cyprus to Beirut.

26 Jan. 1973. Israeli citizen murdered by PLO agents in a street in Madrid.

January 1973. Three PLO terrorists detained in Vienna on 20 January and three others arrested at the Austro-Italian border on 30 January. All six had travelled from Beirut planning to attack Jewish immigrants from the USSR at a Vienna transit camp.

March 1973. Seven el-Fatah agents seized Saudi Arabian Embassy in Khartoum and murdered three diplomats—the U.S. Ambassador, the U.S. Charge d'Affaires and the Belgian Charge d'Affaires. The operation was carried out under personal direction of Yasser Arafat, head of the PLO.

3 March 1973. The Cypriot ship 'Sanya' en route to Haifa with 250 Christian pilgrims sabotaged in Beirut harbour by PLO terrorists.

6 March 1973. PLO attempts to bomb the El Al office at Kennedy Airport and two Israeli banks in New York thwarted. (3 cars loaded with explosives were discovered).

12 March 1973. Murder by PLO agents of an Israeli businessman in Cyprus.

15 March 1973. Dianne Campbell Lefevre, a British medical doctor, and her Palestinian partner, Jamil Abdel Hakim, employed by the PLO, detained in Paris after a planned bombing of the Israel Embassy in Paris had been foiled. A Mercedes car loaded with explosives and driven by PLO agents Sakar Mahmoud El Khalil and Mohammed Tabib Tabab had been seized by the French police at the French-Italian border, this leading to the arrest of the doctor and her accomplice.

19 March 1973. Four suitcases containing weapons and explosives discovered in passenger lounges at Rome Airport, presumably meant for attack by PLO on transit passengers.

4 April 1973. Two PLO agents arrested at Rome International Airport after police found two pistols and six hand grenades on them. The Arab terrorists carried Iranian passports, which, according to the police, were almost certainly forged. It is believed that they were planning to hijack an aircraft.

9 April 1973. Bomb thrown at Israel Ambassador's residence and PLO attack on El Al plane in Nicosia, Cyprus.

11 April 1973. "Molotov cocktail" thrown by PLO terrorists at El Al office —Geneva.

27 April 1973. Italian employee of El Al in Rome murdered by member of "Black September", Zahria Abu Saleh.

27 April 1973. Three PLO terrorists carrying 10 kg. of explosives detained at Beirut Airport while boarding plane for Nice.

19 July 1973. One PLO terrorist failed in an attack on the El Al office in Athens, but seized two hostages. The hostages were released after negotiations with the police and the terrorist was allowed to fly to Kuwait.

20 July 1973. PLO agents hijacked to Dubai a JAL plane en route from Paris to Tokyo. Five days later the plane was flown to Libya and blown up there. (24.7.73). One terrorist was killed in the plane by a grenade explosion and three others were released by the Libyan authorities.

5 August 1973. Two PLO agents threw hand grenades and opened fire with automatic rifles on passengers at the Athens International Terminal, killing five and wounding 54. The terrorists were arrested and sentenced to death. Their sentence was commuted in February 1974.

25 November 1973. KLM aircraft carrying 271 passengers was hijacked by three Arab terrorists in flight between Beirut and Nicosia and finally landed in Dubai. The terrorists were released by the Dubai authorities.

5 September 1973. Five PLO terrorists were caught in Rome while attempting to launch a SAM-7 missile from a position near Rome airport at an Israeli passenger aircraft. Two months later, the terrorists were released on bail.

17 December 1973. A Pan-Am plane was blown up at Rome Airport by Arab terrorists. 31 passengers were killed and 30 wounded, while the five terrorists who committed the crime hijacked a Lufthansa plane with 12 hostages on board (one of the hostages was shot and killed) and flew to Kuwait. The terrorists surrendered to the Kuwait authorities who handed them over to the PLO. The National Palestinian Liberation Front accepted responsibility.

30 December 1973. An assassination attempt was carried out on the life of Mr. Joseph Edward Sieff in London. The PFLP made a statement on 31 December in

Beirut in which it claimed responsibility for the crime.

20 January 1974. One Libyan agent of the PLO was arrested in London, with a bomb in his possession. His target was the El Al office in London.

3 March 1974. Four terrorists hijacked a British Airways plane en route from Beirut, over Yugoslav airspace, and landed the plane at Amsterdam Airport. The passengers disembarked and the plane was burned. The National Arab Youth Organization for the Liberation of Palestine (cover name for the PFLP) accepted responsibility.

14 March 1974. Leabnese police arrested six PLO terrorists in the course of an attempt to hijack a KLM plane.

12 June 1974. Two PLO agents preparing terror attacks at the Cup Games were arrested in Heidelberg, Federal Republic of Germany.

The above list does not include the innumerable attacks carried out by PLO terrorists operating from neighbouring Arab states, and in particular from Lebanon, against Israeli children, women and men on Israeli territory. These attacks include *inter alia* the massacre of children on a school bus near Avivim (22 May 1970), the murder of families of civilians, including children, in Kiryat Shmona (11 April 1974), the slaughter of 24 school-children and the wounding of more than 70 others in Ma'alot (15 May 1974). The PLO or its member groups have accepted responsibility for all these attacks.

The Political Program of the Palestine National Council

The following is the text of the PLO Phased Political Program:

Proceeding from the Palestinian National Charter and the PLO's Political Program which was approved during the 11th session held from January 3-12, 1973, believing in the impossibility of the establishment of a durable and just peace in the area without the restoration to our Palestinian people of all their national rights, foremost of which is their right to return to and determine their fate on all their national soil, and in the light of the study of the political circumstances which arose during the period between the Council's previous and current sessions, the Council decides the following:

1. The assertion of the PLO position regarding Resolution 242 is that it obliterates the patriotic (wataniyah) and national (gawmiyah) rights of our people and deals with our people's cause as a refugee problem. Therefore, dealing with this resolution on this basis is rejected at any level of Arab and international dealings including the Geneva Conference.

2. The PLO will struggle by every means, the foremost of which is armed struggle, to liberate Palestinian land and to establish the people's national, independent and fighting authority on every part of Palestinian land to be liberated. This requires making more changes in the balance of power in favor of our people and their struggle.

3. The PLO will struggle against any plan for the establishment of a Palestinian entity the price of which is recognition [of Israel], conciliation [with it], secure borders, renunciation of the national right, and our people's deprivation of their right to return and their right to determine their fate on their national soil.

4. Any liberation step that is achieved constitutes a step for continuing [the efforts] to achieve the PLO strategy for the establishment of the Palestinian democratic state that is stipulated in the resolutions of the previous National Councils.

5. The PLO will struggle with the Jordanian national forces for the establishment of a Jordanian-Palestinian national front whose aim is the establishment of a national democratic government in Jordan: a government that will cohere with the Palestinian entity to be established as a result of the struggle.

6. The PLO will strive to establish a unity of struggle between the two peoples and among all the Arab liberation movement forces that agree on this program.

7. In the light of this program the PLO will struggle to strengthen national unity and to elevate it to a level that will enable it to carry out its duties and its patriotic and national tasks.

8. The Palestinian national authority, after its establishment, will struggle for the unity of the confrontation states for the sake of completing the liberation of all Palestinian soil and as a step on the path of comprehensive Arab unity.

9. The PLO will struggle to strengthen its solidarity with the socialist countries and the world forces of liberation and progress to foil all the Zionist, reactionary and imperialist schemes.

10. In the light of this program, the Revolutionary Command will work out the tactics that serve and lead to the achievement of these aims.

A recommendation has been added to the political program. The recommendation stipulates that the Executive Committee implement this program:

Should a fateful situation connected with the future of the Palestinian people arise, the Council will be called to hold a special session to decide on it.

> *Voice of Palestine, Cairo,*
> *June 8, 1974, quoted from BBC*
> *Monitoring Service*
> *ME/4622/A/2, June 11, 1974*

Selected Bibliography

George Antonius, *The Arab Awakening—The Story of the Arab National Movement* Hamish Hamilton, London, 1945. Written by an Arab scholar and participant in Arab-Jewish negotiations, this book is often referred to as the "classic study" of Arab nationalism. It offers an account of ideas and events which begins in mid-nineteenth century, and it brings the story forward to the period between the two World Wars.

Shlomo Avineri (Ed.), *Israel and the Palestinians,* New York, St. Martin's Press, 1971. An important collection of a dozen articles by contributors of differing political persuasions which focus on the confrontation between Zionism and Palestinian Arab nationalism.

David Ben Gurion, *My Talks With Arab Leaders,* New York, The Third Press, 1973. Ben Gurion writes of his untiring thirty-years efforts to establish rapport and harmony with numerous Arab leaders and how all of his approaches, many revealed here for the first time, came to naught. This first-hand account should lay to rest, once and for all, that Ben Gurion and company were oblivious to Arab nationalism. Much to the contrary at least this leader gave it perhaps even more import than many Arab leaders would have claimed.

Aharon Cohen, *Israel and the Arab World,* Funk and Wagnall's, 1970. The author, a member of the Left-wing Zionist movement since 1926 and an active participant in efforts toward Jewish-Arab rapprochement, offers a comprehensive account of relationships between Jews and Arabs—with an intensive study of the period of the Mandate.

Sir Geoffrey Furlonge, *Palestine is My Country: The Story of Musa Alami,* New York, Praeger Publishers, 1969. A sympathetic biography of a prominent Palestinian-Arab spokesman.

Sylvia G. Haim (Editor), *Arab Nationalism—An Anthology* (University of California Press, 1962). This very useful anthology offers an inclusive selection of Arab ideologists.

Yehoshafat Harkabi, *Arab Attitudes Toward Israel,* New York, Hart Publishing Co., Inc., 1972. The author, Senior Lecturer in International Relations at the Hebrew University and former Chief of Intelligence of the Israeli Army analyzes the depth of the hatred of both Zionism and Judaism which are manifested in over 100 books written by Arabs and in Arab newspapers.

Susan Lee Hattis, *The Bi-National Idea in Palestine During Mandatory Times,* Haifa, Shikmona Publishing Company, 1970. Originally written as a doctoral dissertation, this well-researched volume examines all aspects of the idea of bi-nationalism from 1922 to 1948. The author, who began this work strongly believing in bi-nationalism, concludes with a very skeptical outlook on the feasibility of this solution for the foreseeable future.

Arthur Hertzberg (Editor), *The Zionist Idea—a Historical Analysis and Reader.* This anthology includes the writings of ideologists who represent the many diverse tendencies of though within the Zionist movement.

Irving Howe and Carl Gershman (Eds.), *Israel, the Arabs and the Middle East,* New York, Quadrangle Books and Bantam Books, 1972. More than twenty distinguished scholars and journalists from the democratic left critically sympathetic to Israel, explore the dynamism of Israeli society and the clash between Zionism and Palestinian-Arab nationalism.

J.C. Hurewitz, *The Struggle for Palestine,* W.W. Norton and Company, New York, 1950. This is probably the most authoritative (primarily) political history of the period from 1936 to 1948, leading to the emergence of the State of Israel.

John Laffin, *Fedayeen: The Arab-Israeli Dilemma,* New York, The Free Press, 1973. A veteran British journalist provides the most up-to-date account of the status and activities of the various *fedayeen* groups. The author reveals that the failure of their struggle against Israel has led some "guerrillas" to become involved in totally non-Arab causes. Based on research of published material and interviews with Israelis and Arabs, including leaders of rank-and-file *fedayeen,* the author explains the total failure of the movement.

David Pryce-Jones, *The Face of Defeat,* New York, Holt, Rhinehart and Winston, 1972. A veteran British journalist provides a realistic portrait of the Palestinian guerrillas. One of the most readable and reliable books on the subject.

Jon Kimche, *The Second Arab Awakening,* New York, Holt, Rhinehart and Winston, 1970. A rewarding history of the half century beginning with the Arab Revolt of 1916 to the aftermath of the Six Day War of June 1967. Particularly informative on inter-Arab tensions and conflicts.

—*There Could Have Been Peace,* New York, The Dial Press, 1973. A stinging, documented critique of the policies of England, France, United States, and Soviet Union with respect to their treatment of the Arab-Israeli conflict. More significantly, Kimche is highly critical of what he portrays as the two-faced political behavior of Chaim Weizmann during the period 1917-1921, and of Golda Meir, since 1967. Strangely, Kimche's hero is Dayan, whom he sees as following the forthrightness of Ben Gurion, yet the author has no discussion of the period of Ben Gurion's leadership. Some of Kimche's major hypotheses would seem to fall flat when compared with Ben Gurion's account in his book, *My Talks With Arab Leaders,* cited above.

F.H. Kisch, *Palestine Diary,* London, Victor Gollancz, 1938. Between 1923 and 1931, Colonel Kisch served as liaison officer between the Zionist Executive and the British Administration of Palestine. The Diary is a rich source of information concerning relations between Jews and Arabs under the Mandate.

Colonel Richard Meinertzhagen, *Middle East Diary 1917-1956,* Thomas Yoseloff, New York, 1959. The author, a British officer of Danish origin, was chief political officer in Palestine and Military Adviser to the Middle East Department of the British Colonial Office. He was in a unique position to report what happened during the years of his career in the Middle East.

Hazem Zaki Nuseibeh, *The Ideas of Arab Nationalism,* Cornell University Press, 1959. A Ph.D. from Princeton University, the author was a member of the Jordan-Israeli Mixed Armistice Commission and the representative of Jordan on the Advisory Council to the United Nations Relief and Works Agency. The book is partly intellectual history and partly analysis of ideas.

Royal Commission on Palestine, *Palestine Royal Commission Report,* His Majesty's Stationery Office, London, 1937. Often referred to as the Peel Report, after the name of the Chairman of the Commission appointed by the British government to investigate the riots of 1936 and to make recommendations, this volumn presents the most comprehensive and objective account of the historical background and the situation in 1936 that one can find.

James Parkes, *A History of Palestine from 135 A.D. to Modern Times,* Penguin Books Inc., London, 1970. Despite the large scope of events signified in the title, more than a third of this book is devoted to the modern period. The basic historical background offered in the first two-thirds is invaluable preface. Although the book is sophisticated and hardly "elementary," it provides a good introduction for the student who is beginning his study of the Arab-Israeli conflict.

Don Peretz, Evan M. Wilson and Richard J. Ward, *A Palestine Entity?* Washington, D.C., The Middle East Institute, 1970. Four essays by American advocates of Palestinian nationalism examining its history, the projections and economics of the Palestinian entity and the role of Jerusalem in that entity.

Y. Porath, *The Emergence of the Palestinian-Arab National Movement, 1918-1929,* Frank Cass, London, 1974. (Distributed in the U.S. by International Scholarly Book Services, Inc., Portland, Oregon). An extensively researched history of the infancy of Palestinian-Arab national consciousness, which developed in reaction to Zionism, and of Palestinian Arab opposition to Syria's ambition to retain Palestine as part of "Southern Syria."

William B. Quandt, Fuad Jabber, Ann Mosely Lesch, *The Politics of Palestinian Nationalism,* Berkeley, University of California Press, 1973. The most important part of this book, Part II, "Political and Military Dimensions of Contemporary Palestinian Nationalism," by William B. Quandt, was originally written for the Rand Corp., as was Part III, "The Palestinian Resistance and Inter-Arab Politics," by Fuad Jabber. Part I, "The Palestine Arab Nationalist Movement Under the Mandate," by Ann Mosely Lesch, is an outgrowth of a doctoral dissertation. The analysis of Quandt, not without shortcomings, is the most comprehensive and objective study available.

Zeev Schiff and Raphael Rothstein, *Fedayeen: Guerrillas Against Israel,* New York,

David McKay Co., 1972. The authors, both members of the staff of Israel's independent daily newspaper, *Ha'aretz*, portray the histories of the major *fadayeen* groups. Of particular interest is the chapter which consists of interviews with a number of *fedayeen* in Israeli prisons.

Christopher Sykes, *Crossroads to Israel 1917-1948*, The World Publishing Company, Cleveland and New York, 1965. The author states that his purpose is to present "an account free of bias." One of his aims becomes clear to the reader—that of exonerating the British Administration. Nevertheless, he presents an invaluable historical account.

Hans E. Tütsch, *Facets of Arab Nationalism*, Detroit, Wayne State University Press, 1965. Does not deal directly with Palestinian Arab nationalism, but rather with various forms of Arab nationalism and, as such, is a very good introduction.

Shabtai Teveth, *The Cursed Blessing*, New York, Random House, 1969. One of Israel's best known journalists, author of the biography of Moshe Dayan, tells the story of Israel's occupation of the West Bank during and after the Six Day War. The author is an obvious sympathizer of Dayan's policies on the West Bank.

Chaim Weizmann, *Trial and Error—An Autobiography*, Harper Brothers, London, 1949. Although the first President of Israel was a controversial figure even within the Zionist movement, his autobiography remains one of the best introductions to an understanding of Zionist aspirations, as well as an account of the relevant events of the first half of this century.

Index

Abdu', Muhammad, 100
Abdullah, the Emir, 2, 70, 77, 114, 183, 203
Acheson, Dean, 199
Afghani, Jumal al-Din al-, 100
Aflaq, Michel, 110
African Institute of the USSR Academy of
  Sciences, the, 229
Alami, Musa, 113
Algeria, 60-1, 66, 79, 156, 191, 234, 254-5, 261
Ali, Azziz Bey, 43
Ali, Muhammad, 100, 110
Allenby, General, 49
Allon, Yigal, 180, 260
Allon Plan, the, 4
American Board of Commissioners for
  Foreign Missions, 98
American University of Beirut, the, 99, 116
Antonius, George, 99, 200
Arafat, Yasser, 5, 114-6, 130, 141, 203-4,
  208-9, 231, 244, 264
    as representative of Palestinians, 128-9,
    131, 139-40, 203-4, 211
    aims for West Bank, 206, 225
    relations with Soviet Union, 132, 232,
    240-2, 246
Arab Congress, the, 200
Arab Covenant, the, 200
Arab Executive Committee, the, 123
Arab Higher Committee, the, 168

Arab Interstate Information Committee,
  the, 226
Arab League, the, 69, 79, 124, 131, 217
  Council, 115, 231
Arab Learned Society, the, 99
Arab Liberation Front, the, 126, 139, 142, 157
Arab National Committee, the, 53
Arab Nationalist Movement, the, 116, 125-6,
  140, 142
Arab Refugees, (see Refugees, UNRWA, etl)
Arab Summit Conference(s), the, 79, 152,
  219, 242
Assad, President, 141
Attari, Samiel, 141
Azm, Sabiq Jolal al-, 113
Azoury, Neguib, 97, 113

Ba'ath Party, the Arab, 115, 118, 126, 200, 242
Balfour Declaration, the, 3, 42, 46-7, 49, 79,
  122, 145, 150, 200-3, 214, 217, 219
Begin, Menahem, 190, 193
Beliaev, I., 229, 239, 240
Ben Gurion, David, 134-5, 226
Bey, Cavid, 101
Bitar, Nadim al-, 113
Black Panthers, the, 64-5
Black September, 117, 226, 231, 258, 263-5
Borochov, Dov Ber, 108
Brezhnev, (Leonid), 229, 240, 244

273

British Mandate for Palestine, the, 2-3, 25-6, 29, 41-2, 53-4, 58, 78-9, 81-4, 122, 144, 150, 194-5
Bustani, Butrus, 99, 100, 106

Cecil, Lord, 46
Central Committee of the Palestine Resistance Movement, the, 139
China, 226, 232, 234
Communist Party, the Israel, 84
C.P.S.U., the, 237
    Central Committee, 233, 242-3
Conference of Arab Refugees, the, 69
Custodian of Absentees' Property, the, 82

Dajany, Arif, 41
Dayan, Moshe, 114, 185, 188, 192
Deir Yassin, 54
D'Estaing, President Valery Giscard, 181
Druze, the, 82, 85, 99-100

Eban, Abba, 67, 170
ed-Din, Dr. Mohammed Salah, 69
Egypt, 18-19, 27, 52
    and Arab refugees, 69, 78
    and Israel, 178-9, 182, 193, 224
    and Jordan, 222
    and the Palestinian organizations, 79, 141, 161, 164, 167, 169, 205, 212, 217, 220, 254-6
    and the Soviet Union, 229, 234, 242, 246-7
    and Syria, 116
    nationalism, 102
Eisenhower, President, 67
Eliav, Arie Lova, 206
Eshkol, Levi, 67, 192

Fahmi, Isma'el, 242
Faisal, King, 49, 70, 122, 201
Families Reunion Scheme, the, 81
Fanon, Franz, 149
Fatah, el, 70, 125, 128, 131, 139-43, 194, 204
    and Arafat, 140
    and Jordan, 129
    and Nasser, 116, 130
    and West Bank, 93
    founded, 115, 219
    ideology, 126, 147-9, 157
    on a Palestinian State, 225
    Soviet relations with, 231-5, 241, 243
    terrorist acts, 221, 226, 244, 255-6, 258, 263-4
Frankfurter, Felix, 201
French, Lewis, 23, 26, 27

Gaza (Strip) the, 2, 19-20, 22-3, 27, 194, 213-4, 217
    as part of Palestinian state, 203-5, 210, 223-4
    attitude to Jordan, 119
    Hussein Plan for, 222

Israel and, 115, 179, 182, 189-90, 192-6, 206
Palestinian organizations and, 159, 163, 211, 220
    refugees in, 53, 55-6, 67, 78, 125, 231
    Soviet attitude to, 232, 245
General Syrian Congress, the, 200
Geneva Peace Conference, the, 3, 5, 79, 129, 140, 159, 161-3, 165, 167, 169-71, 176, 204, 207-9, 211-12, 222, 225, 267
    Soviet attitude to, 229-30, 241-3, 246-7
Ghor-Mudawwarra Agreement, the, 25-6
Ghory, Emil, 52
Glubb, General Sir John, 52
Gordan, Aharon David, 108
Graetz, Heinrich, 103
Grand Mufti of Jerusalem, the, (see Hussaini, Hajj Amin al)
Gromyko, (Andrei), 242

Habash, Dr. George, 116-7, 125, 140-1, 157, 168, 171, 190, 204, 211, 220, 225, 231, 244
Hammami, Said, 224, 226
Hammarskjold, Dag, 2, 67
Hammouda, Yahya, 139
Hamula, the, 82
Hanna, George, 113
Hawatmeh, Nayef, 117, 126-7, 141, 171, 190, 203, 211, 220, 225, 231
H'deb, Musa, 44
Hedjaz, 50, 122
Herzl, Theodore, 97, 103, 108, 188
Hess, Moses, 104-8
Heykal, Mohammed, 69
Hirschmann, Ira, 56
Histadrut (also Histadruth), 44, 65, 85, 107
Hitler, (Adolph), 80, 134, 204
Hiyali, Dr. Abd el Wahab el, 142
Hope-Simpson, Sir John, 26
Hourani, Akhram, 110
Husayni, Musa Kazim al-, 123
Hussaini, Abd el-Kader, 130
Hussaini, Hajj Amin al, 102, 114, 123-4, 130, 182, 200, 214
Hussaini family, the, 113, 123, 140
Hussein, Abd el Kader, 51
Hussein, Sherif of Mecca, 41-3
Hussein, King (of Jordan), 4, 70, 88, 185, 211
    and terrorist organizations, 70, 79, 117, 221
    and the Palestinians, 71, 129, 210
    Israel's attitude to, 177
    on a Palestinian-Jordanian federation, 227
    Palestinian organizations attitude to, 167, 171, 205, 210, 220, 224
    Soviet attitude to, 237, 245
Hussein Plan, the, 4, 117, 222-3

Ibrahim, Muhassan, 126
Institute for Palestine Studies, the, 117-8
International Civil Aviation Organizations (ICAO) the, 254-9
Iraq, 14, 38, 50, 52, 69, 84, 101-2, 122-3, 142,

164, 194, 205, 256
  Jewish refugees from, 58, 60, 66, 72
  Soviet ties with, 230, 234
Islam
  as state religion, 146
  concept of, 100, 102, 108
Israel, the State of, 1, 21, 60, 67, 70-2, 83, 85,
    114, 135, 176-8, 180-1, 184, 187, 190, 214,
    233
  and Egypt, 125
  and Palestinian organizations, 220
  and Arab refugees, 215-6
  attitude to Arafat, 190, 192
  attitude to PLO 180-2, 190, 192, 194
  and West Bank, 88-91, 93, 185, 211
  establishment of, 2, 29-30, 205
Israel Labor Party, the (Mapai), 65
Israeli Arabs, 3, 81-6, 116, 231
Istikal (the Arab Independence Party), 44
Iyad, Abu, 140, 204

Ja'abari, Sheik Ali, 129, 211, 223
Jarvis, C.S., 31
Jebril, Ahmed, 141-2, 190, 211, 225, 256, 258
Jerusalem, 4, 9, 11-12, 28, 42, 52, 64, 107, 114,
    122, 200
  Islamic period, 14-16, 18-19
  Ottoman period, 24, 101, 121
  Arabs in, 78, 81, 83, 86, 209, 211-12, 218
  Hussein Plan for, 223
Jewish Agency for Palestine, the, 2, 41-2, 48,
    61, 184, 264
Jewish Refugees (Immigrants), 58-65
Johnston, Eric, 67
Johnston (Waters) Plan, 73
Jordan, the Hashemite Kingdom of, 24, 52,
    207, 209-10, 214, 217, 221
  and Nasser, 116
  and Palestinians, 79, 86, 90, 92, 129, 223
  Israeli attitudes to, 175-8, 180, 182, 186,
    195-6
  Palestinian organizations and, 70, 117,
    125, 129, 141, 144, 159, 162-5,
    171, 201, 220, 225-6, 232
  refugees in, 53, 55-6, 69-70, 77, 125, 202-3
  relations with West Bank, 194, 205, 211,
    224
  Soviet attitude to, 237, 243, 245, 247
  terrorism from, 256, 263
Jordanian Communist Party, the, 142, 233,
    238, 242, 245
Judaea, 19, 46, 78-9, 176-7, 179, 185, 206-7

Kader, abd el-, 102, 114
Kailany, Rashid Ali al-, 102
Kamhawi, Dr. Walid, 210
Kassem, Az-el-Din-el, 114
Kawakji, Fawzi el, 51-2
Kawakibi, Abdul Rahman al-, 100
Kazem Pasha, Musa, 41
Khalaf, Salah, 140, 225, 231

Khaled, Leila, 53, 257, 262
Khartoum Conference, the, 69
Khattib, Anwar, 211
King-Crane Commission, the, 201
Kissinger, (Dr. Henry), 170, 212, 225, 228-9
Kosygin, (Alexei), 233
Krochman, Nachman, 103
Kudriavtsev, V.L., 242

Lansing (Robert), 47
Lausanne Conference, the, 2
Lawrence, Colonel (T.E.), 50, 101
League of Nations, the, 2, 123, 150, 201
League of Nations Mandate for Palestine,
    the, 25, 29, 77, 113
Lebanon, 27, 60, 73, 99, 112, 193-4, 200, 205,
    211, 240
  Palestinian organizations in, 117, 140-1,
    146, 159, 167, 189, 201, 220-1, 226
  refugees in, 53, 56, 70, 78, 114, 125, 231
  and Israel, 254
  as terrorists' base, 244,
Levi, Shabetai, 53, 256-9
Libya, 55, 60, 205
  and Arab refugees, 67, 78
  and Palestinian organizations, 164, 255,
    259
  Soviet Union and, 230
London Conference, the, 124
Lutef, Abu, 140

McMahon Letter, the, 201

Ma'alot, 133-5, 191, 203, 225, 244, 266
Malik, Abd al-, 15-17
Malik, Charles, 200
Mapam, 84-5
Mapu, Avraham, 103
Marx (Karl and Marxists), 104-5, 108, 140-1,
    236
Matzpen, 117, 155
Mazer, Abd el Mukhsan Abu, 142, 210
Meir, Golda, 65, 67, 135, 185, 190, 206, 222
Milner, Lord, 49
Mukhsan, Zahir, 141, 166, 231
Muslim Brotherhood, the, 115, 130, 140, 235
Muslim General Congress, the, 84

Nashashibi family, the, 113, 123
Nashashibi, Nasir an, 218
Nashashibi, Ragheb, 41
Nasser, President (Abdul Gamal), 69, 84,
    90, 115-6, 125, 129-30, 140-1, 148, 167, 187
Nassur, Adib, 113
National Arab Youth Organization for the
    Liberation of Palestine, the, 258, 266
National Council of the Palestine Liberation
    Organization, the, (*see* PLO National
    Council)
Nazi(s), 60, 101, 103, 151, 182, 226, 233
Nixon, President (Richard), 185, 230

Nordau (Max), 103

Organization of Victims of Zionist Occupa-
tion, the, 258
Palestine, 1, 3, 9, 213
    Arabs in, 21, 23, 26-32, 34-5, 37-8, 49
    British Mandate period, 24-5, 34, 37, 41,
    77, 122
    Islamic period, 10-11, 13-15, 17, 20
    Jews in, 13-14, 18-19, 21, 23, 42-4, 46-8, 50,
    124, 217
    Partition of, 2, 51-2, 125
    Ottoman period, 20-2
Palestinian Arab Congress, the, 122,
Palestinian Arab Executive Committee, the,
    122
Palestine Arab Higher Committee, the, 52
Palestine Land Development Company,
    the, 26
Palestine Liberation Army, the, 70, 115, 139,
    231
Palestine Liberation Organization, the,
    (PLO), 4-5, 77, 115, 128-30, 139-43, 145,
    156, 164, 166-8, 184, 194, 201, 203-4,
    206-7, 242
    aims, 80, 159-65, 170-1, 226, 260-1
    and China, 232
    and Geneva talks, 141
    and Jordan, 205, 222
    and National Covenant, 146, 152-3
    and Soviet Union, 132, 228, 230, 233,
    235-6, 238, 240, 242, 245-7
    and terrorism, 195, 212, 220, 262-6
    as representative of the Palestinians, 79,
    131, 210-11, 223, 231, 267-8
    ideology, 147, 149, 154, 267-8
PLO Emergency Conference, the, 226
PLO Executive Committee, the, 139, 142,
    155, 219, 268
PLO Research Center, the, 139, 150, 223, 225
Palestine Popular Struggle Front, the, 262
Palestine National Assembly, the, 154-7
Palestinian National Congress(es), the, 115,
    126, 128, 139, 143, 145, 168, 218-9, 231
Palestine National Covenant (*also* Charter)
    the, 5, 70, 79, 80, 117, 126, 128, 140, 142-6,
    154, 164, 181, 218, 260, 267
Palestinian National Council(s), the, 80, 128,
    139-40, 143, 145, 151, 162-5, 190, 204,
    218-20, 225, 243, 245, 260, 267-8
Palestine National Front, the, 142, 231, 242
Palestine Struggle Front, the, 256-7, 262
Palestine Royal Commission Report, the,
    22, 24, 26-8, 47, 50, 215
Pasha, Ibrahim, 100
Pasha, Mustafa Selaleddin, 101
Passfield, Lord, 48
Peel Commission Report (*see* Palestine
    Royal Commission Report)
Ponomarev, B., 242
Popular Democratic Front for the Liberation

of Palestine (PDFLP) the, 117, 139, 141,
    171, 203, 225, 231
    ideology, 126, 155
    Soviet Union and, 236, 244
    terrorism, 220
Popular Front for the Liberation of Palestine
    (PFLP) the, 116-7, 139-41, 168, 171, 211,
    219, 225, 231
    aims, 204
    and Egypt, 255
    and National Covenant, 146
    ideology, 126-7, 157
    Israel's attitude to, 190
    role in Arab nationalism, 109, 143
    Soviet Union and, 236, 243
    terrorist acts, 216, 255-9, 264-6
Popular Front-General Command (PF-GC)
    the, 139, 141-2, 190, 219-20, 225, 231,
    262-3
Protocols of the Elders of Zion, the, 60

Qadhafi, Colonel, 102

Rabin, Yitzhak, 175-9, 206, 208
Rahman, Asad Abdul, 225
RASD, the, 226
Refugees, (*see also* Egypt, Lebanon, Syria
    and UNRWA)
    Arab, 21, 29, 53-5, 66-72, 114, 215
    Jewish, 58-65, 72-3
Reese, Dr. Elfan, 72
Rhodes Armistice Agreement, the, 81, 214
Rifai, Zaid el, 204
Rothschild, Baron Edmund de, 48
Royal Institute for International Affairs, the,
    30

Sabri, Hassan, 43
Sadat, President (Anwar), 168, 205
    Soviet Union and, 230, 245-6
Salah, Abdul Jawad, 210
Saiqa, 129, 139, 141-2, 166, 219, 231
Samaria, 19, 78-9, 176-7, 179, 185, 206-7
Saudi Arabia, 77, 116-7, 129, 220, 226, 255
Shelepin, Aleksandr, 233
Shari'a, the, 82, 123, 146
Shoukair, Sheik Assad, 41
Shukeiry, Ahmed (*also* Shuquairy), 200,
    231-3
Simpson Report, the, (*see* Sir John Hope
    Simpson)
Sinai, the, 2-3, 18, 31, 55
Six Day War (June, 1967) the, 60, 78-9, 81, 83,
    85-6, 88, 93, 110, 116, 119, 125, 131, 143,
    150, 159-60, 167-8, 192, 206, 209
    Soviet Union and, 231-2, 239
Soviet Committee on Afro-Asian Solidarity,
    the, 240
Soviet Union, the, 4-5, 101, 128, 184, 203,
    228-30, 232, 234
    and the Arabs, 236, 241, 247

and Israel, 177, 193
and PFLP, 168-9, 244
and PLO, 131, 241, 243
and Saiqa, 141, 167
attitude to the Palestinian organizations, 195, 205, 212, 222, 226, 245-6
attitude to terrorism, 237-8, 244
attitude to Zionism, 235
Stebbens, Harry, 54
Stockwell, General Sir Hugh, 54
Sykes-Picot Agreement, the, 201
Syria, 12, 15, 17-19, 27, 31, 38, 52, 97, 101
and Arab refugees, 53, 56, 67, 70, 78, 114, 125, 195, 203, 205, 223, 231
and Israel, 178, 182, 225
and nationalism, 102, 122, 194, 200-1, 205, 213, 217
and Nasser, 116
and Palestinian organizations, 129, 140-1, 159, 161, 167, 201, 212, 220, 256
and Soviet Union, 230, 234, 247
Jews from, 60, 72
Syrian Communist Party, the, 234
Syrian-Palestinian Congress, the, 123
Syrian Socialist Ba'ath Party, the, 110, 115, 141, 233
Syro-Palestine Committee, the, 44

Talal, Prince Hassan, 221
Tse-tung, Mao, 191, 244
Toukan, Fadwa, 118
Transjordan, the Emirate of, 2-3, 31, 38, 41, 50, 77, 122-3, 189, 200, 207, 221, 224
Turki, Fawaz, 114
Turkish Ottoman Empire, the, 2-3, 10, 20-2, 26-7, 29, 48, 70, 97-8, 100-2, 106, 109, 112, 121-2, 201-2, 206, 213, 217
Ul'yanovskiy, R.A., 242
U.N., the, 69, 73, 129-31, 150, 161, 181, 200, 203-4, 209, 216, 238
U.N. Charter, the, 5, 150, 181, 260-1
U.N. General Assembly, the, 2, 4, 261
Resolutions, 68, 131, 161, 182, 203
U.N. Palestine Conciliation Commission, the, 2, 53, 68
U.N. Partition Resolution, the, 2, 4, 51-2, 54, 114, 150, 160, 162, 167, 202, 213-5, 217, 219
U.N.R.W.A., 28, 53, 55-7, 67, 70-3, 78, 182
U.N. Security Council Resolution 242, the,

79, 117, 131, 140, 151, 161-2, 165-70, 201, 225, 229, 239, 242, 245, 267
U.N. Special Commission (1963), 67
Union of Palestinian Students, the, 115
United States, the, 5, 56, 141, 164, 167-8, 171, 177-8, 193, 201, 207-8
Soviet relations with, 229-30, 234-5, 237, 241-3, 246-7
Urabi, Captain Yussuf, 129

Versailles Peace Conference, the, 122, 202

War of Independence, Israel's, 52-3, 85, 170, 194, 214
War of October, 1973, the, 87, 140, 142, 159-60, 163, 166, 168-70, 184, 204, 221, 229, 239-41
Wazin, Halil al-, (see Iyad, Abu)
Wazir, Khalil el, 115
Weizmann, Chaim, 46, 48, 201-2
West Bank, the, 2-3, 5, 86, 114, 211, 213-4, 217, 220
and Israel, 88, 91, 182, 192, 194-6, 206-7
and Jordan, 194, 222
as a Palestinian state, 203-5, 209-10, 223-4
attitudes of population, 79, 89, 90, 92-3, 118-9, 129
Palestinian organizations and, 140, 142, 144, 159-64, 189-90, 204, 220
refugees on, 88, 202, 231
Soviet attitude to, 232, 245
World Conference of Peace-Loving Forces, the, 240
World Council of Churches, the, 72
World Zionist Organization, the, 122

Yafi, Abdullah al-, 69
Yariv, Aharon, 225
Yaziji, Nasif al, 99
Yom Kippur War, (see War of October, 1973)
Young Arab Society, the, 101

Zionism, 4, 59, 79, 97-8, 98, 104, 107-8, 111, 121, 184, 188, 190
Biltmore Program, 190
First Zionist Congress, 199
Basel Program, 188
— Socialism, 104, 108
Zurayk, Constantine R., 113